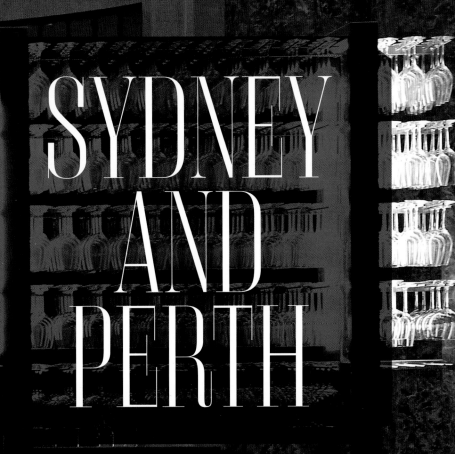

SYDNEY AND PERTH

ROCKPOOL BAR & GRILL

ONCE MORE, LUCK OR DESTINY?

Despite the stress and strain associated with opening Rockpool Bar & Grill Melbourne, Trish, David and I wanted to repeat the steakhouse success in Sydney. The story of Sydney's sister restaurant really began in early 2007 in San Sebastián, Spain, where David and I were holidaying together with our families. We enjoyed an amazing lunch one lazy afternoon in a little fishing village called Kaia, on the outskirts of town. All the seafood on the menu had been brought in by the fishermen fresh that morning and was still swimming around in a tank only seconds before being grilled over the charcoal fire. In essence, it was a seafood version of Rockpool Bar & Grill Melbourne. Suitably inspired, David and I both concluded Sydney would in fact be better suited to a more seafood-centric, summery menu. Once again, the priority was to find a beautiful grand space: we wanted a waterfront location and we wanted to serve really sensational seafood.

A few weeks after our sojourn in Spain, David, who is based in Tahoe in the US, arrived in Sydney to find a property that would fit the brief. The plan was for Trish,

David and I to then lease the space back from him. On Thursday, 28 June at about 11 am, I received a call from David. For a guy who is fairly relaxed most of the time, he sounded positively exuberant! "Well, David, can you see the sea?" This seemed an obvious question given our number one criterion was to find a property that oriented toward the water. "No... but this is Bar & Grill for sure! This is Bar & Grill for sure!" He sounded very excited so Trish and I raced to meet him straight after lunch service at Rockpool Sydney. It was 3 pm and we headed to 66 Hunter Street in the heart of the city. "Wow!" was all I could say. No, it wasn't a waterfront location, but we all agreed it had amazing potential. This was despite the fact it was fitted out with office furniture, featured a grove of plastic palm trees and a staircase that sliced the space in half. But not even those awful palm trees could detract from the soaring ceilings, which featured a plaster relief of the *Flight from Pompeii*. The original detail in the cathedral-high ceilings was balanced by the pearly brilliance of the marble and scaglia walls and the towering three-storey-high green marble columns that stood like sentinels

guarding this expansive space. Adding to the allure of the interior was the fact that it was flooded with light that poured in through gorgeous stained-glass windows.

I met David again the very next day at 10 am to have a closer look at the layout and visualise our plans for the space. The kitchen, the bar, the seating and the wine-storage cellar would all fit beautifully. I called Trish: "Let's go for it!" It was 29 June 2007, and the deal was sealed within just 24 hours and on my fiftieth birthday, too! Perhaps if I had stopped to think about what an expensive undertaking it would be, I might have walked away. But, as with all of the Rockpool restaurants, the Bar & Grill was built on passion and we would find a way to make it work.

THE USUAL SUSPECTS
It was time to round up a new team. While head chef Khan Danis and pastry chef Catherine Adams were slated to return to Sydney, the Melbourne kitchen would now be managed by head chef Paul Easson and second chef Ben Pollard, two talented chefs who had both worked at Rockpool. General Manager, Vanessa, would stay

on to keep Melbourne on track. We loved the Hunter Street heritage-listed premises so much that we also decided to open a second restaurant on the site, Spice Temple, which would be located in the basement of the building. Designer Grant Cheyne, of Bates Smart, was again entrusted with honouring the heritage of the Hunter Street premises and adhering to a demanding brief. Photographer Earl Carter was also deployed to deliver the imagery that would give each restaurant its own distinct character. Meanwhile, David and consultant sommelier Nicole Reimers started work on the mammoth task of putting together one of the world's most extensive wine lists, and Trish and I started planning our budget. Lastly, my beef suppliers were told to expect consumption to be on the rise.

NOW THE PAIN BEGINS

Pain seemed to run parallel to this project every step of the way. Even the project manager, Brian Armour, who was accustomed to tackling very challenging checklists, said it was the most difficult project he'd ever been involved with. Although we were meant to start trading in July 2008, we didn't open for business until 19 March 2009.

This was no ordinary building; we had to squeeze a lot of infrastructure into one of the most amazing Art Deco chambers in the world. But the troubles we had weren't all related to the construction work. We also had to get the budget right, negotiate with council, address corporation constraints with the building's executive committee, manage the ever-increasing cost of the construction process and sort out the shareholder split between Trish, David and myself. The reality was that in June 2008, not long before my 51st birthday, I came very close to walking away from the whole deal. The only thing that prevented me from doing so was the fact that I would have let so many friends down. David and Trish were also suffering. It was an awful 18 months and it was not made easier by the crazy idea of opening Spice Temple. Although the experience was harrowing, it was also a watershed

moment in my life: I emerged with a much better understanding of what I wanted from life and where I could take the brands that I worked with and represented.

ONE MONTH TO GO

How on earth could I have forgotten the brain-crushing stress of opening a restaurant? It had nothing to do with Spice Temple, which had opened for business on 13 January 2009 and was buzzing along nicely. The hardship sprang from the fact that I was working in Spice Temple every day and then, when I had time, hassling the builders and working with the Bar & Grill management staff to get things right.

Rockpool Bar & Grill Sydney was way off schedule and I was extremely stressed out about an important function marked in my calendar for 25 March. To describe the event as being merely "important" was an understatement. It was the Starlight Children's Foundation third Ultimate Dinner, a fundraiser featuring some of the best chefs on the planet, each cooking a course in the Rockpool Bar & Grill kitchen. The star-studded line-up included flamboyant British chef Heston Blumenthal (The Fat Duck) and America's Thomas Keller (Per Se and The French Laundry), alongside our very own Tetsuya Wakuda (Tetsuya's), Guillaume Brahimi (Guillaume at Bennelong) and Peter Gilmore (Quay). But the bad news, according to the builders, was that the restaurant would not be finished until 12 April. No. No. No! That just wouldn't do! The Starlight Children's Foundation was counting on me, and my reputation rested on us opening on time. We fought and struggled and spent a small fortune on accelerating costs to open on 18 March, just one week before these celebrated chefs arrived.

It was déjà vu. The builder had promised me that I would be setting up the restaurant a week out from the official opening date. Yet here we were again, trying to train the staff in a space still swarming with tradesmen. This wasn't a restaurant; it was a building site! To top it off, the cool rooms, refrigeration and air-

conditioning units had all malfunctioned, and smoke was billowing out of the vents. At one stage, we received a letter from Level 10 threatening to take us to council and shut us down. There were so many issues to iron out.

Somehow we managed to avert a total disaster and set up the restaurant on the very night before opening. Add to this the stress of managing the many mechanical hitches, ejecting the builders and trying to fast-track the staff training; the nervous tension and trepidation nearly killed me!

This feeling of anxiousness was further heightened when we had to fork out about $100,000 in wages to pay the Sydney staff in advance for just one week's work. And, to top it all off, one of the sub-contractors had completely stuffed up three of the restaurant's main wine-storage areas. This would prove to be a major problem. David was putting together a huge list and his plan was to store 20,000 wines on the premises. There were five storage areas that spanned the two-storey space so the system for storing the wines had to be precise. The system would rely on an up-to-date inventory that tracked each purchase and catalogued each and every bottle with an individual "locator number". When the sommelier input the data about the wine at the point of sale, a number would then direct staff to the exact location of the bottle. Such a system had to be spot on or we'd never be able to find the bottle that had been ordered. Although we allowed a fortnight to organise the wine cellar, this time was soon swallowed up, and it became painfully clear we would not be able to open Rockpool Bar & Grill Sydney with a proper wine list.

We spent one month working with a small temporary list, which was very disappointing, as wine was such a big part of Rockpool's DNA. Of course, by the time the racking was back on track and the wine was ready to be put away, the wine team were all flat-out working the floor and finding the time to order the bottles was proving impossible. In the end, Nicole and our very own dedicated wine buff David arranged the 20,000 bottles themselves.

It was a painstaking process and it took three long weeks to achieve. David's legacy from that experience was a cortisone injection in his neck, which had seized up due to the physical strain of spending three weeks in a 14°C (57°F) vault sorting through thousands of bottles. In any case we had been to hell and back and survived, and David and Nicole's hard work had paid off — we were thrilled to receive validation for the quality of our wine program when we were awarded *Wine Spectator*'s Grand Award for 2010. This is the premier international wine list award and is not easy to nab. Of the 3700 restaurants that won a wine list award in 2010, only 75 from around the world received a Grand Award. This was not only the first Grand Award in Australia but also the first in the southern hemisphere. It's a testament to our sommelier team and the restaurant in general that we were able to win this award in the first year of being eligible.

THE GFC

Just as things were starting to look up, another major crisis emerged that intensified the pressure of opening one of the most ambitious restaurants Australia had ever seen: the GFC.

I'm often asked, "Was there ever a moment that you wanted to pull the plug on your plan to open two restaurants in the heart of Sydney's financial district at the height of a global downturn?" But how could I even contemplate the abandonment of this grand plan? The builders were halfway through Spice Temple and lots of the Bar & Grill fit-out had been ordered. You can't just up-stumps at that stage of the game. If the question was, "Did you think you were crazy?" or "Did it seem like a bad idea?", then the answer would have been, "Yes!" But despite presenting an upbeat front to all the people who were relying on me, I had started to question my very sanity.

Throughout the entire project I had tried to maintain a positive attitude by focusing on how busy we would eventually be. I had painted a very rosy picture: all the borrowed money would be paid back within a few years and all would be okay. But one of the comments that really rattled me was from a "friend" (yes, you know who you are!) who said, "Neil, this is the middle of Sydney; it isn't Crown with 14 million annual visitors. Not that many people go into the CBD at night." This negative comment came back to haunt me when I left the building late at night and noticed how quiet the city streets were. With a great degree of effort, I pushed my fears away and quietly convinced myself that Sydney needed a great steakhouse and there would be a steady stream of customers who would find its historic city location to be a plus. Again, I focused on the only palatable outcome — success — and my positive outlook returned; if we build it, they will come! Although many things did not work in our favour, the fact our opening was delayed from July 2008 to March 2009 proved a blessing. Compared to other developed countries, our island continent had fared quite well during the fiscal crisis and, six months on, people seemed less concerned about their financial future.

OPENING WEEK

The complete chaos that preceded the Starlight Children's Foundation Ultimate Dinner was a different story! Again, I was forced to train my staff while the builders still hammered away. We had a small window of opportunity to host our family and friends in the week leading up to opening night, which would serve as a practice run for our staff. Invites went out to the 120 people we knew would forgive us the odd sin and, importantly, reveal what we might need to work on. Although we had little time to train our new team of wait staff, I was able to bring them up to speed on my passion for high quality produce and the premise behind the restaurant's meat- and fish-focused menu. Wait staff also had the chance to sample the menu, which meant they understood the subtle nuances of each dish and could field customer queries with confidence. Those first few days were totally crazy and I consequently instructed staff to cap the bookings. Those culinary kings Thomas Keller and Heston Blumenthal would be striding into the kitchen the following week and I didn't want them to see us careening out of control!

Thankfully, the dinner was a huge success. The evening raised more than $220,000 and everyone had a blast. What made the evening feel even more special was the fact that so very few people had been inside the Rockpool Bar & Grill Sydney.

To reveal this sophisticated restaurant on such a wonderful, star-studded occasion only added to the drama and mystique surrounding the space.

The Melbourne experience had taught us a lot about opening a Bar & Grill and all that preparation paid dividends. But the rise in unemployment rates as a result of the GFC had also delivered unexpected benefits: unlike the chronic staff shortage we experienced in Melbourne, we were now able to choose from a more experienced, mature pool of staff, which made it easier to hit our stride. Having talent at the top also helped: General Manager Jeremy Courmadias, Restaurant Manager Tom Sykes and Group Beverage Director Linden Pride orchestrated the floor; while Khan and Catherine kept things under control in the kitchen. Together, this team, this restaurant and the extensive wine list and our over-arching food philosophy all came together to deliver "great dining" as opposed to "fine dining". It is as grand an experience as you can have anywhere in the world and it is right here in Sydney. Of course, its success was built on strong foundations. I know we will do it again, but I ask myself… will it get any easier?

A SOURCE OF GREAT PRIDE

The fact we survived the biggest global economic crisis since the Great Depression is a testament to my dedicated team and our passion and belief in the brand. We won almost every available award in 2009 (including taking out the best new restaurant category for both *The Sydney Morning Herald Good Food Guide* and *Australian Gourmet Traveller Restaurant Guide*) and that has been very gratifying for the staff and myself. But by far the most satisfying thing has been that, as with Melbourne, we have engaged the local population and given them something they themselves are proud of and feel privileged to be part of. In essence, we have created something that has become a revered institution and we have done that through our uncompromising approach to quality. In the end, what has given us the most pride is the fact that our Sydney customers embrace and love our beautiful restaurant.

A THIRST FOR KNOWLEDGE

Rockpool Bar & Grill is about steak, service and a good time but also, very importantly, we are about wine and the relationship to food. Here is a story from David Doyle, my American business partner, about what first drew him to wine, what made him an avid collector and how he came to be involved in Bar & Grill.

A COLLECTOR'S CONUNDRUM

I remember the moment I realised I had a serious problem. I was reading an article about the MGM Grand in Las Vegas, which is one of the world's largest hotels. The article said it would take a person 13 years and eight months to sleep in every one of the hotel's 5000 rooms. It suddenly occurred to me that if I had 5000 bottles of wine and drank one each day, it would also take me more than 13 years to get through them. The problem was that I had, at that point in time, about 35,000 bottles in my cellar, so to drink them all would take me about 96 years! And that's assuming I never, ever bought another bottle.

This also got me thinking, as these sorts of things do, how did I get here? And what am I going to do about it? So begins the tale of how the now-famous Rockpool Bar & Grill Sydney wine list originated.

THE EARLY YEARS

Although I've always been a lover of good food, I never really learnt to appreciate wine until I was in my twenties. Considering the poor quality of what I sampled in the seventies, I could not imagine why anyone would want to drink the stuff for pleasure. It took an incident at a San Diego restaurant to make me understand why wine was worth both drinking and collecting. I was having a lovely meal with my lovely date when a rather obnoxious gentleman sat down at the table beside us.

He had an aversion to green food apparently, and loudly complained during his meal about how much "green stuff" had been presented on the plate. Sitting next to this gentleman and listening to his relentless whining was most unpleasant, particularly given that I was busy trying to impress my female companion. Trying to be discreet, I shot the guy a look that said: "I will kill you if you don't shut up!" He quickly figured out his faux pas and was extremely apologetic. Then, to make amends for his social blunder, he insisted on buying us some Champagne.

Up until that moment, I believed a bottle of bubbly was something that cost $1.99 and had a plastic cork that shot across the room when you opened it. I also believed that if you were intemperate enough to drink any you would have a harrowing hangover the next day. Although I tried to gracefully decline his offer, he ordered two glasses of 1973 Taittinger Comtes de Champagne Blanc de Blancs for our table. What was this? It looked good and smelt great. And that first sip was like an epiphany: the clouds parted, the sun shone through and the angels started singing. I was floored! I had never tasted anything that good, much less Champagne. It was time to re-evaluate my non-interest in wine. As the evening progressed, he also shared with us a 1970 Chateau Latour. Here was yet another amazing wine that did not smell like denatured alcohol but rather

tasted like fruit and earth and God knows what else. We finished off the evening with a gorgeous glass of 1967 Château d'Yquem, which I remember to this day. That dinner proved to be a critical turning point in my life.

At this stage of my working life, my budget would not allow for a bottle of Taittinger every night, so I decided to visit the local wine stores in southern California to brush up on my knowledge. What I soon realised was that my quest to become a connoisseur required careful thought. It was a steep learning curve! I almost always regretted not buying more of the very top drops and often had to off-load many of the more underwhelming wines. To add to my layers of learning, I started to ask for recommendations and conduct more research into the taste, texture and aroma of different wines. As my earning capacity increased, so too did my desire to increase the quality of my collection. So began my quest to go from being a casual wine enthusiast to a bonafide aficionado (read: crazed collector), which has since taken years of dedication.

THE LEARNING YEARS

Following is a basic guide that will help give you a better understanding of what it takes to build a wine cellar.

LESSON 1 When you start out, taste, buy and drink a lot of different wines.

Once you've learnt more about what you like, keep tasting but buy more of the things you really like. As a rabid lover of pizza, I initially drank a fair amount of zinfandel, which is a perfect match for pizza. In fact, the very first case of wine I ever bought was the 1979 Clos du Val Zinfandel from the Napa Valley. It cost me about $US72 which was a fair outlay for me at the time and I thought it would last me for years and years. It didn't. It was gone in record time. Although I loved both pizza and zinfandel, the combination became worn after a while and so I decided to branch out a bit. Armed with $US40, I went down to the local Trader Joe's, a specialty retail store in the US, and selected, at random, a case of $1.99 wines with a few $3.99 splurges. I opened them at a poker night at home and we somehow drank them all!

LESSON 2 There are good and very good wines at nearly every price level, but there is a reason why the very best wines are expensive. Ultimately, you'll find your tastes will change over time. You might shift from, say, zinfandel to the Rhône Valley, from oaky New World wines to white Burgundy, from full-throttle cabernets to Bordeaux and back again. The cellar began to fill up with wines I just didn't really want to drink that night, or any night. At about 1000 bottles it was time to shift my buying patterns. Fortunately my software business was now doing exceptionally well, which afforded me the option of buying better wines. It also meant the mistakes I made were expensive ones. What should I spend my money on?

LESSON 3 Find a wine critic or publication with similar tastes to your own and use trusted contacts and resources to help shape your decisions. There are too many wines in the world to try, and weeding out the good from the bad is too expensive to do on your own. Thinking back to that original bottle of 1970 Chateau Latour, I soon realised that drinking old wine was a good thing. More mature wines had an extra level of complexity and flat-out deliciousness that was addictive. In order to ensure a constant supply, I formulated a two-pronged attack: to buy older wines for drinking now and to cellar the younger ones to give them time to mature and improve.

When you buy old wines, the first thing you learn is that they're often very inconsistent. Some are great, some are okay and some are awful. It's important how the older wines were treated in their youth, namely, from the moment they leave the winery until the minute you buy them. It makes a big difference if they were treated kindly and stored at the right temperature rather than, say, rolling around in the back of a truck during a long-haul drive through the desert. Fill levels, colour, leakage around the capsule, corks pushed up or sunken down are all issues that give you an indication of whether you have a great bottle or something that has no value at all. Let's say you bought a $500 bottle of some supposedly great wine. If it had been sitting on a loading dock years ago somewhere in the sun for a few days, then that bottle would actually now be worth nothing! Finding bottles in this condition happened to me too often, and it made me determined to avoid future tragedies.

LESSON 4 Provenance is everything with older wines. Unless you know where your wine comes from and buy from reliable sources, you may as well just roll the dice. As someone who has been to many excellent tastings and dinners around the world, I have noticed a common thread among those who drink a lot of serious wine: nearly everyone's favourite is either red Burgundy or red Bordeaux. Sure, we all love Champagne, admire the great Italians and guzzle Rhône wines at barbecues with gusto. But if you ask most connoisseurs what their favourite sort of wine is, it is nearly always one of these two. If I were forced to decide on which wine I'd prefer, I would say Burgundy and, in particular, a bottle of 1949 Domaine Comte Georges de Vogüé Musigny Cuvée Vieilles Vignes. This wine was beyond heavenly: it was silky with delicious endless fruit and an incomprehensible smell of flowers, fruit, moss, wood and perfume. I'll never forget it.

LESSON 5 There is something special about Burgundy and Bordeaux. While you may love many different wines, try Burgundy and Bordeaux and buy these when you can. You'll be pleased at how smart you are when you drink them.

ENTER NEIL PERRY

As a committed wine collector, I had been struggling with the issue of what to do with all the wonderful wines I had in storage. Even after building Off the Vine, my own wine storage facility in southern California, I knew I still needed to deplete some of my collection. The classic method of moving wine en masse is to auction it off, although I found that idea rather depressing.

A trip to Italy in 2004 helped move me closer towards finding a solution. I was there holidaying with Neil in a Florence villa owned by famed Italian shoemaker Salvatore Ferragamo. Talk soon turned to restaurants and I was enthralled with Neil's plan to create an American-style steakhouse in Australia. As it happened, Neil's timing was impeccable as I had recently moved away from my software business and was ready to take up a new challenge.

THE WINE VAULT

It was just two years later that Neil, Trish and I toasted the success of the Melbourne restaurant with a top drop plucked from my cellar in California. As a committed wine connoisseur, my goal was to create one of the best wine lists in the world! I had the wine to create the core of the list, and we could fill the gaps with quality wines obtained in Australia. As well as a large number of locally sourced Australian and imported wines, I had devised a wine list that included hundreds of bottles from my own personal collection. Although it kick-started my cause to start putting this glut of wine to good use, Rockpool Bar & Grill Melbourne had limited space for cellaring wine and we hit the wall with 1200 bottles. As luck would have it, Bar & Grill Sydney also helped to address my wine storage woes. When I first stumbled across the building, it was a wreck, with dust and detritus everywhere.

"I felt like a character in a film, an explorer who had discovered an ancient city hidden in a jungle or a tomb lost in the desert sands. This incredible place had only one purpose: to be a Rockpool Bar & Grill."

Yet despite the state of it, it was stunning! I felt like a character in a film, an explorer who had discovered an ancient city hidden in a jungle or a tomb lost in the desert sands. This incredible place had only one purpose: to be a Rockpool Bar & Grill. And, even better, there was ample space for cellaring wine in a large, vacant bank vault!

We created enough storage space for nearly 3500 different bottles, which was still not enough space, so we expanded to an off-site facility to house the overflow. With construction completed, more than 12,000 bottles were shipped to Australia from my Californian cellar. What came next was the arduous process of storing each bottle. In a restaurant environment, bottles need to be located fast and systems had to be put in place to achieve this. I spent more hours than I care to remember clad in cold-weather gear helping to stack each and every bottle in the vault.

NOW WHAT?

The number one challenge with a wine list is to keep it interesting and fresh with wines that represent excellent value and accommodate current trends. We have many of the best wines ever made stored in our cellars and we will continue to replenish this list with interesting, exciting wines. Our talented wine team, headed by Group Wine Director Sophie Otton, sources a range of both young and old wines to keep up with customer demand. While it is easy to focus on the great wines at Rockpool, the real beauty of the wine list is that it also offers great value. Not everyone who walks into our restaurants will spend hundreds of dollars on wine (although that would not be a bad thing). I myself love the great variety of affordable wines available in Australia and we made it a requirement that we would always have at least 350 wines under $100 included on the list. In fact, we have more than 400 wines in that price range, and constantly strive to find great wines that cater to all of our customers.

Oddly enough, it was while jotting down this tale that I decided to take stock of just how many bottles I had left. What I soon realised was that despite my very best efforts to off-load the bulk of my collection, I still have about 37,000 bottles and 101 years of drinking ahead of me. Even at two bottles a day, I have just 50 years to achieve this. Since I'm not one to let a problem like this continue unchecked, it's likely that the future will hold another Rockpool Bar & Grill somewhere else. Neil, Trish and I have created what we think are some of the greatest restaurant experiences in the world. It's our hope that with the continued support of our customers we'll be able to take that experience to customers outside of Australia. Now, time to select a bottle of wine and get that quota down to 36,999!

FINANCIAL MISE EN PLACE

*Trish Richards is my cousin and a very talented woman.
In 1988 we joined forces and established our flagship restaurant
Rockpool on George Street. She brought to the partnership her
wealth of knowledge gained from running her own accountancy
business and being a founding shareholder and finance director
of the Triple M radio network and shareholder of Mid Coast
Broadcasters in Port Macquarie.*

My partnership with Neil spans 23 years, during which time we have opened many restaurants. Each one has been different from the last and they have always surprised us with their own unique set of problems and challenges.

From a financial perspective, the process of opening a restaurant starts with finding the site, then crunching the numbers to determine if the appropriate design and fit-out can be achieved within the budget constraints. Then the lawyers and bankers get on board to negotiate everything from leases to partnership agreements and a liquor license. Credit facilities must be established with the bank and all the necessary documentation completed to everyone's satisfaction. After the building and fit-out budget is drawn up, the next step is to plan a pre-operating budget. This part of the process is always a bit unnerving, as you must plan to spend a substantial amount of money on operating costs with no income to offset the expenditure.

While Neil is busy working with builders and designers to develop a conceptual and creative vision for the restaurant, I begin work on the back-of-house requirements such as: the computer systems, point-of-sale computers, printing facilities, communication systems, website construction, budgets, staffing requirements and all the other financial systems needed to get the business up and running. Because Neil and I have already opened up quite a few restaurants, some of the systems are already in place. But they still need to be replicated for each new restaurant.

Opening one restaurant is stressful enough, but opening two restaurants in the space of two months was never going to be easy. The executive team gets involved in the operation about four months prior to the opening. That's when things shift into overdrive. The new computer systems cannot be installed until construction is complete, so managers and chefs work out of the Rockpool office, which doesn't have the space or facilities to cope with double the number of staff members. Many of these executives want to get set up as soon as possible and start spending money on equipment that, though necessary, was not allocated for in my original budget. It is a constant juggling act.

Recruiting staff is a priority at this point. As well as the act of recruitment, there are staff manuals to make up, codes of conduct, job descriptions and letters of offer to be sent out. Once you have made a commitment to new staff, you start to stress about the building dramas that may delay the opening and, therefore, starting date for staff.

Neil must constantly push the builders to stick to the schedule. He must also solve any problems that may further increase construction costs or delay the opening.

Training key management on the point-of-sale systems is also vital. It's a little difficult as final menus and wine lists are nowhere near complete, so setting up templates becomes a real issue. In between all of this, there's a new payroll system and financial accounting package to set up and we have to register for GST, PAYG, payroll tax, superannuation and all the other statutory requirements. We must also organise all the EFTPOS facilities to be implemented, which cannot be tested until all the phone lines are connected. As we move closer to opening, the accounts department gets inundated with forms: staff employment forms; tax declarations; super fund nomination forms and credit applications for our suppliers. It really is a logistical nightmare!

Although the list seems endless, we somehow manage to process all the information and get the systems up and running and that first week of operation is when they are put to the test. We have a few daily reconciliations to see if the staff training has been effective and we also start to scrutinise the point-of-sale systems. The first payroll is always a test. You have managers getting used to new operating systems, staff not supplying the necessary information to process their wages and information not being received on time.

The best thing about opening is the cash flow! What a joy to see some credit going into the bank account. This is when I start to measure performance against budgets. How many covers are we doing? What is our average spend? Although it's early days, it gives me an immediate feel for the business and whether it will fall in line with my forecasts. We must monitor costs — wages, food purchases, beverage purchases and overheads. It's vital we're not too far out on our expectations as such a large operation could fall into financial difficulties very fast. It takes about six weeks for us to gain momentum and our budget makes allowance for that. More and more issues are resolved as the managers and staff become more proficient at service and therefore have additional time to allocate to back-of-house systems. It's amazing how quickly you forget all the stress of getting a business off the ground when you walk into the restaurant and see it full of happy customers and wonderful staff.

Opening Rockpool Bar & Grill Sydney has been a hectic but wonderful journey.

It's a credit to Neil that he has transformed this amazing building into the world-class restaurant it is today. Neil and I have been in this business together since 1988 and have had some remarkable experiences. Together, we gain a lot of satisfaction from enabling our staff to grow with the business. We've also been very fortunate that David believed our company was worth investing in, as I'm sure the big banks would not have shared his enthusiasm. What a wonderful experience we've had over the years. To be involved in this amazing industry, learning and experiencing so many things about food, wine, travel and business, has been really special. I cherish working with Neil and love his energy, enthusiasm, good humour and sense of integrity. Although the company has evolved a lot since the early days, I have loved every step of the way and look forward to our next exciting adventure.

ROCKPOOL BAR & GRILL

FROM THE EAST TO THE WEST

I distinctly remember walking over to James Packer's table at Rockpool Bar & Grill Sydney one lunchtime in October 2009 — I was filled with trepidation. I had heard on the grapevine he wanted to go to Perth and open a Bar & Grill at his Burswood property. For me Perth was going in the wrong direction. I wanted to go to LA, 14 hours east not 4 hours west, first. He simply shook my hand and said, "Neil, let's do this together in Perth." I was still in no way convinced but I had the feeling there was no turning back!

As it transpired he did get me over to Perth to have a look at the site they had in mind and discuss if it would be at all possible. When I arrived there, I felt the wonderful light the space had and instantly felt a connection with the airiness and fresh feel of the place. That night I sat in the private dining room at Yu with James and John, Crown CEO Rowen Craigie, General Manager Crown Hotels Peter Crinis, Crown Executive VP Todd Nesbit and Burswood CEO Barry Felsted. I had a definite feeling I had brought a knife to a gun fight. What chance did I have of saying no to this group of powerful men? We spoke at length about the opportunities and James was very positive about Perth and what a fantastic city it was. I have since spent a lot of time with him in Perth and his enthusiasm for the place has not waned one little bit.

The next day looking at the site with its wonderful long entrée into the hotel, I could see that this was something special. Of course it took a lot of imagination as at the time it was a huge food court and the entrance was the business centre backing on to the food court. I knew straight away it would work. So I brought Grant Cheyne, who had designed Melbourne and Sydney Bar & Grills, straight over to see the sight. As I was, Grant was taken by the light and the natural beauty of Perth. The natural character of the space meant that Perth was going to be a lighter cousin to its east coast predecessors, with lots of recycled timber and light materials to make up the palette.

As it came to pass, we opened Rockpool Bar & Grill Perth in late January 2011. It was, as with all the other Bar & Grills, a tough opening with huge hours and lots of drama, however the customers have come and they have enjoyed.

We now have three of these amazing restaurants all expressive of the wonderful cities they call home.

SERVICE
AND
THE BAR

ROCKPOOL BAR & GRILL

FINE FORM

THE KEY TO ANY GREAT RESTAURANT

The importance of great wait staff and service should not be underestimated. It's important to have quality training programs in place and a service manual to guide staff. Following are snippets from the service philosophy guide that we use to train front-of-house staff in Melbourne, Sydney and Perth.

ROCKPOOL VISION

The Rockpool purpose and vision addresses the questions of what business we are in and where we are heading in the future. Rockpool values define what Rockpool stands for.

Our purpose is to provide sustainable prosperity for our employees through commitment to quality in leadership and a high-quality dining experience through the use of fresh ingredients and customer service.

Our vision is, as a group, to be "ambassadors for modern Australian cooking here and throughout the world... food professionals with a passion for good food and to have a philosophy of tradition, a sense of hospitality and a genuine commitment to the industry."

Rockpool remains committed to:
> providing superior service, products and brands and maintaining our position within the marketplace
> employee involvement in an environment characterised by opportunities, recognition and respect
> gaining community respect through active leadership and participation in community issues and focusing on involvement and support of appropriate community projects.

ROCKPOOL STYLE OF SERVICE

A Rockpool waiter should:
> be knowledgeable and friendly and know everything about the menu, wine list, suppliers and company history
> be informative, not arrogant; be professional, not casual; be friendly, not stuffy
> adapt service to suit each guest; some want a relaxed meal; others may be in a hurry
> inform guests of any difficulties that may be occurring and be upfront about menu changes
> inform the manager of any scenarios that may have the potential to become problematic
> be as accommodating as possible without compromising the experience of other guests
> smile.

KEY POINTS: TEAM, CONSISTENCY, DETAIL

Service is intangible, engaging, knowledgeable, welcoming and friendly. The idea is to create a lasting memory.

PRODUCT KNOWLEDGE

It's imperative we know where every product comes from and why. This should encompass:
> food: ingredients and cultural origins
> wine: styles and regions, with possible food matches
> bread: maker and ingredients
> butter: origin and significance
> coffee: blend and producer
> tea: producer, ingredients
> cheese: type of milk, origin and age.

CARE PHILOSOPHY

This is a philosophy that should be carried right through from our suppliers to the guests and to each other. Without care you cannot give good service.

ROCKPOOL BAR & GRILL

THE BUILDING BLOCKS OF A GOOD BAR

We searched high and low for our spirit selection so that our guests could experience something new and interesting every time they visited the bar. We trawled auction houses, wine merchants and the internet in quest of rare and specialty spirits from around the world. Our selection will be an ever-changing being, as we strive to keep it fresh and up to date while always challenging your palates to try something new. We dedicate a short introduction to each category of spirit to help those who may be unfamiliar with any of them. We hope you enjoy the fruits of our research.

VODKA

Vodka is perhaps the most simple of all spirits, being made for hundreds of years throughout Eastern Europe. Vodka may be made from any source of starch, though it is most commonly made from wheat or rye that is malted and mashed, then left to ferment. The ferment is then run through a still several times to higher and higher strengths of alcohol, evaporating all impurities (otherwise known as congeners) until it reaches a sufficient purity. It is then filtered and watered down to around 40 per cent alcohol, ready to be mixed with anything and everything.

GIN

Derived from the Dutch spirit genever, this famous incarnation made its way across the English Channel to ravage 1700s London. In what became known as the "gin madness", the British public took to this new elixir with unbridled enthusiasm. A legend was born. Two hundred years later, gin has become a refined spirit with an increasing reputation among bartenders and trade professionals. Spurred by the rebottling and launch of Bombay Sapphire in the mid-90s, gin is once again at the forefront of cocktail development worldwide. Gin is made by infusing a grain alcohol with "botanicals", such as juniper, citrus peel and other flavourings, and redistilled by various means. While juniper is the predominant flavouring, each brand has their own special recipe.

SCOTTISH WHISKY

SINGLE MALTS Let's keep it simple. A single-malt whisky is one that is produced only from malted barley at one single distillery. That's it. Since Glenlivet released the first single malt in 1824, the category has developed a cachet of elegance and complexity that has never wavered. The great beauty of single malts lies in the fact that there are so many different styles and flavour characteristics within this classic style. We've searched high and low to bring you a unique whisky collection unlike any seen in Sydney.

HIGHLAND AND SPEYSIDE WHISKIES These are epitomised by those from the famous region known as Speyside, which has the highest concentration of malt distilleries; over half of those throughout Scotland in fact. Because they cover such a wide region, the styles vary greatly but quite often they tend to be light to medium bodied, showing grassy and floral notes, dried fruit and heather honey, backed up by tones of orchard fruits and spice.

LOWLANDS These tend to be light in body with soft grassy notes, some sweet fruitiness and a lovely maltiness. They make nice apéritif whiskies and are an easy introduction for the novice malt drinker. Our representation has been aged in oloroso and Pedro Ximénez sherry, adding a touch of sherried sweetness to the mix.

ISLAY AND THE ISLANDS The most distinctive and complex whiskies of all are those that hail from Islay, an island located just off the west coast of the mainland. They are known for their strong peatiness, backed up by coastal influences such as sea air, iodine and seaweed. All along and up the coast, the harsh environs take hold of the whiskies, from Arran to Orkney, creating robust, warming drams, perfect for the hip flask on that trek to the end of the loch!

CAMPBELTOWN Once the thriving cradle of whisky production in Scotland and now home to only one working distillery, Campbeltown is still home to two of the finest malts in circulation and rarely seen in Australia — Springbank and Longrow. Their distinctive style is full-bodied and mildly peated, with a wonderfully oily mouthfeel.

BLENDED SCOTTISH WHISKY Blends are made exactly as the name suggests. They are a blend of lighter, grain whiskies and any number of different single malts, forming a satisfying and individual whole that is more easily enjoyed by a wider demographic.

IRISH WHISKEY

From just across the water comes a different dram all together: the Irish pure pot still. Made in just a handful of distilleries these days, the Irish were responsible for one of the liquor industry's greatest breakthroughs: continuous distillation. This meant that a spirit could be produced faster, in higher volumes and with greater purity than its counterparts to the east. The result is a lighter, malty, smooth and, at times, honeyed spirit.

NORTH AMERICAN WHISKEY

Bourbon takes its name from Bourbon County, Kentucky, once the major trans-shipment site for distilled spirits heading down the Ohio and Mississippi Rivers to New Orleans. Barrels shipped from its ports were stamped with the county's name, and bourbon and whiskey became synonymous. A congressional proclamation issued in 1964 declared bourbon an "All American product", whereby strict laws governing its production came into force. Fifty-one per cent of the grain used in making the whiskey must be corn, it must be aged for a minimum of two years in new charred oak barrels and nothing can be added at bottling except spring water. Though technically bourbon can be made anywhere, Kentucky is the only state allowed to put its name on the bottle. And as Kentucky distillers are quick to point out, bourbon is not bourbon unless the label says so. Tennessee whiskies such as Jack Daniel's are produced in exactly the same way except that they are filtered through maple charcoal prior to bottling.

RYE WHISKEY

In the United States rye whiskey is by law made from a mash of at least 51 per cent rye (the other ingredients are usually corn and malted barley). Rye whiskey was the prevalent whiskey of the north-eastern States, especially Pennsylvania and Maryland but largely disappeared after prohibition. One to have withstood the post-prohibition years is Rittenhouse Straight Rye while New York-based Tuthilltown Spirits is the first newcomer to this category since the Twenty-first Amendment took effect in 1933, thus ending the era of prohibition.

CANADIAN WHISKEY

Canadian distillers make predominantly rye-based whiskies. Unlike their counterparts south of the border, the classic method of Canadian whiskey production is to blend the rye (although they don't use rye exclusively) with a relatively neutral grain-based spirit. The distillers can also use sherries or assorted fruit wines to bolster their particular flavour profile. The resultant spirit is smooth, with a lighter body than the spicy, complex straight American rye style.

RUM

Even though the Caribbean is undoubtedly the spiritual and cultural home of rum, the category has no appellation and can therefore be made anywhere that sugarcane is grown. Molasses (the fermentable by-product of sugar production) is believed to have first been discovered by the slaves who worked the cane fields of the Caribbean soon after Columbus brought the first cuttings of the grass to Hispaniola, an island now belonging to Haiti and the Dominican Republic, in the late fifteenth century. Today, rum is recognised as a hugely versatile product perfect for sipping straight or in your favourite cocktail.

RHUM AGRICOLE

Born from the French settlers' desire to create yet another fine spirit to call their own, rhum agricole puts to use knowledge of the distilling techniques used in Cognac production. The rhum is made from distilling fermented sugarcane juice instead of the more widely used molasses. The result is a unique, lighter, dry and more pungent spirit.

CACHAÇA

Cachaça is made from sugar and is classified as another style of rum. Sugarcane has been cultivated in Brazil since the early sixteenth century and has played a major role in the socio-economic history of the country. Cachaça does not have quite so many rules and regulations pertaining to its production, so at times the resulting spirit can have wide variances in quality. However, ours are some of the finest examples available!

TEQUILA

Despite the popular myth that tequila is made from the juice of a cactus, it is actually made from the distilled juice of the blue agave. The heart of the plant, known as the piña, is the main source of the fermentable sugars necessary to make tequila. Working in the Mexican sun with a spade sharpened like a knife, the jimador (or agave farmer) cuts away the leaves to expose the piña (which can weigh up to 90 kilograms). Tequila is categorised by the level of agave it contains and the amount of time it is aged; 100 per cent blue agave is regarded as the finest. Silver tequila, also known as plata or blanco, is generally aged for less than three months and bottled immediately. Those silver tequilas that are 100 per cent agave show the true flavour components of the plant more than any other tequila category — peppery, spicy and perfect for cocktails. The aged varieties reposado (meaning "rested") and añejo (meaning "aged") exhibit more complex spice and richer flavours; both take on more characters from barrelling and show tones of vanilla, caramel, nut and spice.

THE TEQUILA VALLEY The area surrounding the town of Tequila is dominated by the dormant Tequila Volcano that is made up of fertile dark brown earth. The tequila produced from distilleries that source agave from this area tends to be earthy, vegetal and herbaceous when bottled young.

LOS ALTOS (THE HIGHLANDS) The Los Altos region of Jalisco is typified by its red soil. This soil isn't known for being fertile for crops but it does wonders for the agave tequila. Consequently, the best agave come from this area. The unaged tequilas from here have a fruity and spicy bouquet.

COGNAC

Cognac is the most famous and revered of all the world's brandies, produced under very strict guidelines in only six designated sub-regions within the area of Cognac. The best ones hail from a small area in the centre of Cognac, known as Petite Champagne and Grande Champagne. However, each sub-region of Cognac has its own recognisable style. Cognac is primarily made from the ugni blanc, folle blanche and colombard grapes; it is double distilled in pot stills and is aged in French limousin oak. The relative qualities of Cognacs depend on the length of time they have been aged. No Cognac may be blended from spirits less than two years old. Classifications range from VS (very special), which may contain brandies as young as three years old. The next is VSOP (very superior old pale) where the youngest spirit has spent at least five years in wood. Those Cognacs blended from minimum six-year-old spirits may be entitled XO (extra old).

ARMAGNAC

Armagnac hails from the Gascony region in south-west France. There are three main areas of production within this region — Bas-Armagnac, Armagnac-Ténarèze and Haut-Armagnac, of which the first is considered the best. The main differences between Armagnac and Cognac are: Cognac is largely made from the ugni blanc grape whereas the base wine of Armagnac is made from several local varieties; it is aged in a local black oak and not in limousin oak as Cognac is; the continuous still is used as opposed to the pot still; and Armagnac is generally more fragrant, showing more biscuit and violet characters, while also being drier because it isn't adjusted with sugar as with many Cognacs.

PISCO

Pisco is a South American brandy but it is probably more akin in flavour and body to white tequila and possibly cachaça. Debate still rages as to whether its origins lie in Chile or Peru, its two main centres of production. Its etymology lies in the Quechuan Indian language of Peru and Bolivia and from the traditional terracotta pots used for ageing the spirit, also called piscos. Made from aromatic varieties of muscat grapes, Peruvian pisco stays as true to tradition as possible, nowadays aged in stainless steel vats, so that oak plays no part in the ageing process, resulting in a clear, clean and pungent spirit, perfect for mixing with a wide range of fruits and juices.

GRAPPA

Grappa is the national brandy of Italy. It is distilled from the skins, pips and stalks of grapes. Sometimes known as pomace brandy, young grappa is very fiery, but it mellows when matured in wood.

The French also produce a pomace brandy that is called marc. This method of brandy making spread throughout Central Europe and into the great wine regions of the world. Our example at the bar has its origins in the Kamptal region of Austria.

CALVADOS

Calvados is a French brandy made from distilling apple cider. The controlled designation of origin is situated in Normandy, in north-west France, within which the Pays d'Auge is the principal region of production, along with the Domfront, whose Calvados distillate is also based on up to 30 per cent perry (pear cider).

APPLEJACK

Applejack, the lesser known spirit to have its roots in colonial America, is also an apple brandy made from cider, and employs freeze-distillation (known as "jacking") to concentrate and remove all impurities (congeners). It can at times also be fortified with a neutral grain spirit. Known as "Jersey Fire Water", the Laird family recipe for Applejack, originating in 1698, was said to be a favourite of George Washington.

EAU-DE-VIE

Eau-de-vie is a French term meaning "water of life". It is a colourless fruit brandy that is produced by means of fermentation and double distillation. Spirits of this type may come from Hungary, Germany, Scandinavia or any country that grows appropriate fruit for fermentation and distillation. Not typically aged in oak, the product retains the freshness and aroma of the parent fruit.

BEST BAR NONE

During the building of Rockpool Bar & Grill Sydney, one of my old staff members approached me. His name was Linden Pride. *He had started behind the bar at Rockpool in 1999, then went to London to further his knowledge. He has always been fascinated with the tradition and history of the cocktail, so when he returned to Sydney, I welcomed him back with open arms. He has gone on to become the Group Director of Beverages and creates each of the unique bars we have within every restaurant. Here are his words on putting together the feel of the cocktail bar at Bar & Grill Sydney.*

In creating the bar at Rockpool Bar & Grill, Neil and I drew on the idea of the classic American cocktail bar — bespoke, historic, intimate — and placed this in a setting of modern luxury. We wanted the idea of a classic speakeasy with the undertones of "discovery" and "exclusivity" (underpinned by our set of gentlemanly house rules, exclusive spirits and a story behind every drink). The drinks program is based on the notion of innovation through authenticity; classic drinks, premium products, seasonal produce and exceptionally well dressed staff providing world-class service, making the venue both a destination and a unique beverage experience.

Looking to history for our cues, we wanted to re-create a speakeasy drinks list, as it might have existed in the 1880s to 1930s — the original golden age of travel and cocktails. The story-line and direction of our drinks menu gives us a foundation that has heritage, points of inspiration from around the world and tradition to play upon.

To drive home the classic cocktail bar feel, we applied the notion of "curated drinks" to our list of the finest traditional spirits and drink structures. We attempted to source recipes and carry products not seen before and present them to our customers to experience for the first time.

The current evolution of drinks — and the embrace of the market towards them — provided enormous opportunity for Bar & Gill to become a true innovator and market leader within the Sydney and international scene.

The following drinks are just a sample of those collated by myself and ex-Bar Manager of Rockpool Bar & Grill Sydney, Will Oxenham, one of the great bartenders of the world. (Will now manages one of our other bars, The Waiting Room in Melbourne.) Studying the classic recipes — such as the Sidecar, house-made tonic water and ginger beer, and hidden classics including the Adonis, Stinger and the original Mai Tai — gave us a great foundation to work from. We have had many amazing young bartenders come through the Rockpool group and these drinks are testament to their passion, efforts and dedication that makes this one of the great bars of the world.

ROCKPOOL TONIC

Also known as the Rockpool Blush, we created this drink for the Starlight Children's Foundation Ultimate Dinner hosted by Neil at Rockpool Bar & Grill with chefs Heston Blumenthal and Thomas Keller. It relies completely on a great-tasting tonic water — not that generic brands won't taste good, they just won't taste great.

50 ml (1³⁄₄ fl oz) Plymouth gin (see note)
60 ml (2 fl oz/¹⁄₄ cup) house-made tonic water
10 ml (¹⁄₃ fl oz) Campari
slice of orange or ruby grapefruit, to garnish

Simply put all of the ingredients into a big double rocks glass, then fill with ice cubes. Garnish with the citrus slice.

NOTE

Any London dry gin will work here. We prefer Plymouth as it is slightly sweeter and softer, allowing our house-made tonic to shine.

HOUSE-MADE TONIC WATER

2 quinine tablets (see note)
6 lemongrass stalks, smashed & cut into pieces
finely grated zest of 3 ruby grapefruit
finely grated zest of 3 limes
1 teaspoon rosewater
1 teaspoon orange blossom water
2–4 teaspoons citric acid (see note)
450 g (1 lb) caster (superfine) sugar
1–2 teaspoons malic acid (see note)

Fill a large stockpot with 8 litres (280 fl oz) of hot tap water. Add the quinine tablets, lemongrass, citrus zest, rosewater, orange blossom water and citric acid and bring to the boil.

Take off the heat immediately after the liquid boils so as to not lose the freshness of the lemongrass or citrus. Working quickly, strain the mixture, making sure to press the solids in the strainer to extract as much flavour as possible.

Add the sugar to the strained liquid and sprinkle in the malic acid, a little at a time, while stirring to dissolve both the sugar and malic acid. The malic acid will clarify the liquid somewhat.

If needed, add a bit more of both the malic acid and citric acid to achieve the correct acidity — the tonic water should be sharp, but balanced. Makes about 8 litres (280 fl oz). Store in glass bottles in the refrigerator for up to 2 weeks.

NOTE

You can buy quinine tablets and malic acid from health food stores or online.

MEXICAN SOUR NO. 1

Using the wood fire to produce smoke is one of the great tools at our disposal at B & G. In this instance, we smoke our peppers to give them a wonderful savoury complexity that matches perfectly with the sweetness of the tequila. Combined with the light smokiness of the mescal, the flavour of this drink is dynamic, lingering and so sexy.

40 ml (1 1/4 fl oz) smoked red capsicum juice (see method)

20 ml (2/3 fl oz) freshly squeezed lemon juice

10 ml (1/3 fl oz) agave syrup

10 ml (1/3 fl oz) Campari

30 ml (1 fl oz) reposado tequila

15 ml (1/2 fl oz) mescal (be sure it is a premium 100 per cent agave mescal)

10 ml (1/3 fl oz) eggwhite

To make the smoked capsicum juice, char the skin of a small red capsicum over a flame until blackened all over, then place under cold running water and remove all of the skin. Remove the stem and seeds. The capsicum is now ready to juice.

Juice the smoked capsicum to order. Add the juice and remaining ingredients to a cocktail shaker and fill with ice. Shake hard and strain into a wine glass filled with ice.

CITY MUTUAL COCKTAIL

This is a simply delicious cocktail, and perfect for anyone who enjoys a spirit with a little age on it. It is named after the building that houses Bar & Grill Sydney and it is a fitting drink for the period that it was built.

30 ml (1 fl oz) Rittenhouse Straight Rye whiskey

30 ml (1 fl oz) Redbreast Irish whiskey

15 ml (1/2 fl oz) Dolin dry vermouth

10 ml (1/3 fl oz) Bénédictine Liqueur

5 ml (1/6 fl oz) Maraschino liqueur

5 ml (1/6 fl oz) Green Chartreuse

1 finger-sized strip lime zest

Put all of the ingredients, except the Chartreuse and lime zest in an ice-cold mixing glass and stir for about 45 seconds.

Pour the Chartreuse into a coupette (or martini) glass and swirl around to cover the entire inside of the glass.

Using a hawthorn strainer, strain the liquid out of the mixing glass into the prepared glass.

Squeeze the lime zest directly over the glass to extract the citrus oils before dropping it into the glass to garnish.

SCORCHED ALMOND SIDECAR

> Makes 1

A Sidecar is one of the great brandy cocktails and perfect at any time of a meal. Eben Freeman showcased this "fat-washing" technique when he was bartender at Tailor restaurant in Manhattan. Beurre noisette is infused with toasted almonds then mixed with a fine Cognac. It's left to cool overnight to allow the fat to resolidify and separate from the spirit, leaving behind a Cognac with a unique, lingering, nutty finish.

You will need to begin this recipe the day before.

40 ml (1 1/4 fl oz) fat wash Cognac
10 ml (1/3 fl oz) Cognac
10 ml (1/3 fl oz) Cointreau
10 ml (1/3 fl oz) orgeat syrup (see page 71)
20 ml (2/3 fl oz) freshly squeezed lemon juice

Add all of the ingredients to a cocktail shaker and shake hard to combine. Using a hawthorn strainer, strain the liquid out of the shaker and through a fine sieve into a chilled coupette (or martini) glass.

FAT WASH COGNAC

1 x 700 ml (24 fl oz) bottle of VSOP Cognac
250 g (9 oz) flaked almonds
250 g (9 oz) Girgar unsalted butter, chopped

Preheat the oven to 160°C (315°F/Gas 2–3). Pour the Cognac into a metal tub.

Grease and line a tray with baking paper. Scatter almonds evenly across the tray and cook until well roasted.

Melt the butter in a small saucepan over low heat. Add the roasted almonds and stir through the butter thoroughly.

Pour the mixture into the Cognac and stir to combine. Leave the Cognac mixture at room temperature for about 4 hours, then refrigerate overnight.

The next day, the butter should have solidified on the surface of the Cognac. Scoop it off and discard. Strain the Cognac through a fine sieve, then again through a sieve lined with muslin (cheesecloth). Makes 700 ml (24 fl oz). Store in a glass bottle in the refrigerator for up to 3 weeks.

DARK & STORMY

> Makes 1

The national drink of Bermuda, this amazingly refreshing beverage long predates the pre-mixed variety. I love this drink. The kick of the fresh ginger and honey in the ginger beer combined with the rum is one of the truly great beverage pairings. This is served long and dry.

50 ml (1³/₄ fl oz) aged dark rum
10 ml (¹/₃ fl oz) freshly squeezed lime juice
60 ml (2 fl oz/¹/₄ cup) house-made ginger beer
1 lime cheek, to garnish
1 sprig mint, to garnish

Build the ingredients, adding one by one to a highball glass, then add ice cubes and garnish with the lime cheek and mint sprig.

HOUSE-MADE GINGER BEER

600 g (1 lb 5 oz) young ginger, peeled & thinly sliced
600 g (1 lb 5 oz) honey
100 g (3¹/₂ oz) white sugar

Place the ginger and 4 litres (140 fl oz) of water in a large saucepan, bring to the boil and cook for 10 minutes. Remove from the heat and, using a stick blender, blend until the ginger is very finely chopped, then return to the hot stove but turn off the heat. Add the honey and sugar, stir well to combine, cover and leave for 1 hour to infuse.

Strain through a fine sieve or muslin (cheesecloth), cool and chill before using.

To serve, place in a soda siphon and gas with 1 cartridge. Makes 3.5 litres (122.5 fl oz). Store in glass bottles in the refrigerator for up to 2 weeks; after that, the spice will begin to fade.

HOUSE MARTINI

> Makes 1

When properly built, the Martini is the only cocktail that can stand the test of time, taste and fashion. Although it has become drier and drier over the years, the marriage of vermouth, spirit, dilution and temperature rivals that existing between gin and tonic water. Our recipe asks for a 7:1 ratio of spirit to vermouth. Although this is the Rockpool standard, we encourage you to increase the ratio to as close to 1:1 as you dare, a balance that was enjoyed during the founding years of this great drink.

vermouth (Dolin is our brand of choice)
gin or vodka
dash orange bitters

In an ice-cold mixing glass (preferably out of the freezer), add ice-cold gin or vodka and vermouth. Fill the glass with ice and stir for about 30 seconds.

Add a dash of orange bitters and strain into an ice-cold martini glass.

If you are serving the martini with lemon or lime zest, extract the oils of one finger-sized strip of zest over the drink and drop in.

If serving with olives, skewer 2–3 olives and serve on the side of the drink (adding up to 20 ml (²/₃ fl oz) of olive brine to the drink to make it as "dirty" as you wish.

Alternatively, you may serve it with a pickled cocktail onion to create a Gibson.

CHIPOTLE MARGARITA

There are so many tales regarding the origin of the Margarita. Our spicy, savoury recipe takes inspiration from Tommy's Mexican Restaurant in San Francisco. This was made by one of the best barmen I have had the pleasure of working with, Will Oxenham, who moved from Sydney to run our bar at The Waiting Room in Melbourne. His simple, fascinating version of this beverage calls for the marriage of only three ingredients — chipotle tequila, lime juice and agave syrup. It's simply delicious.

You will need to begin this recipe the day before.

50 ml (1³/₄ fl oz) smoked paprika & chipotle fat-wash tequila

20 ml (²/₃ fl oz) freshly squeezed lime juice

15 ml (¹/₂ fl oz) agave syrup (see note)

Add all of the ingredients to a cocktail shaker and shake to combine. Strain into a chilled double rocks glass that you have rimmed with salt (use the juice of an orange to ensure the salt sticks). Fill with ice. This is truly a taste sensation.

NOTE

You can buy agave syrup from health food stores.

SMOKED PAPRIKA & CHIPOTLE FAT-WASH TEQUILA

1 x 700 ml (24 fl oz) bottle of Herradura Blanco tequila

15 g (¹/₂ oz) smoked paprika

1 dried chipotle chilli, blitzed in a spice grinder

250 g (9 oz) Girgar unsalted butter, chopped

Preheat the oven to 120°C (235°F/Gas ¹/₂).

Pour the tequila into a metal tub.

Wrap the paprika and chipotle chilli in aluminium foil and roast for 10 minutes.

Melt the butter in a small saucepan over low heat. Add the paprika mixture and stir through the butter thoroughly.

Pour the butter mixture into the tequila and stir to combine. Leave the tequila at room temperature for about 4 hours, then refrigerate overnight.

The next day, the butter should have solidified on the surface of the tequila. Scoop it off and discard. Strain the tequila through a fine sieve, then again through a sieve lined with muslin (cheesecloth). Makes 700 ml (24 fl oz). Store in a glass bottle in the refrigerator for up to 3 weeks.

ROCKPOOL MAI TAI

> Makes 1

This is one of the favoured drinks of David Doyle. It is such a beautifully simple drink that relies on quality ingredients. Remember this drink will only work with homemade orgeat — which is subtle, nutty and gorgeous. Store-bought bottles of orgeat syrup can be overly sweet and will destroy the complexity of the drink. It's all about the rum.

"I was at the service bar in my Oakland restaurant. I took down a bottle of 17-year-old rum, a fresh lime, added some orange curaçao, and a dollop of French orgeat, for its subtle almond flavour. I stuck in a branch of fresh mint and gave two of them to Ham and Carrie Guild, friends from Tahiti. Carrie took one sip and said, 'Mai Tai – Roa Ae'. In Tahitian this means 'Out of This World – The Best'. Well, that was that. I named the drink Mai Tai." Victor "Trader Vic" Bergeron, 1944.

50 ml (1³/₄ fl oz) aged Jamaican rum

15 ml (¹/₂ fl oz) orgeat syrup

10 ml (¹/₃ fl oz) Cointreau

1 lime, halved

dash Angostura bitters (not essential, but a nice addition)

1 sprig mint

Add the rum, orgeat and Cointreau to a cocktail shaker and fill with ice. Squeeze the lime halves into the shaker and cast aside the husk to use as a garnish. Shake hard and strain into a chilled double rocks glass. Hit the top with a dash of Angostura bitters, if using, and add the mint sprig and lime husk as a garnish.

ORGEAT SYRUP

500 g (1 lb 2 oz) blanched almonds

700 g (1 lb 9 oz) white sugar

50 ml (1³/₄ fl oz) vodka

50 ml (1³/₄ fl oz) brandy

1 bunch mint

40 ml (1¹/₄ fl oz) orange blossom water (optional)

Place the almonds in a bowl, cover with warm water and leave to soak for 30 minutes. Drain and discard the water. Transfer the almonds to a food processor and process until finely chopped. If the mixture gets stuck, you can add some of the water to the food processor.

Transfer the almond to a large saucepan, add 800 ml (28 fl oz) of hot water, bring to the boil and cook for 5 minutes, making sure the mixture doesn't boil over. Strain through a fine sieve lined with muslin (cheesecloth) placed over a bowl. Push down on the solids and squeeze the muslin to extract as much liquid as possible. Discard the almond pulp.

Pour the strained liquid into a clean saucepan over low heat, add the sugar and stir until dissolved, then remove from the heat. Allow to cool for 15 minutes, then add the brandy, mint and orange blossom water. Leave at room temperature for 2 hours. Discard the mint after 2 hours. Makes about 1 litre (35 fl oz/4 cups). Store in a glass bottle in the refrigerator for up to 3 weeks.

ITALIAN SOUR NO. 3

> Makes 1

Inspired by Australian bartender and journalist Naren Young (who is now tending a bar in Manhattan) this drink is a wonderful apéritif or great to enjoy throughout the afternoon. The ingredients are initially shaken without ice. This method of "dry shaking" is used to emulsify the eggwhite.

40 ml (1¼ fl oz) Aperol
20 ml (⅔ fl oz) grapefruit juice
10 ml (⅓ fl oz) Campari
10 ml (⅓ fl oz) Yellow Chartreuse
10 ml (⅓ fl oz) freshly squeezed lemon juice
10 ml (⅓ fl oz) sugar syrup (see note)
10 ml (⅓ fl oz) eggwhite
1 finger-sized strip orange zest
1 finger-sized strip grapefruit zest

Add all of the ingredients, except the citrus zest, to a cocktail shaker and shake vigorously. Fill the shaker with ice and shake once again to combine the ingredients. Strain into a wine glass until half full and top with ice. Squeeze the orange and grapefruit zest directly over the glass to extract the citrus oils. Pop one of the zests into the glass to garnish.

NOTE

To make a simple sugar syrup, dissolve one part white sugar to one part water in a saucepan over medium–high heat. Bring to the boil, then allow to cool before using.

BLOODY MARY

> Makes 1

On a busy lunch (particularly a Friday), we sell upwards of 30 of these between 12.30 pm and 12.45 pm. The acidity of the fresh tomato combined with the natural sweetness of the carrot and spice of the Tabasco makes this a wonderful apéritif. We juice all three vegetables to order (from an operational sense, we have a juice extractor positioned next to our dispense section that has a range of small jugs colour-coded for each juice) and I recommend you do the same if possible.

50 ml (1¾ fl oz) vodka
50 ml (1¾ fl oz) tomato juice
20 ml (⅔ fl oz) carrot juice
20 ml (⅔ fl oz) celery juice
20 ml (⅔ fl oz) freshly squeezed lemon juice
10 ml (⅓ fl oz) Worcestershire sauce
5 dashes red Tabasco sauce
5 dashes green Tabasco sauce
sea salt & freshly ground black pepper
1 small celery stalk, trimmed, to garnish

Add all of the ingredients, except the celery stalk, to a cocktail shaker. Season to taste with salt and pepper and fill the shaker with ice. Roll the shaker forward and back 3–4 times to combine the ingredients. Using a hawthorn strainer, strain the liquid from the shaker into a salt-rimmed wine glass filled with ice. Garnish with the celery stalk.

OUR PINK LADY

> Makes 1

This is more of a twist on a delicious sour that we thought suited the pretty ladies of Rockpool Bar & Grill.

25 ml (⁴/₅ fl oz) Applejack
25 ml (⁴/₅ fl oz) gin
20 ml (²/₃ fl oz) freshly squeezed lemon juice
10 ml (¹/₃ fl oz) grenadine (see opposite)
1 eggwhite
1 finger-sized strip lemon zest

Add all of the ingredients, except the lemon zest, to a cocktail shaker and shake hard to combine. Fill the shaker with ice, then shake hard again. Strain through a hawthorn strainer, then through a fine sieve into a chilled coupette glass. Squeeze the lemon zest directly over the glass to extract the citrus oils.

NEW FASHIONED

> Makes 1

One of the great after-dinner experiences is Ron Zacapa rum from Guatemala. This drink draws some of the great flavours of the spirit to the fore and was inspired by one of our Bar Managers, David Nguyen.

1 cherry, plus one to garnish
1 orange wedge
10 ml (¹/₃ fl oz) spiced sugar syrup
50 ml (1³/₄ fl oz) Ron Zacapa rum
2 dashes chocolate bitters (see note)

Muddle the cherry, orange wedge and spiced sugar syrup together in a double rocks glass. Add the rum and bitters with ice to a double old-fashioned glass and stir about 70 times. Taste to ensure you have the balance between sweet, water dilution and the liquor. Add more ice, if necessary, and garnish with a cherry.

NOTE

You can buy chocolate bitters from specialty liquor shops.

SPICED SUGAR SYRUP

white sugar
10 cloves
2 cinnamon quills
1 vanilla bean, split & seeds scraped
3 star anise
juice of ¹/₂ lime

Dissolve the sugar in an equal amount of water in a saucepan over medium–high heat. Add the spices including the vanilla bean halves, bring to the boil and cook for 5 minutes. Stir in the lime juice and leave to cool overnight. The next day, strain the syrup, discarding the spices. Store in a glass bottle in the refrigerator for up to 1 month.

JACK ROSE

> Makes 1

Anectodal evidence suggests, "Frank J. May, better known as Jack Rose, is the inventor of this very popular cocktail to storm the streets." However, our version draws its heritage from The Old Waldorf-Astoria Bar Book. *This is a crowd-pleasing classic and one of our favourites. As this is such a simple cocktail, we recommend the use of premium ingredients. The lime juice should always be fresh, try making your own version of grenadine with fresh pomegranate and raspberry, and find a Calvados you like (I like a Calvados with only 12 months age on it) in place of the traditional Applejack.*

50 ml (1³/₄ fl oz) Calvados
20 ml (²/₃ fl oz) freshly squeezed lime juice
10 ml (¹/₃ fl oz) grenadine

Add all of the ingredients to a cocktail shaker. Fill with ice and shake hard. Strain through a hawthorn strainer, then through a fine sieve into a coupette (or martini) glass.

GRENADINE

You will need to begin this recipe the day before.

500 g (1 lb 2 oz) rhubarb, tops trimmed & discarded, stalks roughly chopped
2.9 kg (6 lb 8 oz) caster (superfine) sugar
juice of 1 lemon
700 ml (24 fl oz) pomegranate juice (see note)
zest of 2 oranges, removed in strips
1 small handful mint leaves
100 ml (3¹/₂ fl oz) brandy

NOTE

If in season, use fresh pomegranates. You will need about 20–30. First remove the seeds and any white pith, blend the seeds in a blender, then strain the juice. You can use store-bought juice, too.

First you need to make a rhubarb purée. Combine the rhubarb, 300 g (10¹/₂ oz) of the sugar and 200 ml (7 fl oz) of water in a saucepan. The water should cover the rhubarb; if not, transfer to a different pan or add a little more water. Place the pan over medium heat, bring to the boil, stirring to dissolve the sugar. Cook the rhubarb until pulpy. Remove from the heat and, using a stick blender, blend until smooth. Strain through a sieve, discarding the solids. Combine the purée with the lemon juice. You will need 200 g (7 oz) of purée.

To make the grenadine, you want the entire cooking process to be gentle, retaining the freshness and natural sweetness of the fruit.

Place the rhubarb purée, pomegranate juice and 300 ml (10¹/₂ fl oz) of water in a deep-sided saucepan over low heat and whisk to combine. Try not to bring the liquid up to any more than a simmer. When hot, add the remaining 2.6 kg (5 lb 13 oz) of sugar and stir until dissolved, then remove from the heat immediately. It should be a thick, crazy sweet, syrupy liquid at this stage.

Add the orange zest and mint leaves, transfer to a container and refrigerate overnight.

The next day, strain the grenadine and check for sweetness. The best way to do this is to make a Jack Rose or Pink Lady, so start your day right and do it! If it needs more sugar, you will need to gently heat the grenadine and add more, as desired. (Make sure the additional sugar is dissolved, then chill again before using.)

Once you're pretty sure of everything, add the brandy. The brandy works on two levels: it lifts the pomegranate flavour and fortifies the syrup, acting as a preservative. Makes 1 litre (35 fl oz/ 4 cups). Store in a glass bottle in the refrigerator for up to 6 weeks.

THE
RECIPES

ROCKPOOL BAR & GRILL

MY PHILOSOPHY

The philosophy that you will see aired continually throughout this book is one of quality produce and provenance. We need to know where our food comes from and who hunts it, fishes it or grows it for Rockpool Bar & Grill. For these restaurants to hit their heights we must have a tight relationship with our suppliers; we put our trust in them. The reason is simple — we have nothing to hide behind. It is nothing more than great ingredients mixed with the craft of cooking to produce beautiful food that is faithful to the source. There is nothing else to it. Put simply, the quality of our restaurants is defined by our producers.

Therefore, our mantra is sustainable fishing and farming. For us, animals must be humanely treated, live a stress-free life and be able to carry out life in a manner sympathetic to their genetics. Seafood, farmed or wild, must be harvested without harm to its population or habitat or to any other species in its ecosystem.

We shun factory-intensive farmers that produce food at a price point without care for the welfare of the animal. Such food is sad and dreary. Put simply, caring is good for our karma and our enjoyment of taste.

It is so interesting that mankind is so proficient at changing nature and then when issues arise we never really wonder what the cause is. Cause and effect are not really ever thought out. A classic example is milk. We used to have unhomogenised milk. I remember my father would always scoop the cream off the top for his porridge. Somewhere along the way we decided to homogenise milk and make sure it looked the same all the way through with no cream on top. What the hell was wrong with a bit of separation anyway? "What is wrong with that?" I hear you ask. Well three things. It doesn't taste as good, is nowhere near as creamy or sweet and, most importantly, it is fattening.

When milk is in its natural state, the fat molecules are large and our body grabs those first to use as energy. When you smash them and thus suspend them in water (that is, homogenise it) they go into the body and can't be accessed for energy easily, so they get stored as fat. What is our answer to that? Well, instead of going back to drinking real milk we now have about 20 different types of milk, all of them low fat in one way or another. All we need is one really, but us clever humans just can't help ourselves. We have to engineer the "perfect" product to within an inch of its life. Will we ever learn?

RAW AND CURED THINGS

Raw and cured seafood is a cornerstone of Rockpool Bar & Grill. Raw fish in its peak season served with many seasonings is always on the menu. Great beef at Rockpool Bar & Grill is a given but our seafood program rivals it. In reality, if we want to be a great modern steakhouse, we have to do all the other things really well too, not just steak. This has not always been a steakhouse tradition, but I want to bring people to the restaurant even if meat isn't their thing. I want people to know that they can come here for a beautiful plate of raw fish or a piece of cooked fish on a day they are giving beef a break.

I will give you a heads-up on what I believe to be one of the very best ways to start a meal: fresh seafood. And eaten raw. The world's preoccupation with sushi and sashimi seems to back me up, but soy and wasabi, although enjoyable, are by no means the only ways to enjoy raw seafood; Mediterranean style with a few drops of extra virgin olive oil and a sprinkle of sea salt is equally as good. I'm also a big fan of just a few drops of fresh lemon juice. This is the starting point at Bar & Grill.

This is a collection of my favourite raw and cured fish dishes that are easy to prepare and depend on the quality of the fish going into them. I often like to say that simple is hard, and it is so true of these dishes. You hide behind nothing — the quality of the fish is everything.

Nearly all fin fish and shellfish can be enjoyed raw in their natural state. They have a delicate taste and texture. But I will say it again, it does depend on freshness and also how the fish has been handled; well-handled fish improves the taste and texture quality immeasurably. A fresh well-handled fish will taste better every time than a fresh fish that is poorly handled.

I know that it's pretty difficult for the average person to buy super fresh fish to enjoy raw. I say that assuming most folks aren't fishing for their own dinner (if you are, then good luck to you and remember to take lots of ice for a slurry and to spike the larger fish) and that most people reading this book may not live near a fish market or that the great restaurant-quality fresh fish that I get may be beyond your reach. Well don't despair, frozen fish will fit the bill. Not just any frozen fish, though. I'm talking about fish frozen using the best technology. As with fresh, there is frozen and *frozen* — you want the highest quality and it is out there. Remember, if it's crap going into the freezer, it certainly will be coming out.

Frozen fish that is caught really well and expertly frozen is indeed "fresher" than a piece of fish out of the water for a few days — the vast majority of tuna consumed in Japan is from frozen fish. So you're better off sourcing great-quality tuna, prawns (shrimp), scallops, scampi (langoustine) and other fish that you know come from sustainable origins, are well handled and frozen and have been well looked after down the supply chain.

You can then thaw your frozen seafood in your fridge and serve it raw knowing it's of the highest quality and really truly fresh. Get to know your fishmonger well. Generally the most expensive frozen fish and shellfish will be the best — it's usually the most expensive because it will be from Australia and handling something well costs more, so make the investment.

"As with fresh, there is frozen and frozen — you want the highest quality and it is out there. Remember, if it's crap going into the freezer, it certainly will be coming out. Frozen fish that is caught really well and expertly frozen is indeed 'fresher' than a piece of fish out of the water for a few days."

FRESHLY SHUCKED OYSTERS

I guess in any recipe book you have to start with the first recipe. How could you start a chapter about raw seafood eaten at its very best without starting with oysters? Now this isn't so much a recipe as it is a technique. When I say oysters, I don't mean those shucked and washed dead things you see people buy and eat in Australia. I mean a beautiful live oyster waiting to be shucked, with salty brine in its shell, ready to be slurped and eaten. It's probably one of the most perfect and fantastic foods in the world. It's not just raw seafood, it's live seafood.

As a kid, my dad would take me oyster gathering at Bald Face Point in Sydney, New South Wales. His skill with a screwdriver and an oyster shucker were legendary in my family, as was my lack of balance. In my youth, oysters were more closely associated with falling off the rocks and cutting my feet to pieces. Mum was always on standby to pick all the shell bits out of the cut, which was no mean feat with me squealing and squirming. As much as my poor balance was hard on my feet, I soon learnt that oysters could be pleasurable as well, tasting like heaven.

After leaving home, I didn't think much about oysters (although I was very suspicious of the open ones in the market covered in wet paper) until I went to Europe and, once again, tasted magnificent freshly shucked oysters (which once fed the poor of Paris in all their glory).

Well, from then on, in all of my restaurants, I have done the right thing by the wonderful bivalve and simply knocked their shell off and served them straight up. We sell thousands of them every week. They're one of the biggest selling appetisers as they're a perfect light start before jumping into a steak.

It seems that the Australian habit of shucking before buying is now starting to disappear in quality restaurants, and one can get good oysters in most places. Freshly shucked oysters need nothing more than some good-quality rye bread with a smear of great butter. You may add a squeeze of fresh lemon juice and a grind of pepper but that could put a purist's nose out of joint. If you wish, make this simple mignonette sauce — its sharpness goes well with the briny oyster.

live oysters in the shell

MIGNONETTE SAUCE

100 ml (3½ fl oz) Champagne vinegar
2 red eschalots, minced
sea salt & freshly ground black pepper

To make the mignonette sauce, combine the vinegar and eschalot and season to taste with salt and pepper. This makes enough to dress one to two dozen oysters.

To shuck an oyster, place a folded tea towel in one hand. Using the tea towel, hold the oyster firmly on a chopping board with the pointy end facing towards you. Take an oyster knife and gently wedge it between the two shells at the pointy end at a slight angle. Once you've got the oyster knife in, give the knife a turn; the shell should lift up and the muscle that holds the shell shut will snap. Slide the knife up and cut the muscle from the shell and the oyster is ready to serve. Remove any grit around the oyster but do not rinse. You can also cut the muscle (the foot) on the underside and turn the oyster over in its shell for easier eating (this is a good idea if you're serving them as a stand-up canapé). Top with a little mignonette sauce, if desired.

BRENDIE GUIDERA, THE OYSTER WHISPERER

There's only one oyster man for seafood expert John Susman *and that's Brendie Guidera, a pioneer of doing things differently and a man who has a laser focus on producing the best. He is without peer on the west coast of South Australia. John shares what he likes best about Brendie's oysters.*

Brendie Guidera is a rare bird in the oyster business. He is a man of few words, preferring to spend his time with his oysters than with people. It's hard to think of another oyster farmer in Australia who understands his crop so intimately. His brand of Pristine Oyster Farm oysters from Coffin Bay are unique not only in their shape, size and incredible meat-to-shell ratio but also in their characteristic sweetness — unusual in a region renowned for the mouth-puckering, salty zing of most oysters.

Brendie and his family of local fishermen are pioneers in the oyster-farming business in South Australia, a relatively new industry (well, only one generation old) that is now centred around Coffin Bay on the west coast of the Eyre Peninsula. Brendie understood that the environment of Coffin Bay was special, and he chose a sub-region within the bay, known as Longnose, to develop his unique farming methods.

Brendie's focus is on producing an oyster with a small but deep cup and one that is intensely flavoured. The gem of his order sheet is the Kumamoto-style oyster, a small, deep-shelled bivalve, named after the famed Japanese style of farming that Brendie has emulated. The shell of the Kumamoto is about the size of a fifty-cent piece and the oyster inside is plump, creamy, briny and sweet. They look like baby oysters but are the same age as any other harvest-ready Pacific oyster. To develop their flavour and unique shape, the Kumamotos are hung close to the surface of the bay, where the strong current tumbles them against each other, knocking off new shell growth from around the rim and forcing the shell to grow deep.

It's revolutionary for Australian oyster farming. It's never been truer that the proof is in the tasting, as they say.

TATHRA OYSTERS,
THE MIGHTY SYDNEY ROCK

Tathra Oysters are one of Australia's most highly awarded foods. In blind oyster-tasting competitions, they have been judged Australia's best on 15 separate occasions. They received the 2006 Royal Agricultural Society of New South Wales' highest award, The President's Medal — a recognition of a quality product, produced in a sustainable and environmentally friendly way. Sydney rocks don't get any better than those from the Tathra family and that's why I serve them at the restaurant.

The Rodely family have been farming their Tathra Oysters at Nelsons Lagoon on the far south coast of New South Wales for more than 20 years. Nelsons Lagoon is regarded as Australia's most pristine home of the Sydney rock oyster. Situated in Mimosa Rocks National Park, the Tathra Oysters farm is surrounded by verdant green forest.

For Gary Rodely, growing oysters is a labour of love. He attributes the farm's fabulous location to the success of their oysters but there's no doubt that loads of hard work, innovative farming techniques, including very low stocking densities and adjustable growing heights, contribute to their great product, together with, of course, a considerable dollop of passion.

As a child growing up in the Riverina district of New South Wales, Gary always envied his friends whose parents owned farms. "I always wanted to be a farmer, to grow food, to nurture crops or animals," says Gary. "That idea always appealed to me." Years later at the age of 28, Gary happened to be in the right place at the right time to buy an oyster farm on the water at Nelsons Lagoon, and he jumped at the chance to live out his dream of being a farmer combined with his lifelong love of the ocean.

Today, Gary and his wife, Jo, run the farm together with his two children Sam and Brooke, who share their father's enthusiasm and bring their marine science and economic expertise to the family business.

WORKING WITH SCALLOPS

If you ever have the chance to buy live scallops and take them home to shuck, try them raw. They're one of the greatest seafood sensations. So sweet and nutty, firm of texture, with a hauntingly long flavour of the sea and not at all fishy. They're simply sublime, the taste of true heaven. It's a tragedy to me to serve scallops raw unless they're shucked fresh from live. I like to say, if a scallop had a heart, it would still be beating.

THE SCALLOP KING

I'm lucky to buy live scallops directly from a rock-star fisherman called Mark Eather, who is based in Kettering just out of Hobart in Tasmania. What makes his scallops taste so sublime is the way he handles them sustainably.

"First, we catch the scallop from the wild as a minuscule spat, about 0.3 mm in size, in collector bags," says Mark. "The spats attach themselves to these collector bags, which are made of plastic mesh and look like 'pillows' hanging in a water column. When they have grown to 5 mm (¼ inch) in size, they detach from the mesh and fall to the bottom of the outer bag. This is when we service the collectors, then place them into 'lantern cages', basically mesh cages in layers of 10 to 15 that resemble a Chinese lantern, and grow them out to at least 40 mm (1½ inches) on our lines before releasing them — if we released them any smaller, then predators, such as ocky, skate and flathead, would make a meal of them. When they've reached 40-plus mm, we release them onto the sea floor and let them grow naturally for two more years, after which divers harvest them by hand to minimise stress, and they're packed and delivered that morning. So my scallops you eat are around three to three-and-a-half years old.

"After many years of trials, we've found that this Great Bay area produces the amazing flavour synonymous with our scallops, so the end product is a combination of good handling and location."

Mark is so clever. He makes sure most of the scallops in the bay reach maturity by removing them out of the predators' way and he only harvests a percentage of what he returns to the bay. This means we get to enjoy these beautiful treats for a long time.

I love it when his little beauties come in the back door at one of my restaurants. They go straight into the tanks and lay in wait till ordered and then, and only then, are shucked and simply dressed with extra virgin olive oil, lime or lemon juice, perhaps a bit of chilli or maybe served ceviche style. Whichever way, they are to die for.

BEWARE THE SOAKED SCALLOP

It has been recent practice to soak scallops in water with sodium triphosphate. This practice robs the scallop buyer not only of weight but also quality. A soaked scallop loses all its moisture when cooked. A fresh high-quality scallop will be firm and look sparkling; a soaked one will be more opaque and soft. Don't fall for a soaked scallop as the taste and texture is underwhelming. I would hate to think you wondered what all the fuss was about when a truly fresh (dry) scallop can be a wonderful thing.

HOW TO SHUCK A SCALLOP

Hold the scallop with a tea towel by its rounded edge, with the hinged bottom facing up. Identify the difference between the two shells: one is flat and the other rounded. There will be a small gap between the shells. Take a sharp paring knife and push it in, sharp-side of the blade towards the round ends of the shell, move it up with the blade flat against the top flat shell — you're cutting the top of the muscle that opens and closes the shell. This muscle is the scallop. The shell should spring open. You then need to trace around the scallop with the tip of the knife to remove the skirt and gut. You should now be able to pull it off the top flat shell leaving the scallop and its orange roe sitting beautifully in the shell.

THE BEST WAY TO EAT THESE BEAUTIES

Fresh scallops need nothing more than a squeeze of fresh lemon, a drizzle of extra virgin olive oil, a sprinkle of sea salt and a grind of pepper, then straight down the hatch. If you want to add some complexity, however, see page 94 for a couple of flavours that work a treat.

They're also great with a ceviche dressing. Marinate the scallops in lime juice for about 2 minutes, then make a dressing of fresh lime juice, chilli and extra virgin olive oil. You can garnish it with finely diced red and green capsicum (pepper), avocado and tomato, some fresh herbs and season with sea salt and a grind of pepper. Combine with the scallops, then return the scallops to their shells for a nice presentation.

QUEEN SCALLOPS WITH PRESERVED LEMON SALSA & HARISSA

> Serves 4

I'm a really big fan of Moroccan flavours with raw fish and shellfish, and this preserved lemon salsa really hits the mark with any raw seafood. With my cheat's version of making instant preserved lemons (without having to wait the usual six weeks), you have no excuse but to try it.

12 live Queen scallops, shucked, roe on (see page 93)

juice of 1 lemon

sea salt & freshly ground black pepper

2 tablespoons preserved lemon salsa (see page 434)

2 teaspoons my harrisa (see page 344)

1 tablespoon coriander (cilantro) leaves, thinly sliced

Halve each scallop horizontally. Place in a non-metallic bowl, pour over the lemon juice, season with a little salt and marinate for 5 minutes.

Divide between plates, arranging in a circle. Top each with some of the preserved lemon salsa, then a dollop of harissa, sprinkle with the coriander and season to taste with salt and pepper.

QUEEN SCALLOPS WITH LEMON & CORIANDER

> Serves 4

Beautiful fresh scallops have a sweet taste and a firm texture to the bite that merges into a silky mouthful. If they are live or super fresh, there is no other tastier seafood to eat raw. The simplest way to serve them (other than straight out of the shell) is with this easy dressing. You can use this dressing with all manner of raw seafood — it really lifts the flavour, making it more delicious. When tomatoes are ripe and beautiful at the peak of summer, simply tear a couple of peeled and seeded ones into the salad.

12 live Queen scallops, shucked, roe on (see page 93)

juice of 1 lemon

sea salt & freshly ground black pepper

60 ml (2 fl oz/¼ cup) extra virgin olive oil

½ teaspoon coriander seeds, toasted & lightly crushed

1 small handful coriander (cilantro) leaves

Place the scallops, lemon juice and a good pinch of sea salt in a non-metallic bowl and leave to marinate for 5 minutes, then add the olive oil and mix gently to combine.

Divide between bowls, pour over the dressing, sprinkle with the coriander seeds and leaves and season to taste with salt and pepper.

PICKLED BLUE NOSE MACKEREL, APPLE & POTATO SALAD

> Serves 4

This is a take on the classic pickled herring. Blue nose mackerel has a high oil content, making it a great substitute for herring. The vinegar cooks the fish through, giving it a wonderful bite to the texture. Here in Australia, herring is called tommy ruff, which can also be used to make this wonderful dish. I recently had a beautiful starter in a great seafood restaurant called La Cagouille in Paris. They served the herring with a simple steamed ratte potato, starchy and sweet — the sweetness of the natural potato flavour worked a treat with the oily fish. I love the fresh horseradish used in this dish as well, but for convenience you could use a really nice horseradish relish instead. If you don't want to marinate your own, there are very good quality pickled herrings and rollmops (herrings that are rolled up and placed in a jar to pickle) available at delis. But if you can get spanking fresh fish, do dive in and try this recipe.

You will need to begin this recipe 2 days ahead.

PICKLED BLUE NOSE MACKEREL

4 blue nose mackerel
sea salt
60 ml (2 fl oz/¼ cup) white vinegar
1 red onion, thinly sliced
3 fresh bay leaves
2 tablespoons soft brown sugar
1 very small pinch of coriander seeds
1 very small pinch of fennel seeds
1 very small pinch of allspice
½ teaspoon black peppercorns

Clean, fillet and pin-bone the mackerel (see page 256), leaving the skin on. Sprinkle the fillets with the salt and leave for 1 hour at room temperature to cure.

Meanwhile, place the remaining ingredients and 250 ml (9 fl oz/1 cup) of water in a small saucepan and bring to the boil, stirring to dissolve the sugar. Set aside to cool.

Wipe the salt and moisture from the surface of the mackerel and place in a glass container large enough to fit the fillets snugly either lying flat or rolled up. Pour over the pickling liquid, cover and refrigerate for 2–5 days or until firm.

TO SERVE

60 g (2¼ oz/¼ cup) crème fraîche
60 ml (2 fl oz/¼ cup) milk
2 teaspoons grated horseradish root
juice of 1 lemon
pinch of white sugar
sea salt & freshly ground black pepper
200 g (7 oz) pink-eye, pink fir apple or kipfler potatoes, cooked, peeled & thinly sliced
2 Granny Smith apples, cored, halved & thinly sliced
1 small red onion, thinly sliced
1 tablespoon flat-leaf (Italian) parsley leaves, thinly sliced

Place the crème fraîche and milk in a bowl and beat until soft peaks form. Add the horseradish, lemon juice and sugar and season to taste with salt and pepper.

Drain the pickled mackerel and discard the bay leaves and spices. Cut the mackerel into rough 3 cm (1¼ inch) squares and place in a large bowl. Add the potato, apple, onion and crème fraîche dressing and gently mix together.

Divide between plates, sprinkle with the parsley and grind over a good amount of pepper.

CUTTING RAW FISH

I tend to use two methods to cut raw fish. For both methods, the knife you use needs to be sharp. As a matter of fact, you'll find the kitchen a much more enjoyable place to be if you have sharp knives. Learn to sharpen your knives. It isn't rocket science and I find it very satisfying.

HIRAZUKURI METHOD

When the fish is large, such as tuna, swordfish, kingfish and snapper, I cut it into a block. I cut straight down the shoulders, using a sashimi knife, in one sweep of the knife, from the heel to the tip. This gives the fish a straight edge and a pleasing sheen. We tend to cut it into blocks and then slice sashimi style for crudo and other raw dishes. Try to cut each slice in a fluid motion. Hold the heel of your knife against the fish and bring the knife towards you carefully and deliberately. By the time the tip of your knife cuts through the fish, you'll have completed one slice with the knife, then move onto cutting the next slice. It's this clean cutting that gives the fish its sheen. Make sure you wipe your knife with every cut.

Generally, for fish cut hirazukuri, I serve the slices in a straight line, slightly overlapping.

USUZUKURI METHOD

When I need to cut fish that are whole fillets, usually smaller and thinner, but not always, I cut the fish on the bias in thin slices — envisage what sliced smoked salmon looks like and that's what you're trying to achieve. Generally, for fish cut usuzukuri, I normally serve the slices fanned out in a circular shape.

I have given a weight of 90 g (3^1/$_3$ oz) of raw fish per person for the following recipes. I believe that this is ample for a starter, but by all means take it up or down as you desire.

RAW TUNA

> Serves 4

360 g (12³/₄ oz) sashimi-grade tuna fillet
lemon wedges, to serve
60 ml (2 fl oz/¹/₄ cup) extra virgin olive oil
sea salt & freshly ground black pepper

Slice the tuna into 5 mm (¹/₄ inch) thick
slices and arrange on plates. Squeeze over
the lemon, drizzle with the olive oil and
season to taste with salt and pepper.

Tuna is one of the world's great delights in both flavour and texture. The wonderful fatty taste of tuna in good condition and well handled is much sought after, not only in Japanese restaurants but also more and more with chefs serving Mediterranean flavours. It tastes great in its simplest form, so if you do have access to really good fish, don't do too much with it.

In addition to this tuna recipe, I have included other simple recipes in this chapter that would be equally delicious with any number of other fish and shellfish, so don't be dismayed if the tuna isn't great quality on the day you go to the market — you can just swap it for whatever is looking fresh.

Tuna is region specific so it's worth checking to see if the species is under threat, then make decisions based on sound information. In Australia we work hard at managing our local fish stocks, but the same can't always be said of other countries, so be aware of origin and satisfy yourself that the right approach has been taken.

Simple and delicious, this dish is like a carpaccio. If the piece of tuna is too big for you to cut, then cut it in half first so you're dealing with two smaller semicircles. If you're confident in cutting, then leave it as one piece as the dish will look better as large slices on the plate.

I'm also not a big fan of cutting the tuna super thin as you don't really appreciate the taste and texture. Above all, I would never beat the fish out as I have seen people do, as it's already very tender and you would alter the taste and mouthfeel.

You can embellish this dish by serving it with toasted baguette or sourdough, adding chopped fresh or dried chilli, chopped capers or olives or both, or a little sprinkle of finely diced red onion. The addition of fresh herbs would be welcome as well, just make sure you don't add too much.

HAGEN STEHR,
THE KINGFISH KAISER

When John Susman first brought hiramasa kingfish into the kitchen I couldn't believe how good it was. I was not a major fan of farmed fish for no other reason than I thought wild tasted better. When we cut the first raw slice and popped it into our mouths, my opinion changed forever. This fish had great flavour but more importantly it had amazing texture — a real melt-in-the-mouth quality. From that point on, I put it on all my raw plates and called it white tuna.

Hagen Stehr is a living reflection of the can-do spirit. He is the unofficial fuhrer of Port Lincoln in South Australia. With a life story that would never be believed in Hollywood, Hagen Stehr, or the Kaiser, as he is affectionately known, is a true believer that life is all about vision. A defector from the French Foreign Legion, Hagen, found himself in the sixties as a fisherman in Port Lincoln, battling the high seas of the Great Southern Ocean, harvesting southern bluefin tuna — a fish that at that time was worth a mere twenty cents a kilo at the cannery. After the fishery nearly collapsed from over-fishing and the Federal Government imposed significant restrictions to the allowable catch levels, Hagen, along with a small group of entrepreneurial fishermen, started tuna ranching (where a school of tuna is caught in a large purse seine net and towed back to port, where the fish are fed for up to nine months and double in size during that time) and quickly became one of Australia's richest men.

Hagen formed Clean Seas Aquaculture, in 2001, to farm kingfish as a means by which he could master the art of propagating a pelagic fish species from eggs produced in a hatchery, with the intention of replicating this process with southern bluefin tuna. Years later, he had become so enamoured with the yellowtail kingfish, having recognised that its commercial and culinary qualities made it a star in its own right, that he launched full throttle into building the largest kingfish farming operation in the world. (Clean Seas call their farmed kingfish by its Japanese name, hiramasa, to differentiate it from the wild variety.)

All the while, he continued to work on the development of the world's only southern bluefin tuna hatchery. In 2009 Hagen announced that his team of scientists had bred the first southern bluefin tuna in captivity.

Now in his mid-seventies, Hagen's pace, commitment and passion are an inspiration — his innate understanding of the fragility of nature and his drive for a future that has seafood on the table of every celebration makes Hagen Stehr not only a friend of Rockpool but also a true friend of the sea.

HIRAMASA KINGFISH TARTARE

> Serves 4

These garnishes are the flavours you would expect in a traditional steak tartare; they happen to work splendidly with fish. Tuna, salmon and mackerel would be great substitutes. I also like the dressing with raw (green) prawns (shrimp) or scallops. You can, if you wish, incorporate the egg yolk into the dressing — it adds weight and flavour to the dish and you can divide the tartare straight onto four plates and serve. I do, however, like the traditional presentation of the egg yolk on top.

360 g (12¾ oz) sashimi-grade hiramasa kingfish fillet

2 teaspoons finely chopped flat-leaf (Italian) parsley

2 teaspoons finely chopped salted capers

2 teaspoons finely chopped gherkin

2 teaspoons finely chopped red onion

Worcestershire & Tabasco sauce

1 teaspoon dry Japanese mustard

juice of 1 lemon

100 ml (3½ fl oz) extra virgin olive oil

sea salt & freshly ground black pepper

1 egg yolk

toast fingers & lemon wedges, to serve

Coarsely chop the kingfish with a very sharp knife. Place in a bowl with the parsley, capers, gherkin and onion and mix gently to combine.

In another bowl, add a few drops each of Worcestershire and Tabasco sauces. Add the mustard and lemon juice and, using a fork, whisk in the olive oil to make a dressing. Season to taste with salt and pepper. Add to the kingfish and toss gently to combine.

Spoon onto a large plate in a mound, place the egg yolk on top and season with pepper. Serve as a shared plate with toast fingers and lemon wedges on the side.

Mix the egg yolk through the tartare at the table.

RAW SCHOOL PRAWNS

> Serves 4

Little fresh school prawns (we get them live at the restaurant — the advantage of tanks) make a wonderful raw dish. You can marinate them in lemon or lime juice and add some herbs or spices, but when they're good and fresh, I like them served very simply. Like fresh scallops, you'll marvel at how sweet fresh school prawns are. Use wild-caught school prawns for this dish. They can be frozen, if from a quality Australian source — I advise against using frozen imported prawns, as you can't be sure of where they've come from. If using frozen ones, make sure you buy them frozen and thaw them yourself. It works best if you peel them while they're still very cold.

500 g (1 lb 2 oz) raw (green) school prawns (shrimp), peeled & deveined

juice & finely grated zest of 1 lemon

3 dried small chillies, crumbled

sea salt & freshly ground black pepper

60 ml (2 fl oz/¼ cup) extra virgin olive oil

2 tablespoons flat-leaf (Italian) parsley leaves, chiffonade

Combine the prawns, lemon juice and zest and chilli in a bowl and season with a good pinch of salt. Set aside for 5 minutes to marinate.

Add the olive oil and parsley and mix gently. Divide the prawns and dressing between bowls, grind over a good amount of pepper and serve immediately.

SEARED SWORDFISH WITH RED BRAISED VEGETABLES

> Serves 4

This is a classic Rockpool dish that has made its way to the Bar & Grill menus. I have been making these Mediterranean-inspired "red" braised vegetables for years. They're really like a fine ratatouille. They're divine with a creamy sweet-tasting fish such as swordfish or with raw fish. You can also add a dollop of aioli on the fish at the end, or it's pretty good with tapenade, too.

RED BRAISED VEGETABLES

3 eggplant (aubergines)

table salt

180 ml (5²/₃ fl oz) olive oil

1 small handful basil leaves

1 small handful flat-leaf (Italian) parsley leaves

1 tablespoon salted baby capers, rinsed

1 brown onion, finely diced

3 garlic cloves, finely diced

5 anchovy fillets, finely chopped

sea salt & freshly ground black pepper

4 red capsicum (peppers), finely diced

5 tomatoes, peeled, seeds removed (see glossary) & diced

Halve the eggplant and scoop out the seeds and most of the flesh, leaving about 1 cm (¹/₂ inch) attached to the skin. Discard the scooped-out bits. Cut the skin into 1 cm (¹/₂ inch) dice. Lightly salt and set aside for 15 minutes. Rinse and pat dry with paper towel.

Heat 100 ml (3¹/₂ fl oz) of the olive oil in a large heavy-based frying pan over medium–high heat. Cook the eggplant until golden all over. Remove, using a slotted spoon, drain well on paper towel and place in a large bowl.

Return the pan to medium–high heat and, when the oil is hot, add the herbs and fry until crisp. Remove, using a slotted spoon, reserving the oil in the pan. Drain on paper towel, then add to the eggplant.

Add the capers to the hot oil in the pan and fry until crisp. Remove and drain on paper towel, then add to the eggplant.

Discard the oil. Heat the remaining oil over medium–low heat. Add the onion, garlic and anchovy and sauté for 5 minutes or until the onion has softened. Add the capsicum and cook for 5 minutes or until softened. Add to the eggplant mixture.

Add the tomato, season to taste with salt and pepper and gently mix. Makes 1 cup.

TO SERVE

360 g (12³/₄ oz) sashimi-grade swordfish fillet

2 tablespoons extra virgin olive oil, plus extra for drizzling

¹/₃ cup tomato jam (see page 433)

20 black olives, pitted & halved

juice of ¹/₂ lemon

Season the swordfish with salt.

Heat the olive oil in a frying pan over high heat until just before smoking, add the swordfish and cook for about 20 seconds on all sides or until seared and it has a good colour. Remove from the pan and place on a chopping board.

Place the red braised vegetables, tomato jam and olives in a bowl and gently mix.

Spoon the vegetable mixture in the centre of each plate. Using a large, sharp knife, cut the fish into 5 mm (¹/₄ inch) thick slices and arrange on top of the vegetables. Drizzle with a little lemon juice and extra virgin olive oil and season to taste with salt and pepper.

SALMON TARTARE WITH OLIVES

> Serves 4

I call any fish I chop up "tartare", so you will see this from time to time on my menus, although they may vary wildly in ingredients. This is a deliciously simple way to eat raw fish. Here I've used pine nuts and olives — I like to use green olives in this dish as they are not as strong and have a wonderful nutty flavour. Lots of different fish work well in this dish, particularly the oily ones, as the dressing is full-flavoured.

360 g (12³/₄ oz) sashimi-grade salmon fillet, pin-boned

1 teaspoon black mustard seeds, toasted

1 tablespoon salted capers, rinsed & drained

2 French shallots (eschalots), thinly sliced

juice & finely grated zest of 1 lemon

1 tablespoon Dijon mustard

60 ml (2 fl oz/¹/₄ cup) extra virgin olive oil

sea salt & freshly ground black pepper

8 large green olives, pitted & roughly chopped

2 tablespoons pine nuts, roasted

2 spring onions (scallions), thinly sliced into rounds

toast or bruschetta, to serve

Using a sharp knife, roughly chop the salmon and place in a bowl.

Place the mustard seeds, capers, shallot, lemon juice and zest and mustard in a bowl. Using a fork, mix in the olive oil and season to taste with salt and pepper. Add to the salmon.

Add the olives and pine nuts and mix gently.

Divide between plates, season to taste and scatter over the spring onion. Serve with toast or, if you want to go really crazy, my favourite hand-cut fat chips (see page 358).

HOW TO KILL A LOBSTER

Celebrity fishmonger Paul Johnson asks the question: "Do crabs and lobsters feel pain?" in his wonderful book, Fish Forever. *There are a lot of organisations that would have us believe they do, but the science behind it would suggest that they don't feel pain, at least not the way we humans do. With a decentralised nervous system and no cerebral cortex to register pain, it would seem that to be cut in half is as humane a death as possible. I do however think that from a karmic point of view, it's always best to treat living things the way you would want to be treated. So these are two simple ways to dispatch your lobster, kindly, and, if they die without any stress, the texture will be all the better for it.*

METHOD ONE

Fill a basin with enough water to completely cover the lobster. Submerge the lobster in the water, cover with a large chopping board or tray and weigh it down as it will thrash about a bit. You are drowning the lobster. I have heard it is quite a good way to go, but that is just hearsay. Drowning the lobster in fresh water prevents their legs falling off.

METHOD TWO

Place the lobster in the freezer for an hour or two. This puts it to sleep and is by far the easiest way to kill a lobster.

RAW LOBSTER WITH CHILLI & MINT

> Serves 4

I first had lobster raw in Tokyo. I was slightly sceptical of how it would taste, but one mouthful and I was converted for life. The texture of raw lobster is silky and the taste is so sweet. This is a very basic ceviche and works well with any kind of fish or shellfish, not just lobster — use whatever is spanking fresh. Live lobster is amazing, though, and, let's face it, you can't get anything fresher. The lime juice cooks the lobster and tightens up the protein structure, creating a very pleasing texture.

This recipe only uses the flesh from the lobster tail, so rinse and freeze the shell and, when you have a couple saved, use them to make a great stock, soup or sauce.

1 x 750 g (1 lb 10 oz) live lobster
sea salt & freshly ground black pepper
juice of 3 limes
8 mint leaves, chiffonade
1 spring onion (scallion), thinly sliced diagonally
2 wild green Thai chillies or jalapeño chillies, seeds removed
125 ml (4 fl oz/½ cup) extra virgin olive oil

Dispatch the lobster humanely (see opposite). Bring a saucepan of salted water to the boil. Plunge the lobster into the boiling water and cook for 1 minute, then remove and immediately submerge in iced water and leave until cooled. This process makes it easier to remove the meat as it may stick to the shell.

When the lobster is cold, remove from the water bath and place on a chopping board. Run a sharp paring knife around the gap between the head and tail. Using scissors, cut down the two sides of the shell on the belly side. Remove the digestive tract. Remove the tail meat, roughly chop and place in a bowl. Season to taste with salt, drizzle with the lime juice and mix well. Set aside for 3 minutes to marinate.

Add the remaining ingredients and taste for seasoning. Divide between plates, spoon over the dressing from the bowl and grind over a good amount of pepper. Serve immediately.

CRUDO OF KINGFISH, OCEAN TROUT & TUNA WITH HORSERADISH, SHALLOT, CORIANDER & LEMON OIL

> Serves 4

Crudo is Italian for raw and it sounds much better on a menu than "raw fish" — it's amazing how a name change can make a huge difference in sales. This is our sashimi-style dish and, along with the "four raw tastes of the sea" (see page 117), is one of our most popular starters. Here we adopt the Italian method of presenting raw fish, with extra virgin olive oil and lemon juice replacing the traditional soy sauce and wasabi. The crudo idea came from a visit to a wonderful seafood restaurant called Esca in Manhattan on the West side at the beginning of 2000. My friend Johnny Apple who was a respected food critic and a helluva guy, had recommended Esca to me. We went and enjoyed the most beautiful raw razor clam, flake and snapper dressed with only some simple extra virgin olive oil variations. They were called crudo and I immediately fell in love with the idea of serving Italian-style raw fish at Rockpool in Sydney. It has been part of the menu for more than a decade now. I do believe that Esca chef David Pasternak is one of the great fish cooks on the planet. He is the only other chef (along with myself and Sydney chefs Greg Doyle and Stephen Hodges) who I have ever met who cares so passionately about how fish is caught and looked after. If you're ever in New York and need a great meal, you don't have to go much further than Dave's joint.

This dish can be done with one type of fish or as many as you like — shellfish are pretty delicious done this way.

We use native Australian finger limes when in season (instead of the lemon segments) and sprinkle them over the fish. They're often referred to as "lime caviar" as their flesh looks like little round balls. The best way to try them is to pop the little citrus balls in your mouth — they're sour and slightly bitter at the same time, making them an amazing marriage with fish.

120 g (4¼ oz) hiramasa kingfish fillet

120 g (4¼ oz) ocean trout fillet

120 g (4¼ oz) yellowfin tuna loin

sea salt & freshly ground black pepper

40 g (1½ oz) grated horseradish root

40 g (1½ oz) French shallots (eschalots), thinly sliced

40 g (1½ oz) lemon segments (see glossary), finely chopped

1 handful coriander (cilantro) leaves, chiffonade

1 teaspoon coriander seeds, toasted & crushed

lemon oil (see page 435), to taste

Thinly slice each fish into 12 pieces. Place 3 slices of each fish, slightly overlapping, on each plate. Season to taste with salt and pepper. Scatter over the remaining ingredients and drizzle over the lemon oil.

RAW LEATHERJACKET WITH CHERRY TOMATO & CHILLI

> Serves 4

Leatherjacket is another fish that deserves more care. It's very versatile and is a great way to start kids eating whole fish, as the flesh is easy to pick off. As a kid my dad and I spent many a day fishing for leatherjackets. They would be beheaded, gutted, skinned and in the pan before they knew what was happening. This fish, well handled and fresh, is so sweet with a lovely medium flake. It is truly delicious to eat. We serve it pan-fried and deep-fried, both whole and filleted, but when it's raw, it's at its most lovely. It's very rarely served raw, so if you happen to catch some or see a couple that are fresh and looking spanking, dive into it. I promise, you'll rarely eat such good-value seafood.

360 g (12³/₄ oz) sashimi-grade leatherjacket fillets
8 cherry tomatoes, halved
sea salt & freshly ground black pepper
3 dried small chillies
2 teaspoons chopped flat-leaf (Italian) parsley
¹/₂ teaspoon chopped marjoram
juice of 1 lemon
125 ml (4 fl oz/¹/₂ cup) extra virgin olive oil
juice of 1 lime

Using a sharp knife, cut the leatherjacket fillets on the bias into thin slices. Arrange the slices on plates in a circular pattern.

Squeeze the seeds and juice of the tomatoes into a bowl. Roughly chop the flesh and add to the seeds. Season to taste with salt and crumble in the dried chillies. Add the herbs, lemon juice and olive oil and mix gently.

Drizzle the leatherjacket with the lime juice, season to taste with salt and pepper, then spoon over the tomato salsa. Serve immediately.

FLATHEAD CEVICHE

> Serves 4

This is the ceviche we sell the most of at Rockpool Bar & Grill. We feature it regulary on our signature plate, the "four raw tastes of the sea" (see page 117), alternating the flathead with scampi (langoustine). Flathead has a great flavour and texture and, if handled well at capture, really shines as one of the great sashimi fish. We use red, green and yellow capsicum in this dish at the restaurant, but you can easily use just one or two types, if you prefer.

320 g (11¼ oz) sashimi-grade flathead fillet

juice of 2 limes

1 tomato, peeled & seeds removed (see glossary)

½ red onion

½ red capsicum (pepper), seeds removed

½ green capsicum (pepper), seeds removed

½ avocado

4 wild green Thai chillies

1 small handful coriander (cilantro) leaves

1 small handful mint leaves

125 ml (4 fl oz/½ cup) extra virgin olive oil

sea salt & freshly ground black pepper

Using a very sharp knife, cut the flathead into 1 cm (½ inch) dice and place in a large bowl. Add the lime juice and set aside for 3 minutes to marinate.

Cut the tomato, onion, capsicum and avocado into 1 cm (½ inch) dice. Chiffonade the chillies and herbs.

Add the olive oil and a good pinch of salt to the flathead and mix gently. Add the diced vegetables, herbs and chilli and mix gently to combine. Divide between plates and grind over a good amount of pepper. Serve immediately.

SCAMPI CEVICHE

> Serves 4

I'm a big fan of raw scampi. You may have guessed it by now, I love most seafood in its natural state. Like most other crustaceans, scampi has a wonderful natural sweetness. This dish is simple but with a bit of chilli and the crunch of cucumber it hits both taste and texture.

4 scampi (langoustines)

juice of 1 lemon

juice of 1 lime

sea salt & freshly ground black pepper

125 ml (4 fl oz/¹/₂ cup) extra virgin olive oil

1 vine-ripened tomato, peeled, seeds removed (see glossary) & cut into 2 cm (³/₄ inch) dice

¹/₂ large cucumber, peeled, seeds removed & cut into 2 cm (³/₄ inch) dice

2 spring onions (scallions), cut into paper-thin slices diagonally

1 jalapeño chilli, seeds removed & finely diced

1 wild green Thai chilli

Remove the tail meat from the scampi and discard the shells. Remove the digestive tracts from the scampi. Roughly chop the flesh and place in a bowl. Add the lemon and lime juices and a good pinch of salt and set aside for 2 minutes to marinate.

Add the olive oil, mix to combine, then add the remaining ingredients and mix gently. Divide between bowls, spoon over the dressing and grind over a good amount of pepper. Serve immediately.

SQUID INK CEVICHE

> Serves 4

This is a beautiful raw starter, which looks amazing as it's all black. Raw squid has a texture that is so creamy and, like all really fresh seafood, a wonderful natural sweetness to it. We cut all the vegetables and squid into julienne, which adds a textural play. I also like to top it with little croûtons to add a crunchy texture, which you could do too if you want to go to the effort. When you're cleaning the squid, save the ink from the ink sac to use in the dish, or you can buy some — there is really good squid ink coming from Spain and Italy.

1 x 320 g (11¹/₄ oz) sashimi-quality squid

1 teaspoon squid ink

125 ml (4 fl oz/¹/₂ cup) extra virgin olive oil

juice of 2 limes

sea salt & freshly ground black pepper

¹/₂ red capsicum (pepper), cut into julienne

¹/₂ green capsicum (pepper), cut into julienne

¹/₂ Lebanese (short) cucumber, peeled, seeds removed & cut into julienne

2 tablespoons coriander (cilantro) leaves, chiffonade

1 spring onion (scallion), white part only, cut into thin rounds

croûtons, to serve (see page 432)

Clean the squid (see glossary). Cut the squid tube, wings and tentacles into julienne.

Combine the squid ink, olive oil and lime juice in a bowl. Check the seasoning (the squid ink is quite salty). Whisk to incorporate.

Add the squid, capsicum, cucumber and coriander and mix gently. Divide between bowls, spoon over the dressing from the bowl and grind over a good amount of pepper. Scatter over the spring onion and croûtons. Serve immediately.

BLUE NOSE MACKEREL ESCABECHE

> Serves 4

This is something I love doing at the restaurant with any oily fish. The vinegar marinade finishes the cooking process of the fish and it has a wonderful sharpness to it. I have also had escabeche in Spain with chicken, roasted and then marinated. It was delicious with a tomato salad and some crusty bread as a starter. The same can be said of this dish.

You will need to begin this recipe the day before.

4 x blue nose mackerel
sea salt & freshly ground black pepper
plain (all-purpose) flour, for dusting
80 ml (2½ fl oz/⅓ cup) extra virgin olive oil, plus extra for drizzling

ESCABECHE MARINADE

125 ml (4 fl oz/½ cup) sherry vinegar
125 ml (4 fl oz/½ cup) Forum cabernet sauvignon vinegar
1 small red onion, thinly sliced
1 small carrot, thinly sliced diagonally
5 parsley stalks
4 fresh bay leaves
2 dried small chillies, crushed
2 teaspoons white sugar
2 teaspoons sea salt
1 teaspoon coriander seeds, toasted
1 teaspoon black peppercorns, toasted

Clean, fillet (skin on) and pin-bone the mackerel (see page 256).

To make the escabeche marinade, combine all of the ingredients and 200 ml (7 fl oz) of water in a small saucepan, bring to the boil and cook for 5 minutes to allow the flavours to mingle. Keep warm.

Flour the mackerel and season with salt. Heat half of the oil in a non-stick frying pan over medium heat. Cooking half the fillets at a time, shake the excess flour from the mackerel and cook, skin-side down, for 1 minute, then turn over, remove the fish immediately and place, skin-side up, in a container large enough to fit all of the fillets and marinade snugly. Wipe out the pan and repeat with the remaining oil and fillets.

Pour the hot marinade over the mackerel to cover and allow to cool. Cover and refrigerate overnight.

To serve, remove the mackerel from the fridge at least 30 minutes before serving to bring to room temperature. Divide the mackerel, vegetables and spices between plates. Drizzle with olive oil and grind over a good amount of pepper.

FOUR RAW TASTES OF THE SEA

> Serves 4

This is one of the most popular starters at the restaurant. This dish was born at Rockpool in Sydney some years ago and illustrates how lovely, light Mediterranean flavours go so well with raw fish. One of the tastes is always a simple ceviche style — usually extra virgin olive oil spiced with something aromatic such as coriander seed. I love to incorporate my preserved lemon salsa and harissa as a dressing on one of the four tastes as well. If you don't want to go to the trouble of making four separate dressings, you could serve four raw tastes of the sea with the same dressing over each. Feel free to pair the dressings with different tastes or even use other dressings such as the one from the squid ink ceviche (see page 114). Whatever you choose to do, hunting down fish of great quality is the hard part. After that it's child's play.

HIRAMASA KINGFISH WITH SMOKED OYSTER DRESSING

100 g (3½ oz) hiramasa kingfish fillet
4 oysters, shucked on half shell
200 g (7 oz) jasmine tea leaves
200 g (7 oz) soft brown sugar
200 g (7 oz) uncooked white rice
2 spring onions (scallions), thinly sliced
1 cos (romaine) lettuce leaf, blanched, refreshed & finely chopped
1 tablespoon lemon juice
1 tablespoon extra virgin olive oil
sea salt & freshly ground black pepper

Combine the tea leaves, sugar and rice in a small bowl. Cut out a circle of aluminium foil about 20 cm (8 inches) in diameter. Scrunch up the sides to make a round container about 12 cm (4½ inches) in diameter. Pour the tea mixture into the foil container and place in a deep heavy-based saucepan or wok, then place a wire rack on top of the foil. Place the pan over high heat and once the tea mixture starts smoking a lot, place the oysters on the wire rack. Cover with a lid and leave to smoke for 2–3 minutes. Remove the pan from the heat and stand, covered, for 2–3 minutes. Discard the tea mixture. Remove the oysters from their shells.

Finely chop the smoked oysters and place in a bowl. Add the spring onion, lettuce, lemon juice and olive oil, season to taste with salt and pepper and mix gently.

Cut the kingfish into 8 thin slices. Arrange 2 slices on each plate and garnish with ½ teaspoon of smoked oyster dressing. Serve immediately.

OCEAN TROUT WITH PRESERVED LEMON SALSA & HARISSA

100 g (3½ oz) ocean trout fillet
1 teaspoon preserved lemon salsa (see page 434)
1 teaspoon my harissa (see page 344)

Cut the trout into 8 thin slices. Arrange 2 slices on each plate and garnish each with a little of the preserved lemon salsa and a little of the harissa. Serve immediately.

»

FOUR RAW TASTES OF THE SEA
CONTINUED

CEVICHE MIX

¹/₄ red capsicum (pepper), seeds
removed & finely diced

¹/₄ yellow capsicum (pepper), seeds
removed & finely diced

¹/₄ green capsicum (pepper), seeds
removed & finely diced

¹/₄ long red chilli, seeds removed
& finely diced

¹/₈ red onion, finely diced

1 wild green Thai chilli, finely chopped

¹/₄ tomato, peeled, seeds removed
(see glossary) & finely diced

1 tablespoon coriander (cilantro) leaves,
chiffonade

2 tablespoons mint leaves, chiffonade

¹/₄ avocado, finely diced

2 teaspoons extra virgin olive oil

2 teaspoons lime juice

sea salt & freshly ground black pepper

Place all of the ingredients in a bowl,
season to taste with salt and pepper
and mix gently.

SCAMPI CEVICHE

2 scampi (langoustines), peeled
& quartered

juice of 2 limes

2¹/₂ tablespoons extra virgin olive oil

lemon juice, to taste

sea salt & freshly ground black pepper

Combine the scampi, lime juice and olive
oil in a bowl and marinate for 30 seconds.

Remove the scampi from the marinade
and combine with the ceviche mix.

Season to taste with lemon juice, salt and
pepper. Place 2 pieces of scampi on each
plate. Serve immediately.

TUNA WITH GINGER, JALAPEÑO
CHILLI & CORIANDER DRESSING

100 g (3¹/₂ oz) yellowfin tuna loin

2 jalapeño chillies, halved lengthways
& thinly sliced

1 small knob of ginger, cut into julienne

1 small handful coriander (cilantro)
leaves, roughly chopped

1 tablespoon extra virgin olive oil

1 tablespoon lemon juice

sea salt & freshly ground black pepper

Cut the tuna into 8 thin slices. Arrange
2 slices on each plate.

Gently bruise the jalapeños in a mortar
with a pestle. Add the ginger and gently
bruise, then stir through the coriander,
olive oil and lemon juice. Season to taste
with salt and pepper.

Garnish the tuna with ¹/₂ teaspoon of the
dressing. Serve immediately.

RAW FLOUNDER WITH FRESH HORSERADISH

> Serves 4

These flavours are great with any fish you may like to use. Flounder has a very creamy texture and clean sweet taste. I'm a big fan of freshly grated horseradish with raw fish. We use it with various raw dishes at the restaurant. In Australia, we have a very small window when fresh wasabi is available. When it's not around I use fresh horseradish as it's far superior to powdered wasabi or wasabi paste. There is very little real wasabi in the paste so it pales in significance compared to the fresh, which has wonderful complexity. A microplane is a really worthwhile investment for grating all sorts of things, such as fresh horseradish.

400 g (14 oz) flounder fillets
juice & finely grated zest of 1 lemon
60 ml (2 fl oz/¼ cup) extra virgin olive oil
sea salt & freshly ground black pepper
¼ bunch chives, thinly sliced
1 spring onion (scallion), white part only, cut into thin rounds
grated horseradish root, to serve
1 vine-ripened tomato, peeled, seeds removed (see glossary) & finely diced

Using a very sharp knife, cut the flounder on the bias into thin slices and divide between plates.

Combine the lemon juice and olive oil in a bowl and season to taste with salt and pepper.

Drizzle the flounder with the dressing, scatter over the lemon zest, chives and spring onion. Scatter over the horseradish and tomato and serve immediately.

TUNA TARTARE, MOROCCAN EGGPLANT, CUMIN MAYONNAISE & HARISSA

This dish brings together flavours that I have loved since the mid-eighties, which is about the time I started playing around with Moroccan flavours and when I first made the Moroccan eggplant salad out of Robert Carrier's brilliant cookbook, Taste of Morocco. *To this day, it is one of my all-time favourites. I use it on a lot of different preparations, but it's particularly good in this tartare — the heat of the harrisa and the creamy cumin mayonnaise come together to make this dish a real killer. Make sure the eggplant is nicely golden otherwise it can taste a bit wishy-washy — it really needs that caramelisation to taste the best. This garnish is great with cooked fish, seared tuna or swordfish, and it even works well with chicken or barbecued lamb. Master this eggplant salad, the mayo and harissa and you'll have many great dishes at your disposal.*

EGGPLANT SALAD

extra virgin olive oil, for shallow-frying

3 medium eggplant (aubergines), sliced into 1 cm (½ inch) thick rounds

1 handful flat-leaf (Italian) parsley leaves

4 vine-ripened tomatoes, peeled, seeds removed (see glossary) & diced

1 tablespoon cumin seeds, toasted & ground

sea salt & freshly ground black pepper

juice of 1 lemon

Heat 1 cm (½ inch) of olive oil in a large heavy-based frying pan. Add the eggplant and fry, in 3–4 batches, until dark brown all over. Remove with tongs and place in a bowl.

Add the parsley to the hot oil — be very careful as it will spit a fair bit. Reduce the heat to medium, add the tomato and cumin, season to taste with salt and cook for 1–2 minutes, stirring regularly so the cumin doesn't catch on the base of the pan. Return the eggplant to the pan and cook for 5 minutes. Add the lemon juice and season to taste with salt and pepper. Remove from the heat and cool to room temperature to serve.

CUMIN MAYONNAISE

150 ml (5 fl oz) olive oil

½ tablespoon ground cumin

1 egg yolk

1 teaspoon Dijon mustard

lemon juice, to taste

Heat 2½ tablespoons of olive oil with the cumin in a small saucepan over low heat for 5 minutes to gently infuse. Remove from the heat and set aside to cool completely. Combine with the remaining olive oil.

Place the egg yolk and mustard in a bowl. While whisking continuously, very slowly drizzle in the combined oils. As the emulsion starts to form, you can add the oil in a steady stream. Keep whisking while adding the oil, making sure the oil does not sit on the surface as this can cause the mayonnaise to split. Season to taste with lemon juice, salt and pepper. Serve immediately or refrigerate, with plastic wrap pressed directly onto the surface, for up to 1 week. Makes about 185 g (6½ oz/¾ cup).

TO SERVE

300 g (10½ oz) yellowfin tuna loin, diced

1 tablespoon extra virgin olive oil

lemon juice, to taste

sea salt & freshly ground black pepper

½ cup eggplant salad

2 tablespoons cumin mayonnaise

4 chives, finely snipped

harissa oil (see page 344), for drizzling

Combine the tuna and olive oil and toss to coat. Season to taste with the lemon juice, salt and pepper. Place 1 heaped tablespoon of eggplant salad in the base of each bowl. Top with the tuna and a dollop of cumin mayonnaise. Garnish with the chives and drizzle over the harissa oil. Serve immediately.

LEMONGRASS SUGAR-CURED OCEAN TROUT

> Serves about 12

This is my version of gravlax. If you have wild-caught salmon at your disposal, then this lemongrass sugar cure is perfect for it. The classic treatment uses dill as the herb and although I do enjoy it that way this is a little more complex and I like the lift the fish gets from the lemongrass and lemon zest. The salt firms up the flesh of the fish and the curing flavours penetrate well, making this a delicious fish to serve with some horseradish cream and toast. Yellowfin tuna, well all the tunas really, come up a treat when handled this way. If you don't want to cure such a large fish, small oily fish, such as blue nose mackerel, are also great.

You will need to begin this recipe the day before.

OCEAN TROUT

1 x 1.6 kg (3 lb 8 oz) ocean trout

500 g (1 lb 2 oz) caster (superfine) sugar

400 g (14 oz) coarse salt

3 lemongrass stalks, finely chopped

finely grated zest of 2 lemons

2 tablespoons coriander seeds, toasted & crushed

2 tablespoons black peppercorns, toasted & crushed

1 bunch coriander (cilantro), washed & roughly chopped, stalks & all

Clean and fillet the trout, removing each side in one whole piece and leaving the skin intact (see page 256). Using a pair of fish tweezers, run your fingers along the centre of each fillet and remove any protruding pin bones.

Combine the remaining ingredients in a large bowl. Choose a tray not much bigger than the fish and sprinkle the base with one-quarter of the sugar mixture. Place a fillet, skin-side down, on top and cover with half of the remaining mixture. Place the remaining fillet, skin-side up, on top and cover with the remaining sugar mixture. Wrap the whole tray with plastic wrap. Refrigerate for 12 hours, then remove from the fridge. There should be a little liquid in the tray by now. Discard the liquid and turn over the trout. Rewrap the tray and refrigerate for another 12 hours.

TO SERVE

olive oil, for rubbing

freshly ground black pepper

horseradish cream (see page 344) or Zuni pickle (see page 166), to serve

lemon wedges, to serve

toast or buttered rye bread, to serve

Remove the trout from the fridge and rinse the fillets under cold water to remove the sugar mixture. Pat dry with paper towel, then rub the trout with a little olive oil. Place a fillet, skin-side down, on a chopping board and, using a sharp knife, thinly slice the trout off the skin on the bias like smoked salmon slices.

Place a few slices on each plate, grind over a good amount of pepper, top with a dollop of horseradish cream or Zuni pickle and serve with a lemon wedge on the side. Enjoy with toast or rye bread. Store left-over cured trout in the fridge for up to 7 days.

STERLING CAVIAR WITH TOAST & CRÈME FRAÎCHE

> Serves 4

This is not so much a recipe as accompaniments to caviar and a brief discussion about it. These little salty fish eggs, one of the great cured fish dishes, are right up there as one of my favourite foods. As with all great things — truffles, Ibérico ham — it's great to have a lot of it and indulge. Yes it is expensive and getting more so, particularly if you want wild-caught, but it's such a great special treat. We are now getting through some really good farmed caviar, such as Californian-based Sterling Caviar — guilt-free sustainable products that taste great — okay not quite like the wild version, but we humans have stuffed that one up good. At some stage for us, and our children, we will only know of the "legend" of wild-caught caviar. Caviar is best enjoyed with pearl (or ceramic) spoons so that its taste is not tainted by metal.

1 x 30 g (1 oz) jar Sterling Caviar
4 slices white bread
unsalted butter, softened for spreading
crème fraîche, to serve
3 chives, finely snipped

Toast the bread until lightly golden. Butter one side, then cut the crusts off and discard. Cut the toast into triangles.

Using 2 hot spoons, form the crème fraîche into quenelles, place in a small ramekin and sprinkle over the chives.

To serve, simply open the jar of caviar, place on a plate with the toast and crème fraîche.

Cured meats *are one of my favourite ways to start a meal. A piece of ham twirled onto some torn bread is a mightily satisfying way to start. Cured meats, along with cheese, are a wonderful link to ancient times, as many are produced the way they were hundreds of years ago. It's easy to make a beautiful ham plate at home. Find a great butcher or deli that sells these fantastic products, buy two to four different varieties and have them sliced and placed perfectly on wax paper. When you get home, just lovingly unfold, place on a plate and serve in the middle of the table with some good bread and wine. I also like to serve pickles on the side.*

I always enjoyed ham and smallgoods as a youngster. Back in the eighties there were some reasonable prosciutto-style hams produced in Australia, but it wasn't until I travelled to Europe that I appreciated how good they could be. When I tasted San Daniele and Parma prosciutto on my first trip to Italy in 1984, I became a diehard prosciutto lover. I followed that trip up with one to Spain in the early nineties and that clinched the deal. My first taste of jamón Ibérico was astounding. To call it ham is almost an insult, as it's truly sublime and one of the greatest culinary products.

When I came home to Australia, I sought out the best local producers I could find — the quality of smallgoods was increasing all the time in Australia, with the inital focus on raising the right type of pigs. However, I would always lament the fact that wonderful jamón Ibérico and San Daniele were not available in this country.

About the time I was designing the first menu for Rockpool Bar & Grill Melbourne, something wonderful happened. The Federal Government allowed jamón Ibérico, jamón serrano and Italian prosciuttos to be imported (although with no skin and off the bone, so they are not quite as good as in Europe but they're still, damn fine). I was really excited. It was a no-brainer. Rockpool Bar & Grill was going to be all about the best produce and here for the first time we were able to get the greatest hams in the world. The jamón Ibérico arrived first. It was so expensive, but I thought who cares? This wasn't ham. It was the best of the best, the ultimate benchmark and something that should be put on a plate, popped in your mouth and absolutely savoured. You need no other adornment. When it was first on the menu, I labelled it "Best Ham in the World" just to make people understand why I charged so much and what they were about to experience. Well it went off.

Since then, all the other great Spanish and Italian hams have become available in Australia. This has upped the ante with local producers and pushed them to make the best ham they can, so nowadays we always have two different ham plates on the menu: one with all the imported and one with all the local. We dub them "Australia versus the Rest of the World".

These are the hams and cured meats I love to serve at Rockpool Bar & Grill.

JAMÓN IBÉRICO DE BELLOTA JOSELITO GRAN RESERVA

Joselito jamón is produced from the Iberian breed of black pigs. The pigs grow freely and slowly in their natural surrounds, called the dehesa — a diverse habitat with at least four types of oak that produce the pigs' main form of diet, acorns.

The legs are hung and aged in natural cellars — the minimum ageing required to be classified as Gran Reserva is 24 months, although in most cases the period is 36. It is a fine leg ham with golden-rosaceous fat and a soft, oily consistency. It has different tones of red and numerous shiny streaky fat infiltrations that melt on the palate. It has a smooth and delicate flavour.

JAMONDUL JAMÓN SERRANO MILLENIUM GRAN RESERVA

Jamón serrano literally translates to mountain ham. The main distinction between serrano and Ibérico is that serrano is produced from white pigs. Ninety per cent of Spanish jamón is serrano. Jamón serrano should have an attractive nose, deep pink-red flesh, firm texture and taste both salty and sweet. Typically, legs must be aged for a minimum of 12 months, however Jamondul Millenium Gran Reserva is aged for 24.

FRATELLI GALLONI PROSCIUTTO DI PARMA

Parma, a small town in Emilia-Romagna, is renowned for producing the best ham in Italy. The pigs are "mature" heavy beasts that are native to the area and feed naturally. An integral part of their diet is high-protein milk whey that is the by-product of the Parmigiano-Reggiano produced in the area. This is what is believed to give Parma ham its distinctive taste and perfume. The best ham is prized for its sweetness, a quality that depends on the amount of salt used in the processing. In order to control salt content, hams are salted by hand. The legs are then hung and dried naturally for 24 months.

KUROBUTA PROSCIUTTO

Kurobuta pork is the most highly prized pork in Japan and comes from the ancient breed of pig known as Black Berkshire. The meat from the pure strains found in Japan is regarded as the highest quality pork in the world. In Australia, Kurobuta describes a specific type of Berkshire pig raised using Japanese-style nutrition and animal management practices, not forcing growth on their animals as in the modern intensive manner, but allowing them to grow in a slow, natural way that results in juicy, tender, tasty pork.

The fat composition of the prosciutto is soft, white and flavourful, and the meat has a fine, rich texture that is tender and juicy. Many people describe Kurobuta as the Kobe beef of pork production. Kurobuta prosciutto has been aged for a minimum of 18 months, producing a depth of flavour similar to the revered Spanish jamón Ibérico.

KUROBUTA CAPOCOLLO

Capocollo is cured and dried pork neck. The use of this cut produces an amazing, deeply flavoured and finely marbled result.

RODRIGUEZ BROS CHORIZO

Chorizo is a traditional South American style sausage, also referred to as *parrillero*, which literally translates to barbecue sausage. It's a mix of fresh pork and beef, seasoned with herbs and spices, such as oregano, Spanish sweet paprika and garlic.

BLACKMORE WAGYU BEEF BRESAOLA

David Blackmore only raises 100 per cent Japanese Fullblood Wagyu cattle in Victoria. They are not crossed or diluted with any other breed. David feeds his cattle a secret ration for 600 days that allows for slow daily gain, maximising marbling and minimising the laying of external and seam fat. It allows the overall unique flavour to penetrate the whole carcass.

Bresaola is a remarkable, intricately marbled product that is produced from the eye of the topside (from the hindquarter of the animal) and is hand-tied and cured for up to nine months. (Read more about David Blackmore on page 307.)

MONDO DI CARNE PANCETTA

Pork belly is used for this traditional Italian cured meat. The belly is salt-cured, not smoked, then dried for a minimum of three months.

PICKLED VEGETABLES

> Fills a 3 litre (105 fl oz) capacity jar

These pickles are fabulous and easy to make. I love them with ham and bread but they're equally at home in a salad or on a sandwich. As a matter of fact one of my favourite ways is to put them on a beautiful piece of buttered sourdough and just eat them like that. The wonderful full texture and taste of butter is perfect with the sour crunch of the pickle.

You will need to begin this recipe the day before.

8 pickling onions

sea salt

1 litre (35 fl oz/4 cups) rice wine vinegar

1 kg (2 lb 4 oz) white sugar

1 fresh bay leaf

5 black peppercorns

1 bunch radishes, trimmed

6 long red chillies

1 bunch Dutch carrots, peeled & trimmed

10 cauliflower florets

Sprinkle the onion with salt and set aside for 1 hour.

Combine the vinegar, sugar, bay leaf and peppercorns in a large saucepan and bring to the boil, stirring to dissolve the sugar. Transfer to a 3 litre (105 fl oz) capacity heatproof jar.

Add the onions to the jar and set aside for 30 minutes. Add the radishes and chillies and leave for another hour. When the pickling liquid has cooled to room temperature, add the carrots and cauliflower. Cover with the lid and refrigerate for 24 hours to pickle.

SALADS

Salads are really important to the
Bar & Grill concept. If you're heading
into a rich, dry-aged steak, a light salad
is a terrific way to start proceedings.
I like to have several classic composite
salads on the menu. When dining out,
I love to begin the meal with some
starters (a salad, some ham and raw
fish) before sharing a steak and sides.
It's the perfect way to eat at home, too.

Remember, it's important to have
all the salad leaves washed and dried
very well. The home cook will, too
often, dilute a dressing with wet leaves.
That just won't do, so pay attention to
the drying — it's as important as the
seasoning and dressing.

HOUSE-CHOPPED SALAD

> Serves 4

Having an American business partner and also having enjoyed quite a few chopped salads in the States, I wanted to put one on at Bar & Grill. It's a great way to start a meal before launching into a nice big steak. I wanted to have this salad tossed by a waiter tableside and served to the guests directly. The reason for this was clear: all of the ingredients are thinly sliced, so if the salad sits on the pass for five or so minutes waiting for other dishes before it can go out, then it will get soggy. The only way around this was table service. The salad is presented to the customer, dressed, gently tossed, then spooned onto a plate and served. It means my chopped salad is perfect every time.

2 witlof (chicory/Belgian endive) leaves, chiffonade

30 g (1 oz) cooked chickpeas (see glossary)

30 g (1 oz) dried chorizo, julienne

1 jalapeño chilli, seeds removed & julienne

2 cherry tomatoes, thinly sliced

1 small radish, thinly sliced

1/4 cucumber, peeled, seeds removed & julienne

2 radicchio leaves, chiffonade

1 spring onion (scallion), white part only, julienne

2 sorrel leaves, chiffonade

1/4 fennel bulb, julienne

1 very small handful flat-leaf (Italian) parsley leaves, torn

1 very small handful mint leaves, torn

30 g (1 oz) grated Gruyère

croûtons (see page 432), to serve

CHAMPAGNE DRESSING

2 teaspoons extra virgin olive oil

1 teaspoon Champagne vinegar

1 lemon wedge

sea salt & freshly ground black pepper

Arrange the witlof in a straight line on a plate. Next to that, arrange the chickpeas in a straight line followed by the chorizo, jalapeño, cherry tomato (slightly overlapping), radish, cucumber, radicchio, spring onion, sorrel, fennel, herbs and finish with the grated Gruyère. Scatter over the croûtons.

To make the Champagne dressing, combine the olive oil and vinegar in a small bowl, squeeze in the juice from the lemon wedge and season to taste with salt and pepper. Transfer to a sauce boat.

Toss the salad in the dressing at the table and serve immediately.

BEETROOT, MÂCHE & FETA SALAD
WITH PISTACHIO NUT DRESSING

This dish spends a good part of the year on the menu. I love the sweet earthy taste of beetroot. I love it boiled, grated raw or cooked in a salt crust. It also adds killer colour to a dish. We use large beets here and cut them into big discs — it makes for a great presentation. Equally impressive are baby beets of different colours. The salty feta and exotic dressing really turn this into a must-make-often salad.

BEETROOT JELLY

3 medium beetroot (beets)
2 gold-strength gelatine leaves
sea salt
extra virgin olive oil, for drizzling

Peel and chop the beetroot, then juice in an electric fruit juicer. Strain the juice through a fine sieve — you will need 220 ml (7³/₄ fl oz). Heat the juice in a small saucepan over medium heat until warmed.

Meanwhile, soak the gelatine in cold water until softened. Squeeze out the excess water and add to the juice with a pinch of salt, stirring until the gelatine has dissolved. Strain through a fine sieve, then pour into a 29 cm x 21 cm x 2 cm (11¹/₂ inch x 8¹/₄ inch x ³/₄ inch) tray.

Refrigerate for 3 hours or until set, then cut the jelly into 5 mm (¹/₄ inch) cubes. You will only need 24 cubes, so you will have some jelly left over.

ROASTED BEETROOT

2 large beetroot (beets)
2 tablespoons extra virgin olive oil
sea salt

Preheat the oven to 180°C (350°F/Gas 4). Place the beetroot in a baking dish, drizzle with the olive oil, season to taste with salt and add 500 ml (17 fl oz/2 cups) of water. Cover with aluminium foil and bake for 2 hours or until tender when pierced with the tip of a knife. Remove from the oven and keep covered — this will trap the steam and make it easier to peel off the skins. When cooled slightly, rub the skins off the beetroot.

PISTACHIO NUT DRESSING

150 g (5¹/₂ oz) pistachio nuts, roasted & roughly chopped
1 handful mint leaves, finely chopped
1 large handful flat-leaf (Italian) parsley leaves, finely chopped
1 teaspooon rosewater
finely grated zest & juice of ¹/₂ lemon
2 teaspoons caster (superfine) sugar
sea salt & freshly ground black pepper

Place all of the ingredients and 210 ml (7¹/₂ fl oz) of water in a small bowl, season to taste with salt and pepper and mix to combine.

TO SERVE

24 cubes beetroot jelly
extra virgin olive oil, for drizzling
200 g (7 oz) feta
200 g (7 oz) mâche (lamb's lettuce) leaves, washed
juice of ¹/₂ lemon

Slice the roasted beetroot into 5 mm (¹/₄ inch) thick rounds, drizzle with olive oil and season to taste with salt and pepper. Arrange on plates. Spoon over the pistachio nut dressing, crumble over the feta and arrange 6 cubes of beetroot jelly on top of each serve.

Dress the mâche with the olive oil and lemon juice, season to taste and place on the plate. Finish with a drizzle of olive oil.

MODERN-DAY CAPRESE SALAD WITH BURRATA

This is just a bit of fun with the classic Caprese salad. I've used the traditional flavours but substituted burrata for the mozzarella. Burrata is a wonderful cheese — the curd is pulled into a ball, then fresh cream is injected into it — so decadent and delicious. When I first put this on the menu, I simply called it burrata and tomato salad and didn't sell any, then I changed its name. Amazing what a name change can do!

You will need to make the tomato jelly the day before.

12 Johnny Love Bite tomatoes (see notes), quartered

2 ox-heart tomatoes, cut into thin wedges

15 baby basil leaves, torn

80 ml (2¹/₂ fl oz/¹/₃ cup) extra virgin olive oil

2 tablespoons Forum cabernet sauvignon vinegar

sea salt & freshly ground black pepper

2 burrata, halved (see notes)

1 quantity tomato jelly (see page 429)

BASIL OIL

2 bunches basil, leaves picked

250 ml (9 fl oz/1 cup) extra virgin olive oil

To make the basil oil, blanch the basil in boiling water for 5 seconds, then immediately refresh in iced water. Pat dry. Purée the basil and oil in a food processor or blender. Set aside for 10 minutes, then strain through a sieve lined with muslin (cheesecloth). Discard the solids and collect the basil oil. Makes about 350 ml (12 fl oz). (Left-over oil is fantastic in almost anything from salad dressings to pasta sauces or just drizzled over barbecued vegetables.)

Place the fresh tomato and basil leaves in a large bowl. Dress with the olive oil and vinegar and season to taste with salt and pepper. Divide between plates. Top each with a piece of burrata, season the cheese to taste and drizzle with olive oil.

Cut the tomato jelly into 4 cm (1¹/₂ inch) squares. Using a palette knife, lift the jelly out of the container and place 6 squares on each of the plates.

Drizzle basil oil around the plate and serve immediately.

NOTES

Johnny Love Bite tomatoes are available from select greengrocers and farmers' markets. You can buy burrata from specialist cheese stores and Italian delicatessens.

NEW-STYLE PRAWN COCKTAIL

> Serves 4

This is another bit of fun with a classic. There is nothing quite as nice as a bright, delicious-tasting crustacean and cocktail sauce — it's a match made in heaven. We serve all types of seafood with this cocktail dressing. To give it a modern spin, we add small squares of jelly made from sweet ripe tomato water that has a pleasing golden hue. It offers a great texture with each bite — the jelly exploding in the mouth is a perfect partner for the spicy cocktail sauce. You could use lobster or crab in this dish to raise it to another level of luxury.

You will need to begin the tomato jelly the day before.

16 medium cooked prawns (shrimp), peeled & deveined with tails intact

1 quantity tomato jelly (see page 429)

1 head of frisée (curly endive) lettuce, inner tender leaves only

juice of 1 lemon

80 ml (2^1/$_2$ fl oz/^{1}/$_3$ cup) extra virgin olive oil, plus extra to serve

4 cherry tomatoes, quartered

croûtons (see page 432), to serve

COCKTAIL SAUCE

1 egg yolk

1 tablespoon Dijon mustard

1^1/$_4$ tablespoons lemon juice

200 ml (7 fl oz) extra virgin olive oil

200 ml (7 fl oz) vegetable oil

30 g (1 oz) grated horseradish root

300 ml (10^1/$_2$ fl oz) tomato ketchup

3 teaspoons Tabasco sauce

sea salt & freshly ground black pepper

To make the cocktail sauce, place the egg yolk, mustard and lemon juice in a bowl and whisk together. Combine the two oils and, while whisking continuously, slowly add in a thin stream to the egg yolk mixture until all of the oil is added and a thick mayonnaise forms. Add the remaining ingredients and whisk until incorporated. Season to taste with salt and pepper and set aside.

Cut the tomato jelly into 2.5 cm (1 inch) squares.

Place the frisée leaves in a bowl, add half of the lemon juice, drizzle with half of the olive oil, season to taste and gently mix.

Place the prawns in a separate bowl, add the remaining lemon juice, drizzle with the remaining olive oil, season to taste and gently mix.

To assemble, spoon the cocktail sauce onto the centre of each plate, place some frisée leaves on top, arrange 4 tomato quarters around the frisée on each plate and layer 4 prawns on top of each plate of frisée. To finish, place a square of tomato jelly on top of each stack of prawns, drizzle with olive oil and scatter over the croûtons.

BUTTER LETTUCE, AVOCADO, CHERRY TOMATO & JALAPEÑO CHILLI SALAD

I love this simple salad. It's a bit of a favourite at the restaurant. Quite often we will serve this with lobster or swordfish from the charcoal grill. It has a nice bite to it from the jalapeño chilli and you can add as much or little as you like, depending on your heat tolerance. The citrus nature of the jalapeño is great with the creamy avocado texture and the sweetness of the tomatoes.

2 avocados, cut into 1 cm (½ inch) dice
juice of 1 lemon
90 ml (3 fl oz) extra virgin olive oil
sea salt & freshly ground black pepper
20 cherry tomatoes, quartered
1 jalapeño chilli, thinly sliced
2 heads of butter lettuce, leaves separated and washed
croûtons (see page 432), to serve

Combine the avocado, lemon juice and olive oil in a large bowl, season to taste with salt and pepper and mix gently.

Add the tomato, chilli and lettuce and toss gently to coat the leaves in the avocado mixture.

Divide between bowls, layering the avocado mixture and lettuce leaves evenly, finishing with the small delicate leaves on top. Sprinkle with a small handful of croûtons to serve.

KING PRAWN RUSSIAN SALAD WITH AVRUGA

> Serves 4

16 cooked medium king prawns (shrimp), peeled, deveined & halved lengthways

4 medium kipfler potatoes, washed & unpeeled

1 egg

50 g (1³/₄ oz/¹/₃ cup) podded green peas

1 organic carrot inspired by St. John (see page 367), cut into 5 mm (¹/₄ inch) thick slices diagonally

¹/₃ bunch chives, finely snipped

85 g (3 oz/¹/₃ cup) aioli (see page 431)

lemon juice, to taste

sea salt & freshly ground black pepper

extra virgin olive oil, for drizzling

2 tablespoons Avruga

Cook the potatoes in a saucepan of boiling water for 10–15 minutes or until tender. Peel, then cut into 5 mm (¹/₄ inch) thick rounds and place in a large bowl

Cook the egg in a saucepan of simmering water for 8 minutes. Peel and separate the eggwhite and yolk. Grate or push through a fine sieve separately. Set aside.

Cook the peas in a saucepan of boiling water for 1 minute or until tender. Drain and add to the potato.

Add the carrot, chives and aioli to the potato mixture, season to taste with lemon juice, salt and pepper and gently mix.

Divide the potato mixture between bowls and layer the prawns on top. Season the prawns with lemon juice, salt and pepper to taste and drizzle over the olive oil. Scatter over the grated eggwhite and yolk. Place ¹/₂ tablespoon of Avruga on top of each and serve.

This salad is another play on a classic. It can be as simple as vegetables or as extravagant as caviar and lobster. Prawns and Avruga are a good compromise, which stops the price from blowing out, yet elevates the dish and adds a fair degree of good looks. Avruga is, of course, not caviar at all, but pressings of dried smoked herring. In any case, the smoky fish flavour works a treat — and mortgages are thankfully not needed to enjoy this sublime salad.

MY STEAK TARTARE WITH CHIPS

> Serves 4

This is a killer dish and a classic. As with all classics, there's a very good reason for their popularity, but often they're executed poorly. Make friends with your butcher to get the freshest lean beef fillet with flavour. Never buy vacuum-sealed meat for this dish. Beef that has been sitting around for a month or more in a plastic bag of blood would destroy the wonderful freshness. I call this "my steak tartare". Traditionally the beef is minced and presented with all the garnishes around it and an egg yolk on top. A waiter would then dress and mix the tartare for you and serve it, mostly, with toast. I prefer to hand chop the meat and I like chips with mine as it's served in many a Parisian bistro. I make my own dressing and I love it spicy. A spicy lush moist tartare smeared on a hot crisp chip served with lettuce leaves is my idea of heaven. I hate dry tartares, which is the way it's often served.

MAYONNAISE

2 egg yolks
1 tablespoon Dijon mustard
2 teaspoons Worcestershire sauce
5 drops Tabasco sauce
125 ml (4 fl oz/^{1}/$_2$ cup) extra virgin olive oil
125 ml (4 fl oz/^{1}/$_2$ cup) vegetable oil
juice of ^{1}/$_4$ lemon
sea salt & freshly ground black pepper

Place the egg yolks, mustard and Worcestershire and Tabasco sauces in a bowl and whisk together. Combine the two oils and, while whisking continuously, slowly add in a thin stream to the egg yolk mixture until all the oil is added and a thick mayonnaise forms. Add the lemon juice and season to taste with salt and pepper. Press a piece of plastic wrap directly onto the surface and refrigerate for up to 2 days. Makes about 355 g (12^1/$_2$ oz/1^1/$_2$ cups).

TO SERVE

400 g (14 oz) fillet steak
2 tablespoons salted capers, rinsed
4 anchovy fillets, chopped
2 French shallots (eschalots), thinly sliced
4 gherkins (cornichons), chopped
85 g (3 oz/^{1}/$_4$ cup) mayonnaise
2 handfuls mixed salad leaves
extra virgin olive oil, for drizzling
1 large handful flat-leaf (Italian) parsley leaves, chiffonade
hand-cut fat chips (see page 358), to serve

Finely chop the steak with a sharp knife and place in a bowl. Add the capers, anchovy, shallot and cornichon. Add enough mayonnaise to bind the mixture to achieve your desired consistency.

Arrange the salad leaves on plates. Using a large kitchen spoon, shape the tartare into 4 quenelles, placing each one neatly on top of the leaves. Drizzle with a little olive oil and sprinkle with the parsley. Serve with the chips.

WOOD-FIRE GRILLED BABY OCTOPUS WITH OLIVES & HAND-POUNDED PESTO

> Serves 4

This is a salad I make in summer when the cherry tomatoes and basil are at their very best. The key is to hand-pound the pesto in a mortar with a pestle — it's really easy and much easier to clean than a food processor. The pounding, rather than the chopping of a processor, brings out the oils from the basil and makes the pesto incredibly creamy. I don't recommend roasting the pine nuts. It's not traditional and for a good reason because the roasted flavour tends to dominate — the pine nuts are there to add complexity, not to be a major player. The octopus could be poached, or fried in olive oil for this dish, but I love the slight char flavour from the grill.

500 g (1 lb 2 oz) baby octopus, cleaned

HAND-POUNDED PESTO

$^1/_2$ small garlic clove
$^1/_2$ teaspoon sea salt, plus extra to serve
$^1/_2$ bunch basil, leaves picked
$1^1/_2$ tablespoons pine nuts
1 tablespoon freshly grated parmesan
2 tablespoons extra virgin olive oil, plus extra to serve
juice of $^1/_4$ lemon
freshly ground black pepper
$^1/_3$ cup Ligurian olives, pitted
12 cherry tomatoes, quartered
100 g (3$^1/_2$ oz) mixed salad leaves

To make the hand-pounded pesto, place the garlic and salt in a mortar and, using a pestle, pound to a paste. Add the basil leaves and continue to pound. It takes a while to get the basil to break down. Once a thick paste has formed, add the pine nuts and really grind them in with the pestle. The pesto should start to take on a creamy texture. Add the parmesan, olive oil and lemon juice. Season to taste with more salt, if required, and pepper. Transfer to a large bowl and add the olives and tomato.

Heat a barbecue grill plate or chargrill pan to high. Grill the octopus for 5 minutes or until tender, making sure to get some good colour and grill marks — you want that nice barbecue flavour. Cut into bite-sized pieces, add to the pesto and mix well.

To serve, place a small pile of salad leaves on each plate, top with some octopus and pesto and drizzle over some olive oil.

SALAD OF BABY BEETROOT, PICKLED ONION, GRILLED ZUCCHINI, FARRO, FETA & WHITE BEANS

> Serves 4

This is another favourite composite salad of mine. This recipe may look long, but it isn't really. Cooking each item adds weight to the salad and this can be done way before dinner time. Yes, items can be left out but the complexity of simple ingredients together is the charm: creamy white bean purée, earthy beets, the sharpness of pickled onions, the sweet flavour of dried tomatoes, the charred nuance of zucchini and, lastly, the wonderful crunch and nutty flavour of farro. At the restaurant, we grill the zucchini over the wood-fired grill, but at home the barbecue is ideal. Farro is an ancient wheat that is very low in gluten, and it has a thoroughly enjoyable flavour.

ROASTED BEETROOT

4 small red beetroot (beets)
12 small golden beetroot (beets)
1½ tablespoons Forum cabernet sauvignon vinegar, plus extra for drizzling
1½ tablespoons extra virgin olive oil, plus extra for drizzling
sea salt & freshly ground black pepper

Preheat the oven to 180°C (350°F/Gas 4). Place the beetroot in a roasting tray, drizzle with the vinegar and olive oil, add 2½ tablespoons of water, season to taste with salt and pepper and mix to coat. Cover with foil and roast for 30 minutes or until tender. Remove and keep covered — this will trap the steam and make it easier to peel off the skins. When cooled slightly, rub the skins off and cut into halves or quarters.

To serve, drizzle the beetroot with the vinegar and olive oil and season to taste.

COOKED FARRO

50 g (1¾ oz) farro
1 very small handful flat-leaf (Italian) parsley leaves, chiffonade

Place the farro in a small saucepan, cover with water and bring to the boil. Cook for 20–25 minutes or until tender. Drain and spread out on a plate to cool.

To serve, toss the farro with the parsley.

GRILLED ZUCCHINI

½ zucchini (courgette)
1 tablespoon Forum cabernet sauvignon vinegar, plus extra for drizzling
extra virgin olive oil, for drizzling
sea salt & freshly ground black pepper

Heat a barbecue grill plate or chargrill pan to high. Coat the zucchini with the vinegar and olive oil and season to taste with salt and pepper. Grill, turning the zucchini 90 degrees every few minutes to achieve good grill marks. Cook until tender, then set aside to cool.

To serve, cut into half moons, drizzle with the vinegar and olive oil and season to taste with salt and pepper.

WHITE BEAN PURÉE

160 g (5⅔ oz) jarred white beans, drained
1 small garlic clove, roughly chopped
1¼ tablespoons extra virgin olive oil
lemon juice, to taste
sea salt & freshly ground black pepper

Blend the beans, garlic and olive oil in a food processor until smooth. Season to taste with the lemon juice, salt and pepper.

TO SERVE

40 g (1½ oz) jarred white beans, drained
1 pickled onion (see page 429), halved & thinly sliced
100 g (3½ oz) feta, cubed
12 semi-dried cherry tomatoes halves (see page 429)

Place 1 heaped tablespoon of white bean purée in the middle of each plate and, using the back of a spoon, spread it out to make a wide circle. Scatter a few white beans on top of the purée.

Divide the roasted beetroot and grilled zucchini between the plates, making sure all of the ingredients are visible. Top with a few slices of pickled onion, semi-dried cherry tomatoes and cubes of feta. Top with the farro to finish.

WOOD-FIRE GRILLED EGGPLANT, ROASTED PUMPKIN & CHILLI SALAD WITH GOAT'S CURD

> Serves 4

This is a dish we serve in winter. It brings together the use of our wood-fired grill and the charcoal oven. The charred caramel flavour of the eggplant combines with the sweet pumpkin, creamy goat's curd and heat from the chilli to make this simple salad that is super delicious and complex both in flavour and texture. You can barbecue both the eggplant and pumpkin or roast the pumpkin and pan-fry the eggplant slices for colour.

CHARGRILLED EGGPLANT

1–2 large eggplant (aubergines), trimmed

1 tablespoon extra virgin olive oil, plus extra for brushing

lemon juice, to taste

sea salt & freshly ground black pepper

1 large handful flat-leaf (Italian) parsley leaves, torn

6 sprigs thyme, leaves picked

Heat a barbecue grill plate or chargrill pan to medium. Slice the eggplant lengthways into about 8 mm (³/₈ inch) thick slices — you'll need 12 slices. Brush with olive oil and season to taste with lemon juice, salt and pepper. Grill the eggplant for 3–5 minutes on one side or until cooked through, making sure to get good chargrill marks. Turn the eggplant over and cook the other side, being careful not to overcook each slice.

Place on a plate, drizzle over the tablespoon of olive oil, scatter over the herbs and season to taste with lemon juice, salt and pepper. Cover and refrigerate until needed.

ROASTED PUMPKIN

600 g (1 lb 5 oz/about ¹/₄) Japanese pumpkin (winter squash), seeds removed

3 garlic cloves, unpeeled

10 sprigs thyme

100 ml (3¹/₂ fl oz) extra virgin olive oil, plus extra for drizzling

sea salt & freshly ground black pepper

4 French shallots (eschalots), thinly sliced diagonally

1 large jalapeño chilli, thinly sliced

2 teaspoons coriander seeds, toasted & crushed

lemon juice, to taste

Preheat the oven to 200°C (400°F/Gas 6). Cut the pumpkin into 3–4 wedges and place in a heavy-based roasting tray with the garlic and thyme, drizzle with the olive oil and season to taste with salt and pepper. Roast for 25–30 minutes or until the pumpkin is tender. When cool enough to handle, remove the skin, cut each wedge into 3–4 bite-sized pieces and place in a large bowl. Cool to room temperature.

Add the shallot, jalapeño and coriander seeds, drizzle over some olive oil and season to taste with lemon juice, salt and pepper.

TO SERVE

¹/₃ heaped cup goat's curd

extra virgin olive oil, for drizzling

Divide the marinated chargrilled eggplant between plates. Top with 3 pieces of roasted pumpkin and spoon over the shallot, jalapeño and coriander seeds. Top with a heaped tablespoon of goat's curd, drizzle over more olive oil and grind over a good amount of pepper.

PRAWN, NECTARINE & HAZELNUT SALAD

> Serves 4

This is a wonderful, light, composite summer salad of beautiful colours and textures. The sweetness of the nectarines goes so well with the salty taste of the prawns and the extra flavour and nuttiness from the hazelnut oil takes it to the next level. What's even better is that this dish is easy to prepare as it's all about the ingredients.

16 cooked large prawns (shrimp), peeled & deveined

1 witlof (chicory/Belgian endive), leaves separated & washed

1 red witlof (chicory/Belgian endive), leaves separated & washed

2 heads of baby cos (romaine) lettuce

sea salt & freshly ground black pepper

2 tablespoons hazelnut oil

juice of 2 limes

2 yellow nectarines

80 g (2¾ oz) hazelnuts, roasted & roughly chopped

1 small handful flat-leaf (Italian) parsley leaves, chiffonade

Halve each prawn at an angle and place in a large bowl. Roughly tear the witlof and baby cos leaves and add to the bowl. Season to taste with salt and pepper. Drizzle with the hazelnut oil and lime juice, a little at a time to achieve the required balance.

Cut the cheeks off each nectarine and thinly slice each cheek on an angle.

Divide the salad between wide bowls or plates, arrange the nectarine slices on top and sprinkle with the hazelnuts and parsley.

WOOD-FIRE GRILLED VEGETABLES & GOAT'S CURD SALAD

> Serves 4

We think of this as a bit of a signature dish because it uses our wonderful wood-fired grill, the heart of the restaurant. Each vegetable is grilled to a tender texture with a smokiness from the fire that is truly amazing. Seasoned with Forum red wine vinegar and extra virgin olive oil and teamed with creamy goat's curd, this is a really memorable salad. You can achieve a pretty good result on a home barbecue. The vegetables are also nice roasted.

200 ml (7 fl oz) extra virgin olive oil

2 zucchini (courgettes)

1 leek, white part only, washed

1 red capsicum (pepper)

$1/2$ eggplant (aubergine), cut into 4 wedges

4 spring onions (scallions), white part only

12 vine-ripened cherry tomatoes

sea salt & freshly ground black pepper

$2^1/_2$ tablespoons Forum cabernet sauvignon vinegar

20 black Ligurian olives, pitted

1 tablespoon balsamic vinegar

100 g ($3^1/_2$ oz) fresh goat's curd

juice of 1 lemon

baby basil leaves, for garnishing

Preheat a barbecue grill plate to high. Place all of the vegetables in a large tray, drizzle over 80 ml (2 fl oz/$^1/_3$ cup) of the olive oil to coat the vegetables and season to taste with salt and pepper. Chargrill the vegetables, except the tomatoes, until tender. Increase the heat to high, blister the skins of the tomatoes, then remove from the grill.

Remove the skins and seeds of the capsicum, the skins of the tomatoes and the outer layers of the spring onions and leek. Cut all of the vegetables into bite-sized pieces and place in a large bowl.

Dress the vegetables with the red wine vinegar, 100 ml ($3^1/_2$ fl oz) of the olive oil and season to taste. Place on a baking tray and reheat under a medium grill (broiler).

Combine the olives, balsamic vinegar and remaining olive oil and season to taste. Arrange the hot vegetables on plates, top with the olive salad, then a quenelle of goat's curd. Season to taste with salt and lemon juice and garnish with a few basil leaves.

ANCHOVY, BABY COS & POACHED EGG SALAD WITH GREEN GODDESS DRESSING

> Serves 4

This dish is loosely based on the Caesar salad. I love it because the Ortiz Reserve de Familia anchovies are to die for. They are in fact one of my favourite foods. I love them on toast, in salads, laying them on a steak, just about anywhere really. They're so sweet and tasty that I doubt even anchovy haters wouldn't love these. As if the anchovy factor wasn't enough, then there is the slow-cooked egg. What's not to love about a slow-cooked egg? These are great on anything. In this salad they break up and enrich the dressing. This is a truly delicious way to ease into a steak course at the restaurant and would work perfectly for you at home, too.

2 heads of baby cos (romaine) lettuce, washed

80 ml (2½ fl oz/⅓ cup) extra virgin olive oil

juice of 1 lemon

4 eggs, poached (see glossary)

6 Ortiz Reserve de Familia anchovy fillets, halved diagonally

100 g (3½ oz/1 cup) freshly grated parmesan

croûtons (see page 432), to serve

GREEN GODDESS DRESSING

3 tablespoons mayonnaise (see page 431)

1½ tablespoons chopped chives

1½ tablespoons finely chopped flat-leaf (Italian) parsley leaves

2 teaspoons finely chopped tarragon leaves

2 teaspoons lemon juice

60 g (2¼ oz/¼ cup) crème fraîche

sea salt & freshly ground black pepper

To make the green goddess dressing, process the mayonnaise, herbs and lemon juice in a blender or small food processor. Gently fold through the crème fraîche to combine and season to taste with salt and pepper.

Halve the baby cos, then slice each half into thirds. Place in a large bowl, drizzle with the olive oil and lemon juice and season to taste.

Spoon 2 tablespoons of the green goddess dressing onto the centre of each plate. Place 3 pieces of cos on each plate creating a bed for the poached egg. Place a poached egg in the centre of the cos, season to taste with salt, then lay 3 pieces of anchovy over the cos. Sprinkle over the parmesan and some croûtons.

SALAD OF PRAWN, CALAMARI, OCTOPUS, MUSSELS & CLAMS WITH ROCKET & SMOKY POTATO

> Serves 4

From the moment the wood-fired grill is lit, we utilise every aspect of it. We place cherry tomatoes, and kipfler potatoes that have been boiled and skinned on trays above the grill to soak up the wonderful smoke, and we grill the vegetables for the salads alongside a rotisserie of pork or beef shoulder. A great way to simulate our wood-fired grill is to place wood chips in an iron box and smoke in a barbecue — sit your potatoes on the resting rack to absorb the smoke. Presto, you'll have a salad just like ours.

8 raw (green) large prawns (shrimp), peeled & deveined with tails intact

200 g (7 oz) cleaned calamari tubes

100 g (3½ oz) cleaned baby octopus (or replace with braised octopus, see right)

16 mussels, scrubbed & beards removed

16 clams (vongole), purged

8 large kipfler potatoes, unpeeled

sea salt & freshly ground black pepper

wood chips, soaked in water

2 anchovy fillets, chopped

85 g (3 oz/⅓ cup) aioli (see page 431)

lemon wedges

100 ml (3½ fl oz) dry white wine

2 handfuls rocket (arugula)

extra virgin olive oil, for drizzling

Place the potatoes in a saucepan of water, bring to the boil and cook until tender. Drain and, when cool enough to handle, peel and roll in a little salt and pepper.

Preheat the barbecue to high and get it nice and hot with the lid down, about 20 minutes should do it. Place the soaked wood chips in a fire box and place the fire box on the bottom of the hot barbecue, directly on top of a burner, and close the lid. It should take about 5–10 minutes to start smoking. Place the potatoes on the resting rack or a tray over the barbecue but not directly over the heat so they take on the smoky flavour without being cooked further. Leave for 1 hour for the smoke to infuse.

Slice the potatoes into 2 cm (¾ inch) thick rounds and place in a bowl. Add the anchovy and aioli and squeeze over a lemon wedge. Season with salt and pepper.

Place the wine in a large saucepan, preferably with a glass lid, and bring to the boil. Add the mussels and clams, cover and cook, shaking the pan occasionally. Remove the mussels and clams as soon as they open. Discard any that do not open. Remove the meat from the shells and place in a large bowl. Discard the cooking liquid.

Heat a barbecue grill plate or chargrill pan to high and grill the prawns, calamari and baby octopus until just cooked. Slice the calamari and octopus and add to the mussels and clams. Add the rocket, drizzle over some olive oil and season to taste.

Divide the potato mixture among plates and top with the seafood.

BRAISED OCTOPUS

1 kg (2 lb 4 oz) octopus tentacles

200 ml (7 fl oz) brine from a jar of olives

100 ml (3½ fl oz) olive oil

5 sprigs dried Greek oregano, leaves picked

½ bunch thyme

finely grated zest & juice of 1 orange

20 Ligurian olives, pitted & crushed

4 garlic cloves, crushed

Bring 3 saucepans of water to the boil. Add the octopus to one pan. When it comes back to the boil, remove the octopus and transfer to pan number two. When that comes back to the boil, remove the octopus and transfer to pan number three. When that comes back to the boil, remove the pan from the heat and allow the octopus to cool in the water for 15 minutes.

Meanwhile, add the remaining ingredients to a separate saucepan, adding enough water to dilute the olive brine until it's nicely salty but not too much. Bring to the boil, then simmer for 5 minutes to cook out the garlic.

Add the octopus to the braising liquid and simmer for 40 minutes or until tender. Cool in the braising liquid, then peel off the skin and slice into rounds. Add to the other seafood.

WARM SALAD OF WOOD-FIRE GRILLED QUAIL WITH SMOKY TOMATO & BLACK OLIVES

> Serves 4

This dish rocks my world. It has all my favourite things: wood-fire grilled quail, smoked tomatoes, black olive and Forum red wine vinegar. You can of course substitute the quail for the chicken or even some quality veal. If smoked tomatoes are beyond you, just oven-dry some yourself and add them to the mix. The important thing here is the combo of tomatoes and black olives, which is heaven. Make sure you use quality black olives, so you get out of this dish what you put in.

4 quails, butterflied

sea salt & freshly ground black pepper

70 ml (2¼ fl oz) extra virgin olive oil

16 smoky semi-dried cherry tomato halves (see page 428)

50 g (1¾ oz) Ligurian olives, pitted & chopped

1 small handful mint leaves, finely chopped

1 small handful flat-leaf (Italian) parsley leaves, finely chopped

1½ tablespoons Forum cabernet sauvignon vinegar

Flatten out the quails and season inside and out with salt.

Heat 2 tablespoons of the olive oil in a large heavy based frying pan over medium–high heat or heat a barbecue grill plate or chargrill pan to hot and lightly brush the quails with oil. Cook the quails on each side until browned and cooked through.

Combine the smoky tomato halves, olives, herbs, vinegar and remaining olive oil in a large bowl.

Cut the quails into quarters and add to the bowl. Season to taste with salt and pepper, toss well to coat and serve.

SANDWICHES

Sandwiches are the backbone of our bar menu. We have lots of bruschettas and such on the menu because it's part of the DNA of the restaurant. We have a wonderful wood-fired grill and we want to use it for just about everything we can, including toasting our bruschetta.

The Wagyu burger looms large over the bar menu. It would be about 75 per cent of the food orders on any given day. We do, however, have a range of other sandwiches, burgers and bruschettas that I love. These are great recipes for a weekend lunch with a good glass of wine. Make sure you use good-quality bread to make the bruschetta, and it's best when it's a day old.

DAVID BLACKMORE'S FULLBLOOD WAGYU HAMBURGER WITH BACON, GRUYÈRE & ZUNI PICKLE

> Serves 4

I guess my love affair with the humble hamburger started when my father took me, at the age of about six, down to the local milk bar. That was in the early sixties when there were many of these kinds of places and you paid in pounds and pennies. (Gee that makes me feel old.) This was way before the dreaded fast-food joints arrived and turned the mighty burger into a commodity. I still remember pulling back the wax paper and eating a yummy burger, the juices running down my fingers and arms. Perhaps it's only my nostalgia talking, but those simple milk-bar burgers seemed so fresh and delicious. From that time on I have made it my mission to eat burgers around Australia to find my favourite. It's the perfect food, really. All the flavours of the burger in every bite. And it's my fave way of eating: with my hands.

So, making one of the world's great burgers was my mission at Bar & Grill. Lofty statement, I know. But I think I might have pulled it off. This burger is a contender. Every burger should be about the meat. Enter David Blackmore's Fullblood Wagyu (see page 307). It is without doubt the best Wagyu produced outside of Japan. One of the reasons for my burger's success is that the wonderful fattiness of the Wagyu picks up the smoky quality of the wood-fired grill perfectly. When you partner such great meat with other great ingredients, you're halfway there to the best burger.

Those other great ingredients I'm talking about are Judy Rodgers' pickles. I was inspired by her great burger at Zuni Café in San Francisco. I have borrowed the pickle recipe from her wonderful book and it's important that I give her credit for a significant part of what my burger is all about. I call them Zuni pickles on the menu. (I hope she doesn't mind.)

To finish, I simply add Schulz Bacon, the best smokehouse bacon in Australia, nutty Gruyère and our house-made tomato and chilli relish. Pastry Chef Catherine Adam's brioche buns are the inspired crowning glory.

It can be hard to get David's great beef, but do try to at least use Wagyu. If not, use beef chuck steak and ask your butcher to mince it for you. (Using minced meat from the supermarket is bound to bring mediocrity to your burger and disappointment. Sadly there are no shortcuts for the quality of the beef.) This is a great recipe for the barbecue. If you need to use a pan, make sure you use a cast-iron one and get it really hot — a good caramelised crust on the patties is one of the keys to the right flavour.

You can use tomato ketchup and mustard, but it won't be the same. And, very sorry, but no beetroot, egg or pineapple here, thanks.

»

DAVID BLACKMORE'S FULLBLOOD WAGYU HAMBURGER WITH BACON, GRUYÈRE & ZUNI PICKLE
CONTINUED

RED ONION PICKLE

3 red onions, cut into 3 mm (⅛ inch) thick rounds

345 g (12 oz) caster (superfine) sugar

750 ml (26 fl oz/3 cups) rice wine vinegar

4 cinnamon quills

1 tablespoon whole cloves

2 dried long red chillies

2 fresh bay leaves

1 tablespoon black peppercorns

2 star anise

To make the brine, combine all of the ingredients, except for the onion, in a large saucepan and bring to the boil. Reduce the heat and simmer for 3 minutes. Remove from the heat and set aside to infuse for 1 hour.

Return the brine to the stove and bring back to the boil. Transfer the brine to a 2 litre (70 fl oz) capacity sterilised jar and refrigerate until completely chilled.

Meanwhile, blanch the onion in boiling water for 20 seconds. Remove the onion and refrigerate until chilled. When onion is chilled, repeat the whole process again. This process will ensure a crunchy pickle.

Add the onion to the brine, seal the jar with the lid and refrigerate. Store for up to 3 months if unopened. Makes about 500 g (1 lb 2 oz).

ZUCCHINI PICKLE

4 green zucchini (courgettes), thinly sliced lengthways

1 brown onion, thinly sliced lengthways

1 tablespoon sea salt

500 ml (17 fl oz/2 cups) cider vinegar

250 g (9 oz) caster (superfine) sugar

1 teaspoon brown mustard seeds

1 teaspoon mustard powder

1 teaspoon ground turmeric

Place the zucchini and onion in a bowl, sprinkle with salt, cover with iced water and set aside for 1 hour.

Combine the remaining ingredients in a saucepan over medium heat, bring to the boil and cook for 3 minutes, then cool. Transfer to a 2 litre (70 fl oz) capacity sterilised jar and refrigerate until chilled.

Drain the zucchini and onion and add to the brine. Seal the jar with the lid and refrigerate overnight. Store for up to 3 months if unopened. Makes about 500 g (1 lb 2 oz).

TO SERVE

800 g (1 lb 12 oz) coarsely minced Wagyu beef

4 rashers bacon

4 brioche burger buns, halved & toasted

4 slices Gruyère

tomato & chilli relish (see page 432), to serve

zucchini pickle, to serve

red onion pickle, to serve

4 cos (romaine) lettuce leaves

1 vine-ripened tomato, sliced

extra virgin olive oil, for drizzling

sea salt & freshly ground black pepper

Knead the mince with your hands until it becomes sticky and the meat binds together. Form into 4 patties.

Heat a barbecue or chargrill pan to high. Cook the patties, turning once. Cook until medium-rare.

Meanwhile, heat the grill (broiler) to hot and grill the bacon until crisp.

Top each patty with cheese, then the bacon and cook on the barbecue until the cheese has softened.

Place each patty on a bun base, top with some relish and pickles and sandwich with the bun tops.

Serve with the lettuce and tomato on the side, drizzled with olive oil and seasoned to taste with salt and pepper.

ARTICHOKE & MUSHROOM BRUSCHETTA

> Serves 4

I love these muted simple flavours that remind me of an Australian late winter moving into spring. Don't underestimate how good this can be. It's simple, direct and tasty. You can, of course, use preserved artichokes if you want to take a short cut, but once you get into the groove of cleaning fresh ones, it's quite straightforward.

MUSHROOM SPREAD

50 g (1¾ oz) Swiss brown mushrooms, thinly sliced

50 g (1¾ oz) field mushrooms, thinly sliced

2 tablespoons extra virgin olive oil

10 g (⅓ oz) unsalted butter

1 garlic clove, finely chopped

1 sprig thyme, leaves picked

100 ml (3½ fl oz) pouring (single) cream

sea salt & freshly ground black pepper

Heat the olive oil and butter in a saucepan over medium–high heat, add the mushrooms and sauté for 5 minutes or until golden. Add the garlic and thyme and cook for 1 minute. Add the cream, bring just to the boil, then reduce to a simmer and cook for 5 minutes or until slightly thickened and reduced. Purée with a stick blender or in a blender until smooth. Season to taste with salt and pepper. Serve warm or at room temperature.

ARTICHOKES

8 baby artichokes

juice of 1 lemon

2 tablespoons extra virgin olive oil

1 garlic clove, finely chopped

1 anchovy fillet, chopped

1 dried long chilli, seeds removed & finely chopped

2 French shallots (eschalots), finely diced

1 small handful flat-leaf (Italian) parsley leaves, chiffonade

To prepare the artichokes, fill a saucepan with enough water to cover all of the artichokes and add a little of the lemon juice. Trim the artichoke stems. Cut the top of the artichokes. Peel away and discard the tough outer leaves to expose the pale yellow-green leaves. Peel the tough outer layer from the stems. Place each artichoke in the pan as you finish trimming it. Bring the pan to the boil, then reduce to a simmer and cook for 15–20 minutes, depending on their size, until the artichokes are tender when pierced with a skewer. Drain and quarter lengthways.

Heat the olive oil in a frying pan over low heat, add the garlic, anchovy, chilli and shallot and sauté until the shallot has softened. Add the artichokes and stir through for about 5 minutes or until warmed through. Add the remaining lemon juice and parsley and season to taste with salt and pepper. Keep warm until serving.

TO SERVE

4 x 2 cm (¾ inch) thick slices white sourdough

100 g (3½ oz) Parmigiano-Reggiano, shaved

extra virgin olive oil, for drizzling

Chargrill the bread on both sides until crisp or cook under a grill (broiler). Spread each slice of bread with a good layer of mushroom spread, top with the artichokes and parmesan and drizzle with some olive oil.

WAGYU BRESAOLA WITH MUSHROOM TOAST

> Serves 4

When I first tasted David Blackmore's bresaola, I loved it. What's not to love about anything made from David's extraordinary Wagyu! (Read about him on page 307.) The high marbling of the Wagyu tastes so luxurious, and when paired with a crisp mushroom sandwich, with its texture and rich earthy taste, it's a simple and sublime thing.

400 g (14 oz) Blackmore Wagyu Beef bresaola, thinly sliced

50 g (1^3/$_4$ oz) unsalted butter

2 tablespoons extra virgin olive oil, plus extra for dressing

200 g (7 oz) Swiss brown mushrooms, sliced

200 g (7 oz) field mushrooms, sliced

2 garlic cloves, chopped

sea salt & freshly ground black pepper

1 handful flat-leaf (Italian) parsley leaves

lemon juice, to taste

^{1}/$_2$ loaf white sourdough bread

clarified butter, melted, for brushing (see glossary)

2 handfuls rocket (arugula)

Heat the butter and olive oil in a frying pan over medium–high heat until melted. Add the mushrooms and cook until softened. Add the garlic, season to taste with salt and pepper and sauté for another minute. Add the parsley and season to taste with lemon juice. Remove from the pan and chop to a fine paste.

Trim the crusts from the sourdough, then, using a very sharp serrated knife or on a meat slicer, slice the loaf into 3 mm (^{1}/$_8$ inch) thick slices. Trim each slice to make a 10 cm x 5 cm (4 inch x 2 inch) rectangle. You'll need 8 rectangles. Spread a thin layer of mushroom paste over half of the rectangles and sandwich with the remaining rectangles.

Brush sandwiches with clarified butter and cook under a hot grill (broiler) until golden and crisp on both sides. Drain on paper towel.

Divide the bresaola between plates. Cut each sandwich into 2 fingers and place on top of the bresaola. Dress the rocket with olive oil and lemon juice, season to taste and divide between the plates.

SARDINES WITH CHILLI ON BRUSCHETTA

> Serves 4

My father used to love eating tinned sardines on toast. I think the brand was King Oscar. I've always been a fan of eating fresh ones — just grilled and served with a little lemon juice and extra virgin olive oil — but somewhere along the line memories of my father and his tinned sardines stuck with me and the thought of tinned ones started to appeal to me. I tried some one day and, hey, I loved them too! I just mash them on bruschetta, add some lemon juice, oil, pepper and chopped chilli and there you have it, a wonderful nibble with a pre-dinner drink or, in our case, a great bar snack. Serve these alongside the Ortiz anchovies bruschetta (see below) and perhaps the preserved tuna bruschetta (see opposite) — these will make a lovely plate of food to pass around while having a drink before dinner.

4 x 2 cm (¾ inch) thick slices of sourdough baguette, cut on the diagonal
1 garlic clove
4 good-quality tinned sardines
sea salt & freshly ground black pepper
extra virgin olive oil, for drizzling
1 long red chilli, thinly sliced

Toast the baguette slices and rub with the garlic clove. Top each slice with a sardine (lightly mashed first if you like), season to taste with salt and pepper, drizzle over olive oil and top each with a slice of chilli. Warm under a hot grill (broiler) and serve.

ORTIZ ANCHOVIES WITH SMOKY TOMATO BRUSCHETTA

> Serves 4

The Ortiz anchovies and smoky tomato elevates this from simple to special. If you don't feel like smoking the tomatoes, then just substitute a halved fresh tomato.

4 x 2 cm (¾ inch) thick slices of sourdough baguette, cut on the diagonal
1 garlic clove
12 smoky semi-dried cherry tomato halves (see page 428)
4 Ortiz or other good-quality anchovy fillets
sea salt & freshly ground black pepper
extra virgin olive oil, for drizzling

Toast the baguette slices and rub with the garlic clove. Top each slice with 3 smoky tomato halves and an anchovy fillet, season to taste with salt and pepper and drizzle over some olive oil. Warm under a hot grill (broiler) and serve.

PRESERVED TUNA, WHITE BEAN, CHILLI & SILVERBEET BRUSCHETTA

> Serves 4

This began as a simple salad, then morphed into bruschetta at home for my wife, Sam, and I. As a matter of fact, barely a week goes by in summer without us tossing some preserved tuna, white beans and cherry tomatoes together with red wine vinegar and extra virgin olive oil, then eating it with toast rubbed with garlic and a drizzle of oil. We love it because it's simple to put together and healthy. At the restaurant, I add the intense dark green flavour of silverbeet braised with a touch of chilli. It's a killer combination.

PRESERVED TUNA

300 g (10½ oz) sashimi-grade tuna fillet
4 sprigs oregano, leaves picked
4 sprigs thyme, leaves picked
finely grated zest of ½ orange
¼ garlic clove, thinly sliced
1½ tablespoons extra virgin olive oil
sea salt & freshly ground black pepper

Cut the tuna into 2 even pieces — log shapes work best.

Combine the oregano, thyme, orange zest, garlic and olive oil in a large bowl and season to taste with salt and pepper. Add the tuna and turn to coat well in the marinade. Wrap each log of the tuna in plastic wrap, but don't wrap too tight as this will damage the flesh. Twist the ends like a bonbon and secure each end with a knot, then wrap each log in aluminium foil, twisting the ends to secure.

Fill a saucepan, big enough to hold both logs of tuna, with water and bring to the boil. Gently place the logs into the water, then remove the pan from the heat. You may need to weigh down the logs with a small plate to keep them submerged. Set aside for 20 minutes. Remove and place in a bowl of iced water to cool. Leave wrapped until ready to serve.

BRAISED SILVERBEET

½ bunch silverbeet (Swiss chard), washed, stalks discarded & leaves finely shredded
100 ml (3½ fl oz) olive oil
5 French shallots (eschalots), thinly sliced
2 garlic cloves, thinly sliced
2 good-quality anchovy fillets, finely chopped
1 dried long red chilli, seeds removed & finely chopped

Heat the olive oil in a large saucepan over medium heat. Add the shallot, garlic, anchovy and chilli and cook until the anchovy has dissolved and the shallot has softened. Add the silverbeet and 125 ml (4 fl oz/½ cup) of water. Reduce the heat to low, cover and cook for about 30 minutes or until most of the liquid has evaporated and the silverbeet is very soft and has a slippery appearance. Season to taste with salt and pepper and set aside to cool to room temperature.

WHITE BEAN & CHILLI

200 g (7 oz) cooked cannellini (white) beans
12 small cherry tomatoes, quartered
1½ tablespoons extra virgin olive oil
4 long red chillies, chargrilled, peeled & sliced
1 large handful flat-leaf (Italian) parsley leaves, chopped
juice of 1 lemon
sea salt & freshly ground black pepper

Combine all of the ingredients in a bowl and season to taste with salt and pepper.

TO SERVE

4 thick slices sourdough bread
1 garlic clove
extra virgin olive oil, for brushing
freshly ground black pepper

Chargrill the bread on both sides until crisp or cook under a grill (broiler). Rub one side with the garlic clove and lightly brush with some olive oil.

Unwrap the preserved tuna, gently flake into bite-sized pieces and add to the white bean and chilli.

Spread the braised silverbeet evenly on top of each slice of sourdough and place in the centre of each plate. Spoon over the tuna mixture and finish with a good grind of pepper.

WOOD-FIRE GRILLED ASPARAGUS BRUSCHETTA WITH TOMATO, RICOTTA & BASIL

> Serves 4

Asparagus is best in spring and early summer. These local beauties are great boiled, pan-fried or eaten raw. Here they are grilled over our wood-fired pit. This can be simulated at home by simply barbecuing the asparagus. The dish itself is so simple and you can swap the ricotta for goat's cheese, if you wish. You can also pan-fry the asparagus and the result will be just as pleasing.

12 spears green asparagus

juice of 1 lemon

extra virgin olive oil, for drizzling

sea salt & freshly ground black pepper

4 x 2 cm (³/₄ inch) thick slices sourdough bread

1 garlic clove, halved

2 vine-ripened tomatoes, thickly sliced

12 basil leaves

100 g (3¹/₂ oz) fresh ricotta

Trim the bottom 3 cm (1¹/₄ inches) from the asparagus spears and peel the bottom half of each spear. Heat a barbecue or chargrill pan to medium and cook the asparagus, rotating with tongs, until tender. Cut each asparagus spear in half and place in a bowl. Drizzle with the lemon juice and olive oil and season to taste with salt.

Toast the slices of sourdough on the grill, then rub each side with the garlic clove. Drizzle with olive oil and season to taste with salt.

Arrange the tomato and basil leaves on top of the toast and season to taste with salt and pepper. Lay 3 of the asparagus bottoms on top, then place 3 of the asparagus heads crossed over the bottoms. Top with some ricotta and drizzle with olive oil to finish.

PRAWN ROLL

What's not to like about prawns and mayonnaise? We make brioche torpedo rolls to serve this on at the restaurant, but white bread works fine too, just make sure that it's soft; I always feel that soft bread is the go here. I like my roll really spicy, so I add a good hit of Tabasco. If you really want to spoil your friends, substitute the prawns for crab or lobster.

20 cooked medium king prawns (shrimp), peeled, deveined & chopped

1 tablespoon chopped flat-leaf (Italian) parsley

1 tablespoon finely chopped tarragon

3 small French shallots (eschalots), finely chopped

4 brioche dinner rolls, halved

4 cos (romaine) lettuce leaves, washed & finely shredded

sea salt & freshly ground black pepper

SPICY MAYONNAISE

2 egg yolks

1 tablespoon Dijon mustard

finely grated zest & juice of 1 lemon

$1/2$ teaspoon cayenne pepper

150 ml (5 fl oz) vegetable oil

$2^1/_2$ tablespoons extra virgin olive oil

To make the spicy mayonnaise, place the egg yolks, mustard, lemon zest and juice and cayenne pepper in a large bowl and whisk together. Combine the two oils and, while whisking continuously, slowly add in a thin stream to the egg yolk mixture until all the oil is added and a thick mayonnaise forms.

Add the prawns, parsley, tarragon and shallot to the mayonnaise and gently mix to combine.

Lightly toast the brioche rolls.

Meanwhile, add the lettuce to the prawn mixture and season to taste with salt and pepper.

Spoon the prawn mixture onto the warm rolls and serve immediately.

FRIED FISH BURGER WITH CHILLI MAYONNAISE

> Serves 4

I love eating this when I feel like something a little lighter — now that sounds crazy when we're talking about fried battered fish on a bun, but let me tell you, when compared to the Wagyu burger (see page 165), this is a "light" snack. There is a sandwich in New Orleans called a Po Boy. It's essentially crumbed or battered oysters that are fried and sandwiched in a bun with spicy sauce. You could replace the fish here with fried oysters, prawns or soft-shell crab. Heaven.

CHILLI MAYONNAISE

2 egg yolks
1 tablespoon Dijon mustard
juice of ¼ lemon
5 drops Tabasco sauce, or to taste
250 ml (9 fl oz/1 cup) Rockpool oil (see note)
2 tablespoons salted chilli paste (see page 433)

Place the egg yolks, mustard, lemon juice and Tabasco sauce in a bowl and whisk together. While whisking continuously, slowly add the oil in a thin stream to the egg yolk mixture until it is all added and a thick mayonnaise forms. Stir through the salted chilli paste.

NOTE

Rockpool oil is a blend of one part extra virgin olive oil to one part olive oil.

BEER BATTER

375 ml (13 fl oz/1½ cups) beer
170 g (6 oz) plain (all-purpose) flour
1 teaspoon bicarbonate of soda (baking soda)

Pour the beer into a large bowl. While whisking, gradually sprinkle in the flour and whisk until thickened and smooth. Stir in the bicarbonate of soda.

TO SERVE

4 x 60 g (2¼ oz) leatherjacket fillets or other similar white fish
vegetable oil, for deep-frying
plain (all-purpose) flour, for dusting
sea salt
4 brioche buns, halved
2 cos (romaine) lettuce leaves, thickly sliced
1 large vine-ripened tomato, sliced

Cut each leatherjacket fillet into 2 fingers (about 10 cm x 2 cm/4 inches x ¾ inches).

Heat the vegetable oil in a deep-fryer or in a deep, heavy-based saucepan to 180°C (350°F).

Lightly dust the leatherjackets in the flour, shaking off the excess, dip in the beer batter, then deep-fry until golden all over. Drain on paper towel and season lightly with salt.

Lightly toast the brioche buns under a hot grill (broiler). Spread the bases with the chilli mayonnaise and top with the lettuce and tomato. Place the fried fish in the buns, sandwich with the tops and serve.

THE RECIPES
SANDWICHES

179 | THE RECIPES
SANDWICHES

STEAK SANDWICH WITH TOMATO & CHILLI RELISH

> Serves 4

Take steak, bread, relish and salad and there you have it. I have had this on the Qantas first-class menus forever and I suspect there may be a revolution if it ever came off and with good reason—because it's damned delicious. The simplest things in life are often the best. Once you've made a batch of the relish, you'll see how easy it is to make. The rest comes down to really good bread and a very nice piece of steak and you'll be in never-fail territory. Instead of minute steaks, you could roast a nice piece of beef sirloin and carve off thick slices. Now that's upping the ante and making it a royal event.

8 x 100 g (3½ oz) minute steak fillets
extra virgin olive oil, for brushing
sea salt & freshly ground black pepper
2 baguettes, halved lengthways
4 cos (romaine) lettuce leaves
2 vine-ripened tomatoes, thinly sliced
tomato & chilli relish (see page 432),
for spreading

Heat a barbecue grill plate or chargrill pan to high. Brush the steaks with a little olive oil and season to taste with salt and pepper. Cook the steaks for 1 minute each side for medium-rare. Remove and allow to rest while you get ready to assemble.

Lightly toast the baguette halves under a hot grill (broiler). Place the lettuce on the bases, top with the tomato, then the steaks, a good spoonful of tomato and chilli relish and sandwich with the tops. Halve each baguette crossways and serve.

HOT STARTERS

These hot starters give you an insight into the hot entrées the kitchen dishes out. These are simple produce-driven dishes. Buy well and you will eat well. You want the taste of the ingredient to really shine through. This principle applies to all of the recipes in this book. These dishes use basic simple techniques: roasting, sautéing and frying, so don't be afraid to add them to your dinner party repertoire. Don't forget that if all your prep is done beforehand and you're organised, it will give you plenty of time to relax and enjoy time with your guests.

EMPANADAS

> Makes 12

These empanadas started out as a bar snack at Rockpool Bar & Grill Sydney. Head Chef Angel Fernandez, who works closely with Executive Chef Khan Danis, is Chilean and his love for empanadas meant we had to put them on the menu. They proved so popular that we put on a seafood and vegetarian version as well. Now we couldn't live without them. This recipe is from his mother and I feel very privileged that he has shared it with us. Spend a day making a big batch of these and freeze them. You can then pull them out as you need them — they will take a moment longer to fry from frozen. The pebre is a salsa commonly served with empanadas in Chile but I also like them with my harissa (see page 344).

BEEF FILLING

200 g (7 oz) minced (ground) beef
125 ml (4 fl oz/^{1}/$_2$ cup) extra virgin olive oil
2 large brown onions, finely chopped
4 garlic cloves, finely chopped
1 teaspoon smoked paprika
1 teaspoon ground cumin
^{1}/$_2$ teaspoon chilli powder
^{1}/$_4$ bunch oregano, leaves picked & chopped
sea salt & freshly ground black pepper
^{1}/$_2$ bunch flat-leaf (Italian) parsley, leaves picked & chopped

Heat half of the olive oil in a saucepan over low heat. Add the onion and cook, stirring, for 2 minutes or until they start releasing their moisture and have softened. Strain through a sieve, discarding the juices.

Return the pan to medium heat and add the remaining olive oil. Add the beef and garlic and cook until browned. Return the onion to the pan, add the spices and oregano and cook for 5 minutes. Season to taste with salt and pepper, stir through the parsley and set aside to cool.

EMPANADA DOUGH

150 g (5^1/$_2$ oz/1 cup) plain (all-purpose) flour
50 g (1^3/$_4$ oz/^{1}/$_3$ cup) self-raising (self-rising) flour
^{1}/$_2$ teaspoon table salt
40 g (1^1/$_2$ oz) unsalted butter, melted

Place the flours and salt in a large bowl. Add the melted butter and mix until well distributed. Add 185 ml (6 fl oz/^{3}/$_4$ cup) of warm water and knead until a smooth dough forms. Cover with a tea towel and set aside for 15 minutes to rest.

PEBRE SAUCE

1 large vine-ripened tomato, peeled, seeds removed (see glossary) & diced
^{1}/$_2$ red onion, finely diced
2 jalapeño chillies, finely diced
2 garlic cloves, crushed
60 ml (2 fl oz/^{1}/$_4$ cup) good-quality white wine vinegar
^{1}/$_2$ bunch coriander (cilantro), chopped

Combine all of the ingredients with 60 ml (2 fl oz/^{1}/$_4$ cup) of hot water and season to taste. Cover and refrigerate until needed.

TO ASSEMBLE

2 boiled eggs, each cut into 6 pieces
12 Kalamata olives, pitted
24 raisins
vegetable oil, for deep-frying

Roll the empanada dough into a cylinder, then cut into 12 even pieces. Roll each piece out into a 12 cm–15 cm (4^1/$_2$ inch– 6 inch) diameter round. Divide the beef filling between the rounds, top each with a piece of boiled egg, an olive and 2 raisins. Fold the dough in half to form a semicircle. Press the edges together, crimping with your fingers to seal them.

Heat the vegetable oil in a large heavy-based saucepan or deep-fryer to 180°C (350°F). Deep-fry the empanadas, 3 at a time, until golden and crisp.

Serve the empanadas with the pebre sauce for dipping.

CHARCOAL-OVEN ROASTED KING PRAWNS

> Serves 4

These roasted, marinated prawns are super delicious. You can cook them on a barbecue or under a grill (broiler) or even pan-fry or roast them. The prawns we use at Rockpool Bar & Grill are the Spencer Gulf king prawns — a beacon of best-practice sustainable fishing (read about them on page 188).

12 raw (green) large king prawns (shrimp), unpeeled, halved lengthways & deveined

1 small handful sage leaves

1 small handful oregano leaves

1 small handful coriander (cilantro) leaves

1 small knob of ginger

1 garlic clove

2 dried long red chillies

finely grated zest & juice of 1 lemon

125 ml (4 fl oz/½ cup) extra virgin olive oil, plus extra for drizzling

sea salt & freshly ground black pepper

1 small handful flat-leaf (Italian) parsley leaves, chiffonade

lemon wedges, to serve

Arrange the prawns, cut-side up, on a tray.

Preheat the oven to 250°C (500°F/Gas 9) or a barbecue grill plate to hot.

Finely chop the herbs, ginger, garlic and chilli. Combine in a bowl, add the lemon zest and olive oil and season to taste with salt and pepper.

Spread the marinade over the prawns. If using the oven, roast the prawns for about 5 minutes or until cooked through. If using a barbecue, place the prawns, cut-side down, on the barbecue and cook for 5 minutes, pressing down on the prawns to caramelise the flesh.

Remove from the oven or barbecue, squeeze over the lemon juice to taste and season with salt and pepper. Drizzle with the olive oil, sprinkle with the parsley and serve with the lemon wedges.

ROCKPOOL PRAWNS,
STARS OF AUSTRALIAN FISHING

Most prawns in Australia and around the world are treated with metabisulphite. This is a chemical that stops oxidisation, which causes black spots. Metabisulphite is used in the prawn industry to preserve the aesthetic of the prawn rather than its freshness. For me, the major concern about the use of metabisulphite is the taste and texture. A treated prawn doesn't have the same sweet taste or slight crunch in texture. The Spencer Gulf Prawn Fishery in South Australia is not only a shining beacon in sustainable fishing but also produces untreated prawns. These are the prawns of choice at Rockpool Bar & Grill. Seafood expert John Susman has spent some time at the Spencer Gulf Prawn Fishery and shares his insider knowledge.

If there is an iconic Australian seafood, then surely it must be the king prawn, in no small thanks to the work of the original *Crocodile Dundee*, Paul Hogan, and the hundreds and thousands of holidaymakers every year in Australia who grab a cold beer, a kilo of prawns and spend the summer listening to the cricket.

Since the early nineties, prawn farming throughout the world has had a dramatic effect on the availability of prawns, both in the number of species and forms available. Concurrently, there has been a dramatic decrease in the availability of sustainably caught, premium wild prawns. Like elsewhere in the world, the Australian wild-prawn fisheries are under stress from over-fishing, years of bad practices and diminishing stocks.

There is, however, a standout fishery: Spencer Gulf Prawn Fishery in South Australia. This fishery is somewhat unique due to its geographical location, cold-water environment and the existence of only one prawn species in the fishery. The southern king prawn (*Melicertus latisulcatus*) has a wide distribution over the colder waters of the Indo-Pacific region, with the world's largest known population in the Spencer Gulf region.

The fishery harvests around 2000 tonnes of prawns each year, a volume that has been constant for nearly 40 years. Unlike many wild-prawn fisheries in other parts of the world, the Spencer Gulf Prawn Fishery remains in positive growth after nearly 40 years of commercial fishing. This means that there are more prawns growing wild in the fishery every year than were caught the previous year. Their remarkably stable history of catches is the result of appropriately conservative management strategies, suitable environmental conditions for spawning and recruitment and highly productive juvenile habitats. It is the leading example of how long-term fishery management plans and proactive fishing practices can deliver both short- and long-term sustainability and a truly great-eating crustacean.

The fishery is restricted to about 65 nights per year of catching and the grounds are closed during the key prawn spawning and juvenile times from January to February and July to October. Fishing in other months lasts a maximum of 12 nights, from the last to the first quarter of the moon phase.

Harvest strategies for each period are determined on the basis of data collected during regular fishery-independent and fishery-dependent surveys. The fishery can change its harvest strategies at an hour's notice to achieve the best results for the fishermen, the prawns and the environment. Incredibly, these practices were in place nearly a generation before it was fashionable or legislated to do so.

Trawling is undertaken at night, from sunset to sunrise, using the demersal otter trawl technique. Fishing is undertaken using double-rigged trawl gear, which ensures that the nets do not drag along the seabed, reducing both the impact on the sea floor itself and limiting the number and volume of by-catch species. Remarkably, there is less than one per cent by catch, the majority of which is returned alive to the sea.

Over the past 40 years, considerable technological advances have been made in the way the catch is handled. These practices include: advanced by-catch management systems with the use of "crab bags" to exclude mega-fauna by-catch; "hoppers" for efficient sorting of the catch and rapid return of by-catch; "graders" to sort the prawns into marketable-sized categories; and on-board super-freezing facilities that enable full processing. The vessels are among the most technologically advanced commercial boats afloat, but instead of using this technology to increase catches, it's used to improve the quality of the limited catch.

As one of the most iconic of all Australian prawns, the Spencer Gulf king prawn is characterised culinarily by a crisp firm bite and sweet rich flavour. A naturally beautiful looking prawn, in its "green" or raw state, the prawn is peach coloured with a distinctive blue tip on its tail. When cooked, it turns pale pink and is regarded by Neil as one of the tastiest eating king prawns to be had.

While the sustainable nature of the fishery gives it a distinct market advantage, it is this superb eating quality of the Spencer Gulf king prawn that Neil identified, and also heralded by flavour-driven chefs in Japan, Spain and Italy that has prompted fishermen, including Rockpool supplier, Andrew "Pugs" Puglisi (also the founder of Kinkawooka, read more about him on page 197), to further modify their handling to deliver eating excellence. Key to the process has been Rockpool's commitment that has allowed Pugs and his team in the Spencer Gulf to eliminate the use of antioxidants (most commonly sodium metabisulphite), reduce harvest times and commit to better packaging and freezing techniques, safe in the knowledge that their extra effort will deliver the best possible eating prawn to the guests at Rockpool.

Pugs and his team have backed themselves, their best-practice fishing and handling methods and, most importantly, the ultimate eating qualities of their catch in the process. Their innate respect for their harvest is a shining example of how the contemporary wild-catch fisherman is working symbiotically with both nature and the appreciative chef.

As far as being prawn stars, Pugs and the Spencer Gulf prawn fishermen are delivering star quality to Rockpool — seafood that is genuinely special, absolutely sustainable and bloody delicious. It's what you might call a win-win.

"Their innate respect for their harvest is a shining example of how the contemporary wild-catch fisherman is working symbiotically with both nature and the appreciative chef."

GLOBE ARTICHOKES SAUTÉED WITH MINCED PRAWN ON SOFT WHITE POLENTA WITH FONTINA

> Serves 4

This is a dish that I've been cooking for some time at Rockpool. I love the creamy fine porridge-like texture and taste of white polenta, but yellow polenta will do nicely too. The Fontina adds a lift to both the texture and flavour. You can swap out the ingredients and change it to your liking, though. You could, for example, simply sauté mushrooms with garlic and serve on top of the polenta, or you could substitute the prawns for crab or the artichoke for slices of zucchini (courgette).

6 raw (green) large king prawns (shrimp), peeled, deveined & chopped

4 large globe artichokes

1 lemon, halved

sea salt

100 g (3^1/$_2$ oz) white polenta

80 g (2^3/$_4$ oz/^{2}/$_3$ cup) freshly grated Fontina

50 g (1^3/$_4$ oz/^{1}/$_2$ cup) freshly grated parmesan

50 g (1^3/$_4$ oz) unsalted butter

80 ml (2^1/$_2$ fl oz/^{1}/$_3$ cup) extra virgin olive oil

1 garlic clove, finely chopped

Chop the prawns and set aside.

To prepare the artichokes, fill a large bowl with water and squeeze in half of the lemon. Working with one artichoke at a time, trim the stem to 3 cm (1^1/$_4$ inches). Cut 2 cm (3/$_4$ inch) from the top of the artichoke. Peel away and discard the tough outer leaves to expose the pale yellow-green leaves. Peel the tough outer layer from the stem. Cut in half lengthways and remove the furry choke. Place the artichoke halves in the bowl of water as you finish preparing them. Drain the artichokes. Place in a saucepan of salted water and bring to the boil, then reduce the heat to a simmer and cook until tender when pierced with a skewer. Drain and set aside.

Fill a large saucepan with 600 ml (21 fl oz) water, add salt and bring to the boil over high heat. Pour in the polenta and cook, stirring with a whisk, for 2 minutes. Reduce the heat to low and cook, stirring occasionally with a wooden spoon, for 50 minutes or until smooth. Stir in the Fontina, parmesan and butter. Remove from the heat and keep warm.

When the polenta is nearly ready, heat the olive oil in a frying pan over medium–high heat. Add the artichokes and cook until browned.

Add the chopped prawn and garlic and cook for 1 minute or until the prawn meat is cooked through. Season to taste with lemon juice, salt and pepper.

To serve, spoon the polenta onto plates and top with the artichoke and prawn mixture.

PEA, BACON & CHILLI BROTH WITH GNOCCHETTI

> Serves 4

Peas and bacon are a match made in heaven. This is a dish I cook at home all the time when I want a quick meal (you can make the dish in the time it takes to boil the pasta) and it has found its way from my home repertoire to the restaurant. It was inspired by a great pasta dish that Armando Percuoco makes at his Sydney restaurant, Buon Ricordo. You can use any pasta, but just make sure the size of the pasta isn't a whole lot bigger than a pea. You can cheat and use frozen peas, but I find the best thing is French or Italian tinned peas because they're so sweet and creamy; the sauce will look a little greyer, but the flavour is exquisite.

400 g (14 oz) gnocchetti

1 garlic clove, finely chopped

1 dried long red chilli

40 g (1 1/2 oz) butter

60 ml (2 fl oz/1/4 cup) extra virgin olive oil

125 g (4 1/2 oz) cold-smoked speck, finely diced, skin reserved

1 anchovy fillet, chopped

300 g (10 1/2 oz) podded green peas (about 750 g/1 lb 10 oz unpodded)

1.8 litres (63 fl oz) white chicken stock (see page 436)

juice of 1/2 lemon

1 small handful flat-leaf (Italian) parsley leaves, chiffonade

sea salt & freshly ground black pepper

Cook the gnocchetti in a large saucepan of boiling salted water until al dente, then drain.

Meanwhile, place the garlic, chilli, butter and 2 tablespoons of the olive oil in a large frying pan over low heat and cook until the garlic is just starting to colour. Add the speck and anchovy, cook until the speck starts to crisp a little, then add the peas, reserved speck skin and stock. Bring to the boil, then reduce the heat to a simmer and cook until the liquid has reduced by one-third.

Add the gnocchetti, lemon juice, parsley, the remaining olive oil and season to taste with salt and pepper. Discard the skin. Serve in warmed soup bowls.

ANDREW "PUGS" PUGLISI,
THE MUSSEL-BOUND DIAMOND

*Pugs is a brilliant guy, gentleman and fiercely proud fisherman.
We are so proud to have his products as part of the Rockpool
group's menus. His prawns and mussels are wonderful.
The mussels are full and sweet, particularly in early spring
when he has small new season mussels. They're a real treat.
Seafood guru John Susman is a fan too. He tells us why.*

Andrew "Pugs" Puglisi has been a friend of Rockpool for a long time, supplying his Spencer Gulf king prawns that have featured on Rockpool's menu for nearly 20 years, and now more recently his deliciously sweet mussels from Boston Bay.

Pugs is at the vanguard of the new generation of Australian fishermen: committed, commercial and professional. The ocean is as much a part of his DNA as good food and family. His dad, Bob, a fifth-generation fisherman from Puglia, Italy, settled in Port Lincoln in South Australia, where his only son, Pugs, followed him onto the sea. Bob and Andrew, already pioneers in Australian fishing with the Spencer Gulf Prawn Fishery (see page 188) and the farming of southern bluefin tuna as their credentials, approached the development of the Kinkawooka Shellfish Mussel Farm with the primary goal of producing a great eating mussel.

With a rich heritage of both fishing and cooking from their homeland, the Puglisi family knew that the unique waters and sunny Mediterranean climate of Boston Bay, surrounding Port Lincoln, was ideal for growing the native blue mussel.

Pugs, a keen trencherman, undertook a mission of visiting mussel farms, processors and mussel restaurants around the world, learning about growing and harvesting techniques, environmental protection management and, most importantly, tasted all the resulting mussels. Taking the best of what he had learnt, Pugs designed and built a mussel farm that utilised the unique marine environment of Boston Bay and our indigenous blue mussel species to produce a delicious, naturally sweet mussel. He returned to France in 2006 to learn about their unique mussels from the south-west region, the petit bouchot, with the aim of possibly replicating it in Boston Bay. After three hard years of trial and error, Kinkawooka released Australia's first "bouchot-style" mussel at Rockpool Bar & Grill Sydney. Needless to say, they were little pots of gold.

STEAMED MUSSELS WITH JOSELITO JAMÓN IBÉRICO, CHILLI, TOMATO & CHICKPEAS

> Serves 4

This is a great one-pot dish. I often have this after service when I'm hungry and feel like the taste of the sea. It's such a satisfying meal with the nutty chickpeas and the silky pasta. I use the same wonderfully silky pasta squares we use to make the goat's cheese tortellini (see page 215), but you could easily use papardelle, cut or broken into pieces.

32 mussels, scrubbed & beards removed

24 x 3 cm (1¼ inch) pasta squares

2 tablespoons extra virgin olive oil, plus extra for drizzling

½ red onion, thinly sliced

1 garlic clove, thinly sliced using a mandolin

1 dried long red chilli, seeds removed & finely chopped

1 anchovy fillet

20 g (¾ oz) Joselito jamón Ibérico, finely diced

300 g (10½ oz) vine-ripened tomatoes, halved & sliced

100 ml (3½ fl oz) white chicken stock (see page 436)

100 ml (3½ fl oz) white wine

600 g (1 lb 5 oz) cooked chickpeas (from 200 g/7 oz dried)

juice of ½ lemon

1 handful flat-leaf (Italian) parsley leaves, chiffonade

sea salt & freshly ground black pepper

toasted crusty bread, to serve

Bring a saucepan of salted water to the boil. Add the pasta and cook until al dente. Drain and set aside.

Heat the olive oil in a wide-based saucepan, preferably with a glass lid, over medium–low heat. Add the onion, garlic, chilli, anchovy and jamón and cook until the onion and garlic have softened. Add the tomato and cook for 20 minutes or until softened and creamy.

Add the stock, wine and chickpeas and bring to the boil. Add the mussels, cover and cook, shaking the pan occasionally, until the mussels have opened. Discard any that do not open.

Add the pasta, lemon juice and parsley, drizzle with the olive oil and season to taste with salt and pepper. Serve in warmed bowls with a slice of crusty bread.

LOBSTER OMELETTE WITH PRAWN SAUCE

> Serves 4

Omelettes are great. If you have a few eggs in the house you can always make a fine meal. My wife, Sam, and I eat them at home often, whether truffle, ham and cheese, or crab, prawn or lobster. Whatever you choose to put in your omelette, keep in mind that it should already be cooked, so you only need to warm it during the omelette-making process. Make sure you use good-quality eggs from chickens that have not been raised in cages. With a salad and a good glass of wine, you really couldn't ask for more.

OMELETTE

8 eggs

Crack the eggs into a large bowl and whisk until well combined and smooth. Pass through a fine sieve, then refrigerate for 2 hours to rest.

PRAWN SAUCE

200 ml (7 fl oz) extra virgin olive oil
1 kg (2 lb 4 oz) prawn heads
4 carrots, finely diced
1 brown onion, finely diced
4 stalks celery, finely diced
1 leek, white part only, washed & finely diced
2 sprigs thyme
2 fresh bay leaves
200 ml (7 fl oz) port
100 ml (3½ fl oz) white wine
1.5 litres (52 fl oz) white chicken stock (see page 436)
4 vine-ripened tomatoes, quartered
sea salt & freshly ground black pepper
300 ml (10½ fl oz) thickened cream
2 teaspoons Tabasco sauce
juice of ½ lemon
10 g (⅓ oz) unsalted butter

Heat half of the olive oil in a heavy-based saucepan over low heat. Add the prawn heads and crush with a wooden spoon to help release the flavours and colour. Add 1 tablespoon of the remaining olive oil, increase the heat to medium and cook for about 15 minutes or until nicely coloured.

Meanwhile, heat the remaining olive oil in a saucepan over medium–low heat. Add the carrot, onion, celery, leek and herbs and cook for 10 minutes without colouring the vegetables too much. Add the port and wine and cook until the liquid has reduced by half.

Add the stock and tomato and stir to combine. Add to the prawn heads, bring to a simmer and cook for 20 minutes. Season to taste with salt. Strain through a fine sieve placed over a bowl and discard the solids. You will need 200 ml (7 fl oz) of prawn sauce. (Left-over sauce can be used as a soup base.)

Place the cream in a saucepan, bring to the boil and simmer until reduced by one-third. Add the Tabasco and the prawn sauce and simmer until reduced by half. Strain through a fine sieve placed over a bowl. Add the lemon juice and butter to the strained sauce and stir to combine. Check the seasoning and keep warm until serving.

TO SERVE

160 ml (5¼ fl oz) extra virgin olive oil
40 g (1½ oz) unsalted butter
sea salt
200 g (7 oz) cooked lobster meat

Heat a frying pan over high heat. Add 2 tablespoons of the olive oil and a small knob of the butter. When the butter is foaming, add 185 ml (6 fl oz/¾ cup) of the beaten egg to the pan and season with some salt. Using a spatula, scrape the setting egg into the centre of the pan to create a ribbon effect and tilt the pan so that the beaten egg runs out to the edge. Once the egg is just set, lay one-quarter of the lobster across the centre of the omelette, fold one side of the omelette over the lobster, then the other side to create a barrel shape. Slide the omelette onto a plate and keep warm in the oven. Repeat with the remaining olive oil, butter, beaten egg and lobster to make 3 more omelettes. Spoon some of the prawn sauce over the top and serve.

CHARCOAL-OVEN ROASTED SQUID & PORK BELLY

> Serves 4

The charcoal oven imparts a slight smoky flavour and a wonderful moistness to anything that is cooked in it. This dish is like a little tapa where the ingredients are thrown in and cooked in extra virgin olive oil, then served with a couple of slices of bruschetta to soak up the juices. We change the ingredients to create different dishes, but they all have oil as the common thread. Now you probably won't have one of these ovens, but never fear, the squid and pork can be thrown on a barbecue or even cooked in a preheated 200°C (400°F/Gas 6) oven. If you want to infuse the dish with charcoal-roasted flavour, cook the squid and pork in a small charcoal barbecue and cover with the barbecue lid for part of the cooking process so that the meat absorbs the charcoal flavour.

You may need to begin this recipe the day before.

500 g (1 lb 2 oz) pork belly

1 x 400 g (14 oz) squid

sea salt & freshly ground black pepper

1.15 litres (40 fl oz) extra virgin olive oil

1 red onion, thinly sliced

2 garlic cloves, thinly sliced using a mandolin

2 long red chillies, thickly sliced

⅓ cup semi-dried cherry tomatoes (see page 428)

juice of 1 lemon

crusty sourdough bread, to serve

Coat the pork belly in 2 tablespoons of salt and refrigerate for 3 hours or preferably overnight.

Preheat the oven to 90°C (194°F). Pat the pork dry with paper towel and wipe away any excess salt. Warm 1 litre (35 fl oz/4 cups) of the olive oil in a saucepan over low heat. Place the pork in a roasting tray with at least 3 cm (1¼ inches) of space around the edges. Cover the pork with the warm oil and roast for 4–6 hours or until tender.

Remove from the oven and allow to cool slightly, then remove the pork from the oil. Set the pork aside to cool completely. Remove the skin and discard. Slice the pork into bite-sized pieces (about 4–5 per serve) and set aside.

Clean the squid (see glossary). Score the inside of the squid tube in a crisscross pattern, then cut into bite-sized pieces. Cut the wings and tentacles into 3 cm (1¼ inch) lengths.

Heat a heavy-based saucepan or cast-iron casserole over medium–high heat. Add the remaining olive oil and when hot, add the pork, squid, onion, garlic, chilli and tomatoes. Cook for 5 minutes or until the onion has slightly caramelised and the squid is cooked through, then stir to distribute the heat. Remove from the heat. Add the lemon juice and season to taste with salt and pepper. Serve straight away with crusty sourdough bread.

PETER "REEVSO" REEVES,
THE CLAM KING

I love the nutty taste of clams and the firm texture they have. I also know that when we have Peter's clams in the house, they will be live and full of sea water, which is why they add so much flavour to any dish you cook. It is that wonderful sea brine flavour that comes from the clams that I love so much. I wish I could bottle it and add it to every seafood dish we make! John Susman *gets down to what makes these clams so delicious.*

Peter "Reevso" Reeves has shoulders as broad as he is tall. They're the shoulders of a bloke who spends six months in the surf and six months digging clams. He's a quiet fellow with a permanent deep tan and a face etched by salt. Reevso is the sort of knockabout bloke who knows the swells and eddies of the Great Southern Ocean better than most. An avid surfer, Reevso has been hand-harvesting the sand clams of Coffin and Venus Bays in South Australia for years. Like all of the Rockpool suppliers, there is something special about him.

The licence for harvesting the *Katelysia* clam, commonly known as vongole in Australia, is a highly quota'd fishery, meaning a "total allowable catch" is prescribed and only that amount can be harvested by the fishermen. In addition, the licence holder must only fish for the clams using a hand rake.

To harvest clams that are full, rich and sweet, Reevso needs to know the exact spot on any given day where the conditions are perfect as the conditions can change quickly and the clams are only full, rich and sweet for a restricted amount of time and then they deteriorate. Standing in chest-deep water for up to eight hours, hand-raking the sub-tidal sandbanks for clams, is no job for the faint-hearted. Reevso, with his intimate knowledge of the coastline, the water, the tides and the clams, is as unique as the clams that he catches.

CLAMS STEAMED WITH JAMÓN SERRANO, WHITE WINE & FLAGEOLET BEANS

> Serves 4

This is a dish I eat at home all the time, and when I do eat it at the restaurant I do so without sharing it as I love it, love it, love it. I'm addicted to the salty flavour of the sea, the nutty taste of the clams and the deep richness of the ham. We serve a lot of ham plates, so we use the end of the leg for dishes such as this one. On occasion, I have used jamón Ibérico, which takes it to the next level. Make sure your clams come from a good supplier as often they can be quite gritty. A welcome addition to this dish would be some strips of fresh squid, quickly sautéed, then braised with the clams as they open, or mussels or pipis mixed in with the clams, too.

500 g (1 lb 2 oz) clams (vongole), purged
2 tablespoons extra virgin olive oil
1 French shallot (eschalot), finely diced
1 garlic clove, finely chopped
60 ml (2 fl oz/^{1}/$_4$ cup) white wine
50 g (1^3/$_4$ oz) jamón serrano, finely diced
100 g (3^1/$_2$ oz) tinned flageolet beans, drained
50 g (1^3/$_4$ oz) unsalted butter
lemon juice, to taste
sea salt & freshly ground black pepper

Heat the olive oil in a large saucepan, preferably with a glass lid, over low heat. Add the shallot and garlic and cook for 2 minutes without colouring. Increase the heat to high, add the clams and wine, cover and cook, shaking the pan occasionally. Remove the clams as soon as they open. Discard any that do not open.

Add the jamón and beans to the pan, reduce the heat to low and stir in the butter. Season to taste with the lemon juice, salt and pepper. Return the clams to the pan and stir to combine. Serve immediately.

CREAM OF OYSTER, LEEK & POTATO SOUP

> Serves 4

This is a simple delicious chowder with a wonderful creaminess and a great taste of the sea. I'm a big fan of oyster soup when it's done right. It's light and delicate but the oyster flavour still comes through. The butter really enhances the flavour, so don't be tempted to leave it out. On occasion, I serve this with some bruschetta on the side. If you really don't want to shuck your own oysters, you could use jarred ones — I won't tell anyone. The juice from the jar will add good flavour. Or you can replace the oysters with mussels — just steam them open with a little wine, strain the juice and add the mussel meat and juices right at the end.

24 freshly shucked oysters (see page 87), brine reserved

50 g (1³/₄ oz) unsalted butter

80 ml (2¹/₂ fl oz/¹/₃ cup) extra virgin olive oil

2 large leeks, cut into 5 mm (¹/₄ inch) dice

100 ml (3¹/₂ fl oz) dry vermouth

100 ml (3¹/₂ fl oz) white wine

1.5 litres (52 fl oz) white chicken stock (see page 436)

4 large kipfler potatoes, boiled, peeled & cut into 1 cm (¹/₂ inch) thick slices

100 ml (3¹/₂ fl oz) pouring (single) cream

lemon juice, to taste

sea salt & freshly ground black pepper

finely snipped chives, for garnishing

Heat half of the butter and the olive oil in a large saucepan over medium heat. Add the leek and cook for 5 minutes or until softened. Add the vermouth and cook until reduced by half, then add the wine and cook until reduced by half again.

Add the stock and cook until reduced by half. Add the potato, reserved oyster brine and cream and simmer for 2 minutes. Add the oysters and simmer for 1 minute, making sure not to overcook the oysters. Stir in the remaining butter and season to taste with the lemon juice, salt and pepper. Garnish with the chives to serve.

FRIED SQUID, RADICCHIO & CHILLI SALAD WITH ROMESCO SAUCE

> Serves 4

When I opened Rockpool Bar & Grill Melbourne I figured that I needed to have fried calamari on the menu, as it would be a perfect starter to share before moving on to steaks. Having just been to Spain, I had fallen in love with the sauce, Romesco, and it seemed to me that it would be a perfect match for the fried squid. As it turned out, it has become a bit of a signature and one of the most popular dishes.

ROMESCO SAUCE

1 head garlic
1 red capsicum (pepper)
4 long red chillies, seeds removed
50 ml (1³/₄ fl oz) vegetable oil
10 g (¹/₃ oz) crustless white sourdough bread
2 vine-ripened tomatoes, peeled, seeds removed (see glossary) & quartered
4 hazelnuts, roasted
4 blanched almonds, roasted
1 teaspoon sherry vinegar
1 tablespoon extra virgin olive oil
lemon juice, to taste
sea salt & freshly ground black pepper

Preheat the oven to 200°C (400°F/Gas 6). Place the head of garlic, capsicum and chilli in a roasting tray and roast. When the chilli is just roasted and soft, remove from the oven. When the capsicum is tender, remove from the oven. When the garlic is tender, remove from the oven. Peel the skin from the chilli and capsicum and remove the seeds. Roughly tear the capsicum and chilli flesh and place in a food processor. Squeeze the garlic cloves from their skins into the food processor.

Heat the vegetable oil in a small frying pan over medium heat. Tear the bread into chunks, add to the pan and fry until light golden. Add to the food processor.

Add the tomato, nuts, vinegar and olive oil to the food processor and purée until smooth. Season to taste with the lemon juice, salt and pepper.

TO SERVE

1 x 500 g (1 lb 2 oz) squid
seasoned plain (all-purpose) flour, for dusting
vegetable oil, for deep-frying
¹/₂ head radicchio, leaves roughly chopped
2 large handfuls rocket (arugula) leaves
sea salt & freshly ground black pepper
2 tablespoons balsamic vinegar
80 ml (2¹/₂ fl oz/¹/₃ cup) extra virgin olive oil

Clean the squid (see glossary). Cut the squid tube, wings and tentacles into bite-sized pieces. Dust in the seasoned flour, shaking off any excess.

Heat the vegetable oil in a deep-fryer or deep heavy-based saucepan to 180°C (350°F). Fry the squid until light golden. Drain on paper towel.

Combine the radicchio and rocket in a bowl, season to taste with salt and pepper, drizzle with the vinegar and olive oil and toss to combine.

Divide the salad among plates, top with the fried squid and serve with the romesco sauce on the side.

WHITE ASPARAGUS WITH SHIITAKE MUSHROOMS, SLOW-COOKED EGG, BURNT BUTTER & PARMESAN

> Serves 4

Slow-cooked eggs are one of my favourite things ever. They pair perfectly with all types of salads. Here I've partnered them with white asparagus and shiitake mushrooms. The burnt butter and parmesan take it to the next level, but you could just drizzle with extra virgin olive oil, if you like. The nice thing about white asparagus is that it has quite a muted, soft flavour compared to its green brother, so it goes well with the creamy egg, nutty parmesan and earthy mushrooms.

28 spears white asparagus

4 eggs

80 ml (2½ fl oz/⅓ cup) extra virgin olive oil

8 French shallots (eschalots), left whole

12 shiitake mushrooms, stems removed

sea salt & freshly ground black pepper

juice of 1 lemon

50 g (1¾ oz) unsalted butter

100 g (3½ oz) freshly grated parmesan

½ small handful flat-leaf (Italian) parsley leaves, chiffonade

To slow-cook the eggs, heat a saucepan of water to 60°C (140°F). Place the eggs in the pan and cook for 2 hours, making sure the temperature remains constant. Alternatively, poach the eggs (see glossary).

Heat the olive oil in a frying pan over low heat. Add the shallots and cook for 20 minutes or until tender and golden.

Remove the woody bases from the asparagus and peel the spears from just below the tips.

Once the eggs are cooked, add the asparagus and mushrooms to the shallots and cook until tender. Season to taste with salt and pepper and dress with the lemon juice.

Heat the butter in a small frying pan over high heat and cook for 1 minute or until nut brown.

To serve, lay the asparagus spears on serving plates and arrange the mushrooms and shallots in a circle over the asparagus to create a base to hold the egg in place.

Very carefully crack the eggs into the circles formed by the mushrooms and shallots. Sprinkle with the parmesan, then spoon the burnt butter over the egg, being careful not to scoop up any of the burnt milk solids. Grind over some pepper and sprinkle with the parsley.

LICENSEE, JEREMY JOHN COURMADIAS, LIQO660010182
ROCKPOOL
BAR & GRILL ★ SYDNEY
ROCKPOOL
BAR & GRILL ★ SYDNEY

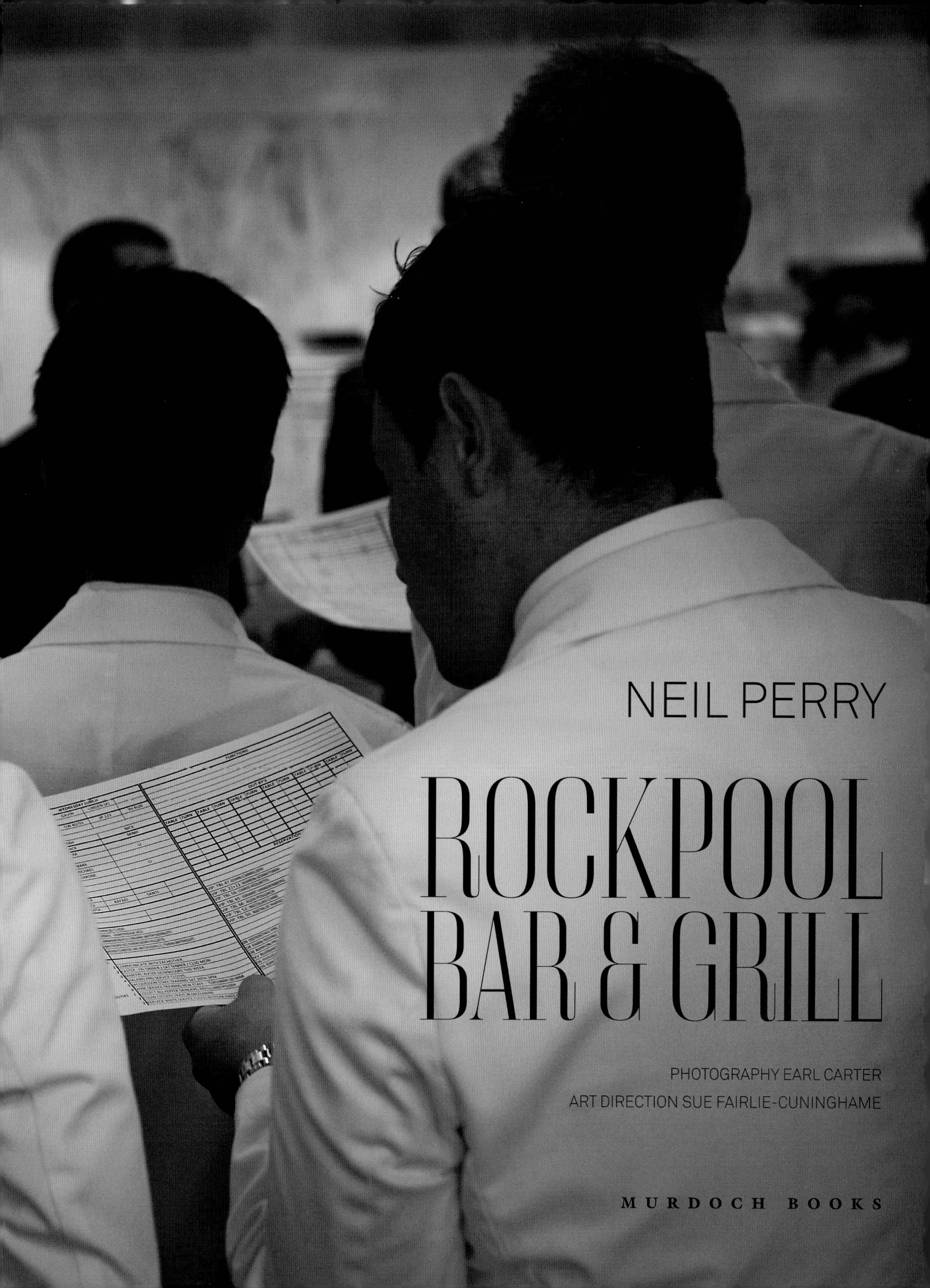

NEIL PERRY

ROCKPOOL BAR & GRILL

PHOTOGRAPHY EARL CARTER
ART DIRECTION SUE FAIRLIE-CUNINGHAME

MURDOCH BOOKS

DEDICATION

This book is dedicated to the memory of David Band, style guru, graphic designer and awesome artist. He is responsible for the graphic identity of all my restaurants. In fact, he has been and always will be a very important part of the Rockpool family. Most importantly, he was a wonderful man and a great friend. His legacy will live on in his great art and style and in his beautiful family.

WELCOME

This is the Rockpool Bar & Grill cookbook. It is more than just a collection of recipes. It is really a journey through the experience that is Rockpool Bar & Grill. It is about service, wine, cocktails, ambience, food and, most importantly, about what makes the place live and breathe every day — the producers and suppliers who love what they raise or catch and the environment that it comes from.

This book is about the people who make the place run, our amazing staff. It's also about the people who come and love it, our beautiful customers.

I hope that it gives you an insight into what it takes to run a restaurant and also sends you into the kitchen to prepare and cook this wonderful produce-driven food.

The older I get the more I realise that the natural food we have on this planet is at its best when well treated and cooked simply. It would be hard to say there is something more delicious than an amazing piece of cheese, such as Gruyère or parmesan, made as it has been for centuries. This is simple eating at its best.

Throughout this book, I have asked some of our amazing suppliers to tell you their story as I could never do justice to the passion that they have. I hope it goes some way to explaining why small, caring farmers and fishermen are a better option than industrially raised food that has neither good taste nor humanity attached to it.

It seems strange to me that since World War II, in the drive to never feel hunger in the developed world, we have driven the cost of food production down so low that it does neither us nor the environment any good. If the planet is to be saved, I fear we shall have to do it ourselves. We, the consumers, must take responsibility and demand change, for in the hands of the multinationals, the world is in peril of destruction through the web of deception that is spun all in the name of advancement and plenty and the cry of 'farm fresh' when it is a blatant lie.

In any case, at its heart, this book is meant to inspire the cook, so shop well, cook well, eat well and live a happy life.

CONTENTS

THE STORY

14 | MELBOURNE

17 | A Brand: By Luck or Design?
28 | Opening Two Great Restaurants: Khan Danis
31 | My First Ferrari: Vanessa Crichton

32 | SYDNEY AND PERTH

35 | Once More, Luck or Destiny?
42 | A Thirst for Knowledge: David Doyle
49 | Financial Mise en Place: Trish Richards
53 | From the East to the West

54 | SERVICE AND THE BAR

57 | Fine Form
59 | The Building Blocks of a Good Bar
63 | Best Bar None: Linden Pride
64 | Rockpool Tonic
66 | Mexican Sour No. 1
66 | City Mutual Cocktail
67 | Scorched Almond Sidecar
69 | Dark & Stormy
69 | House Martini
70 | Chipotle Margarita
71 | Rockpool Mai Tai
72 | Italian Sour No. 3
72 | Bloody Mary
74 | Our Pink Lady
74 | New Fashioned
75 | Jack Rose

THE RECIPES

79 | My Philosophy

82 | RAW AND CURED SEAFOOD

87 | Freshly shucked oysters
89 | Brendie Guidera, The Oyster Whisperer
91 | Tathra Oysters, The Mighty Sydney Rock
93 | Working With Scallops
94 | Queen scallops with preserved lemon salsa & harissa
94 | Queen scallops with lemon & coriander
95 | Pickled blue nose mackerel, apple & potato salad
96 | Cutting Raw Fish
97 | Raw tuna
99 | Hagen Stehr, The Kingfish Kaiser
100 | Hiramasa kingfish tartare
100 | Raw school prawns
101 | Seared swordfish with red braised vegetables
103 | Salmon tartare with olives
106 | How to Kill a Lobster
107 | Raw lobster with chilli & mint
109 | Crudo of kingfish, ocean trout & tuna with horseradish, shallot, coriander & lemon oil
112 | Raw leatherjacket with cherry tomato & chilli
113 | Flathead ceviche
114 | Scampi ceviche
114 | Squid ink ceviche
115 | Blue nose mackerel escabeche
117 | Four raw tastes of the sea
119 | Raw flounder with fresh horseradish
120 | Tuna tartare, Moroccan eggplant, cumin mayonnaise & harissa
124 | Lemongrass sugar-cured ocean trout
125 | Sterling Caviar with toast & crème fraîche

126 | CURED MEATS

129 | Pickled vegetables

130 | SALADS

135 | House-chopped salad
136 | Beetroot, mâche & feta salad with pistachio nut dressing
138 | Modern-day Caprese salad with burrata
139 | New-style prawn cocktail
140 | Butter lettuce, avocado, cherry tomato & jalapeño chilli salad
142 | King prawn Russian salad with Avruga
143 | My steak tartare with chips
145 | Wood-fire grilled baby octopus with olives & hand-pounded pesto

147 | Salad of baby beetroot, pickled onion, grilled zucchini, farro, feta & white beans
148 | Wood-fire grilled eggplant, roasted pumpkin & chilli salad with goat's curd
152 | Prawn, nectarine & hazelnut salad
155 | Wood-fire grilled vegetables & goat's curd
156 | Anchovy, baby cos & poached egg salad with green goddess dressing
157 | Salad of prawn, calamari, octopus, mussels & clams with rocket & smoky potato
159 | Warm salad of wood-fire grilled quail with smoky tomato & black olives

160 | SANDWICHES

165 | David Blackmore's Fullblood Wagyu hamburger with bacon, Gruyère & Zuni pickle
167 | Artichoke & mushroom bruschetta
171 | Wagyu bresaola with mushroom toast
172 | Sardines with chilli on bruschetta
172 | Ortiz anchovies with smoky tomato bruschetta
173 | Preserved tuna, white bean, chilli & silverbeet bruschetta
174 | Wood-fire grilled asparagus bruschetta with tomato, ricotta & basil
176 | Prawn roll
177 | Fried fish burger with chilli mayonnaise
179 | Steak sandwich with tomato & chilli relish

180 | HOT STARTERS

185 | Empanadas
187 | Charcoal-oven roasted king prawns
188 | Rockpool Prawns, Stars of Australian Fishing
191 | Globe artichokes sautéed with minced prawn on soft white polenta with fontina
192 | Pea, bacon & chilli broth with gnocchetti
197 | Andrew "Pugs" Puglisi, The Mussel-bound Diamond
198 | Steamed mussels with Joselito jamón Ibérico, chilli, tomato & chickpeas
199 | Lobster omelette with prawn sauce
200 | Charcoal-oven roasted squid & pork belly
203 | Peter "Reevso" Reeves, The Clam King
205 | Clams steamed with jamón serrano, white wine & flageolet beans
206 | Cream of oyster, leek & potato soup
207 | Fried squid, radicchio & chilli salad with romesco sauce
209 | White asparagus with shiitake mushrooms, slow-cooked egg, burnt butter & parmesan

210 PASTA

215 | Seared king prawns with goat's cheese
tortellini, burnt butter, pine nuts & raisins
219 | Octopus braised in red wine, tomato
& olives with saffron pappardelle
221 | Spanner crab, roasted cherry tomato
& spicy prawn oil with semolina noodles
225 | Wagyu Bolognese with hand-cut fettuccine

228 MAIN PLATES

230 | Crisp leatherjacket with "crazy water"
233 | Green lip abalone steak meunière
234 | Seared crisp snapper with smoky
cherry tomatoes, borlotti beans
& green olive butter
235 | Wood-fire grilled swordfish with broad
beans & olive tapenade
237 | Seafood stew with spicy mussel
& saffron broth
238 | Grilled lobster with fennel & herb butter
243 | Classic lobster thermidor
245 | Confit duck with roasted mango
246 | Wagyu chuck braised in red wine
with gremolata & potato purée
247 | Corned Wagyu silverside with slow-cooked
carrots & mustard sauce
248 | Lentil & ricotta eggplant moussaka
251 | Vegetable tagine

252 FROM THE CHARCOAL OVEN

255 | The Charcoal Oven
256 | Seafood 101
258 | Sustainable Seafood
263 | Snapper
265 | Whole John Dory
266 | Mark Eather, The Fisher God
268 | Whole red mullet
271 | Lakes & Coorong Fishery,
A Sustainable Harvest Enterprise
273 | Coorong yellow-eye mullet
274 | Grilled swordfish steak

278 FROM THE WOOD-FIRED ROTISSERIE

280 | Wood-fired rotisserie chicken with Tuscan
bread salad
283 | Poultry of Burrawong, No Ordinary Birds
287 | Looking the Animal in the Eye
288 | Pigeon with roasted red capsicum,
red grape & radicchio salad
291 | Melanda Park Pork, A Rare Breed
in Pig Farming
292 | Wood-fired rotisserie loin of pork

294 FROM THE WOOD-FIRED GRILL

297 | Beef 101
303 | Wagyu sirloin, rib-eye or fillet
303 | Wagyu rump, topside or skirt
307 | David Blackmore's Dry-aged Fullblood
Wagyu Beef
313 | Cape Grim's Dry-aged, 36-month-old
Grass-fed Beef
314 | Grass-fed T-bone
315 | Grass-fed fillet
315 | Grass-fed rib-eye on the bone
319 | Rangers Valley Dry-aged,
300-day-grain-fed Beef
321 | Grain-fed rib-eye on the bone
321 | Grain-fed sirloin on the bone
324 | Slow Cooking
325 | Slow-roasted rib of beef
329 | White Rocks Veal, Australian-bred
Champions
331 | Wood-fire grilled White Rocks Veal cutlet
333 | Maylands Farm Lamb, Setting the
Australian Standard
337 | Wood-fire grilled lamb cutlets with
mint jelly

338 CONDIMENTS AND SIDES

342 | Barbecue sauce
344 | My harissa
344 | Horseradish cream
345 | Modern béarnaise
349 | Anchovy butter
349 | Herb butter
350 | Café de Paris butter
351 | Marchand de vin butter
354 | Sautéed zucchini with garlic & mint
354 | Long-braised, melting Roman beans
with herbs
355 | Braised cavolo nero & silverbeet with
chilli, garlic & parmesan
355 | Creamed silverbeet
358 | Hand-cut fat chips
359 | Kipfler potatoes sautéed with
Wagyu fat & rosemary
360 | Potato purée
361 | Mac 'n' cheese
362 | Charcoal-oven roasted pumpkin & sweet
potato with garlic yoghurt & burnt butter
363 | Mushy peas with slow-cooked egg
365 | Potato & cabbage gratin
366 | Sautéed mixed mushrooms
367 | Organic carrots inspired by St. John
370 | Onion rings
372 | Cauliflower & cheese
373 | Green beans with creamy anchovy, chilli
& lemon dressing & almonds
374 | Boiled mixed greens with extra virgin
olive oil & lemon
377 | Radicchio, cos & endive salad
with palm sugar vinaigrette
379 | Cabbage & parmesan salad
379 | Tomato basil salad

382 CHEESE

385 | The Cheese Course
387 | Raw Milk Cheese

388 DESSERTS

391 | A Memorable Ending: Catherine Adams
393 | Muscat de Beaumes-de-Venise granita
with mango ice-cream & fruit salad
395 | Chocolate pudding with cherry compote
397 | Strawberry tart with balsamic vinegar
ice-cream
399 | Summer fruit tart with rose cream
402 | Syllabub with rhubarb & strawberry
compote
405 | Lemon meringue cupcakes
407 | Ricotta fritters with ricotta ice-cream
& citrus
413 | Passionfruit pavlova
415 | Rice pudding with apricots
& candied almonds
417 | Crème renversée
418 | Warm rhubarb & strawberry pudding
421 | Prune & Armagnac crème brûlée
424 | Salted butter caramels
425 | Passionfruit marshmallows

426 BASICS

428 | Semi-dried cherry tomatoes
428 | Gremolata
429 | Tomato jelly
429 | Pickled onions
431 | Mayonnaise
432 | Tomato & chilli relish
432 | Croûtons
433 | Tomato jam
433 | Salted chilli paste
434 | Preserved lemons
434 | Preserved lemon salsa
435 | Quick preserved lemons
435 | Lemon oil
436 | White chicken stock
436 | Rendered Wagyu fat
438 | Veal stock
439 | Crème pâtissière
440 | Sweet pastry
441 | Praline

445 GLOSSARY

447 THANK YOU

450 INDEX

THE
STORY

MELBOURNE

ROCKPOOL BAR & GRILL

A BRAND: BY LUCK OR DESIGN?

The building of the Rockpool Bar & Grill brand began in 1989 with the opening of Rockpool, my flagship restaurant on George Street in The Rocks in Sydney. Some two decades on, Rockpool Bar & Grill Melbourne was born. What many of my restaurant regulars don't know is that meat — and in particular beef — was always destined to assume a starring role on one of my menus! In fact, it has always been central to my passion for cooking: my late father, three brothers and uncle have all been butchers and my culinary education began by learning to celebrate every cut of meat. The only reason my first restaurant, Blue Water Grill, and later Rockpool both had a seafood bias was because, back in those days, the quality of meat required to run a high-end steakhouse simply wasn't available in Australia. It was only in the nineties, when Australian farmers began delivering a world-class grade of meat, that I began to seriously contemplate the challenge of opening a Rockpool Bar & Grill.

The steakhouse concept received a nudge in the right direction in 2004 when John Alexander called me to discuss his grand plan of creating a world-class dining precinct in Melbourne. The development of a smart new dining space, which had the full support of Crown owners, James and Kerry Packer, was part of his vision to completely revitalise the Crown property portfolio. I felt honoured to be invited to be part of such an ambitious dining precinct at Crown. There was just one problem: I was a whisker away from opening up a Rockpool in London. I had found a great property in Mayfair and was ready to sign on the dotted line. How could I possibly be part of the project in Melbourne when I might well be risking millions of pounds on the other side of the world? Although opening up a London restaurant had been a long-held dream of mine, it was also very flattering for Rockpool to be recognised as a well-known Australian brand, and I gave the proposal due consideration.

As it happened, fate intervened and made the decision for me. The London project faltered, so in 2005 my business partner Trish Richards (read about her on page 49) and I went down to Melbourne to have a look at several sites that were still on offer at Crown. John was still keen to see us involved in the project and invited us to inspect the sites that would later become Nobu, Bistro Guillaume and Giuseppe Arnaldo & Sons. Although they were all fantastic, we remained unconvinced it was right for us to take a risk on a Melbourne restaurant. I had long since vowed that if we were to open another restaurant, the space had to speak to us; it had to be vibrant and exciting and have an energy and soul we connected with. Sure, we loved visiting the city and savoured the buzzing, competitive dining scene, but we knew little about how to conduct business in Melbourne and still dreamt of opening a restaurant overseas.

It was not long after this visit that John again urged me to meet with him in Melbourne to outline how Rockpool would sit within the context of Crown's revamped restaurant scene. John spent much of the afternoon outlining his plans; he was keen to seal the deal and felt my involvement would encourage other restaurateurs to follow suit. Later that evening, I joined John and Crown CEO Rowen Craigie for dinner to discuss the finer details of the project. We met at Cecconi's at Crown, an amazing, warm, airy space with high ceilings, grand columns and sweeping

"What I didn't bank on was that telling him turned out to be a defining moment in my career. As well as loving the idea, John said he believed in the Rockpool brand and trusted my food philosophy and dedication to delivering on quality. But he also said do anything I liked, as long as Rockpool is in the name."

views of the cityscape. After enjoying a pleasant meal and a bottle of 2001 Antinori Tignanello, I said to them, "If I could have this space, I would commit in a heartbeat." John replied, "I will call you in the morning." He did. "It's yours!" he said. He also gave me a timeline: we had to open late 2006. It was a moment of clarity — Neil Perry and Trish Richards were going to open a Rockpool in Melbourne! The site was everything I'd been searching for and more. It had presence and beauty and was very dynamic. It was perfect.

With a site secured, a designer engaged and John and Rowen satisfied, next came the question: what style of restaurant would best fit the venue? Trish and I both agreed the traditional fine-dining Rockpool restaurant would get lost in such a cavernous space. My idea of opening a steakhouse again sprang to mind and when I told Trish, she immediately joined in my excitement. Our next hurdle was to sell the idea to John. Naturally, I hoped he'd be enthusiastic about a steakhouse that served the best-quality produce the country had to offer. What I didn't bank on was that telling him turned out to be a defining moment in my career. As well as loving the idea, John said he believed in the Rockpool brand and trusted my food philosophy and dedication to delivering on quality. But he also said do anything I liked, as long as Rockpool was in the name. John is an astute businessman and a big part of his investment was about backing the Rockpool brand. So began Rockpool Bar & Grill Melbourne.

BUILDING ROCKPOOL BAR & GRILL

Saying "yes" was the easy part. What followed my decision to sign on the dotted line was a chaotic 12 months of managing the project from the initial concept to completion, negotiating with a raft of new suppliers we'd never dealt with and, most importantly, recruiting a talented team of staff to commit to what would be a massive undertaking. A staff of some 100 would be required to run the Bar & Grill, and one glimpse of that wage bill was enough to frighten me half to death! After setting up Bar & Grill in Melbourne, my plan was to resume my life and work in Sydney and return fortnightly to oversee operations. I therefore had to hand over the day-to-day running of the restaurant to a team I could trust. Rockpool's head chef Khan Danis and his wife, pastry chef Catherine Adams, were two of my most talented and loyal Sydney staff members and I was confident they would work as hard as I would to maintain the quality and consistency of the food. Together, we started talking to our would-be suppliers and designing a menu to suit the very best seasonal produce.

While we were busy engineering the menu, the restaurant was ready to be rebuilt. Enter Crown project manager Talis Sterns and Bates Smart Architects head designer, Grant Cheyne. I've always understood that a detailed brief is everything to a designer. Grant had to understand what the restaurant would deliver, what it stood for and how the food, wine, ambience and service would come together to fulfil that brand promise. If you're ever going to make that name over the door into a brand, it has to be somewhere that both staff and customers can enjoy and appreciate. I had learnt the hard way that if this didn't drive

the restaurant there was a good chance it wouldn't survive. The premise was simple. As with Rockpool, this had to be world-class; it had to be grand, spacious and intimate; and it also had to nod to the many great American steakhouses that would influence the menu. Grant is a kindred spirit. Here was a designer who had worked with many architects I admired, had experience in hospitality and who understood why I insisted on so much detail with regard to how the restaurant would work for the staff as well as the customers. Talis, on the other hand, was a hard-nosed project manager who considered all the critical aspects of the design and knew what was required to deliver the project on time and within budget. It was their shared expertise, complementary style and dedication to quality that resulted in a beautiful restaurant that met the brief and was only two weeks late! Given that most things that could go wrong *did* go wrong, this was nothing short of a miracle.

While the builders concentrated on constructing the shell of the restaurant, the interior started to take shape. Injecting some soul into the space began with the basics: graphics, crockery, cutlery, computers, the reservations system, point of sales, glassware, menu design and more. The staff, of course, would be the real heart and soul of the space. We had the kitchen management team in place, so it was time to find someone to lead our front-of-house staff.

Trish and I both agreed we needed to appoint a local for this all-important role. It would need to be someone who understood and could implement the Rockpool service philosophy (see page 57). But, if we wanted to crack the cut-throat Melbourne restaurant scene, they would also need

to understand the customers we wanted to attract and have a good idea of how Melburnians liked to be treated. I didn't want them to think I was some arrogant Sydneysider showing them how to suck eggs; in fact, I felt very humbled to be given the opportunity to come to a city renowned for its food and wine and offer something unique. I wanted to win their hearts and minds on quality and the front-of-house staff were integral to that plan.

After placing a newspaper advertisement for a general manager in *The Age*, I travelled to Melbourne to conduct interviews. Although there were some exceptional candidates, both Trish and I were blown away with the qualities that Vanessa Crichton (read about her on page 31) brought to the interview table. She was imminently employable. In addition to her experience managing Taxi Dining Room and Lower & Upper House, she was confident, friendly and enthusiastic. Vanessa has since gone on to become one of the best managers I've ever had the pleasure of working with and remains a constant source of inspiration for the staff. Vanessa puts all of her energy into the role and runs Rockpool Bar & Grill Melbourne as if it were her own.

While chef Khan, my former right-hand man at Rockpool, worked on our supplier base, he and Vanessa also started hiring the floor and kitchen staff. Vanessa's team included some of her former colleagues from Taxi, and Khan also managed to woo a few ex-Rockpool team members our way. Rockpool Bar & Grill Melbourne was starting to shape up.

"We'd worry about the money later! Trish and I have always put our stringent standards for quality before any concerns about cash, which has helped establish Rockpool as an enduring brand."

BUILDING AN IMAGE

I very much wanted Rockpool Bar & Grill Melbourne to have its own image: a look and feel that would help to develop the brand's identity. It needed to be the sort of place whereby if a person saw a particular image, they would instantly link it to the restaurant. I had worked as a consultant for Qantas for more than a decade and, during that time former Qantas CEO Geoff Dixon taught me much about building brand loyalty. Think of the iconic image of the flying kangaroo and the theme song, *I Still Call Australia Home!* It's clear to people around the world that these two components connect to Qantas. I, too, wanted an indelible image that reflected the Rockpool brand. To discuss possible strategies for success and the metaphorical packaging of my product, I turned to my great friend, photographer Earl Carter. After a brief brainstorming session, it became clear that our brand identity should be all about the beef.

But it wasn't just about the produce; it was about provenance, too. It was about the bulls, about the strength of the lineage and about the quality that extends down the line through good breeding. To get the message across, Earl photographed some prize bulls and digitally manipulated the images to make them look like eighteenth-century paintings; they are truly magnificent! To further bolster the restaurant's brand identity, I met with David Band, a contemporary artist, genius graphic designer and mad Scotsman to boot. David tapped into all the elements of my brand strategy and, using Earl's images as inspiration, designed a menu layout that also captured the essence of the brand.

GETTING THE FUNDING
AND PARTNERSHIPS

At this point, Trish and I had been in business together for 18 years, and we were very proud that our relationship had survived both major triumphs and failures. We were also proud we'd kept our reputation intact and never short-changed any of our staff or suppliers. Despite the ups and downs, we still had this beautiful restaurant called Rockpool, which was voted, five times, as being one of The S.Pellegrino World's 50 Best Restaurants. Added to this I'd also carved out a television career presenting on the LifeStyle Food Channel, written a few cookbooks and continued my role as a consultant to Qantas. These successes had helped to strengthen the profile of Rockpool and made it, alongside Tetsuya's, one of only two Australian restaurants recognised around the world at that time. That's precisely why we were lured to Crown and part of why we have been so successful there ever since.

As far as funding Rockpool Bar & Grill Melbourne, there were two clear paths we could take. First, we could get a bank loan and own the equity down the track. Alternatively, we could, for the first time, bring an external associate into the Rockpool fold. Both Trish and I thought long and hard about this decision. Although we felt confident the steakhouse idea would be successful, we were still nervous about the size and scope of the project and the fact it was located in Melbourne; we both agreed an additional business partner would help alleviate some of those concerns. My friend David Doyle (read about him on page 42) was an obvious choice. I met David, an American businessman, when he strolled into Rockpool many years ago. Since then, David and I have travelled together to some of the world's best restaurants, both in Australia and overseas, to indulge our passion for food and wine. David was my first and only choice because I knew cash would not be his primary concern; he would be more interested in ensuring Rockpool Bar & Grill Melbourne was a success. We'd worry about the money later! Trish and I have always put our stringent standards for quality before any concerns about cash, which has helped establish Rockpool as an enduring brand. As it turns out, my hunch about David was right on the money: he was keen to get involved.

"The truth was I was quietly imploding. I had come from a fine-dining restaurant with a huge reputation and I was about to serve a steak with a piece of lemon on the side and tell Victorians it was the best ever. Would they believe me? I knew it was true, but would they stop to taste the difference? Were they ready for such a pared-back approach or would I be run out of town as a fraud?"

COME OPENING NIGHT

It was a mad scramble to open, as scheduled, in the first week of October 2006. We needed to ready ourselves for the *Australian Gourmet Traveller Restaurant Guide* Awards dinner. It might sound bonkers to book a function so early after our launch date, but I've always found that a deadline helps propel me towards the finish line. The *AGT* Restaurant Awards dinner was also an important occasion for John Alexander, as he wanted to officially announce the expansion of Crown. Unfortunately, we were still in a state of chaos the week before opening! I had to call staff in to unpack the front-of-house, arrange the kitchen equipment, organise uniforms, wine and furniture, and I still had the bloody builders in! There was no front desk, the phones weren't connected, the dishwasher was faulty, and the noise from the builders made it impossible to conduct training programs or tastings. But by far the biggest problem we had was the fact we couldn't take the waiters and staff through the space to familiarise them with the flow of service. There we were begging the builders to finish the kitchen so we could begin the mammoth task of organising it. There were 100 staff members all running around and nothing was in its place. We simply had to get organised.

As it happened, we had just one day in the kitchen before opening night. I had said we would open on the Thursday; instead, we opened the following Tuesday — tired and stressed out of our minds all before we'd served a single customer. It was hell! Even though everything that could go wrong did, Khan and Vanessa stayed cool, the staff remained good-humoured, and we somehow managed to set up. Most importantly, the wood-fire grill was ready to go, so the staff could finally sample some aged beef and understand what I'd been banging on about. And, hallelujah, we also got the dishwasher going! But boy was it touch and go! So much for a relaxed week of briefing the staff and testing the menu on family and friends. The very next day we'd be serving the paying public.

As with most restaurant openings, all hell was breaking loose. No one knew where anything was, we were all working together for the first time and things weren't going to plan. In order to cope, I had to stay calm and show some leadership and hope my attitude had a positive effect on the staff. Although I had great support from Khan and Vanessa and their management teams, the truth was I was quietly imploding. I had come from a fine-dining restaurant with a huge reputation and I was about to serve a steak with a piece of lemon on the side and tell Victorians it was the best ever. Would they believe me? I knew it was true, but would they stop to taste the difference? Were they ready for such a pared-back approach or would I be run out of town as a fraud? At this stage the F-word was flying freely around the restaurant. We weren't using the expletive in an aggressive way; it was more a case of, "What the f--k are we doing?" and, "Whose f--king idea was this?" Well, it was my f--king crazy idea, so I had to take control and hope my flock would follow.

At the briefing before service on opening night, I told the team: "Guys you're about to go to hell and back. If we get through it, it will be twice as easy tomorrow and when we get through that, it will be easier again the next day. By the time we get to the end of the week, if you haven't gone mad or resigned, we will be on the road to building a great team." I'm pleased to say many of those front- and back-of-house staff are still with us today and do indeed share that sense of kinship that emerges from the chaos of opening a restaurant.

AFTER THAT ONE NIGHT THE HARD WORK STARTS

Khan, Vanessa and I worked together every day, around the clock, for the next three weeks. We were all exhausted. I was living out of a hotel room and missing my beautiful wife Sam, my then two-year-old daughter Macy, little Indy, who was just six weeks old at the time, and my eldest daughter, Josephine. It was difficult not seeing my wife and children for long tracts of time, but it was also essential for me to take the time to entrench the Rockpool philosophy in the hearts and minds of our staff. It wasn't easy. We had underestimated the fact that the really experienced waiters in Melbourne had jobs they wouldn't leave. It was close to Christmas and they didn't realise this was in fact a Rockpool. We hadn't given a licence to Crown; it didn't own us; and I wasn't a consultant! Back then all the best waiters in the city seemed happy to sit back and wait and see if we would be a success. Although we had put together

a great management team, the only wait staff we found were inexperienced and had to learn on the job. With really busy lunchtime services and an average of 300 covers each night, we were feeling the pain. Vanessa and the team were working hard, but silly mistakes were being made. Finally, after a gruelling first month, we started to function as a team and I felt so proud of this wonderful bunch of waiters. This core group was soon joined by more-experienced wait staff with a deeper understanding of what the Rockpool brand was built on.

The Saturday lunch before our first Christmas, I sat down with the entire staff for a festive lunch. We had a feast of turkey and Catherine made a lush dessert. We had a glass of wine to toast our success: I told them how proud they should be of their efforts. We had so many regulars that loved the restaurant and in three short months Rockpool had become an exciting new addition to the Melbourne dining scene. My biggest fear was about acceptance; I was terrified of being told I was a Sydney upstart that didn't take the Melbourne market seriously. As it happened, my biggest fear was washed away; Melbourne embraced Rockpool Bar & Grill as its own and that is largely due to my loyal, fantastic staff. I returned home to Sydney on Christmas Eve after three long months. It was great to see my family again and to cuddle my wife and children, who had paid a high price for the restaurant's opening success.

KEEPING UP THE MOMENTUM

The next year was fantastic! I came down every other week and the restaurant flourished. The strength of the team had also intensified; it was amazing to see Vanessa and Khan take ownership of the business and to put all of their energy into it. The amazing suppliers had delivered on their promise and the food was fantastic. We ended up building two more dry-ageing rooms for the beef. It was a great surprise and pleasure for Trish, David and myself to win *The Age Good Food Guide 2007* Restaurant of the Year and the *Australian Gourmet Traveller* New Restaurant of the Year. I guess we did what we came to do: create a world-class restaurant in Crown. We also knew that the hard work had just begun because we wanted it to be as great as it could be not just now but for the next 10 years and beyond.

OPENING TWO
GREAT RESTAURANTS

*Khan Danis is my right-hand man. Khan joined me as a junior
at the original Rockpool, and now he is the Executive Chef
of the ever-expanding Rockpool Bar & Grill restaurants. He shares
his opening-night memories.*

When Neil invited me to help with the opening of a new steakhouse, I was over the moon. He told me we'd be cooking aged meats over a wood fire, and the idea really appealed to my sense of taste. I had always loved cooking outdoors, over wood fires, on backyard barbecues and campfires. Plus, it would be a completely new way of cooking for us in a commercial sense. We were wood-fire virgins! The whole idea was, in equal parts, both scary and exciting. Moving to a new city and opening a massive restaurant based on an entirely new concept sounded crazy. How were we going to keep the fire going in the middle of a mad service? Were people even going to turn up? Some were saying there was no way Melbourne would accept us because we were from Sydney and others were saying no one would come to Crown for a "dining experience". The imperative to get this one right was huge.

We met some really passionate suppliers, including John Christopoulos and George Lucas of Ocean Made Seafoods; Leo Donati from the well-known Carlton butcher shop, Donati's; and Peter Cannavo from Flavours Fruit and Veg, to name a few. With the help of these amazing suppliers we hit the ground running. No request was too hard for them and their quality produce really helped shape the menu.

The next step was to hire kitchen staff. I engaged 10 chefs who I had cooked with in the past at Rockpool Sydney. They were the heart and soul of the kitchen and without their knowledge of our philosophy, the opening would have been so much more stressful. They were friends I could trust and I'm in their debt to this day. We barely had time to keep on top of the prep work let alone find staff to replace the ones that were dropping off like flies because they were either unsuitable or uncommitted. If I could compare our situation to a football game, it felt like we had to complete a whole game playing with only 10 men and without any reserves. In fact, it was like playing a complete season without any replacements for injured players. I couldn't tell if we were winning or losing; it felt like we were only just playing the game.

The number of people coming through the doors was insane! We were doing huge numbers and getting lots of compliments but I really hadn't tasted the results for myself as a diner, only sampling food as it was cooked. I couldn't tell if they were well-deserved compliments or just kind words of encouragement. After about three months, my partner Catherine and I had our first meal in the restaurant. It was only then that I finally understood why it was worth doing what we were doing. Sitting in this amazing space with a comfortable club-like atmosphere, we had a simple meal of aged yearling rump cooked medium-rare, a side of boiled cabbage, leek and broccolini, as well as mac 'n' cheese. The steak had been transformed by the smoky fire from a good piece of aged meat into something absolutely delightful. The side dishes did nothing to hinder our appreciation of the tasty, juicy steak, but simply enhanced it because of the simplicity. There was no pool of rich sauce to mask the true flavour of the aged meat. After 20 years of working in kitchens, I felt like I had found a way of cooking that was really true to my own personal taste.

Not long after, a prominent Melbourne restaurateur told me there was no way we could keep up this momentum. My immediate response to his comment was over my dead body. There was no way in hell we were going to let our hard work go to waste. As it turned out, my words could well have come true because some months later I was diagnosed with bowel cancer. I'm proud to say that the team we had in the kitchen and on the floor barely missed a beat and performed like true champions. And, after a period of treatment and surgery, and with support from my wife Catherine, Neil, my colleagues, friends, family and fantastic medical staff, I recovered in time for round two: the opening of Rockpool Bar & Grill Sydney. Even though I knew we were on a winning team, the second opening presented us with a whole host of new obstacles. But as my wise friend Neil keeps telling me, "If it was easy, everyone would be doing it!" No truer words have been spoken.

MY FIRST FERRARI

Vanessa Crichton is the General Manager of Rockpool Bar & Grill Melbourne, Spice Temple and The Waiting Room. She manages a team of some 250 staff to ensure the smooth running of all three Melbourne restaurants. Here is her story.

When I made the decision to make hospitality my career I left behind seven years of university study. I thought to myself, "If hospitality is going to be my career of choice, then I'm going to make it my mission to manage the best restaurant in Australia."

When Neil Perry called to offer me the job of General Manager of Rockpool Bar & Grill Melbourne, I was ecstatic and immediately popped open a bottle of Champagne. It was not long after I had finished the first glass that I stopped to contemplate what a massive undertaking it would be... I thought, "How on earth am I going pull this off?"

It seems much of the population in Melbourne thought the same thing. Despite being constantly told: "That's a huge job you have there!" I was determined not to let Neil and Trish or myself down.

From the start, the restaurant build was on a tight schedule: it had been booked out to host one of the biggest events on the culinary calendar: the *Australian Gourmet Traveller Restaurant Guide* Awards. No matter what happened over the next three months, WE HAD TO OPEN in the second week of October 2006. Oh, the horror! We seemed to face a new crisis every day and endured so many hardships and hassles before opening that I came to believe Bar & Grill Melbourne was cursed. There were issues surrounding every aspect of the build: plumbers left splattered in sewage

from burst pipes; custom-made kitchen equipment that didn't fit; and, a brand-spanking new dishwasher that didn't work. We had to plead with the project managers just to let us on site to train the staff on how to use the point-of-sale system.

With just one week to go until opening night, the constant delays with construction meant we still hadn't moved the furniture in, unpacked the crockery or taken delivery of some 30,000 bottles of wine. But that was just the beginning. The phone and computer lines failed, I had no office and I was trying to recruit staff during one of Australia's worst labour shortages. I was also competing for a limited pool of skilled labour with two other high-profile restaurants due to open the same week. I quickly had to modify my modus operandi: I would ignore what little experience the applicants had and focus on hiring people who I thought would complement the Rockpool culture. If I liked them and the interview felt right, they could develop their skills on the job. I'm proud to say I still have some of those staff members working with me to this day.

Of course, opening night was not without its challenges. As I walked towards the staff to deliver my first pre-service briefing I had to sidestep a ladder with two workmen perched on top! Moments later, I found the climate-control wine towers had flooded. The fact that we had a film crew there to document the chaos for perpetuity

added to the intensity. When would it all end? Thank goodness Neil never ever wavered in his vision for the venture. It was because of his supreme confidence and calm under pressure that I was more determined than ever not to let him down. To my absolute relief, it did come together. The restaurant looked spectacular, the food was sensational and my team of young, inexperienced wait staff had risen to the challenge. The *Australian Gourmet Traveller Restaurant Guide* Awards dinner was a huge success, and just 12 months later the magazine awarded us New Restaurant of the Year.

One night after service, not long after opening, I told Neil that managing this high-end restaurant was akin to "driving a Fiat Bambino around the bends of the Amalfi Coast on two wheels". Neil appreciated the analogy, but added: "You're not in a Bambino; you're driving a Ferrari!" Once again, Neil was right. Even though setting up the restaurant was one of the most challenging experiences of my career, its ongoing success makes it a pleasure to drive.

PASTA

Most of our pasta is made by hand on the premises. Our pasta has been a cornerstone of Rockpool in Sydney and I wanted to continue the tradition at Bar & Grill too. The pasta is cooked to order, which makes all the difference, as pre-blanching pasta leaves you with a less than perfect dish. Have a crack at making pasta at home: pasta machines are affordable and it's a very tactile and wonderful thing to do. Sitting down to a bowl of noodles that you have made for friends and family is a very satisfying thing.

SEARED KING PRAWNS WITH GOAT'S CHEESE TORTELLINI, BURNT BUTTER, PINE NUTS & RAISINS

> Serves 4

This dish is a Rockpool classic and has been on the menu at George Street almost since day one. When I started Bar & Grill Melbourne, it was the first pasta dish I put on the menu. After many years I took it off the menu at George Street but as soon as I started writing the menu for Bar & Grill Sydney, I knew I had to bring it back. Now, it's a classic Rockpool Bar & Grill dish. The combination of silky pasta dough, goat's curd, king prawns, sweet nutty raisins, pine nuts and burnt butter sauce is to die for.

GOAT'S CHEESE TORTELLINI

350 g (12 oz) floury potatoes, unpeeled, such as kipfler, bintje, pink-eye or King Edward
150 g (5½ oz) fresh goat's curd
lemon juice, to taste
sea salt & freshly ground black pepper
150 g (5½ oz/1 cup) baker's (hard) flour, plus extra for dusting

Cook the potatoes in boiling salted water for about 20 minutes or until tender.

Meanwhile, place the goat's curd in a bowl and season to taste with the lemon juice, salt and pepper. Spoon into a piping bag fitted with a small plain nozzle and refrigerate until needed.

Drain the potatoes and, when just cool enough to handle, peel them. While the potatoes are still warm, pass them through a potato ricer or food mill. Add the flour, season to taste with salt and mix until a soft dough forms.

The dough deteriorates as it gets cold so try to work quickly to roll it out and make the tortellini. Divide the dough in half. Cover one-half with a tea towel to keep warm.

Feed the other half through a pasta machine on the widest setting. Dust the dough with a little flour each time you put it through if it's sticking, but it shouldn't be necessary. Keep feeding it through the widest setting. After about the third time through, the dough will start to come together, but don't expect it to look as smooth as normal pasta dough. Reduce the machine to setting 5, fold the pasta sheet into thirds (this is called a book fold) and, using a rolling pin, roll out the seam-end evenly. Make sure that the width of the dough is the width of the pasta machine, then feed the dough through the machine. Increase the machine setting to 10 and feed the dough through. Reduce the settings one notch at a time and feed the dough through each setting until you reach setting 3. It should become silkier and smoother with each time you pass it through the machine. The pasta sheet is not as thin as normal ravioli, but it does have a sexy mouthfeel. Be very careful not to use too much flour in the last rolling through or on your work surface, as the flour stops the tortellini from sticking together.

»

SEARED KING PRAWNS WITH GOAT'S CHEESE TORTELLINI, BURNT BUTTER, PINE NUTS & RAISINS
CONTINUED

Lay the pasta sheet on a surface and trim the edges with a pizza cutter. Halve the sheet lengthways, then cut 3 cm (1¼ inch) squares from each half. It's important that the squares are perfect because you fold them in half to make a triangle. (I love to use these pasta squares in the steamed mussels with Joselito jamón Ibérico, chilli, tomato & chickpeas, see page 198.)

Pipe a large marble-sized amount of goat's curd mixture in the top left-hand corner of each square. Fold the bottom right-hand corner to the top to form a triangle to envelop the filling. You should have triangles with the point facing to the top left.

Fold the base of the triangle up so it is level with, and covers, the top point. You should have a long skinny piece of pasta with a bump in the middle.

Pick up the pasta, with the top point of the triangle facing away from you, and wrap it around your index finger.

Squeeze the two ends together where they overlap, then remove your finger — you shouldn't need water for the ends to stick.

Place on a floured tray and shape the remaining pasta squares.

Repeat with the remaining half of the pasta dough. The tortellini will keep in the refrigerator, covered, for 1 day, or can be frozen for up to 6 months. (You can cook them from frozen using the same method as fresh.)

TO SERVE

8 raw (green) large king prawns (shrimp), peeled & deveined

60 g (2¼ oz/⅓ cup) raisins

freshly brewed English Breakfast tea

2½ tablespoons extra virgin olive oil

20 goat's cheese tortellini

40 g (1½ oz/¼ cup) pine nuts, roasted

50 g (1¾ oz/½ cup) freshly grated parmesan

200 g (7 oz) unsalted butter, chopped

Place the raisins in a heatproof bowl and cover with the hot tea. Set aside to soak for 1 hour. Drain.

Bring a large saucepan of salted water to the boil. Add ½ tablespoon of the olive oil, then the tortellini. Cook until the tortellini float to the surface. Remove with a slotted spoon and keep warm.

Meanwhile, heat half of the remaining olive oil in a heavy-based frying pan over high heat. When the oil starts to smoke, add half of the prawns and cook for 1–1½ minutes each side — be careful not to overcook them, they should still be opaque in the middle. Remove from the pan and keep warm. Repeat with the remaining oil and prawns.

Arrange 5 tortellini on the outer rim of each bowl and place 2 prawns in the middle. Scatter the raisins and pine nuts over the prawns and sprinkle the parmesan over the pasta.

Add the butter to the same pan that you cooked the prawns in, place over high heat and cook for 1 minute or until nut brown. I don't worry about removing the milk solids from the butter as they have a nice flavour, but make sure you do not burn them. If they're burnt, then so is the butter, so throw it out and start again — black butter will spoil the dish. Spoon some hot butter over the tortellini and serve immediately.

OCTOPUS BRAISED IN RED WINE, TOMATO & OLIVES WITH SAFFRON PAPPARDELLE

> Serves 4

I love this dish as the octopus braises and becomes incredibly meaty tasting. It's the perfect marriage with the red wine and it becomes so intense and complex. Just a great dish.

SAFFRON PAPPARDELLE

300 g (10½ oz/2 cups) plain (all-purpose) flour, plus extra for dusting

½ teaspoon sea salt

2 x 55 g (2 oz) eggs

pinch of saffron threads, soaked in 1 tablespoon hot water

Sift the flour and salt together into a large bowl and make a well in the centre. Place the eggs and saffron water in a bowl and beat together with a fork. Pour into the flour well and, using a spoon, combine with the flour. Tip onto a floured surface and, using your hands, bring the dough together and knead for 5 minutes or until smooth and elastic. Form into a disc, wrap in plastic wrap and set aside for 30 minutes to rest.

Roll the pasta through a pasta machine to around 1.5 mm (¹⁄₁₆ inch) thick. Divide the dough into 2 pieces. Roll each piece through the pasta machine, starting at the widest setting, until 1.5 mm (¹⁄₁₆ inch) thick. Roll up the pasta sheet and cut into 25 cm x 3 cm (10 inch x 1¼ inch) strips. Unroll the pappardelle and hang over a bar or rod to dry, or spread out flat, dusted with plenty of flour, over a large tray to dry.

BRAISED OCTOPUS

1 kg (2 lb 4 oz) baby octopus, cleaned

100 ml (3½ fl oz) extra virgin olive oil

½ carrot, diced

½ brown onion, diced

½ leek, white part only, diced

2 garlic cloves, finely chopped

½ dried long red chilli, seeds removed & finely chopped

4 cherry tomatoes, halved

20 Ligurian olives, pitted

1 litre (35 fl oz/4 cups) red wine

1 fresh bay leaf

finely grated zest of ½ orange

5 sprigs thyme, leaves picked

sea salt & freshly ground black pepper

Cut the octopus into bite-sized pieces. Heat half of the olive oil in a large saucepan over high heat. Add the octopus and cook for 1 hour or until tender. Remove from the pan and set aside.

Return the pan to medium heat, add the remaining oil, the carrot, onion, leek, garlic and chilli and cook for 10 minutes or until softened.

Add the tomato, olives, wine, bay leaf and octopus and simmer for 20 minutes or until the octopus is just starting to become tender.

Add the orange zest and thyme. Check the octopus again to make sure it's tender enough to just hold its shape and reduce the sauce by one-third. Check the seasoning.

TO SERVE

gremolata (see page 428) or chiffonade parsley, to serve

Bring a large saucepan of salted water to the boil. Add the saffron pappardelle and cook until al dente. Drain and add the pasta to the braised octopus. Cook for about 1 minute or until the starch from the pasta has thickened the sauce — it should be wet but not soup-like. Divide among bowls and serve scattered with gremolata or parsley.

SPANNER CRAB, ROASTED CHERRY TOMATO & SPICY PRAWN OIL WITH SEMOLINA NOODLES

> Serves 4

The semolina noodles soak up the shellfish oil and make this dish lip-smackingly good. It's almost impossible to sit at the bar with my eldest daughter, Josephine, and not have her order it — I completely understand her addiction. This dish is equally great with prawn or lobster, and if you don't feel like making the noodles, good-quality spaghetti or linguine are yummy with it too.

SEMOLINA NOODLES

210 g (7½ oz) semolina flour, plus extra for dusting
½ teaspoon sea salt
2 x 55 g (2 oz) eggs
1 egg yolk
1 teaspoon extra virgin olive oil

Sift the flour and salt together into a large bowl and make a well in the centre. Place the eggs, egg yolk and olive oil in a bowl and beat together with a fork. Pour into the flour well and, using a spoon, combine with the flour. Tip onto a floured surface and, using your hands, bring the dough together and knead for 5 minutes or until smooth and elastic. Form into a disc, wrap in plastic wrap and set aside for 30 minutes to rest.

Using a rolling pin, roll the dough out to flatten slightly. Set a pasta machine on the widest setting and lightly dust the rollers with flour. Feed the dough through the machine. Reduce the settings one notch at a time and feed the dough through each setting. If the dough becomes sticky, lightly rub flour onto both sides of the pasta sheet. When you reach the second-last setting, fold the pasta sheet into thirds (this is called a book fold), then turn it 90 degrees and feed the dough through the machine, starting on the widest setting again and working through to the second-last setting. Repeat the book folding and rolling process twice more. On the final time, feed the pasta through twice on the second-last setting.

Using a sharp knife, cut the sheet into 25 cm (10 inch) lengths. Attach the noodle-cutter attachment to the machine and feed the pasta sheets through, one at a time, catching the noodles with your hand. Hang the noodles over a bar or rod or spread out flat, dusted with plenty of flour, over a large tray to dry.

SPICY PRAWN OIL

1 tablespoon shrimp paste
2 stalks lemongrass, roughly chopped
1 small knob of ginger
3 garlic cloves, roughly chopped
2 coriander (cilantro) roots, scraped & roughly chopped
2 French shallots (eschalots), roughly chopped
6 wild green Thai chillies, roughly chopped
2 kaffir lime leaves
1 teaspoon sea salt
350 ml (12 fl oz) olive oil
250 g (9 oz) prawn shells

Preheat the oven to 180°C (350°F/Gas 4). Wrap the shrimp paste in aluminium foil and roast until fragrant. Be careful it doesn't burn or it will be bitter. Unwrap and transfer to a blender or food processor. Add the lemongrass, ginger, garlic, coriander root, shallot, chilli, lime leaves, salt and 200 ml (7 fl oz) of the olive oil and blend to a fine paste.

Heat the remaining olive oil in a saucepan over high heat. Add the prawn shells and cook until they become a rich red colour, crushing the prawn heads to extract the flavour. Add the paste, reduce the heat to medium–low and cook for about 30 minutes or until the rawness of the paste is cooked out. Pass through a coarse sieve, pushing the paste through with a wooden spoon. You will only need 200 ml (7 fl oz).

»

SPANNER CRAB, ROASTED CHERRY TOMATO & SPICY PRAWN OIL WITH SEMOLINA NOODLES
CONTINUED

ROASTED CHERRY TOMATOES

20 cherry tomatoes
2 tablespoons extra virgin olive oil
sea salt & freshly ground black pepper

Preheat the oven to 200°C (400°F/Gas 6). Place the tomatoes on a baking tray, drizzle with the olive oil and season to taste with salt and pepper. Roast until the skins blister. Remove and discard the skins. Return the tomatoes to the oven and continue to roast for 15 minutes to release the juices and improve the flavour. Remove from the oven and check the seasoning.

TO SERVE

240 g (8½ oz) picked spanner-crab meat
80 ml (2½ fl oz/⅓ cup) olive oil
200 ml (7 fl oz) spicy prawn oil
60 ml (2 fl oz/¼ cup) lemon juice
1 small handful flat-leaf (Italian) parsley leaves, chiffonade
sea salt & freshly ground black pepper

Bring a large saucepan of salted water to the boil. Add the semolina noodles and cook until al dente. Drain.

Meanwhile, heat the olive oil in a large frying pan over medium–high heat. Add the crabmeat and cook for 2–3 minutes or until translucent. Add the roasted tomatoes, 200 ml (7 fl oz) of prawn oil and noodles and toss lightly to coat. Add the lemon juice and parsley and season to taste with salt and pepper.

WAGYU BOLOGNESE WITH HAND-CUT FETTUCCINE

> Serves 4

The Wagyu makes this Bolognese rich and creamy. I love the extra silkiness it seems to bring to the dish and, although, you could just use spaghetti, I feel the extra width of the fettuccine is important to pick up the sauce.

HAND-CUT FETTUCCINE

300 g (10½ oz/2 cups) plain (all-purpose) flour, plus extra for dusting

½ teaspoon sea salt

2 x 55 g (2 oz) eggs, lightly beaten

Sift the flour and salt together into a large bowl and make a well in the centre. Pour the beaten egg into the well and, using a spoon, combine with the flour. Tip onto a floured surface and, using your hands, bring the dough together and knead for 5 minutes or until smooth and elastic. Form into a disc, wrap in plastic wrap and set aside for 30 minutes to rest.

Roll the pasta in a pasta machine to around 1.5 mm (¹/₁₆ inch) thick. Divide the dough into 2 pieces. Roll each piece through a pasta machine, starting at the widest setting, until 1.5 mm (¹/₁₆ inch) thick. Roll up the pasta sheet and cut into 2 cm (³/₄ inch) thick strips. Unroll the fettuccine and hang over a bar or rod to dry or spread out flat, dusted with plenty of flour, over a large tray to dry.

WAGYU BOLOGNESE

400 g (14 oz) minced (ground) Wagyu

2 tablespoons extra virgin olive oil

1 onion, finely chopped

4 garlic cloves, finely chopped

1 small carrot, finely diced

1 stalk celery, finely diced

80 g (2³/₄ oz) speck, finely diced

sea salt & freshly ground black pepper

400 ml (14 fl oz) full-bodied red wine

1.2 kg (2 lb 10 oz) vine-ripened tomatoes, peeled, seeds removed (see glossary) & diced

2 sprigs thyme, leaves picked & chopped

Heat the olive oil in a large, deep-sided frying pan over medium heat. Add the onion, garlic, carrot, celery and speck, season to taste with salt and cook, stirring occasionally, for 15 minutes or until the vegetables have caramelised but are not burnt.

Add the minced Wagyu, season with salt and cook, breaking up the beef with a spoon, for 5 minutes or until the beef is well browned.

Add the wine and bring to the boil, then reduce to a simmer and cook until the liquid has reduced by half.

Add the tomato and simmer for about 45 minutes or until thickened. Add the thyme and check the seasoning.

TO SERVE

1 very small handful flat-leaf (Italian) parsley, chiffonade

freshly grated parmesan, to serve

freshly ground black pepper

Bring a large saucepan of salted water to the boil. Add the fettuccine and cook until al dente. Drain.

Toss the pasta with the Bolognese and divide among bowls. Garnish with the parsley, grind over some pepper and serve with the parmesan.

MAINS

MAIN PLATES
FROM THE CHARCOAL OVEN
FROM THE WOOD-FIRED
ROTISSERIE
FROM THE WOOD-FIRED GRILL

The main courses at Rockpool Bar & Grill are built around the power of the wood-fired grill and charcoal oven, but we also serve dishes that either have sauces or garnishes and these are on the menu under the heading main plates. These dishes aren't served with a lemon wedge as with most of our beef and seafood, but are complete dishes that in the most part just need a simple green salad to make a meal. These run from fish dishes to great braises and the wonderful lobster thermidor. There are some nice skills on offer here and each of these dishes is well worth the effort.

CRISP LEATHERJACKET WITH "CRAZY WATER"

I love crazy water or "aqua pazza" as it is called in Italy. This sauce is so easy to make. Normally you would poach fish or a combination of fish and shellfish in it, which is what I do a lot at home. It is truly delicious, especially when the tomatoes are in full season and sweet. For the restaurant, I decided to play around with the texture of the fish, so instead of using the crazy water as a braising medium, I use it as a sauce; the fish is fried — crisp batter encasing meltingly tender steamed fish — then placed on top. Might I suggest that I've actually improved on a classic? You be the judge.

CRAZY WATER

125 ml (4 fl oz/½ cup) extra virgin olive oil
5 garlic cloves, thinly sliced
1 dried long red chilli, chopped
sea salt
3 vine-ripened tomatoes, roughly chopped
2 tablespoons flat-leaf (Italian) parsley leaves, roughly chopped

Heat the olive oil in a saucepan over medium–low heat. Add the garlic and chilli, season to taste with salt and cook for 1 minute without colouring.

Add the tomato, parsley and 125 ml (4 fl oz/½ cup) of water. Bring to the boil and cook for 2 minutes, then remove from the heat. Keep warm until serving.

BEER BATTER

225 g (8 oz/1½ cups) plain (all-purpose) flour
500 ml (17 fl oz/2 cups) chilled beer
½ cup ice cubes

Place the flour in a bowl and, while whisking continuously, gradually add the beer, making sure there are no lumps. Add the ice cubes, season to taste with salt and refrigerate until needed.

TO SERVE

600 g (1 lb 5 oz) leatherjacket fillets
1.5 litres (52 fl oz) vegetable oil
seasoned plain (all-purpose) flour, for dusting
aioli, to serve (see page 431)

Cut the leatherjacket fillets into 12 even-sized pieces.

Heat the vegetable oil in a large heavy-based saucepan or deep-fryer to 180°C (350°F).

Dust the leatherjackets in the seasoned flour, shaking off any excess, then dip into the beer batter. Carefully drop 3 pieces at a time into the oil and cook until crisp and golden all over. Remove and drain on paper towel.

Divide the crazy water among bowls and top with the fish. Serve immediately with aioli on the side.

GREEN LIP ABALONE STEAK MEUNIÈRE

If Rockpool Bar & Grill is about one thing, it is about the produce. In green lip abalone, we have one of the greatest ingredients ever. To me they're as good as truffles and foie gras — and they are a local product to boot. Along with mud crab, I reckon they're the best thing to come out of the ocean. I love them done many ways: thinly sliced and stir-fried, confit, cooked Chinese steamboat style or just beaten out slightly and pan-fried, the way it's cooked here — they become rich and delicious with a haunting taste of the sea. I remember the first time I tried this in 1990 at Sam's Grill, a San Francisco institution. I fell in love straight away and have been cooking it ever since.

2 x 600 g (1 lb 5 oz) live green lip abalone
plain (all-purpose) flour, for dusting
30 g (1 oz) unsalted butter
1 very small handful flat-leaf (Italian) parsley leaves, chiffonade
extra virgin olive oil, for drizzling
sea salt & freshly ground black pepper
lemon wedges, to serve

Remove the abalone from their shells, removing all guts from the meat. Dust the abalone in flour, shaking off any excess.

Heat the butter in a frying pan over medium–high heat. When it starts to foam, add the abalone, reduce the heat to medium and spoon the butter over the abalone regularly so it cooks evenly. Cook for 5 minutes each side. Remove the abalone from the pan and return the pan to the heat. Slice into 2 mm ($^1/_{16}$ inch) thick pieces and arrange on plates.

Add the parsley to the pan on the heat and spoon the pan juices over the abalone, drizzle with the olive oil and season to taste with salt and pepper. Serve with plenty of lemon wedges.

SEARED CRISP SNAPPER WITH SMOKY CHERRY TOMATOES, BORLOTTI BEANS & GREEN OLIVE BUTTER

I opened Rockpool Bar & Grill Melbourne before I discovered the wonderful charcoal grill oven that is the centre of the fish program at the Bar & Grill in Sydney, so the fish dishes in Melbourne have garnishes that create what I call a finished dish, rather than a piece of grilled fish with a wedge of lemon mirroring the beef menu as in Sydney. This is one of my Melbourne favourites and it moves off and on the menu in various forms — in the height of summer it may be garnished with roasted tomato and Forum red wine vinegar; in autumn it may have artichokes and fennel with it. Here we smoke cherry tomatoes, add them to slow-cooked beans and toss them together to make a delicious little salad under the fish. The crust on the snapper is an El Bulli concept. First the bread is frozen to make slicing easier, then it's cut super thin using a meat slicer. It's then laid over the skin of the fish and the flesh proteins cause the bread to adhere to it, which creates a wonderfully thin, crisp crust. The green olive butter is a killer with any seafood or barbecued meat — make a large roll and freeze what you don't use.

GREEN OLIVE BUTTER

125 g (4¹/₂ oz) unsalted butter, cubed & at room temperature

50 g (1³/₄ oz) green olives, pitted & finely chopped

juice of 1 lemon

sea salt & freshly ground black pepper

Place the butter, olives and lemon juice in a bowl, season to taste with salt and pepper and mix to combine. Spoon onto a sheet of baking paper or aluminium foil and roll into a log shape about 35 cm (14 inches) long and 4 cm (1¹/₂ inches) in diameter. Wrap in plastic wrap, twisting the ends to secure and refrigerate until firm. Cut into 1 cm (¹/₂ inch) thick slices to serve. Refrigerate any left-over butter for up to 2 weeks or many months in the freezer.

TO SERVE

4 x 200 g (7 oz) snapper fillets, skin on

¹/₂ loaf sourdough (from the centre of the loaf)

600 g (1 lb 5 oz) podded fresh borlotti beans (about 1 kg/2 lb 4 oz unpodded)

12 cherry tomatoes

60 ml (2 fl oz/¹/₄ cup) extra virgin olive oil

2 tablespoons flat-leaf (Italian) parsley leaves, chiffonade

1 tablespoon Forum cabernet sauvignon vinegar

clarified butter (see glossary), for cooking

Trim the crusts from the loaf of sourdough and discard. Place the loaf in the freezer and leave until frozen.

Place the borlotti beans in a saucepan filled with cold water, bring to the boil, then reduce to a simmer and cook for about 30–40 minutes or until soft in the middle. Drain.

Using a meat slicer or electric knife, slice the loaf of bread into paper-thin slices. You will only need 4 slices. Place a slice of bread on a chopping board and place a snapper fillet, skin-side down, on top. Cut out around the fish through the bread and discard the off-cuts. Repeat with the remaining bread and fillets.

Heat a barbecue or chargrill pan to high. Roll the tomatoes around on the grill for 10–20 seconds or until the skins blister. Remove the skins, keeping the tomatoes whole.

Heat the olive oil in a frying pan over medium heat. Add the tomatoes and borlotti beans and cook for about 4 minutes or until warmed through. Add the parsley and vinegar and season to taste with salt and pepper.

Meanwhile, heat the clarified butter in a frying pan over medium–low heat, add the fish, bread-side down, and cook until the bread is golden and crisp, then turn over and cook the other side for 1 minute or until just cooked.

Divide the tomato mixture between plates and top with a piece of fish, bread-side up. Place a slice of green olive butter on top of each fish and serve immediately.

WOOD-FIRE GRILLED SWORDFISH WITH BROAD BEANS & OLIVE TAPENADE

> Serves 4

Swordfish is perfectly suited for cooking on a wood-fired grill; its high oil content handles the charred flavours from the grill beautifully. Here fresh broad beans add a wonderful nuttiness and the tapenade adds a deep salty flavour that pairs well with the fish. Tapenade is easy to make and is fantastic to have in the fridge, ready at any moment, to add flavour to whatever you're cooking.

OLIVE TAPENADE

50 g (1³/₄ oz) salted capers
10 small black olives, pitted
2 anchovy fillets
crushed black peppercorns, to taste
extra virgin olive oil, for drizzling

Soak the capers in water for about 1 hour, making sure they're not too salty. Drain, then roughly chop.

Roughly chop the olives and anchovy fillets, combine with the capers and peppercorns and drizzle with the olive oil. Set aside until needed.

TO SERVE

4 x 200 g (7 oz) pieces of Pacific swordfish loin (see page 274)
600 g (1 lb 5 oz) podded broad (fava) beans (about 1.8 kg/4 lb unpodded)
1 small handful flat-leaf (Italian) parsley leaves, chiffonade
1 small handful mint leaves, chiffonade
80 ml (2¹/₂ fl oz/¹/₃ cup) extra virgin olive oil
juice of 1 lemon
sea salt & freshly ground black pepper

Bring a saucepan of water to the boil. Blanch the broad beans for about 30 seconds. Drain, then peel off the outer skins and discard. Place the beans in a bowl, add the herbs, olive oil and lemon juice and season to taste with salt and pepper. Keep warm until serving.

Heat the barbecue to medium–high. Grill the swordfish for 2 minutes each side or until just cooked through.

Divide the broad beans among plates and top with a piece of fish. Spoon the olive tapenade on top.

SEAFOOD STEW WITH SPICY MUSSEL & SAFFRON BROTH

> Serves 4

Originally a dish at Rockpool, George Street, Executive Chef Khan Danis wanted to put it on the Bar & Grill menu in Melbourne. The spicy intensive flavour of the broth paired with seafood makes it a winning combination. It has a permanent home at all Bar & Grills now. You can add any seafood you like, but don't omit the mussels — they're essential to the broth as their salty juices give the sauce a rich deep taste of the sea.

ROASTED TOMATO SAUCE

2 vine-ripened tomatoes, cores removed
3 teaspoons extra virgin olive oil
sea salt & freshly ground black pepper
1/2 teaspoon white sugar
1 teaspoon Forum cabernet sauvignon vinegar
1 teaspoon chopped tarragon
1 teaspoon chopped thyme

Preheat the oven to 180°C (350°F/Gas 4). Coat the tomatoes in olive oil and season to taste with salt and pepper. Roast until they collapse and the juices release. Cool, then peel off their skins.

Place the tomatoes in a small saucepan over low heat. Add the sugar and vinegar and cook until the tomatoes have broken down and the sauce has thickened. Stir in the herbs and season to taste.

PASTE

1 tablespoon coriander seeds, toasted
1 tablespoon fennel seeds, toasted
1 tablespoon white peppercorns, toasted
1/2 carrot, chopped
1/2 red onion, chopped
1/2 large fennel bulb, chopped
3 garlic cloves, chopped
3 red birdseye chillies, chopped
3 kaffir lime leaves, very finely chopped

1 stalk lemongrass, inner part chopped
45 g (1²/₃ oz) knob of galangal, chopped
70 ml (2¹/₄ fl oz) vegetable oil

Finely grind the coriander and fennel seeds and peppercorns in a mortar using a pestle or in a spice grinder. Transfer to a blender, add the remaining ingredients and blend until a smooth paste forms.

TO SERVE

200 g (7 oz) baby octopus
1 x 400 g (14 oz) calamari
800 g (1 lb 12 oz) mussels, scrubbed & beards removed
2 tablespoons white wine
1/4 teaspoon saffron threads
70 ml (2¹/₄ fl oz) vegetable oil
1 kg (4 lb 8z) snapper bones, cut into 5 pieces
1 tomato, diced
2 tablespoons tomato jam (see page 433)
3 kaffir lime leaves, bruised
1 litre (35 fl oz/4 cups) white chicken stock (see page 436) or water
4 x 100 g (3¹/₂ oz) snapper fillets
250 g (9 oz) clams (vongole), purged
8 raw (green) king prawns (shrimp), peeled & deveined
40 g (1¹/₂ oz) unsalted butter
60 g (2¹/₄ oz/¹/₄ cup) crème fraîche
aioli (see page 431) & croûtons (see page 432), to serve

Clean the octopus and calamari (see glossary). Score and cut the calamari into 8 pieces. Place the mussels and wine in a heavy-based saucepan over high heat. Cover and cook, shaking the pan occasionally until the mussels have opened. Strain through a sieve placed over a bowl. Add the saffron to the hot strained liquid and set aside. Remove the mussels from their shells and set aside.

Heat the vegetable oil in a large saucepan over medium heat. Add the paste and cook for about 20 minutes or until fragrant and split.

Add the snapper bones, tomato, tomato jam, lime leaves and mussel meat and cook for 5 minutes. Add the saffron liquid and stock, bring to a gentle simmer, reduce the heat to medium–low and cook for about 30 minutes. Season to taste with salt. Pass through a potato ricer or food mill, then pass through a sieve, pushing down on the purée until dry.

Transfer the soup to a large wide-based saucepan over low heat. Add the snapper fillets, calamari, octopus, clams, prawns and roasted tomato sauce, bring to a very gentle simmer and cook until the seafood is cooked and the clams have opened. Remove the seafood, using a slotted spoon, leaving the liquid in the pan, and divide among warmed serving bowls. Add the butter and crème fraîche to the pan, whisk to combine, then ladle over the seafood. Serve with the aioli and croûtons.

GRILLED LOBSTER WITH FENNEL & HERB BUTTER

> Serves 4

Whenever you want to spoil yourself or friends, pull this dish out. The slight smokiness of the lobster from the wonderful charcoal oven and the taste of the flesh with the herb butter soaked in is amazing. The complexity of the smoke and herb-flavoured butter doesn't overpower but enhances the natural lobster sweetness.

FENNEL & HERB BUTTER

4 garlic cloves, peeled
1/2 small leek, halved lengthways
100 g (3 1/2 oz) fennel, roughly chopped
1/2 bunch sage leaves
1/2 bunch oregano leaves
1/2 bunch tarragon leaves
1/2 bunch chervil leaves
1/4 bunch flat-leaf (Italian) parsley leaves
1/2 bunch English spinach leaves
juice of 1 lemon
500 g (1 lb 2 oz) unsalted butter, cubed & at room temperature
sea salt & freshly ground black pepper

Preheat the oven to 200°C (400°F/Gas 6). Place the garlic, leek and fennel in a roasting tray and roast for 15–20 minutes or until softened. Cool slightly, purée with a stick blender or in a blender until smooth, then pass through a fine sieve, discarding the solids.

Place the fennel mixture in a food processor. Finely chop all the herbs and spinach and add to the food processor.

Add the remaining ingredients and process until well combined. Season to taste with salt and pepper.

Spoon onto a sheet of baking paper or aluminium foil and roll into a log shape about 35 cm (14 inches) long and 4 cm (1 1/2 inches) in diameter. Wrap in plastic wrap, twisting the ends to secure and refrigerate until firm.

TO SERVE

4 x 700 g (1 lb 9 oz) live Southern rock lobsters
400 ml (14 fl oz) white wine
lemon wedges, to serve

Preheat the oven to 250°C (500°F/Gas 9) or heat a barbecue to hot.

Dispatch the lobsters humanely (see page 106). Bring a saucepan of salted water to the boil. Plunge the lobsters, one at a time, into the boiling water and cook for 1 minute, then remove and immediately submerge in iced water and leave until cooled. This process makes it easier to remove the meat as it may stick to the shell.

When the lobsters are cold, remove from the water bath and place on a chopping board. Run a sharp paring knife around the gap between the head and tail. Using scissors, cut down the two sides of the shell on the belly side. Remove the digestive tract.

Place, cut-side up, in 2 large roasting trays, season the meat with salt and add half of the wine and 100 ml (3 1/2 fl oz) of water to each tray. Roast or barbecue, with the lid closed, for 5 minutes.

Remove the lobster from the oven or barbecue. Cut the butter into 1 cm (1/2 inch) thick slices and place 4 over each lobster half. Roast or barbecue for another 5 minutes or until the meat is just firm. Cut each lobster half into 4 pieces each and place in a large serving bowl.

Meanwhile, melt the remaining herb butter in a saucepan and pour over the lobster pieces. Serve with lemon wedges on the side.

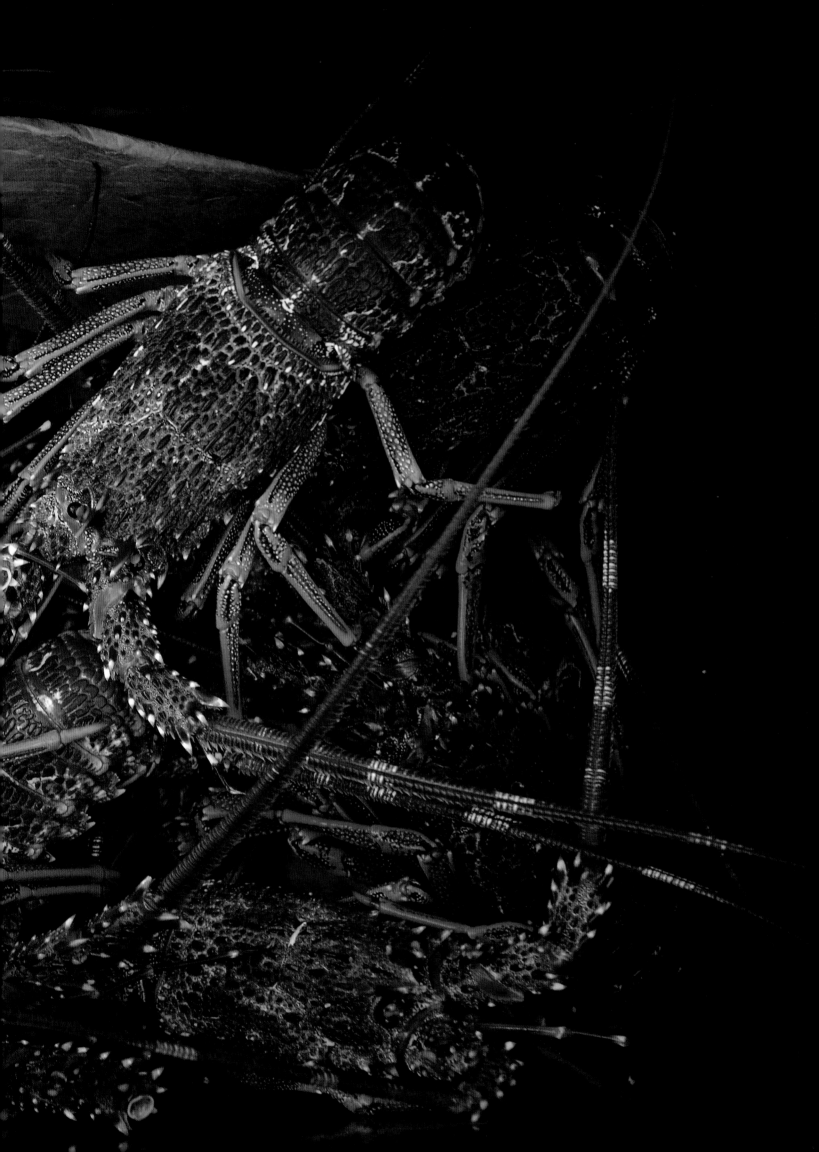

CLASSIC LOBSTER THERMIDOR

> Serves 4

When we first started talking about the menu at Rockpool Bar & Grill Sydney, we jokingly said perhaps we should bring back a few retro dishes, things that harked back to the thirties and really invoked a feeling of grandness. Well, as it turned out, that joke seemed to make some sense. Lobster thermidor was one of the first dishes my business partner, David Doyle, and I threw around. Thermidor has a lot of good things going for it, but, as is often the case with most classics, it has been done fairly poorly over the past decades; all too often a restaurant would boil the lobster, mix it with a very heavy béchamel and add too much cheese. As a result, it has had a fairly ordinary wrap in most people's minds. It is, in fact, a simple dish, so there are easy places to muck it up. My updated version takes it back to its roots: kill a lobster, set the flesh, make a fresh sauce and sprinkle a hint of cheese over it as it goes under the grill. This is a great dish to split between two or four people.

WHITE SAUCE

1 litre (35 fl oz/4 cups) milk
1 small onion
1/2 teaspoon black peppercorns
1 fresh bay leaf
60 g (2 1/4 oz) unsalted butter
35 g (1 1/4 oz/1/4 cup) plain (all-purpose) flour
2 teaspoons hot English mustard
sea salt & freshly ground black pepper

Combine the milk, onion, peppercorns and bay leaf in a small saucepan over medium heat, bring to a simmer, then remove from the heat and set aside for 15 minutes to infuse. Strain, discarding the solids. Keep the infused milk warm.

Melt the butter in a small saucepan over low heat. Stir in the flour. While whisking continuously, gradually add the infused milk, making sure there are no lumps.

Once all the milk is added and the sauce is a thick consistency, add the mustard and season to taste with salt and pepper. Cover the surface directly with baking paper and simmer very gently for 15 minutes, making sure the sauce doesn't catch on the base of the pan.

TO SERVE

4 x 650 g–700 g (1 lb 7 oz–1 lb 9 oz) live Southern rock lobsters
60 g (2 1/4 oz) unsalted butter
125 ml (4 fl oz/1/2 cup) brandy
1 small bunch tarragon, roughly chopped
25 g (1 oz/1/4 cup) freshly grated parmesan
lemon cheeks, to serve

Preheat the oven to 180°C (350°F/Gas 4).

Dispatch the lobsters humanely (see page 106). Bring a saucepan of salted water to the boil. Plunge the lobsters, in batches, into the boiling water and cook for 1 minute, then remove and immediately submerge in iced water and leave until cooled. This process makes it easier to remove the meat as it may stick to the shell.

When the lobsters are cold, remove from the water bath and place on a chopping board. Using a large knife, halve each lobster lengthways and remove the digestive tract. Remove the tail meat and cut into large pieces.

Place the shells, cut-side up, on baking trays and roast for 10 minutes.

Meanwhile, heat the butter in a large deep-sided frying pan over medium heat. When it starts to foam, add the lobster meat and cook until half cooked and starting to turn opaque. Add the brandy, carefully ignite and allow the alcohol to burn off.

Add the white sauce and simmer until the lobster meat is cooked. Check the seasoning and stir through the tarragon.

Heat a grill (broiler) to high. Spoon the lobster mixture into the shells and sprinkle with the parmesan. Grill (broil) until golden. Serve with lemon cheeks on the side.

CONFIT DUCK WITH ROASTED MANGO

> Serves 4

Duck confit is a classic for one reason — it's delicious. I think it's one of the two favourite duck dishes in the world hands down (the other being Peking duck, of course). The meaty flesh soaks up the duck fat, becoming tender and rich, and the long, slow cooking enhances the great flavour and texture of the duck. Although I do like duck rare, I don't believe it ever compares with the rich flavour derived from the meat being well cooked. I garnish this dish with mangoes in summer, figs in early autumn and sautéed apples in winter, but any fruit that has a nice sweet-acid balance goes well with the rich duck meat.

At the restaurant we vacuum-seal the duck and its fat in a Cryovac bag and steam it in our Combi Oven at 70°C (158°F) for 6 hours until it's tender. I've included an alternative method to simulate this slow-cooking process at home.

You will need to begin this recipe the day before.

2 x free-range or organic whole ducks
1 litre (35 fl oz/4 cups) warmed duck fat
1½ tablespoons extra virgin olive oil, plus extra for drizzling
2 mangoes, cheeks removed & peeled
1 tablespoon apple balsamic vinegar
sea salt & freshly ground black pepper

MARINADE

8 small red eschalots, sliced
8 garlic cloves, sliced
2 large handfuls flat-leaf (Italian) parsley leaves
1 small handful thyme leaves
1 small handful rosemary leaves
125 g (4½ oz) fine sea salt
60 g (2¼ oz) white peppercorns

To make the marinade, pound all of the ingredients together in a mortar with a pestle or process in a food processor to a coarse paste.

To prepare the ducks, working with one at a time, remove the neck, wishbone and wing tips and discard. Halve lengthways, using kitchen scissors to cut down both sides of the backbone. Discard the backbone. Rub the marinade into the skin and meat and refrigerate for 24 hours to marinate.

The next day, wipe the excess marinade off the duck halves and place in a saucepan large enough to fit the duck halves snugly. Cover with the duck fat and place over low heat. Attach a thermometer to the side of the pan to keep check of the temperature — you want it to be 70°C (158°F). Cook for 6 hours.

Preheat the oven to 180°C (350°F/Gas 4).

In an ovenproof frying pan large enough to fit the duck breasts and legs, heat the olive oil. Add the duck, skin-side down, then place in the oven and roast for 10 minutes.

Turn the duck over, add the mango cheeks to the pan and return to the oven for a further 6 minutes.

Remove from the oven and place the duck on a chopping board. Cut the legs in half at the joint where the thigh and leg meet. Place the legs on serving plates.

Remove the breast from the bone and slice. Place on the legs. Place a mango cheek next to each duck and drizzle with the apple balsamic vinegar and olive oil. Grind over a good amount of pepper and sprinkle with salt.

WAGYU CHUCK BRAISED IN RED WINE WITH GREMOLATA AND POTATO PURÉE

> Serves 4

We buy whole bodies of David Blackmore's Fullblood Wagyu, so along with all the wonderful grilling and rotisserie cuts come the secondary or braising cuts. Our braises end up with the most unique texture because of the heavy marbling of the Wagyu. We're so lucky to have these cuts of such high quality; the brisket, chuck, round, silverside and short ribs are not secondary cuts to us, but meat that we feel privileged to have. At the restaurant we vacuum-seal the chuck and braising mixture in a Cryovac bag and steam it in our Combi Oven at 70°C (158°F) for 18 hours. I've included an alternative method to simulate this slow-cooking process at home.

BRAISED WAGYU CHUCK

1 x 1 kg (2 lb 4 oz) piece of Wagyu chuck
80 ml (2½ fl oz/⅓ cup) extra virgin olive oil
1 onion, cut into large dice
1 carrot, cut into large dice
1 stalk celery, cut into large dice
1 head garlic, halved
50 g (1¾ oz) prosciutto, chopped
500 ml (17 fl oz/2 cups) port
1 litre (35 fl oz/4 cups) red wine
10 sprigs thyme
2 fresh bay leaves
10 black peppercorns

Preheat the oven to 150°C (300°F/Gas 2).

Heat the olive oil in a large heavy-based ovenproof saucepan over medium heat. Add the onion, carrot, celery, garlic and prosciutto and cook for 10–15 minutes or until the vegetables are very caramelised to bring out their natural sugars — this is one of the main flavours you're trying to achieve in your sauce. Once coloured, add the port and cook until the liquid has reduced by half. Add the wine, thyme, bay leaves and peppercorns and continue cooking until the liquid has reduced by half again.

Just as the braise is nearly ready, heat a large heavy-based frying pan over high heat until very hot. Add the beef and seal on all sides.

Add the beef to the braise, cover and cook in the oven for 3–4 hours or until the beef is fork tender. (Alternatively, gently simmer the beef, covered, over low heat.)

Remove the beef from the sauce and keep warm. Strain the sauce through a fine sieve placed over a bowl and discard the solids.

TO SERVE

80 ml (2½ fl oz/⅓ cup) extra virgin olive oil
1 onion, finely diced
1 carrot, finely diced
1 stalk celery, finely diced
3 garlic cloves, thinly sliced
1 leek, white part only, finely diced
2½ tablespoons aged balsamic vinegar
soft brown sugar, to taste
sea salt & freshly ground black pepper
potato purée (see page 360), to serve
gremolata (see page 428), to serve

Heat the olive oil in a large frying pan over medium heat, add the onion, carrot, celery, garlic and leek and cook for 10 minutes or until starting to colour and caramelise.

Add the strained sauce from the braised Wagyu chuck and vinegar to the pan and cook until the sauce has reduced to form a thick glaze. Add a little sugar to sweeten, if needed, and season to taste with salt and pepper.

To serve, cut the beef into 4 pieces and place each on a plate. Serve with a quenelle of potato purée and sprinkle with the gremolata.

CORNED WAGYU SILVERSIDE WITH
SLOW-COOKED CARROTS & MUSTARD SAUCE

> Serves 4

This dish reminds me of my childhood. My father would cook corned beef all the time and we loved it with white sauce, mustard on the side and cauliflower and boiled carrots. It was one of Dad's favourite dishes and I was pretty happy when I knew it was on for dinner. We corn our own beef at the restaurant — the advantage of having whole bodies of Wagyu and an in-house butcher. If you don't want to corn your own silverside, you can buy it already corned from a good butcher — it's possible to even find corned Wagyu. At the restaurant we vacuum-seal the silverside and court-bouillon in a Cryovac bag and steam it in our Combi Oven at 70°C (158°F) for 18 hours.

You will need to begin this recipe 2 weeks ahead.

CORNED WAGYU SILVERSIDE

1 x 1 kg (2 lb 4 oz) piece of raw Wagyu silverside
400 g (14 oz) sea salt
6 g (¹/₅ oz) sodium nitrate (see note)
1 quantity court-bouillon

To brine the silverside, combine it with the salt and sodium nitrate and 2 litres (70 fl oz) of water in a container, making sure the beef is completely submerged. Cover and refrigerate for 2 weeks.

Following this, remove the corned beef and discard the brine. Place the beef in a large saucepan, cover with cold water and bring to a simmer, then drain and repeat simmering with fresh water 3 more times. (If you are using already corned beef, you will need to do this blanching step too.)

Place the blanched silverside in a saucepan over medium–low heat. Add the court-bouillon and just enough water to cover and gently simmer for 3 hours or until tender.

NOTE

Sodium nitrate is available from butcher stores and online.

COURT-BOUILLON

1 carrot, julienne
1 brown onion, sliced
1 stalk celery, julienne
1 fresh bay leaf
2 black peppercorns
200 ml (7 fl oz) dry white wine

Combine all of the ingredients in a saucepan, bring to the boil, then reduce to a simmer and cook for 30 minutes.

MUSTARD SAUCE

You'll need a 1 litre (35 fl oz/4 cup) heat-sensitive cream siphon and cartridges for this recipe.

25 g (1 oz) unsalted butter
2 tablespoons plain (all-purpose) flour
100 ml (3½ fl oz) veal stock (see page 438)
½ tablespoon crème fraîche
2 g (¹/₁₆ oz) mustard powder
2 tablespoons Dijon mustard
sea salt & freshly ground black pepper

Combine the butter and flour in a saucepan over medium heat and cook, stirring, for about 5 minutes or until golden. Gradually whisk in the stock and 300 ml (10½ fl oz) of water and simmer for 10 minutes. Remove from the heat, stir in the crème fraîche, mustard powder, Dijon mustard and season to taste with salt and pepper.

Pour the sauce into a cream siphon and screw on the lid. Screw in a cartridge to aerate the sauce, then shake vigorously.

Place the siphon in a warm water bath until ready to serve.

TO SERVE

4 organic carrots inspired by St. John (see page 367)

Remove the corned Wagyu silverside from the court-bouillon and cut into 4 pieces. Place a piece of beef on each plate with a slow-cooked carrot and pump some mustard sauce from the siphon alongside.

LENTIL & RICOTTA EGGPLANT MOUSSAKA

This is a dish I first put on the Qantas menu in 1997 and I have loved it ever since. All the textures and flavours combine to create a very satisfying meal that is surprisingly light and delicious. This can easily be made and reheated at a later date — I think it's better once the flavours have settled together after a couple of days.

EGGPLANT

4 large eggplant (aubergines), cut lengthways into 5 mm ($^1/_4$ inch) thick slices
table salt
extra virgin olive oil, for shallow-frying

Place the eggplant on a tray, sprinkle with some salt and set aside for 30 minutes. Pat dry to remove the salt and moisture.

Heat 1 cm ($^1/_2$ inch) of the oil in a frying pan over medium–high heat. Shallow-fry the eggplant, in batches, until golden on both sides. Drain on paper towel and set aside.

RED CAPSICUM SAUCE

2 kg (4 lb 8 oz) red capsicum (peppers)
120 ml (4 fl oz) extra virgin olive oil
lemon juice, to taste
sea salt & freshly ground black pepper

Preheat the oven to 220°C (425°F/Gas 7). Coat half of the capsicum in 100 ml ($3^1/_2$ fl oz) of the olive oil and roast for 20 minutes or until the skins start to blister. Place in a bowl, cover with plastic wrap and set aside to steam. When cool enough to handle, peel off the skins and discard the seeds. Roughly chop the flesh.

Juice the remaining capsicum in an electric juicer. Place in a heavy-based saucepan and bring to the boil. Reduce the heat to a simmer, add the chopped capsicum and simmer for about 20 minutes. Pass through a mouli (food mill).

Return the sauce to a clean saucepan over medium heat and bring to a simmer, stirring occasionally. Season to taste with salt and pepper and cook for 15 minutes or until thickened. Add the remaining olive oil and check the seasoning. Keep warm until serving. Just before serving, add lemon juice to taste.

»

LENTIL & RICOTTA EGGPLANT MOUSSAKA
CONTINUED

BRAISED LENTILS

150 g (5½ oz/⅔ cup) green lentils
450 ml (15¾ fl oz) vegetable stock
100 ml (3½ fl oz) extra virgin olive oil
600 g (1 lb 5 oz) onions, finely diced
sea salt & freshly ground black pepper
600 g (1 lb 5 oz) red capsicum (peppers),
seeds removed & finely diced
4 garlic cloves, finely chopped
300 ml (10½ fl oz) red wine
60 g (2¼ oz/¼ cup) tomato paste
(concentrated purée)
1 cinnamon quill
600 g (1 lb 5 oz) tinned whole Roma
(plum) tomatoes, roughly chopped
1 small bunch flat-leaf (Italian) parsley
leaves, roughly chopped

Place the lentils in a saucepan, cover with
cold water and bring to the boil. Drain
and rinse well. Return the lentils to the
pan and place over medium heat. Add the
stock, bring to the boil, then simmer until
all of the liquid is absorbed and the lentils
are just tender. Set aside.

Heat the olive oil in a separate heavy-
based saucepan over low heat. Add the
onion, season to taste with salt and cook
for 10 minutes or until softened but not
coloured. Add the capsicum and garlic
and cook for 15–20 minutes or until they
are starting to brown slightly. Add the
wine and simmer until reduced by half.
Stir in the tomato paste and cook for
2–3 minutes. Add the cinnamon, chopped
tomato, season to taste with salt and
pepper and simmer for about 15 minutes
or until the sauce has thickened. Add the
lentils and parsley and stir to combine.
Check the seasoning and set aside.

RICOTTA BÉCHAMEL

25 g (1 oz) unsalted butter
25 g (1 oz) plain (all-purpose) flour
pinch of freshly grated nutmeg
sea salt & freshly ground black pepper
250 ml (9 fl oz/1 cup) milk, warmed
250 g (1 cup/9 oz) ricotta
1 egg, lightly beaten
25 g (1 oz/¼ cup) freshly grated
parmesan

Melt the butter in a heavy-based saucepan
over low heat. Add the flour and cook,
stirring continuously, for 2 minutes or
until golden. Add the nutmeg and season
to taste with salt and pepper.

While whisking continuously, gradually
add the milk, making sure there are no
lumps after each addition. Once all the
milk is added and the sauce is a thick
consistency, remove from the heat and
cool slightly.

Add the ricotta and whisk until smooth,
then add the egg and parmesan and
whisk until smooth. Check the seasoning
and keep warm until needed.

TO ASSEMBLE

Decrease the oven to 200°C (400°F/Gas 6).

Lightly grease 4 x 350 ml (12 fl oz) capacity
ramekins and line the bases with baking
paper. Reserve 4 eggplant slices, then
line the base and side of each ramekin
with the remaining slices, overlapping,
if necessary, with enough eggplant
overhanging the edge to cover the top.

Divide half of the braised lentils between
the ramekins, then top with half of the
ricotta béchamel. Place an eggplant slice
on top, then repeat the process with the
remaining lentils and béchamel until the
ramekins are full. Fold the overhanging
eggplant over to enclose the filling and
cover with aluminium foil. Bake for
10–15 minutes or until warmed through.

To serve, invert each ramekin onto a plate,
spoon the red capsicum sauce on top and
finish with a grind of pepper.

NOTE

You can also make one large moussaka
instead of individual ones. Use a 1.5 litre
(52 fl oz) capacity baking dish. There is
no need to line the base with paper or the
side with eggplant. To serve, divide the
moussaka among 4 plates and serve with
the red capsicum sauce.

VEGETABLE TAGINE

> Serves 4

This is an old Rockpool Sydney dish that's still on the menu there today. I'm in love with Moroccan flavours and this dish delivers great taste and a wonderful array of vegetable textures. My wife, Sam, and I eat this at home at least every couple of weeks. It usually comes out on a Sunday night when I'm looking for something really yummy, but light on protein. You can use any vegetables you love. At Rockpool, we have a lot of different baby vegetables grown especially for us. One of my favourite veggies to is small red radishes — try them, I think you'll love them as much as I do.

CHERMOULA

1 red onion, roughly chopped

4 garlic cloves, roughly chopped

1 bunch coriander (cilantro), stalks, roots & all, roughly chopped

1 bunch flat-leaf (Italian) parsley, including stalks, roughly chopped

1 heaped teaspoon sea salt

1 tablespoon ground cumin

1 tablespoon ground coriander

1 1/2 tablespoons ground chilli

1 tablespoon ground turmeric

2 teaspoons sweet paprika

1 1/2 tablespoons ras el hanout

185 ml (6 fl oz/3/4 cup) extra virgin olive oil, plus extra for covering

juice of 1 lemon

Place all of the ingredients, except the olive oil and lemon juice, in a food processor and process for 1 minute. With the motor running, gradually pour in the olive oil until a thick paste forms. Stir through the lemon juice. Spoon into a sterilised jar, cover with a layer of olive oil and refrigerate for up to 4 weeks. Makes about 500 g (1 lb 2 oz/2 cups).

TO SERVE

2 1/2 tablespoons extra virgin olive oil

1 carrot, diced

1 red onion, diced

2 garlic cloves, finely chopped

100 g (3 1/2 oz) chermoula

1 1/2 tablespoons honey

7 cherry tomatoes, halved

sea salt & freshly ground black pepper

steamed couscous, to serve

Heat the olive oil in a frying pan over medium heat, add the carrot, onion and garlic and cook for 5 minutes or until softened.

Increase the heat to high, add the chermoula and cook for 5 minutes or until the paste is just sticking to the base of the pan.

Add the honey and cook, stirring, for 1 minute. Add 1 litre (35 fl oz/4 cups) of water and the tomato, bring to the boil, then reduce the heat to a simmer and cook for 20 minutes. Season to taste with salt and pepper.

Divide among bowls and serve with the steamed couscous on the side.

This is only a selection of seafood from the charcoal oven that I've chosen to put in the book. In reality any fish you like can be cooked and served in the manner suggested in the recipes. During the different seasons, we use whiting, blue-eye trevalla, coral trout, Tasmanian trumpeter, red emperor, kingfish, ocean trout, flathead, bar cod, bass groper, mulloway (jewfish), sardines, mackerel, flounder, tuna and barramundi. It's great to cook smaller fish whole. Cooking these on the bone means they'll stay wonderfully moist. Don't underestimate the power of sea salt, freshly ground pepper and lemon juice when cooking fish; these three things in concert make fresh seafood taste wonderful.

THE CHARCOAL OVEN

It can be quite funny how things work out. When I was putting together Rockpool Bar & Grill Sydney in 2009, my flagship restaurant Rockpool on George Street had been placed in The S.Pellegrino World's 50 Best Restaurants for the seventh consecutive year and I was invited to attend the awards in London. I was talking to my great mate John Susman and he mentioned that there was a sustainable seafood fair in Brussels he thought I should go to. He suggested we should take a side trip together from there to Dartmouth, a small fishing village in the south of England, to enjoy a day's fishing and to attend dinner for the Australia versus England Fishing Cup. This was, I suspected, really just an excuse for a piss up. However, as all the fishermen I respected and whose products I used were going to Dartmouth, I decided it would be a good chance to catch up with everyone. As fate would have it, it was one of the best decisions of my life.

The night of the fishing cup we ate at celebrity fishmonger Mitch Tonks' new place The Seahorse Restaurant. We ate well and drank too well, but the most exciting thing about the day wasn't that Australia won the fishing cup, it was what I saw in Mitch's kitchen: a charcoal oven. It imparted a great flavour to the fish. Straight away I knew I needed something like this to complement the wood-fired grill planned for Bar & Grill Sydney. It was perfect. We could present fish in the same way we served the beef and the smoky flavours from the charcoal would enhance all the beautiful fish we wanted to showcase. At the back of my mind I was thinking Sydney was a real seafood town and that the new Bar & Grill had to have a strong platform for fish as well as being a steakhouse.

As soon as I got back home, I started working with the builders of our wood-fired grill to make a charcoal oven. With my input, Greg Thompson designed it. It turned out to be perfect, but I had one problem... where was I going to put it? By the time I had made my trip to London and Dartmouth, the kitchen design was fixed and signed off on. Then the day arrived when the wood-fired grill and charcoal oven were delivered. The grill arrived first and it took about four hours to get it into place. Just as the job was nearly done, the charcoal oven arrived. There was a possible space up near the larder that I thought it could go. The guys installed it there, but when I saw it in place, I knew it couldn't stay there; the heat generated by the oven would have killed the larder guys.

I stood there faced with a really hard decision: say nothing and live with it for the rest of my life or ask the question: could the oven be moved, and we would just have to suffer the delay — as it was, we were already on a knife's edge to finish the kitchen on time. I took a deep breath and decided to fess up. "Guys, I've totally screwed up this thing. I really need the oven to be down there," pointing to the end of the grill line. The problem with that was the only way to get the oven in was to move the grill out again. With amazingly good humour, the guys added another three hours of work to their day to put everything in the right place. I'm so lucky that it all worked out perfectly. And now I have the best kitchen. Oh, but what a disaster it could have been.

SERVING

I love to serve all fish at the restaurant quite simply with a wedge of lemon and a drizzle of extra virgin olive oil to allow the natural expression of the flavours of the particular species to shine through.

I also like to serve a small herb salad on the side and a sauce boat of aioli (see page 431), allowing guests to use as little or as much as they wish.

For a simple herb salad, pick the leaves of coriander (cilantro), parsley, mint, dill, tarragon and mix with French shallot (eschalot) slices and spring onion (scallion) rounds. Season with sea salt and freshly ground black pepper and dress with extra virgin olive oil and lemon juice.

SEAFOOD 101

When buying fish, it's important to select the most vibrant, handsome looking specimen you can. For a whole fish, it's easy to tell if it's fresh by looking at it. The eyes should be clear and shiny and the fish should smell of the sea — a sweet fresh smell, not a fishy one. The gills should be bright red (not brown or grey) and the scales should be shiny and tight, not loose and falling off. The texture of the fish should be firm. To test for firmness, run your finger along the flesh from the back of the head to just past the fin (the shoulder of the fish), it should quickly spring back to shape, even if the fish is a soft-fleshed fish. Shellfish should be either live or look bright and vibrant. Seafood, such as oysters, mussels and clams (vongole) should be heavy and full of salt water. Squid and octopus should be vibrantly coloured and shiny.

HANDLING OF SEAFOOD

Fish are cold-blooded creatures. This means that the enzymes and bacteria present in them start breaking down the flesh at much lower temperatures than in warm-blooded animals. For this reason, cold-chain management is the most important consideration when it comes to handling seafood. Within the Rockpool Group, we use fishermen who follow the traditional Japanese stress-minimising catch methodology. Briefly, the fish are line caught, immediately spiked in the brain (iki-jime killed) and placed in an ice slurry. This reduces the body temperature rapidly and brings on rigor mortis. As a result the fish is less damaged by stress and the best flavour and texture are preserved. All of our fish come in whole, under ice, and are dry filleted each day. The fillets are then kept in a cool room at 0°C (32°F) until needed.

Like meat and poultry, fish is about 70 per cent water, the rest being made up of protein, fats, minerals and vitamins. The big difference between fish and meat or poultry is the lack of connective tissue, which can be a positive and a negative. No connective tissue means that fish is naturally tender but the bad news is that this makes it very easy to overcook, ending up dry or even falling apart. Overcooking is the single biggest problem to be aware of but, if you look after your fish and cook it perfectly, you'll have a very good chance of cooking seafood better than the average restaurant — you certainly don't have the time pressures that professional chefs have.

When buying seafood, either take an esky with an ice brick in it to carry the seafood home or make the trip quickly. Remember not to buy seafood too far in advance — you don't want to store it in the refrigerator for more than two days, if that.

FILLETING WHOLE FISH

I completely understand people's reluctance to fillet fish at home. It's messier than just bringing fillets home and you have to get rid of the waste — and if you're not diligent in cleaning, a little scrap may accidentally get hidden away somewhere and stink out the kitchen. By all means purchase fillets to use in the recipes in this chapter (or even just be inspired by them, if that's what you're more comfortable with).

But let's get back to the reasons why it's better to fillet your own fish (assuming that it has been well looked after before you get it). One, you can tell very easily whether the fish is fresh. Two, you can make sure you dry fillet it. By this I mean the opposite to wet filleting, which is how 99 per cent of all fish are filleted. These fish are rinsed in fresh water as they're being filleted to make the process quick and easy — I hate standing at the fish market watching beautiful fish being sloshed through tubs of running water. Once a fish is dead it shouldn't see water again. The fresh water will only dilute the oils that give the fish its flavour and you will end up compromising both the flavour and texture. If you have a good fishmonger, you can always ask them to dry fillet the fish for you. Explain what you want and by all means watch them do it — they're so used to the water its hard to get them to stop, but perhaps you casting an eye over the process will keep them honest.

To dry fillet, you need a bit of time, a board and a damp cloth or some heavy-duty paper towel. First, scale the fish. Lay it on a chopping board and draw the back of a large knife or scaling tool against its scales from the tail to the head. If you're serving fish whole or it's a large fish that you want to serve with the skin on, it's essential to remove all of the scales. If you're going to skin the fish, then just remove the scales around the perimeter of the fish, so your knife doesn't slip when you cut into it. Scaling can be a messy job, so keep using your damp cloth or paper towel to wipe the board clean, removing the scales and sea slime as they get in your way. Alternatively, you could ask your fishmonger to scale the fish and wipe it (but not wash it) for you. I remember as a young kid, Dad would always scale the fish on the beach or in the river water, then fillet it at home.

Next comes the gutting and filleting. Place the fish on the board and cut the belly open. Remove the guts and discard. Make a cut behind the head and cut a line from the back of the head to the tail, then down the other side from the stomach to the tail. Depending on how big the fish is, slide your knife into the backbone all the way to the tail or, if large, cut to either side of the backbone and then work your knife over it to release the fillet. Turn the fish over and repeat the process. Remember, use a damp cloth as needed and don't wash the fillet in water!

COOKING FISH IS ALL IN THE MIND

No matter how you decide to cook your fish, you need to remember one thing: when you remove the fish from the heat source it continues to cook. If the fish is cooked perfectly in the pan or oven or under the grill (broiler), then, sadly, you'll have overcooked it by the time you start to eat it. Think residual heat: the hotter the cooking method, the more the fish will continue to cook on resting. There is a game you can play in your mind: as the

fish is cooking the heat penetrates from both sides and meets in the middle, even if cooking one side at a time. Now, as the "doneness" of the fish is indicated by the heat meeting in the middle of the fish, the fish needs to be removed from the heat when it's three-quarters of the way cooked each side. Imagine as a waiter picks up the fish the two sides are getting closer and closer; as the waiter puts it down they are starting to join; just as the customer plunges the fork into the fish, there's just enough residual heat for the two sides to meet. I get my staff to visualise the gentle embrace of the two sides at the moment of being perfectly cooked. The important thing is to really get a sense for what you think would be perfect.

What I have the staff do to make sure the fish is cooked perfectly is push a cake skewer into the flesh; if you feel a slight resistance as you push the skewer through the thickest part of the fish, then it's time to take it off. If you have trouble pushing it through, then it needs more time. If you have no resistance, your fish is probably perfect — but, as stated before, by the time you get it out to the table it will be overcooked.

If you're cooking oily fish, such as tuna or salmon, you want to cook rare — just imagine a nice warm strip of flesh running through the centre. It's quite good to think about what is happening to all the things you cook and, like Tigger, you will get it right most of the time. Having said that, there is another way to tell when a larger piece of fish is cooked — simply insert a digital thermometer into the fish and when it reads 48°C–50°C (118°F–122°F), the fish is cooked.

LIGHTING A CHARCOAL FIRE

You can re-create the experience of our charcoal oven using charcoal in a Weber or other type of barbecue with a domed lid. I find the best way to light charcoal or bricket fires is with a chimney starter. Simply place firelighters on the grill in the barbecue base and light. Fill the chimney starter with charcoal and place on top of the firelighters. Wait till the charcoal is glowing red — this should take about 20 minutes — then wearing gloves, take the handle of the chimney starter, tip the hot charcoal out and spread over the base. Place the lid on the barbecue and in about 10 minutes it should be ready to use. Cooking in this type of

environment will create a nice smoky fish that is moist and delicious. Either cook the fish directly on the grill plate or, do as we do at the restaurant, cook the fish in a cast-iron saucepan with the barbecue lid closed.

SMOKY FLAVOUR FROM WOOD CHIPS

You can cook fish just as easily in a gas barbecue with a lid using wood chips to achieve the smokiness we get from the charcoal oven. Using a metal fire box filled with wood chips is the easiest method. Preheat the barbecue to high and get it nice and hot with the lid down, about 20 minutes should do it. Place wood chips that have been soaked in water in a fire box and place the fire box on the bottom of the hot barbecue, directly on top of a burner, then close the barbecue lid. It should take about 5–10 minutes to start smoking. Place the fish in a cast-iron frying pan or an aluminium foil roasting tray, place on the barbecue, close the barbecue lid and cook for about 5 or so minutes, depending on the thickness of the fish. Fire boxes and different types of wood chips are available at barbecue stores. This smoking will hold you in good stead for cooking meat (such as loin of pork, see page 292; or chicken with Tuscan bread salad, page 280) on the barbecue as well.

IN THE OVEN

You can cook fish in the oven with great success. This really is the simplest method and a very good way to cook any kind of fish at home, but it won't have that smoky complexity that you get from the barbecue. I usually cook fish at 200°C (400°F/Gas 6). I find that fish cooks well and keeps moist at this temperature, but you can go higher if you wish. Just oil and season the fish, then place in a roasting tray or in an ovenproof cast-iron frying pan and roast in the oven. For a standard portion size of 180 g–200 g (6¹/₃ oz–7 oz), a thin fish such as John Dory will cook in 5 minutes, while thicker steaks such as blue-eye trevalla will take about 12 minutes. If the fish is a thick slice, you can add a little stock or water to the base of the pan to keep the fish moist, but only add just enough so the liquid is almost gone by the time the fish is cooked.

SUSTAINABLE SEAFOOD

When talking about sustainability, eliminating the commercial fishing industry is not *the solution. I find this view particularly ridiculous, but believe me it is bandied about a fair bit, mainly by the lot who think the right to have a rod in their hand and go fishing outweighs my right to eat fish... b---s---t to that. We need to be aware that there are many players involved in the sustainable seafood debate. And each of those players, including governments, industry bodies, amateur anglers and the Greens, have their own view of the argument.*

The most important thing for us, as consumers, is to know the provenance of our seafood (all our food, for that matter). Knowing where our fish are caught may help us to know if they're caught in accordance with a particular system that has the biomass of the species at heart. If you live in Australia, we are safe in the knowledge that our government is working with all the players to keep our seafood industry vibrant for the future. Likewise, if you live in the US or England, authorities there are focusing heavily on sustainability and working towards consumers being better educated.

You will also have to be ready to value it and pay for quality. Seafood should be treated the way we treat beef. By that I mean cows don't only have fillets, rib-eyes and sirloins — but we have to use the whole animal and get value from every cut for it to be sustainable; this is the same with fish. In many countries only white-fleshed, broad-flaked, mild-tasting fish are considered special enough to attract a decent price. We must value *all* fish — believe me, I have tasted very few species that aren't delicious when well handled and served fresh. Eating across the board and not targeting just a few species is important for our fish stocks to remain healthy. We need to support fishermen who have the quality of their fish and the health of the environment at heart. These people have a love of the ocean and a desire for the ability to fish to go on forever.

All around the world there are government quotas on fish species that seem like a good idea, however

I would value a system where every kilo of fish brought up over the side of a boat has value to the fisherman and the community and should be taken to market. The destruction of fish via by-catch is huge. There are heaps of stories about high-quality non-quota fish being thrown away dead as the fishermen are not allowed to bring it in to market under the quota system. There must be a better method than this; having several species targeted by the same hook and line, say.

Since the middle of the twentieth century, when large-vessel, net fisheries emerged, the world's wild fish stocks have been steadily depleting. This is occurring at a rate that is not only alarming, but at a rate that is also going to have irreversible consequences if we don't take the time to see how we might develop sustainable fisheries based on best-practice wild-caught fishing and aquaculture.

The Marine Stewardship Council (MSC), an international non-profit, independent charity has been working since 1997 to do exactly that. It investigates and awards fisheries that exercise good sustainability practices the right to bear the MSC label on their products. There are more and more similar brands that will guide consumers in the right direction. It must be said that in Australia and New Zealand we have very well managed fish stocks, although the tussle between angler and professional fisherman is destined to go on forever — that is if the fish last that long.

NOT A ONE-SIZE-FITS-ALL CONCEPT

John Susman, an advocate for sustainable seafood shares with us what sustainability means to him.

"Sustainable seafood is an ethic. It is also a market trend, a movement and an ideal, but mostly it is an overused, abused, hackneyed cliché, exploited by those wanting to get on — or perhaps make sure they are seen to be on — the green bus.

"Sure, there are a gaggle of easy-to-swallow, bite-sized and often empirical certifications that exist in good faith to give the buyer confidence that what they're purchasing is sustainable but, more often than not, they are generalisations, fashioned out of proprietary science or, worse, global assumptions.

"The truth is that sustainable seafood is not a 'one-size-fits-all' concept that can be conveniently prescribed against a set of tick-a-box ideals. Not only is it a truly localised issue but it is also determined by the species in discussion (its breeding cycle, its life cycle, its feeding cycle and demands), the habitat in question and the culinary and commercial expectations of the consumer. This is no discussion for the faint-hearted or those prone to supporting a cause purely for the grandstanding goodwill effect it may generate.

"That said, the whole world is searching for a clear definition. I think the following is a good start: sustainable seafood is farmed or wild seafood harvested without harm to its population or habitat or to any other species in its ecosystem.

"Translating this simple sounding concept into purchasing decisions at Rockpool has been the culmination of nearly 25 years of hard labour. Neil and I have long believed that there is a natural equilibrium between great-eating seafood and catchers and growers, who really care for the environment from which they harvest. The innate, symbiotic relationship between a fisherman and his ocean is true sustainability at work. In my experience, the best producers of seafood are, by nature, the most vigilant environmentalists.

"We live in a global village these days and sustainability is, indeed, a global issue, but, when it comes down to it, seafood sustainability is not only the responsibility of the catcher or grower but also the responsibility of all of us. Simply, if we are serious about the sustainability of the seafood we eat, it's about respecting its value and being prepared to pay a premium for what is genuinely premium, sustainable seafood. We should undertake to celebrate, not denigrate wild-capture seafood for its remarkable uniqueness and further appreciate that aquaculture or the farming of seafood is not merely the only means by which the broader community outside of Rockpool can enjoy the wonders of seafood, but also a means by which pressure can be put on catchers of wild fish and seafood to best look after what they catch and to best preserve the stocks from which they harvest.

"If we're committed to the concept of sustainability, then we must also be committed to the need to undertake due diligence on many unchartered waters. It is our responsibility to ask as many questions of our supplier, farmer or fisherman as possible. Know what we are getting, where it comes from and how it was harvested or raised. Merely deferring to the thoughts of the 'sustainable' agencies is a dangerous and narrow view comparable to making a donation to a charity to rid yourself the nuisance of the telemarketer soliciting donations. In the confusing and often murky waters that are sustainable seafood take the lead of Rockpool and buy 'best in class and best in season'. This is at least a good start."

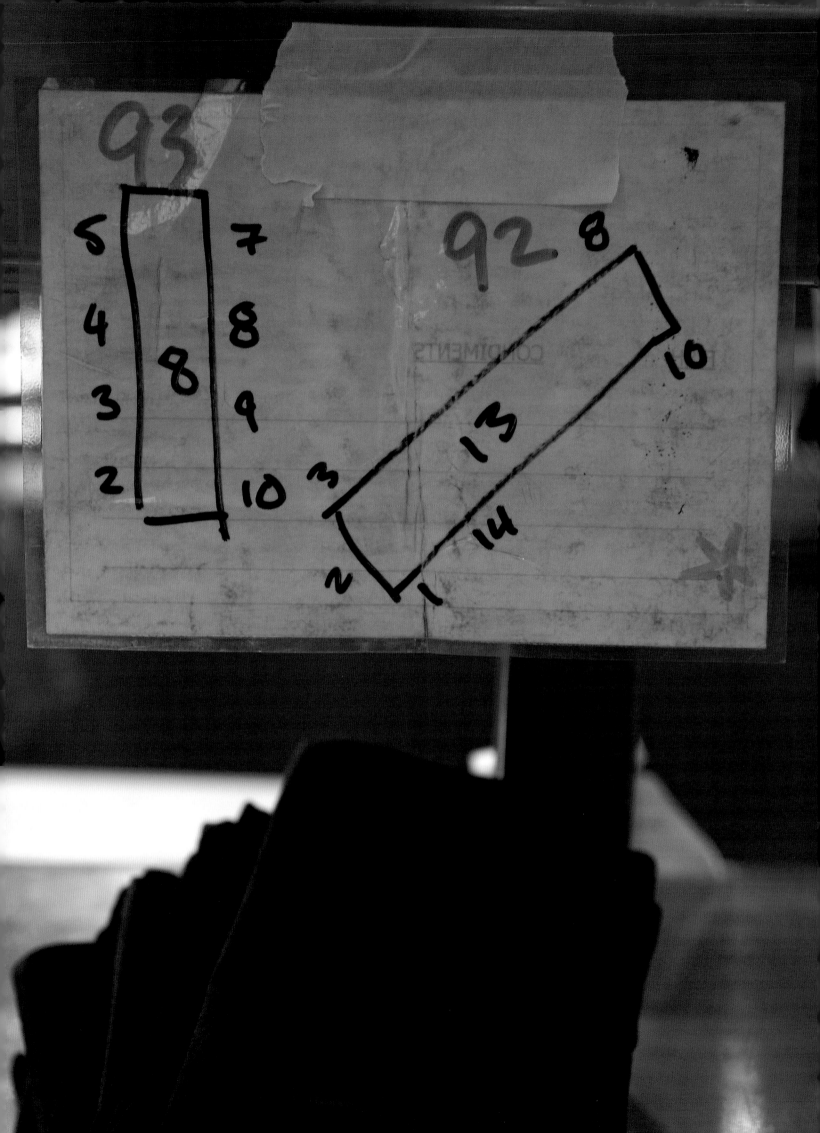

SNAPPER

> Serves 4

Snapper is a handsome fish caught in most places up and down the Australian coastline. We use fish from different parts of the country, from the New South Wales coast to Victoria and South Australia, as the seasons change across the country. We buy three to five kilo snappers and cut them into large steaks. They are mild flavoured and firm textured. Watch out, however, as they're lean and can overcook in a heartbeat. A beautifully cooked piece of snapper is a wonderful thing, an overcooked piece is a tragedy.

4 x 200 g (7 oz) snapper fillets, skin on
sea salt
extra virgin olive oil, for drizzling
herb salad (see page 255), aioli (see page 431) & lemon wedges, to serve

Heat the barbecue or grill (broiler) to extremely hot or the oven to 200°C (400°F/ Gas 6). Season each side of the fillets with salt and drizzle with the olive oil. Place in a heavy-based roasting tray or frying pan, add a splash of water, close the barbecue lid and cook for 8–10 minutes or until just cooked through. Remove from the pan and set aside for 1 minute to rest.

Place a piece of fish on each plate, sprinkle with salt, drizzle with the olive oil and serve with a wedge of lemon. Serve with the herb salad and aioli on the side.

WHOLE JOHN DORY

> Serves 4

John Dory is a sweet firm-fleshed fish, which has always enjoyed the limelight in restaurants, mostly because it has very little fish flavour, making it popular among those who want to eat fish, but prefer it mild. Having said that, it's a very tasty fish and really great when cooked whole, which makes it harder to overcook, keeps it moist and gives it extra flavour. It's also very easy to eat as there is just one central bone to navigate, making it a great specimen to start the kids eating whole fish with.

4 x 500 g (1 lb 2 oz) John Dory
sea salt
extra virgin olive oil, for drizzling
herb salad (see page 255), aioli (see page 431) & lemon wedges, to serve

Heat the barbecue or grill (broiler) to extremely hot or the oven to 200°C (400°F/Gas 6).

Scale and gut the fish (see page 256). Remove the heads and snip off the fins. Season each side of the fish with salt and drizzle with the olive oil. Place in a heavy-based roasting tray or frying pan, add a splash of water, close the barbecue lid and cook for about 7 minutes or until just cooked through. Remove from the tray and set aside for 1 minute to rest.

Place a fish on each plate, sprinkle with salt, drizzle with the olive oil and serve with a wedge of lemon. Serve with the herb salad and aioli on the side.

MARK EATHER, THE FISHER GOD

Mark Eather is a fisherman with great passion, not just for catching seafood but treating them perfectly so they are at their peak for eating. I've had a working relationship with Mark for more than 15 years. Here is his story.

"What makes your product so bloody special?!" an exporter/competitor asked me after we achieved another Grand Champion award at Tsukiji Market in Tokyo, the greatest stage in the world for quality seafood. That has been one of the more magnanimous queries from one of my competitors, but not nearly as eloquent as that from a patriarch of a very well known New South Wales fishing family: "You can f--k off! We're not going to all that trouble and hard work!" For every fan, there have been a sea of foes, including one East-coast trawler operator: "Eather is kidding, I'm a much better fisherman than him. I catch 10 times what he does and in half of the time." The same trawler operator also threatened me with "going for a swim out on the shelf", if I didn't stop lobbying against his destructive methodology in the mid-nineties. (I can't print my exact response to him but it was along the lines of self-fornication!) It's been a long journey to get to where we are now and it wouldn't have been possible without help on the way.

THE BEGINNING

Almost 30 years ago in Eden in New South Wales coast, I met by chance a Japanese tourist, Mr Masuko, who was impressed by the lengths I was going to in looking after my fish. Mr Masuko happened to be well connected in the Tokyo seafood industry and he played a pivotal role in launching my product on the Japanese market.

The Japanese consume most of their seafood raw, so any "taint" in the flesh is immediately obvious to the palate. Just as we humans produce adrenaline when under stress, seafood produces a similar substance called adenosine triphosphate, which in poorly handled, non-iki-jime-treated fish can cause adverse reactions in the natural constituents of the flesh to the point where it has an offensive, almost "metallic" flavour with a really strong "fishy aftertaste" to the palate.

Centuries ago the Japanese developed the iki-jime processes to avoid this "taint" and obtain pristine and unspoiled flesh in their seafood. In précis, the art of true iki-jime involves the reduction of stress to an absolute minimum using a quick-catching technique (usually individually line caught), immediate and precise bleeding and killing (I assure you that split seconds actually do matter), then immediate rapid chilling to 0°C (32°F). It may sound like a lot of work and trouble for a small amount of product but the results are exquisite whether consumed raw or cooked. The fastidious treatment of the fish does not just stop on the vessel either; the cool chain needs to be maintained right through, with specialty handling during the processing phase, including totally dry processing (fresh water should never contact the flesh, ever!) to the moment the product is prepared, prior to consumption.

A REVOLUTIONARY POSSE

All of those years ago in the early nineties, the domestic market did not (yet) appreciate our product, so the only way for us to survive was to export. For many years, our brand of seafood, Mark W Eather, was more famous overseas, winning numerous awards and accolades in Japan, USA and Europe, than at home in Australia, where it was relatively unknown.

In the early nineties, a local Sydney restaurateur asked me why we didn't supply our product locally. He had recently visited Tsukiji Market in Tokyo and marvelled at the wonderful produce there. He remarked to the market attendant that he wished he could obtain such wonderful fish for his restaurants back in Australia and the attendant incredulously replied, "But this is Mark-san fish from Sydney, Australia!"

When he returned, he sought out a meeting with me and I explained my background and processes to him. I could sense a synergy — passion, pride, dedication, respect and uncompromising desire to achieve perfection. He said he wanted to "take the seafood used in his restaurants to another level, one never before seen in Australia". Over the ensuing weeks I trialled several products with him and met with his chefs and staff to explain the iki-jime process in its totality and they all sampled and appreciated the immense difference attained from so much attention to detail.

This guy was the real deal and he wasn't just talking the talk. He was actually walking the walk and putting his hand in his pocket to fund a whole culture change. Finally, for the first time in our wonderful country, superb quality seafood was going to be served as it should be. The restaurateur, of course, was none other than Neil Perry. Make no bones about it, people: HE changed the face of Australian restaurant seafood and continues to, to this day. Other wonderful friends were soon to join Neil and Kylie Kwong (Neil's then star apprentice) as co-pioneers in the cause. They included Sydney chefs Khan Danis, Tetsuya Wakuda, Greg Doyle and Stephen Hodges. Each and every one of them deserve a special mention for their contributions and for enriching my life and skills accordingly.

COLLECTIVE CONSCIOUSNESS

I was introduced to fishing by my wonderful granddad when I was four or five years old. Forty-odd years later I can say that I still learn something new and exciting every day. I have been blessed to have an absolute goddess in my day-to-day nurturing in my mum, Judy, together with a long, long list of outstanding individuals, who have been my role models and have taught me the wonders of damn hard work coupled with an open mind, a willingness to change, to listen objectively, to learn, to love unconditionally, to not take a backward step (when you're right that is!) and not to die wondering.

Many articles and testimonials over the years have acclaimed our seafood as "having no peer", "simply the best", "sublimely exquisite", "divinely incomparable". I am humbled by such accolades, but very special mention needs to be made of my wonderfully loving, incredibly hard-working and supportive family, in particular, my late gorgeous wife and soul mate, Michelle, our adored sons and Michelle's incredible mum Patricia (another goddess) and dad Jack (who regularly out-fishes me!). I truly could not have continued to function without their massive and cherished support. When I use the terms "we" or "our" in my story, it is simply an abbreviation for all of their names, collectively. And, of course, thanks goes to Mr Masuko from my serendipitous meeting some 30 years ago and who remains one of my Japanese mentors.

WHOLE RED MULLET

> Serves 4

These are not red mullet as known in Europe — they don't quite have that sweetness — but they're damn good eating. These little fish (also called barbounia or goatfish) are not often seen and rarely used. They have a medium to strong flavour and delicate flesh. They're pretty little things and, for me, just how I love fish to taste — sweet but with a good hint of fish oil that gives a pleasant lasting taste. It's always important to make sure these oily fish are super fresh, otherwise that pleasant fish flavour can become overbearingly fishy.

12 x red mullets

sea salt

extra virgin olive oil, for drizzling

herb salad (see page 255), aioli (see page 431) & lemon wedges, to serve

Heat the barbecue or grill (broiler) to extremely hot or the oven to 200°C (400°F/Gas 6).

Scale and gut the fish (see page 256). Season each side of the fish with salt and drizzle with the olive oil. Place in a heavy-based roasting tray or frying pan, add a splash of water, close the barbecue lid and cook for about 5 minutes or until just cooked through. Remove from the tray and set aside for 1 minute to rest.

Place 3 fish on each plate, sprinkle with salt, drizzle with the olive oil and serve with a wedge of lemon. Serve with the herb salad and aioli on the side.

LAKES & COORONG FISHERY, A SUSTAINABLE HARVEST ENTERPRISE

This is a rather long piece about a rather small fish, the Coorong yellow-eye mullet, but it's important to highlight the length Garry Hera-Singh and the Southern Fisherman's Association have gone to sustain this marvellous fish at the Lakes & Coorong Fishery. This is a story about water, about what a crazy country we have and how many years of very bad decisions have caused one of the greatest waterways in our country to almost stop flowing. For the health of the whole system, not just the Coorong yellow-eye mullet, enough water must run to allow this mighty river to live and flourish.

A PRIME LOCATION

The Lower Murray Lakes and Coorong region is situated at the tail end of the largest freshwater catchment in Australia, the Murray–Darling Basin, where the river system meets the Southern Ocean. The Lower Murray system includes Lakes Alexandrina and Albert while the Coorong region is comprised of two shallow, hypersaline lagoons spanning 100 kilometres by two kilometres (three in some places). The Coorong is the largest area of estuarine habitat in South Australia. Originally the Lower Murray Lakes and Coorong lagoons used to be joined, but in 1940 a system of barrages were completed to stop salt water ingress from storm surges and low-river flow events. The freshwater lakes are now separated from the Coorong lagoons, massively altering the system negatively and reducing the estuary to 11 per cent of its previous size. This is just one example of how the ecosystem in this area has changed. Most of the Murray–Darling Basin has been significantly modified for the worse since European settlement

through the introduction of water-flow management measures, water-extraction systems, the associated barriers (such as weirs, locks, dams, bunds and regulators) to fish migration, the proliferation of exotic fish species and pollution from agricultural run-off.

The fishery includes three separate, but closely linked areas of waters consisting of freshwater, estuarine and marine ecosystem components: the Lower River Murray lakes (Lake Alexandrina and Lake Albert); the Coorong lagoons; and the coastal marine waters adjacent to the Sir Richard and Younghusband peninsulas.

A SOLUTION TO AN ENVIRONMENTAL DISASTER

Estuarine conditions provide an extremely nutrient-rich habitat in which fish and other aquatic species thrive. Estuarine conditions occur near the Murray mouth only when freshwater is available from excess rainfall in the Murray–Darling Basin catchment that is not captured in man-made dams. When this takes place, the majority of the freshwater flows out to sea, however, some mixing occurs in the

north lagoon of the Coorong, resulting in an increased salinity gradient southwards along the north lagoon into the south lagoon. During prolonged periods of no freshwater flows to the Coorong, high evaporation during summer has driven salinities in the southern lagoon to reach five to seven times that of seawater — this happened in 2010. Most birds and fish species can tolerate salinities quite comfortably just above seawater, but once salt loads go beyond one-and-a-half times that of seawater, the food chain starts to disappear. Consequently the birds and fish move back to more favourable areas with lower salinities. Sometimes this can be hundreds of kilometres away from the Coorong region.

The Murray mouth completely closed in 1981 and almost completely in 2002, presenting major ramifications for the ecology in the Lake Alexandrina, Lake Albert and Coorong region. A very successful dredging program spearheaded by many groups (including us) who lobbied the government, has been underway since 2002. In view of there being no major freshwater outflow from

LAKES & COORONG FISHERY,
A SUSTAINABLE HARVEST FISHERY
CONTINUED

Lake Alexandrina and Lake Albert since 1996 (due to drought, over-extraction and over-allocated water resources), dredging has provided cool oxygenated seawater to the tidal areas within the Coorong creating the above-mentioned ideal conditions. This has allowed uninterrupted annual migrations of all species of fish, including yellow-eye mullet, between the ocean and Coorong lagoons.

THE FISHERY

The Lakes and Coorong Fishery (L&CF) is a small-scale fishery catching a number of species, using many different methods (multi-species and multi-method is uncommon practice in Australia). The fishery operates within an internationally significant wetland recognised under the Ramsar Convention in 1985 and within the boundaries of the Coorong National Park. Fishing enterprises have been carried out in the Lower Murray Lakes and Coorong region since the mid-1800s. In 2010 there were 32 fishers holding 36 licences in the L&CF; from the 32 licences approximately 20 fishers harvest Coorong yellow-eye mullet.

Yellow-eye mullet are widespread throughout Southern Australia (and in small quantities in New Zealand) with most of the South Australian commercial catch coming from the Coorong region — indeed, 70 per cent of the state's total catch for the past 25 years comes from here. Catches in the Coorong have ranged from 130 tonnes to 365 tonnes per year since 1983. However, mullet catches pre-barrage construction were often in excess of 450 tonnes per annum. (Pre-barrage catches are a good indicator of the levels of degradation this region has suffered and highlight the potential for the fishery if society addresses some of the issues

that are not only faced in this region but all over the Murray–Darling Basin, mainly over-allocation and over-extraction of river water primarily by farmers and irrigators.) The lack of adequate refrigeration and ice supply restricted the potential size of the mullet catch before barrage construction.

Many local fishing families specialise in processing yellow-eye mullet, which is considered a regional delicacy. Up until recently, Coorong yellow-eye mullet was sold exclusively within South Australia, with 86 per cent eaten locally. It wasn't well known outside of South Australia, then in 2008 the fishery under the leadership of GHS and us at the Southern Fishermen's Association achieved a major milestone and received Marine Stewardship Council certification. With the increasing demand from consumers, particularly those from New South Wales and Victoria, wanting fish sourced from accredited sustainable fisheries, the MCS certification meant that the mullet was now being sent interstate in addition to the South Australian market.

SUSTAINABILITY

The most significant highlight for the fishery to date has been Marine Stewardship Council (MSC) certification in 2008. The MSC is an international and independent non-profit organisation that is setting the world standard for responsible fisheries management. It uses consumer purchasing power to reward environmentally responsible fishery management and practices.

Part of maintaining a healthy environment is conveying a true picture and understanding of how fishing and fisheries work to the wider community, who are increasingly distant from the resource. In 1997, the L&CF community

chose MSC certification as a way to convey to the public their commitment to a well-managed and sustainable fishery. Four species were selected out of a possible nine harvested in the fishery to be MSC certified. These were pipi, mulloway, golden perch and, of course, Coorong yellow-eye mullet. After nearly 10 years from the date we first set on our course for independent and international certification, the L&CF was the world's first multi-species and multi-method fishery to be successfully MSC certified in 2008. The scientific scrutiny and rigour that was required to assess us has dispelled many myths and ill-perceived perceptions about our gill-net fishery.

THE UNIQUE FLAVOUR

The key difference affecting the flavour between the Coorong yellow-eye mullet and other Australasian yellow-eye mullet is the time it spends in a significantly different salinity environment within the Coorong. The Coorong is noted for its three different aquatic regimes: hypersaline (salinities higher than seawater); marine (salinity equivalent to seawater) and estuarine (brackish, salinities lower than seawater). They provide a diverse range of aquatic flora and fauna, such as invertebrates, insect larvae, marine worms and microscopic crustaceans and molluscs and numerous types of aquatic weeds. This translates to a wide range of foods available all year round for fish. This cornucopia of food combines with very high evaporation levels during the summer, so the salinities are generally above seawater, meaning that the Coorong yellow-eye mullet has a unique flavour-enhancing environment to those of mullet found elsewhere in Australia.

COORONG YELLOW-EYE MULLET

> Serves 4

Coorong yellow-eye mullet is one of my very favourite fish to eat — I'd eat it a couple of times a week when it is available at the restaurant. It is the closest thing we have to European red mullet; it has a delicate white flesh with a haunting sweet fish flavour from its wonderful oils. I think it is like King George whiting on steroids!

12 x Coorong yellow-eye mullet
sea salt
extra virgin olive oil, for drizzling
herb salad (see page 255), aioli (see page 431) & lemon wedges, to serve

Heat the barbecue or griller (broiler) to extremely hot or the oven to 200°C (400°F/Gas 6).

Scale, gut and fillet the fish, leaving the skin intact (see page 256). Season each side of the fillets with salt and drizzle with the olive oil. Place in a heavy-based roasting tray or frying pan, add a splash of water, close the barbecue lid and cook for about 3 minutes or until just cooked through. Remove from the tray and set aside for 1 minute to rest.

Place 6 fish fillets on each plate, sprinkle with salt, drizzle with the olive oil and serve with a wedge of lemon. Serve with the herb salad and aioli on the side.

GRILLED SWORDFISH STEAK

> Serves 4

The decision to eat swordfish can be a very emotional one for some people. Yes, it is long lived and the Atlantic species is endangered. This should not confuse the issue for its Pacific cousin, which I believe, at present, is an under-utilised resource. The Atlantic swordfish is a species that has collapsed and all but disappeared as a commercial fish in the United States, whereas the Pacific swordfish catch is mainly a by-product of tuna fishing. They're caught by long lining, a method employed in Australia using hook technology that stops the catching of sea birds and turtles. I believe we have a very sustainable fish on our hands and it means you can sit down to a nice plate of grilled swordfish with a clear conscience.

Being an oily fish, swordfish is perfect for grilling or barbecuing. Cook it about medium-rare to medium rather than well done or it will be dry and flavourless. Cooked perfectly, it will melt in your mouth with heaps of flavour and have a buttery texture.

4 x 200 g (7 oz) Pacific swordfish steaks
sea salt
extra virgin olive oil, for drizzling
herb salad (see page 255), aioli (see page 431) & lemon wedges, to serve

Heat the barbecue or grill (broiler) to extremely hot. Season each side of the swordfish steaks with salt and drizzle with the olive oil. Place on the barbecue or under the grill and cook for about 3 minutes, rotating the steaks 90 degrees halfway through so you get a cross pattern on the fish. Turn the steaks over and cook for another 2 minutes, rotating the steaks 90 degrees halfway through again. Remove from the heat and set aside for 1 minute to rest.

Place a piece of fish on each plate, sprinkle with salt, drizzle with the olive oil and serve with a wedge of lemon. Serve with the herb salad and aioli on the side.

One of the great benefits of having a wood-fired grill is you can easily set up a wood-fired rotisserie. It's such a wonderful way of cooking, especially poultry and pork. It's the original form of roasting and I love any kind of bird or beast cooked this way. As the meat turns slowly, it rotates from the fierce heat near the coals to the softer heat at the top, the juices flow back down the meat, increasing the juiciness of whatever you're cooking and, most importantly, infusing it with the wonderful smokiness of the embers burning underneath. There is something incredibly satisfying about cooking over wood and charcoal. I guess in a sense, as a cook, it takes you back to where it all began.

WOOD-FIRED ROTISSERIE CHICKEN WITH TUSCAN BREAD SALAD

> Serves 4

The Rockpool Bar & Grill menu reads: "Man first roasted birds over fire; I see no reason why it still isn't the best method today." The wood-fired rotisserie is one of the cornerstones of the restaurant. I love watching the chicken as it turns slowly over the embers, glowing red with heat, turning the skin golden and imparting a wonderful smokiness. Two things are really important for the success of this dish. First, you must get a really terrific free-range or organic chicken and, second, don't overcook it.

If you're using a gas barbecue, you can simulate the smokiness by using soaked wood chips (see page 257). And, very important, don't close the barbecue lid! The bird needs to cook without too fierce a heat. I find that closing the lid makes it happen all too quickly for the delicate nature of the bird's flesh. And remember to rest it. We serve the chicken with a Tuscan bread and tomato salad in summer, with white beans through winter, and peas and broad (fava) beans at other times of the year.

2 x 1.5 kg (3 lb 5 oz) free-range or organic chickens

sea salt & freshly ground black pepper

60 ml (2 fl oz/¼ cup) extra virgin olive oil, plus extra for rubbing

4 x 3 cm (1¼ inch) thick slices sourdough bread, crusts on

1 garlic clove

400 g (14 oz) cherry tomatoes, halved

1 handful flat-leaf (Italian) parsley leaves

2 tablespoons red wine vinegar

aioli (see page 431), to serve

Prepare the rotisserie. Remove the wing tips and trim the excess fat from the chickens. Season the chickens liberally with salt and rub with some olive oil. Thread the chickens onto the rotisserie and cook for 35–40 minutes or until golden and cooked through. Remove from the rotisserie and set aside for 10 minutes to rest.

Meanwhile, heat a chargrill pan to high and toast the bread on each side until crisp. Rub both sides with the garlic clove. Cut the bread into 2 cm (¾ inch) cubes and toss with the tomato, parsley, olive oil and vinegar, and season to taste with salt and pepper.

To serve, cut the chicken into desired pieces and serve with the bread salad and aioli on the side.

POULTRY OF BURRAWONG, NO ORDINARY BIRDS

I love Grant and Trudi Jolliffe's chickens. All the energy that goes into a bird that lives stress free comes back in spades in flavour and texture. The grazing and movement in open spaces coupled with the fact the birds are killed on the farm, add up to a firm and delicious skin and a depth of flavour in the meat. They are the equal of any great chicken I have eaten in Europe. Here is Grant's story.

My dad has kept birds all of his life. We had birds when we were growing up, too, because Dad was very big on self-sufficiency. How many we kept depended on where we were and how much land we had. I remember helping Dad pluck and dress the meat chooks we'd raised. If we had any left-over, we'd sell them to friends and neighbours. We thought the chickens were good and the feedback was so strong that we thought one day we could make this into a business.

We first looked at a chicken farm up near Gympie in south-east Queensland back in 1997 but my wife Trudi and I hadn't been married long and it just wasn't the right time. I said to Dad that one day we would find the right place. After 10 years of hunting around looking for the perfect place, planning and preparation, three children and a stint in the army, finishing up as a peacekeeper in Timor, the time was right for a change and a call from my dad got the ball rolling.

Dad had seen an ad in *The Land* (a rural newspaper servicing New South Wales) for Burrawong, an organic quail farm on the mid-north coast of New South Wales, that ticked all of our boxes. It had the right location for access to markets — almost exactly halfway between Sydney and Brisbane and only a few kilometres off the highway — and it had an organically certified processing facility as well, which meant we could control the whole process from start to finish. It was perfect.

After purchasing the farm, we raised quails for a short while but then stopped and decided to concentrate on chickens and later on ducks, too. To raise quails, they need to be in covered pens to stop them flying away, but chickens and ducks (once they're big enough to look after themselves) can be left outside in their enclosures down on our flats. Our birds get to live outside and we think that's the way it's got to be. Our outdoors approach to raising chickens and ducks is definitely harder, especially when the river floods and we've got to get them up onto high ground quick smart. Generally, there are more things that are out of our control, too; sizes can vary week to week and there are seasonal fluctuations — our ducks do better in winter, whereas our chickens go better when it's warmer. But for us, there's not really a choice about how to raise our chickens and ducks, it's the only way. We're able to produce healthier birds with better texture and flavour.

Burrawong is a big jump from raising a few birds when we were growing up to doing what we do now. We've learnt a lot and we're still learning, but we don't want to get too big. There are three generations living and working here now and the operation is at a size we can manage and still deliver a quality product. We think that's pretty good. To have people recognise that and have great restaurants serving our chickens and ducks is the icing on the cake.

LOOKING THE ANIMAL
IN THE EYE

One of the great things about being a passionate chef is you get to meet a lot of wonderful like-minded people: producers, fishermen and suppliers (whose role is to help grow the businesses of the producer and often guide them to grow what the market wants). Grant Hilliard and Laura Dalrymple of Feather and Bone supply our Burrawong chickens. This is their story.

There are lots of very rewarding moments in our business, but one of the best is when we see a grower and a chef who are introduced by us start to form their own relationship, shaped by their mutual passion for the product. This is what has happened with Neil and his team of chefs and a couple of our producers.

Essentially, we connect people with similar attitudes about farming and sustainability. We develop relationships with producers. We visit their farms and learn as much as we can about what they do and how they do it. Then we introduce their product to potential customers and, if the fit is right, we manage the whole exercise of delivering the product from the farm (or the abattoir) to the customer.

Our business is built around the desire to know as much as we possibly can about every stage of the life cycle of the produce we sell and then to pass that information on to the customer. To borrow novelist Jonathan Safran Foer's phrase, we want to open up "the line of sight" between the farm and the consumer. It's great when we find ourselves in a circular relationship with our producers and customers, where they are as engaged with each other as we are with each of them. This sort of exchange can only lead to greater understanding and appreciation of everyone's contribution and continued improvement in the quality of the product from the farm through to the diner's plate.

Sustainably produced food is incomparably better than food grown on efficiency-based farms. But it's also more variable and less predictable, so it takes real understanding and passion for a chef running a restaurant to commit to buying sustainably raised produce. There are a growing band of these chefs in Australia who are increasingly concerned with the ethics of the product and who are incorporating these concerns into their restaurants. They want the integrity of the producer to be reflected in the final product on the plate but they don't want to compromise on quality. Our role is to find producers who feel the same way about the whole process and then align them together.

We believe there's a fundamental link between the way an animal is raised and the way it tastes. Where you find passionate, maverick farmers who put the welfare of their land and animals first, you will almost certainly find exceptional produce.

We don't shy away from the fact that we're all about eating animals. But we believe that, if you're going to farm, kill and eat animals, then you have an obligation to treat every step of the process with the greatest respect and consideration possible. We're a work in progress, but we're doing our best to run a business that practises this kind of respect and consideration. It's the only way we feel we can look the animal in the eye.

PIGEON WITH ROASTED RED CAPSICUM, RED GRAPE & RADICCHIO SALAD

> Serves 4

Pigeons are one of my favourite birds. They have a great texture and nice gamey flavour that really makes them one of the go-to game meats in Australia. Glenloth are the best producers we've come across. Their pigeons have a wonderful depth of flavour and the skin is always a delight to eat. We cook them on the rotisserie and I recommend this, if you have one on your barbecue, but they're equally delicious seared straight on the barbecue to give a nice charred flavour that enhances the richness of the breast and skin. These birds are awesome with fruits, such as figs, peaches, plums and cherries that cut through the richness of the meat. To top it off, I love to serve them with either radicchio or endive for their bitterness, which cuts through the sweetness of the fruit.

4 x pigeons (squabs)

2 tablespoons extra virgin olive oil, plus extra for drizzling

1 red capsicum (pepper)

sea salt & freshly ground black pepper

12 radicchio leaves, washed

120 g (4¼ oz) red grapes, halved

2 tablespoons balsamic vinegar

1 tablespoon 20-year-old aged balsamic vinegar

Preheat the oven to 220°C (425°F/Gas 7). Drizzle some olive oil over the capsicum to coat and place in a roasting tray. Roast for 15–20 minutes or until the skin starts to blister. Place in a bowl, cover with plastic wrap and set aside to steam. When cool enough to handle, peel off the skin and discard the seeds. Cut the flesh into julienne, place in a bowl and set aside.

To prepare the pigeons, working with one at a time, remove the neck, wishbone and wing tips and discard. Using kitchen scissors, cut down both sides of the backbone and remove. Open up the pigeon flat and lightly rub both sides with some olive oil and season with salt and pepper.

Heat a barbecue flatplate to hot. Cook the pigeons, turning several times, until the skin is golden and the meat feels firm when pressed. Be careful not to overcook them, as pigeon is best served medium-rare. Remove from the heat and set aside for a few minutes to rest.

Meanwhile, add the radicchio leaves and grapes to the roasted capsicum, dress with the 2 tablespoons of olive oil and balsamic vinegar, season to taste and toss to combine.

Place the pigeons on a chopping board. Remove the legs, thighs, wings and breast meat by slicing from the centre against the breastbone in long strokes.

To serve, divide the salad among plates and arrange the pigeon meat on top. Drizzle with the aged balsamic vinegar, some olive oil and season to taste.

MELANDA PARK PORK,
A RARE BREED IN PIG FARMING

Pork is one of the most intensively farmed animals on earth.
Buy free-range and organic pigs (and chickens). It's much better
for your karma and, more importantly, tastes so much better.
Lee McCosker, founder of Melanda Park Free Range Pork
and author of Free Range Pig Farming — Starting Out, *a book*
that now sets the industry standard for genuine true free range,
need not worry about her karma. This is her story.

I could never be described as "just a pig farmer". Pigs are my passion and if I'm not working with them in the paddock, then I'm usually working to promote free-range production. I'm particularly concerned with truth in labelling and lobbying hard for a national definition of the term "free range" to protect our industry and allow producers to differentiate their product, a product that deserves to be set apart from pork that is intensively farmed.

I describe my pigs as the biggest time wasters. I lose so many hours just leaning on a fence or sitting in a paddock observing their antics and interactions with one another. They're such unique individuals, each with their own personality. How anyone can justify locking them up in tiny cages or confining them to overcrowded sheds is beyond my comprehension. The only answer I have is that the people who produce pork in this manner have never taken the time to lean on a fence and learn a little about these fascinating animals.

Pigs have the incredible ability to infuse the flavour of their environment into their meat. Feed a pig fish meal and its fat tastes like fish; feed a pig dog food waste and the meat tastes like dog food; let a pig lie in its own excrement all of its life and it tastes like...

We try to raise our pigs in an environment that is as close to nature as possible — plenty of trees for shade, long grasses to rest in, scrubby hiding areas, plenty of grazing, mud wallows and lots of opportunity to display the very piggyness of the pig.

The grain in our pigs' diet is grown only 10 kilometres away on similar terrain to our own. Their nutrition is balanced with fresh produce (leafy vegetables, fruits and herbs) to deliver desirable fat coverage and flavour. However, the flavour is not just about what they're fed; the environment in which they live is just as important. Sun, wind and rain on their backs and dirt underfoot, the ability to root through the earth and consume what they find in it; plenty of room to run and explore; raised without drugs or fear and fed a good diet — this is the recipe for flavourful, wholesome pork.

The breeds of pigs used at Melanda Park are also very different to the breeds of super genetics of intensive farming. The sow lines are a blend of old-fashioned lines of Large White and Landrace that are now being mixed with the English Large Black (or Cornish) pig. The genetic pool of the world's pig population is shrinking fast, with intensive producers seeing no value at all in the heritage breeds because they carry more fat, are slower growing and are usually dark in skin colour. We have a small herd of pure Cornish pigs but they're extremely difficult to market because they're very fat animals. The cross we produce reduces the amount of fat in the meat when compared to the pure lines but still leaves us with a nice coverage.

We do not force the growth of our animals either with modern genetics, drugs or hormones. As a result the pigs grow a little slower and are five to six months of age before they're sent off for slaughter. The pigs get to live a free and natural life right up until the day they leave the farm.

WOOD-FIRED ROTISSERIE LOIN OF PORK

> Serves 6

This is a great way to cook a whole loin of pork. You should try it out, if you have a rotisserie on your barbecue. The skin becomes crisp crackling and the meat inside stays moist and delicious. You can add any kind of seasoning or herbs you like to the meat before you roll and tie it.

We buy our pigs whole and remove the loin with some belly attached from the cutlet section down to the rump. This is seasoned simply with salt and pepper and tied, then cooked over the wood-fired grill. We cook it for about an hour and then check the core temperature with a meat thermometer (a must when cooking whole joints of meat such as this). When the core temperature reaches 55°C we take it off and rest it. The temperature then increases as it rests and by the time we serve it, it's a rosy moist cut of pork with a meltingly tender interior and crisp crackling. The smokiness from the fire is fabulous, making this dish really worth the effort. If you're using a gas barbecue, you can simulate the smokiness by using soaked wood chips (see page 257).

You will need to begin this recipe the day before.

1 x 1.6 kg (3 lb 8 oz) loin of pork, tied
sea salt & freshly ground black pepper
extra virgin olive oil, for drizzling
aged balsamic vinegar, for drizzling

Leave the pork uncovered in the fridge overnight to allow the skin to dry.

The next day, rub a generous amount of salt into the skin and allow the loin to come to room temperature.

If you have a rotisserie on your barbecue, prepare it. If not, preheat the oven to 180°C (350°F/Gas 4). Thread the pork onto the rotisserie or place in a roasting tray, if using an oven. Cook the pork and after 45 minutes insert a meat thermometer into the centre to check the core temperature — you want it to read 55°C (131°F). Remove from the rotisserie or oven and set aside for 20 minutes to rest.

Place the pork on a chopping board and cut it into 2 cm (³/₄ inch) thick slices. I find it easier to use a bread knife to cut through the crisp crackling. Arrange on a serving plate, drizzle with the olive oil and vinegar and season to taste with salt and pepper.

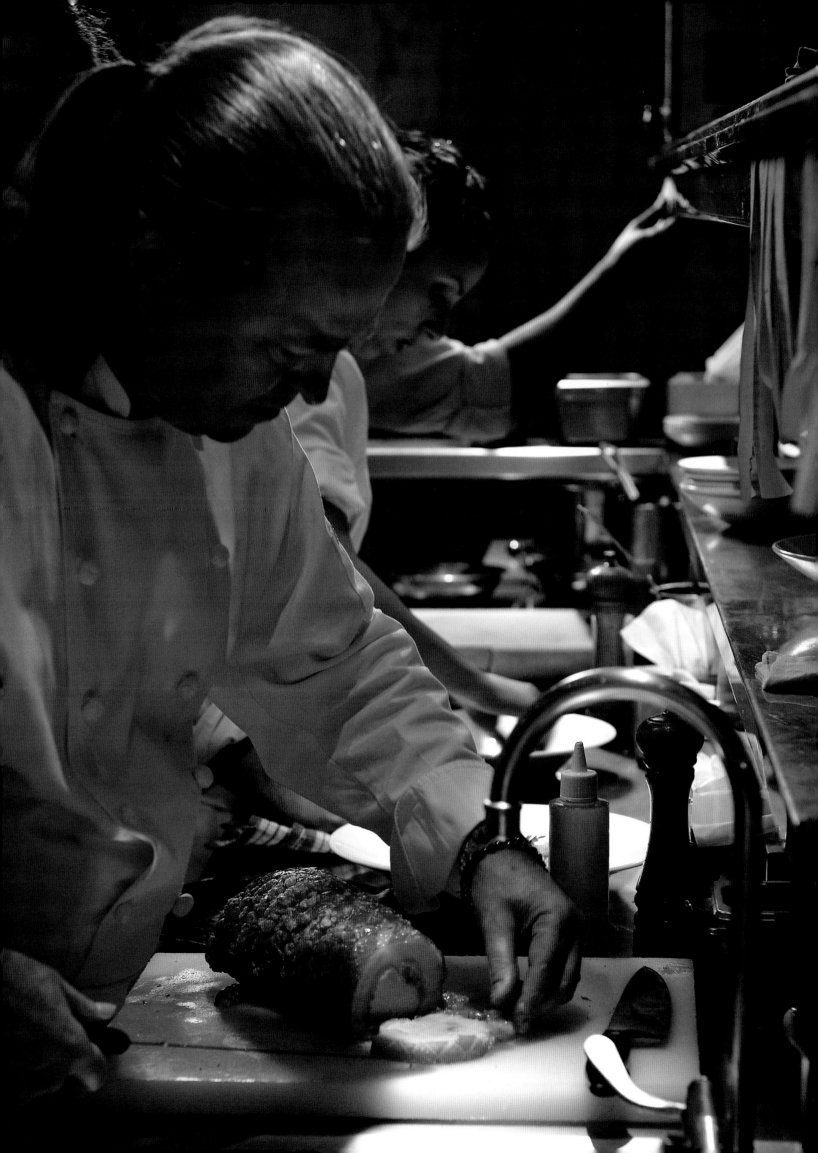

In my opinion, cooking on the wood-fired grill is the very best way to pay homage to a piece of beef, veal or lamb that has been well handled. The quality and type of meat you buy and where you buy it from in this big beautiful world is entirely up to you. Use the recipes in this section as a guideline — cook your beef to the degree of doneness you prefer and by all means use fire, gas, a pan or the oven, whichever suits, and enjoy your steak with condiments and all the sides you wish — this is how to eat great meat.

BEEF 101

So here we are at the pointy end of what Rockpool Bar & Grill really is. Yes, it is a lot of things, but first and foremost it is a steakhouse. So what do you need to be a great steakhouse? Great beef, of course! To have great steaks you need two things: top-quality beef and the ability to treat it well and manage it.

Once you take control of the beef from the suppliers who have cared for it in life, you are charged with the care in its passing. There are two big things I wanted to achieve with Rockpool Bar & Grill: one was to source the best beef in the country, and the other was to have a relationship with my suppliers to make sure we could do the right thing by them, look after their product and make sure it was seen as best it could be. And in order for me to showcase their beef in the best possible light for the diner, I knew I had to dry age the beef *and* I had to do it on the premises.

I knew I wanted to have both grass-fed beef and Wagyu on the menu, and my American partner, who was brought up on US prime all-corn-fed beef, convinced me that we needed grain-fed, too.

GRASSY NIRVANA

I wanted to find the best grass-fed cattle and it was important to me that they were of the same quality as the great beef of Argentina and Europe, where the cattle are not only grass fed but are also older, typically 36 months; in Australia older beef is really hard to find as we consume most of it as yearling at 14 to 18 months old. Why? Because we forgot what our teeth are for and rate tenderness above taste! I wanted all of my steaks, not just the grass-fed, to be from older cattle with great beefy flavour.

Our grass-fed needed to come from lush pastures. Enter Peter Greenham and his co-op of farmers from Cape Grim in Tasmania (read more about Cape Grim beef on page 313). Imagine lots of green grass, clean water, no growth hormones and older beef. I had found Nirvana.

AUSTRALIA'S BEST WAGYU

Next task was the Wagyu. Not as easy as you may think. Most Wagyu in Australia is cross-bred, mainly from F1 cattle, usually a Holstein or Hereford crossed with a Wagyu sire. Most Wagyu breeders don't really have the feeding regime right; that's as important as anything else to making great-tasting Wagyu — it's not just about great marbling but also about texture and great complexity of flavour. To be honest, I wasn't really a fan of Australian Wagyu; I had tasted too many that were not in the same class as the beef I had tasted in Japan.

Then in early 2006 I tasted David Blackmore's Fullblood Wagyu through Anthony Puharich from Vic's Meat. I loved it instantly. This was the foie gras of beef, exploding with flavour (caramel and popcorn) and with a wonderful full-beef taste. This was the first time I seriously rated our Wagyu; I've since tried lots of other Wagyu in Australia and the US and nothing comes close to David's.

NEXT CAME THE REAL TRICK: GRAIN-FED BEEF

The grain-fed beef presented me with a big problem. Also called lot-fed, this type of beef is akin to battery chicken and intensive pork farming; the animals don't do much moving around and are usually fed twice a day so they gorge themselves when the food is there. Not only do the cows put on 1.8 kilograms (4 lb) a day, but also their systems can't assimilate the grain properly (as they were never meant to eat anything other than grass) and they become sick. As a result, they live most of their life feeding off antibiotic slurries.

Add growth hormones to the mix, used by most but not all lot-fed cattle farmers, and you have a very unhappy animal. These cows are sort of athletes on steroids, with the aim to maximise growth so the return is better. This can't be good for them (or us) and the very notion that they're living an unhappy life as a piece of protein growing out of natural proportion is something I find abhorrent. Grain-fed beef goes against every aspect of our philosophy at Rockpool: all the products we use must come from non-factory farms, must practise humane treatment of the animal (a happy life and a stress-free life creates great tasting food and is better for our karma and health as well) and must have an all-natural approach, so no growth hormones, no antibiotics.

At this point I wasn't sure grain-fed could be an option, even given my partner Dave's great love of it. Enter once more Anthony from Vic's. He knew all the reasons I was against lot feeding. He also knew something I didn't know, that there was someone out there doing as David Blackmore was doing, making sure that their cattle were only putting on daily what weight they could handle.

That company was Rangers Valley in New South Wales. Their aim was to create an amazing grain-fed product. They had the same philosophy as us: no growth hormones and no antibiotic slurries. The cattle were free to roam in the feedlot, fed when they wanted and fed slowly over a longer period of time, which is a very expensive way to do it but is the only way to get the best tasting and humanely treated beef. This meant that the slaughter age was around 30 months, so the meat had a strong beef flavour, not that tender, washed out flavour of yearling. It was exactly what I wanted.

THE TRIFECTA

I had, to the best of my ability, got together the best grass-fed, Wagyu and grain-fed beef in the country. Fantastic! I had relationships with the producers and I could go out and help build their brands and ours to the consumer. I had also earned their trust and convinced them to send me their best cattle fresh, not vacuum-packed, which meant I could dry age it so the diner could really taste the difference. This was the best outcome I could have imagined.

DRY AGEING

The two methods of ageing beef are vacuum-packing (Cryovac-ed) and dry ageing. In reality, vacuum-packing simply gives beef a longer shelf life. To me, the longer beef spends under vacuum, the more diminished the quality of taste becomes. That doesn't mean that vacuum-packed meat isn't good for something; it's good for those who don't want waste and want to be able to sell all they buy; it's good for beef that is being flavoured, braised, stir-fried or just about anything except for when it's simply cooked on a grill and presented in all its glory. Vacuum-packed beef always has a cardboard, liverish taste to me and it also releases its juices during cooking more easily. If you're going to seek out the best steak you can, then a dry-aged one is by far the best. As a matter of fact, if you're going to have a great steakhouse, then it's the only way to age beef!

However, dry ageing isn't best for everything. Dry-aged beef can dry out easily if overcooked and, once that happens, you've lost all those nuances of flavour that you've tried so hard to put in. I've heard people say that grass-fed beef doesn't dry age well and that only grain-fed beef should be dry aged. That's rubbish! Our grass-fed Cape Grim is amazing when aged for 50 to 70 days and we've taken it up to 80 days with great success.

So what is dry ageing? Well, it's exactly that. Whole joints are aged on the bone in a controlled environment, adding tenderness and flavour. This happens in two ways. For the first 14 to 20 days, the natural enzymes in the beef work away at breaking down the protein strands and fat molecules. These are broken and made shorter so the beef becomes more tender. They give off gases and add complexity to the flavour. At this stage, when the enzymes are spent, an interesting thing continues to happen — the juices in the beef are continually concentrating, making the beef more and more flavourful, less juicy albeit, but the trade-off is great complexity of flavour. Think of it like taking a stock and reducing it down to a demi-glace — what you're doing is driving off water and concentrating the flavour; the same is happening to the beef. The resulting meat is denser and less juicy, so it has a lot less tolerance during cooking — I hate taking well-aged beef past medium-rare — and you don't need to rest it for as long. If you do cook it beautifully, though, you'll be rewarded with the most delicious steak you've ever tasted.

We dry age on the premises in our purpose-built dry-ageing rooms. We always have and always will. It's an essential part of the restaurant's DNA. For us we have to have total control of the cold-chain management. Dry ageing is something that can't be done at home. Why? Because you can't control the environment (temperature, air circulation and humidty) for it to be safe and get the best results. Our dry-ageing rooms sit at an average temperature of 0°C (32°F) — the motors cut out at 0.05°C (33°F) and cut back in at 1°C (34°F). This means the core temperature of the product sits at about 0°C. To maintain air circulation, we have at least six large in-built fans that move the air around the room swiftly; if the moisture takes too long to dry on the exterior, bacteria can take hold, making the surface slimy, spoiling some of the meat and affecting the taste. We also have constant ultra-violet light for bacteria destruction. Lastly, the humidity must be right. We run our rooms around 85 per cent — too low and the beef dries out too quickly; too high and mould forms. I know some American steakhouses promote mould growth, but I don't like that slight blue cheesy taste the meat gets.

So there you have it. Impossible to do at home, so find a good butcher and ask if they can do it for you. You may have to buy a rib of beef, then wait as it ages, loses weight and develops its flavour. If you live in Australia, you can always order some from Victor Churchill butcher shop in Woollahra, Sydney — they deliver meat all over the country. It's owned by father and son team, Vic and Anthony Puharich of Vic's Meat, who have helped me tremendously in sourcing our amazing beef.

Dry ageing is an expensive process. I buy in five-bone ribs of Cape Grim, weighing about 10 kilograms (22 lb 8 oz) each. I have space in the dry-ageing rooms to hold 700 of them. I age them for about 50 to 60 days — a long time since paying for them — then my in-house butcher prepares the cuts for me. He strips it back, takes the cap that covers the rib-eye off, trims the sides and back and cuts the bones down. We end up with about 3.6 kilogram (8 lb 1 oz) of beef ready to be cut into rib-eyes on the bone. And we end up binning about 70 per cent of what we bought, which hikes up the cost per kilo for us. I believe it's well worth the effort and the price our guests pay. They must too, as many keep coming back.

COMPOSITION

Meat is mainly muscle that is made up of 75 per cent water. This is why overcooking is easy and shrinkage due to cooking at too high a heat is a problem. Protein makes up the next 20 per cent. It coagulates during cooking, which gives us "doneness". It's also the reason for tough meat, which occurs when the steak is cooked too quickly. About five per cent is fat, which varies from cut to cut. Fat is important, as it keeps the meat juicy and tender. And let's not forget that fat is flavour, so a well-marbled piece of beef will taste stronger than other pieces. Meat also contains a small amount of carbohydrate, which causes it to brown on the outside, giving great flavour and a pleasing appearance. Meat, of course, has much larger muscle fibres than poultry and needs special consideration when carving — make sure you cut across the grain for a tender chew.

There are two main cuts of beef: primary and secondary cuts. Leaner cuts (or those with not a lot of connective tissue) are known as primary cuts and include fillet, sirloin, rib-eye, rump, topside and round. In most cases, primary cuts are cooked with dry heat. A good rule of thumb is that the smaller the primary cut, the higher the heat.

Those with a lot of connective tissue, the harder-working muscles, are often referred to as secondary cuts. They include shank, brisket, chuck, short rib and silverside. Secondary cuts should generally be cooked with moist heat; the heat should be gentle, not fierce, so never boil but gently simmer to avoid ending up with tough meat. The connective tissue starts to melt at around 53°C–55°C (127°F–131°F), allowing us to braise and slow roast these cuts successfully. Once all the connective tissue has turned to gelatine, the meat becomes melt-in-the-mouth tender.

RESTING

I cannot stress how important it is to rest meat properly. It always amazes me how many people ask, "What?" when I talk about resting. Though we read about it often, the message still doesn't seem to get through. So here it is: meat will taste better and be more tender if you rest it after cooking. It makes perfect sense. When you apply heat to the surface of meat, the juices rush away from the heat, as it is driven out of the shrinking surface cells, to the middle of the meat (and beyond if you keep cooking it). However, if you take your cooked piece of meat and put it in a warm place, the heat will subside and, through a process of reverse osmosis, the juice will move back to the outside and fill any cells that haven't been damaged completely. This results in a crunchy, tasty crust and a melting interior. The meat will also relax and the final product will be a tastier, juicier and more tender product. You can see this when you cut a piece of meat removed straight off the heat. It will "bleed" when you cut it, as all the juice is trapped in the middle. If you cut it after resting, it will be pink all the way through and release much less juice. As a rule, the larger the piece of meat, the longer it needs to rest. Generally, you should rest the meat for half the cooking time. We don't rest our beef as long as normal beef as all of our beef is dry aged and less juicy.

Don't forget, as a piece of cooked meat rests, its internal temperature rises. This is due to the residual heat that keeps cooking the meat after it's removed from the heat source. The higher the heat during the cooking, the more it will continue to cook — conventional temperature cooking will raise the meat's core temperature by 6°C–8°C (43°F–46°F), which means your rare meat may turn medium and so on, therefore you need to always take your meat out of the oven, off the grill or out of the pan before it reaches the desired final core temperature.

It's a slightly different situation for slow-roasted cuts of meat, as the cooking temperature is not too far off the final core temperature you want the meat to be after resting. The cut will take a lot longer to cook, but it won't need to rest as long. In this case, the temperature increase that occurs during resting is likely to be about 2°C (36°F), but I discuss that in more detail on page 324.

TEMPERING

This process is simple. Take the meat from the fridge, salt it, oil it and leave it on a plate or tray and allow it to come to room temperature. This is a very important part of the cooking process at Bar & Grill and it's very easy to do at home, as you have enough time, usually, and you know what you're cooking. Tempering the meat means it will cook more evenly and the salt will start to penetrate the outside of the beef. As the beef cooks and the juices push to the middle, the salt flavour will influence the inside of the beef; the juices will then flow back through the process of reverse osmosis, developing the flavour of the beef.

BUILDING A WOOD-FIRED GRILL

One of my favourite parts of the day at Rockpool Bar & Grill is about 10.30 am when the wood-fired grill is lit. At 8 am when the first kitchen crew arrive, a young apprentice is given the job of cleaning out the ashes of the previous night's fire; the pit is too hot to clean the night before as the ashes hold quite a bit of heat in them. After it's cleaned out, firelighters are placed on the bottom, then kindling is placed on top and around that a teepee of wood logs is built.

We use ironbark, which is a slow and intense burning wood, perfect for creating the heat we need to crust the steaks with a gentle smoke flavour. The wood burns down for about an hour-and-a-half till they're red glowing embers that are ideal for cooking food quickly. For the rest of the day timber is added to both ends of the fire and the glowing coals are pushed to the middle, to ensure we're using the heat from the coals to cook and not flames from fresh wood. When you're building a wood or heat-bead fire to cook over at home, you apply the same principle.

WAGYU SIRLOIN, RIB-EYE OR FILLET

> Serves 4

Perhaps this is only my opinion but quality Wagyu needs to be cooked medium-rare. Less than that, at rare, the fats have not had a chance to start melting and move back through the meat to lubricate and flavour it and thus the true silky texture of Wagyu is not realised. This is a rich full-flavoured steak — a 200 g portion per person is more than enough.

4 x 200 g (7 oz) premium Wagyu steaks
sea salt
extra virgin olive oil, for drizzling
lemon wedges, to serve

Heat the barbecue, either using wood, charcoal or gas, or grill (broiler) until extremely hot. Season each side of the steaks with salt, drizzle with the olive oil and set aside to come to room temperature.

Cook one side of the steaks for about 2 minutes, rotating the steaks 90 degrees halfway through the cooking time so you get a crisscross pattern. Turn the steaks over and cook for another 1½ minutes. Remove from the heat and set aside for a few minutes to rest.

Place a steak on each plate, sprinkle with salt, drizzle with olive oil and serve with a wedge of lemon.

WAGYU RUMP, TOPSIDE OR SKIRT

> Serves 4

These cuts are some of my favourites as they're full of flavour. Try and get a hold of David Blackmore's Wagyu, which melts in the mouth with an amazing texture.

4 x 260 g (9¼ oz) Wagyu leg steaks
sea salt
extra virgin olive oil, for drizzling
lemon wedges, to serve

Heat the barbecue, either using wood, charcoal or gas, or grill (broiler) until extremely hot. Season each side of the steaks with salt, drizzle with the olive oil and set aside to come to room temperature.

Cook one side of the steaks for about 4 minutes, rotating the steaks 90 degrees halfway through the cooking time so you get a crisscross pattern. Turn the steaks over and cook for another 3 minutes. Remove from the heat and set aside for a few minutes to rest.

Slice each steak into 5–6 slices, then form the meat back into its original shape and place a steak on each plate. Sprinkle with salt, drizzle with olive oil and serve with a wedge of lemon.

DAVID BLACKMORE'S
DRY-AGED FULLBLOOD WAGYU BEEF

It's important to know that there are Wagyu producers and there are Wagyu *producers.* David Blackmore *and his family's story is not only one about great-tasting beef but it's also a story about the humane treatment of animals. There is a blanket notion that mass intensive farming of animals is wrong. Yes, intensive corn feeding of cows in overcrowded pens is wrong, but don't throw the good out with the bad. The term grain-fed can be confusing for people as there are those who are doing it right.*
David is the leading example. This is his story.

THE GENE JACKPOT

I'm a fifth generation Australian farmer. I saw my first Wagyu cattle in 1988 at McGregor Research Farm at Texas A&M University. These were two F3 (87.5 per cent) Wagyu cows. They had been crossbred from bulls exported from Japan in 1976 for research by the University of Colorado. I immediately put plans in motion to get these genetics into Australia. I was aware of Wagyu cattle and the unbelievable beef that Japanese farmers produced. Also, at that time there was a report from the Australian Meat & Livestock Corporation that forecast if the quality of the Australian beef being exported to Japan could increase by one grade, it was worth $200 million per year to the Australian beef industry. I had seen in Japan that Fullblood Wagyu crossed with other breeds (predominantly Holstein) actually increased the beef three grades. I realised that here was an opportunity to increase the beef quality in Australia and to make our farming operation more commercially viable.

My wife, Julie, and I started breeding with these F3 bloodlines but were continually frustrated with the inconsistency of the carcass results. This was mainly due to two things: the Wagyu genetics were old — Japan only started progeny testing in 1976 and it took at least 10 years for them to identify their best genetics; and these Purebred Wagyu had been derived from other breeds. Purebred is the definition of crossbreeding from Wagyu for four generations, using a Fullblood sire over another breed of cows, that is first cross (F1) 50 per cent Wagyu. A Fullblood Wagyu bull bred with that progeny equals F2 (75 per cent Wagyu). When F4 is reached (93.7 per cent or higher) then it can be called a Purebred. It can never be 100 per cent Fullblood, even after many generations. Fullblood is the definition when all genetics both male and female bloodlines originate from the Wagyu breed. There is no contamination of any other breed or bloodline. The Japanese are very strict about this description.

In 1991 I heard about Fullblood female Wagyu that were being shipped from Japan to the US for the first time. Australian protocol has banned the import from Japan of all semen, embryos or live cattle. It was only the arrival of these cattle in the US that allowed

us to bring Wagyu genetics into Australia for the first time. One of the largest shipments (there was also four other smaller shipments) was coming from Mr Shogo Takeda, one of the premier breeders in Japan, who had been breeding Wagyu since the fifties. His bloodlines were considered extreme, being larger and more robust than traditional Japanese Wagyu. I recognised that out of all the Wagyu in Japan, Mr Takeda's were the cattle that would best suit Australian conditions. I realised that here was a once-in-a-lifetime opportunity to obtain bloodlines that would eventually enable us to produce the best Wagyu outside of Japan.

Two like personalities met when I was introduced to Mr Takeda — both passionate individuals with the will to work hard to achieve the same goal. Our friendship endures today. Mr Takeda is in his mid-eighties but he still has the enthusiasm of someone starting out. He calls me his best student. He is my mentor. The most important thing we had to understand was that things that worked on Japanese farms weren't necessarily going to work in Australia. It was here that my 40 years' experience of farming was important. It was up to us — the breeders — to determine what was going to work in Australia.

TRIAL AND ERROR

It hasn't been easy at all. Wagyu are more difficult to raise and need to be managed differently from traditional beef cattle. Not only had we shifted our farms twice to find the best areas for raising the cattle but there also was nowhere in the Western world I could get advice on breeding and feeding for marbling. It was continual trial

and error — and error was expensive. We had to trial all the genetics from all the shipments that left Japan and when we selected bad ones it took us four years (the time it takes from conception to carcass) to rectify the problem.

We also encountered similar issues with our feed rations, critical to achieving that desirable marbling and texture of Wagyu in Japan. It took us 18 months (the feeding period it takes to make a good carcass) to discover if we were on the wrong track, and then we had to correct the problem. Once we were achieving consistent high-quality marbling, we weren't satisfied that we had the texture and flavours in our beef that matched the Japanese Wagyu, but small changes to our ration have now corrected this.

From 12 to 14 months of age our steers are fed a "secret" ration for 550–650 days. The feed is free of antibiotics, growth hormones and genetically modified products. Administering a precise feeding regime is critical to ensuring that our Wagyu achieve a marbling score of nine-plus — higher than Australia's highest score. The ration is based on traditional Japanese methods but it has been modified to suit the available Australian ingredients.

THE HOME RANGE

Our home farm is at Alexandra in Victoria's high country. It consists of 101 hectares (250 acres) of Goulburn River flats with more than two kilometres of river frontage and natural lagoons which we've replanted with native vegetation. The property consists of permanent irrigation, which is important in achieving consistent growth rates in our young cattle. Once our cattle are weaned from their mothers at

10 months of age, they spend three to four months on these beautiful pastures.

We lease a further 506 hectares (1250 acres) consisting of river flats through to hilly country with outcrops of native vegetation in the surrounding Alexandra district. This country is ideally suited for 400 younger cows to raise their calves in a warm natural environment giving us ideal growth rates in our calves.

Our third property is on the northern outskirts of Melbourne. It's a 1214-hectare (3000-acre) open-range farm with cyprus plantations that offer warmth and protection for the cattle. The cattle graze on the natural pastures all year round and are supplemented with cereal hay during winter. This property carries 600 breeding cows that raise their calves naturally. This healthy and stress-free environment offers the calves a great start in life, reducing the risk of disease and allows them to reach our targeted growth rates.

Once the steers reach 12 to 14 months of age, they go to our open-sided and covered feeding facility where they're finished on our secret feed ration.

SUSTAINABLE FARMING

I don't like to use a whole heap of b---s---t words that have become cliché to market products. These points sum up our ethos.

STRESS-FREE ANIMALS PRODUCE OUR AWARD-WINNING BEEF

We strive to eliminate all areas of stress from: climate extremes; feed variations, quality and quantity; animal husbandry, nurturing and handling; and genetics, including structural correctness, temperament and robustness. Any stress in an animal's life will affect the meat quality.

WE HONOUR PROVEN TRADITIONAL FARMING METHODOLOGY, WHILE INCORPORATING NATURAL, MODERN AND BIOLOGICALLY SOUND IMPROVEMENTS

Proven methods and history give the ability to study past successes (or failures) to achieve a consistent high-grade product. This includes lifetime traceability from conception to restaurant through DNA parent verification. We use the proven latest technology to enhance the older proven traditional methodology. One example is pasture — new pasture varieties have different strengths passing on higher protein, energy, minerals and nutrients; some are more drought tolerant in our changing climatic conditions; some with high growth rates in winter, some in summer. These variations alleviate feed stress to our cattle.

SUSTAINABLE FARMING DOES NOT INCLUDE ABUSIVE USE OF CHEMICALS AND ANTIBIOTICS OR ANY USE OF GROWTH HORMONES

Biological (organic) fertilisers enhance the natural biology happening in the soil, allowing plant uptake of naturally processed minerals and nutrients. When eaten, these are passed into the animal.

Chemicals are needed for "on the spot" control of introduced weed species, such as the cursed blackberry that could take over our natural lagoons and waterways. These kind of chemicals are not and should not be used in a blanket manner, though.

No antibiotics are used in the feed ration. When the ration consists of only natural feed products and the grain content is low, the animals' natural stomach bacteria can do their own work and have no requirement for antibiotics or Rumensin (used to balance the high acidity that forms in a cow's stomach from the presence of grain and that would kill the animal). This is the reason for the beer story: beer equals yeast equals bacteria, which means a natural working stomach.

Beer does not enhance marbling or the quality of the beef. But it is important in the health of the animal. If an animal gets sick or bored, it will stop eating and the bacteria in the stomach can die. If you give an animal a bottle of beer (stout is better as it contains more yeast) you are actually giving the animal new bacteria in its stomach to make it feel hungry and it will start eating again. We have a rule on our farm that if an animal is sick and it is given a bottle of beer, my staff insist that they need one too. When our calves are born we give them a dose of probiotics which is like Yakult and gets their stomachs working with bacteria from the day they are born. These are all natural "medicines" that keep our cattle healthy. Yes, the beer story is true, but it is only used when animals are sick.

Some antibiotics are needed to save an individual animal's life, but should not be applied to the total herd. We believe it's better to let the herd build up its own natural immunities.

We do not use any growth hormones (which are banned in chickens but not cattle). Apart from the unknown effects on humans, we believe natural weight gain is preferable to eliminate animal stress and to enhance quality not quantity.

OUR LEGACY TO THE NEXT GENERATION MUST BE A PROFITABLE AND SUSTAINABLE FARMING BUSINESS

Sustainable should also include the profitability of the business. Farming is not sustainable if the business is bankrupt!

TRACEABILITY

A very important part of our business is the traceability of our cattle throughout the whole process. This includes prior to conception. For years the Japanese Wagyu Registry Association, called Zenwa, has required the nose print of each animal on their registration certificate. Each nose print is unique and identifies each individual animal in the same way as a fingerprint.

Every aspect of our animals' lives is recorded including DNA verification of parentage of each animal; and pedigrees can be accurately traced for 10 to 12 generations. We have a full history on each animal including health, performance and quality, from birth to carcass. This has given us a database second to none, enabling us to continue to improve our genetics and management.

SUSTAINABLE SUCCESS

I am assisted greatly by my wife Julie and two of our four children, Danielle and Ben, who now work full-time in our business. We are very dedicated and passionate about our cattle and beef.

It's important to manage the entire production process, including farm management, animal husbandry, genetic selection, the feeding facility, processing and distribution. These are all vital ingredients for producing the best quality Japanese Wagyu beef.

A mate said to me recently, "Blackie, you're an overnight success, it's just taken you 20 years to achieve it!"

Would I do it again? Most definitely! I just wished I had found the Wagyu when I was 20 years younger!

CAPE GRIM'S DRY-AGED, 36-MONTH-OLD GRASS-FED BEEF

*Our grass-fed beef needed to come from lush pastures.
Enter Peter Greenham and his co-op of farmers from Cape Grim
in Tasmania. Imagine a place where the rains come across the seas
straight from the Antarctic, delivering what many believe to be the
cleanest rain on earth. Imagine lots of green grass, clean water,
no growth hormones and older beef. This is Peter's tale.*

The island state of Tasmania is renowned for its pristine environment and vast natural wilderness areas. Surrounding wild oceans stretch towards Antarctica and protect it from the influences of the industrialised world. Farming has been an important industry on the island since the earliest days of settlement. Much of the land has been nurtured by successive generations of families for more than 150 years. The island is blessed with rich fertile soils, generous rainfall, pure water and exceptionally clean air. In these conditions it's no surprise that Tasmania lays claim to some of the best grazing lands on earth.

And nowhere are these grazing lands better than in the Cape Grim region in the north-west. It faces the full fury of the Roaring Forties, winds that blow halfway around the globe bringing with them abundant rain and air measured at the nearby scientific research station to be the most pure in the world.

From the rugged coastline through to the foothills, the landscape is dotted with farms, where cattle graze contentedly on knee-high pastures. Their owners favour the traditional methods of farming based on patience and steady work. This isn't industrialised farming. There is no rush to accelerate growth rates and get the cattle off to market. They're given time to grow and fatten naturally, to develop the rich flavour so well known to previous generations before lean, young, tasteless beef became the norm. These farmers produce British breed cattle of outstanding quality, arguably the best grass-fed beef in the world — succulent, flavoursome, tender and lightly marbled.

Until a few years ago the existence of this incredible taste experience was largely a secret, known only to the locals. Then my family bought the Smithton abattoir, right in the heart of this lush landscape. We've been involved in the meat industry for six generations and quickly recognised the potential the region's grass-fed beef offered. We also knew it would be especially suited to dry ageing, which further enhances and develops the unique flavours in the beef.

We set about establishing and promoting the Cape Grim Tasmanian Natural Beef brand, which is now becoming widely known across Australia and in overseas markets. To protect the traditions behind the product, I created the Cape Grim Natural Beef Producer Group, which currently has 800 farmers and is growing. The group aims to maintain the integrity of the old production methods while taking advantage of technology that allows the tracing of every carton of Cape Grim beef back to the farmer who produced it. Consumers can even view pictures of the farmer and his property.

Members of the group formally agree not to use growth-promoting hormones, antibiotics or any genetically modified feedstuffs. Their cattle are fed only on grass or silage (preserved pasture). All Cape Grim beef is graded under the Meat Standards Australia eating quality system that is administered by Meat & Livestock Australia. The grading system uses indicators, including breed, age, colour and marbling, to accurately predict the eating quality of each cut. Cape Grim beef consistently ranks in the top 4 of the 18 available grades within the system — a result rarely, if ever, matched anywhere in Australia. But that's no surprise to the locals. They know they've been eating the best grass-fed beef in the world for generations.

GRASS-FED T-BONE

> Serves 4

4 x 500 g (1 lb 2 oz) T-bone steaks
sea salt
extra virgin olive oil, for drizzling
lemon wedges, to serve

Heat the barbecue, either using wood, charcoal or gas, or grill (broiler) until extremely hot. Season each side of the steaks with salt, drizzle with the olive oil and set aside to come to room temperature.

Cook one side of the steaks for about 7 minutes, rotating the steaks 90 degrees halfway through the cooking time so you get a crisscross pattern. Turn the steaks over and cook for another 5 minutes. Remove from the heat and set aside for a few minutes to rest.

Place a steak on each plate. Sprinkle with salt, drizzle with the olive oil and serve with a wedge of lemon.

As with the rib-eye, the T-bone from our Cape Grim 36-month-old beef is so large we cut quite thick 500 g steaks, but you can use whatever your butcher recommends. It's often nice to cut a very thick 1 kg (2 lb 4 oz) steak and cook it for two or three, then carve it off the bone.

GRASS-FED FILLET

> Serves 4

We only age our grass-fed fillets for a week as they're tender and have as much flavour as they're going to have. We have experimented with ageing some on the bone before and it does make them a little more interesting when cooked on the bone.

4 x 260 g (9¼ oz) fillet steaks
sea salt
extra virgin olive oil, for drizzling
lemon wedges, to serve

Heat the barbecue, either using wood, charcoal or gas, or grill (broiler) until extremely hot. Season each side of the steaks with salt, drizzle with the olive oil and set aside to come to room temperature.

Cook one side of the steaks for about 6 minutes, rotating the steaks 90 degrees halfway through the cooking time so you get a crisscross pattern. Turn the steaks over and cook for another 5 minutes. Remove from the heat and set aside for a few minutes to rest.

Slice each steak into 5–6 slices, then form the meat back into its original shape and place a steak on each plate. Sprinkle with salt, drizzle with the olive oil and serve with a wedge of lemon.

GRASS-FED RIB-EYE ON THE BONE

> Serves 4

I love grass-fed steak. It's the natural taste of beef with no other influence. Ours have a long clean taste due to the dry-ageing process and the natural age of the beef. This cut is specific to the large Cape Grim 36-month-old beef we get so, unlike yearling, we split some of the bones to get the right weight. Feel free to use a 500 g (1 lb 2 oz) yearling rib — just adjust the cooking time a bit.

4 x 360 g (12¾ oz) rib-eye steaks on the bone
sea salt
extra virgin olive oil, for drizzling
lemon wedges, to serve

Heat the barbecue, either using wood, charcoal or gas, or grill (broiler) until extremely hot. Season each side of the steaks with salt, drizzle with the olive oil and set aside to come to room temperature.

Cook one side of the steaks for about 5 minutes, rotating the steaks 90 degrees halfway through the cooking time so you get a crisscross pattern. Turn the steaks over and cook for another 4 minutes. Remove from the heat and set aside for a few minutes to rest.

Slice each steak into 5–6 slices, then form the meat back into its original shape and place a steak on each plate. Sprinkle with salt, drizzle with olive oil and serve with a wedge of lemon.

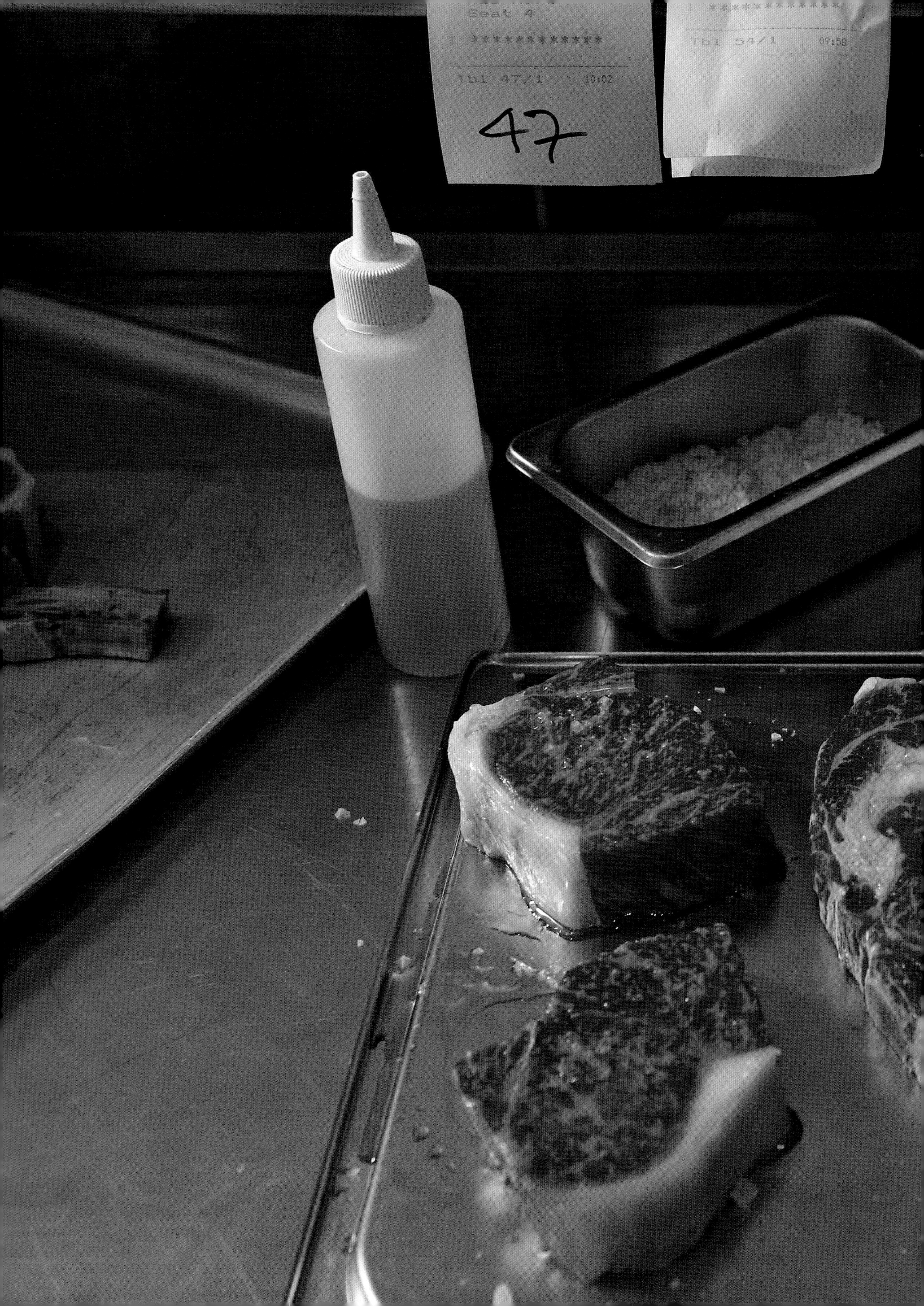
Seat 4
1 ************
Tbl 47/1 10:02
47
Tbl 54/1 09:58

RANGERS VALLEY DRY-AGED, 300-DAY-GRAIN-FED BEEF

Rockpool Bar & Grill receives the very best that Rangers Valley has to offer, their top five to ten per cent. Rangers Valley hand-selects carcasses with a focus primarily on the consistency of marbling in each body. Don Mackay, Managing Director, gives us the lowdown on what sets Rangers Valley apart from the herd.

Rangers Valley is unlike any other beef producer in the world, bringing together the philosophies of Japanese and Australian beef farmers to consistently produce the best Black Angus beef available across the globe.

Rangers Valley was originally established as a sheep property in 1839 in the pristine New England Tablelands near Glen Innes in northern New South Wales. Named by the original owner, Mr Oswald Bloxsome, after his family's property in Gloucester, England, the property was well known for producing high-quality wool. In 1988 the Japanese Marubeni Corporation purchased Rangers Valley and transformed it from a sheep property to a world-class producer of grain-fed beef. Marubeni is a significant Japanese trading house (trading in agricultural commodities) with a history dating back to 1858. Marubeni saw the opportunity to develop Rangers Valley as the premium Australian grain-fed beef supplier based on the use of Japanese expertise.

Originally, Rangers Valley products were only sold to Japan with very limited quantities available to other markets, however, in recent years we have carved out a niche and are now established in more than 15 countries due to the beef's consistent high quality and uniqueness.

Rangers Valley has implemented a number of production standards that are unique in Australia and based on the highly regarded Japanese model for producing quality beef of taking the utmost care of each and every animal every step of the way.

A natural enviroment is key. The pristine New England Tablelands at an altitude of 1000 metres (3280 feet) ensures a cool climate and optimal conditions for cattle to grow. These are similar conditions to where the best Japanese Wagyu are bred.

We take tremendous care of each animal. This includes highly trained staff inspecting each animal every day of the year to make sure they're healthy and stress free. A well-cared-for animal will ultimately produce the best beef.

Rangers Valley has only 100 per cent Black Angus steers due to their superior marbling and eating quality traits compared with other British, European and *Bos indicus* cattle breeds. Our Black Angus cattle are hand-selected by Rangers Valley directly from farmers, many of whom have worked with Rangers Valley for more than 20 years.

The average age of our cattle is between 27 and 30 months. Older cattle have more flavour than yearling cattle, which is more commonly sold in Australia. While the older animals will have more connective tissue, good dry-ageing programs will unlock the tenderness by breaking down this connective tissue and intensifying the flavour.

Japanese experts are utilised to monitor our specialised feed rations to ensure natural and slower growth rates with a focus on marbling. Rangers Valley Black Angus steers are fed on a strict vegetarian diet and grow at approximately one kilogram per day — around half the rate of many other grain-fed suppliers.

Also, we feed twice as long as many other suppliers averaging 300 days for Black Angus. This brings out more flavour and marbling.

All of our cattle have never been treated with hormones. This ensures a natural growth rate for each animal and provides a high level of safety to our customers.

And we only administer antibiotics on an individiual case-by-case basis, not mass medication, because we have a strong ethical responsibility to each animal to care for its welfare and provide it with the best life possible. However, we do not administer any antibiotics within the last 100 days of feeding to ensure there's no possibility of residues in the meat.

GRAIN-FED RIB-EYE ON THE BONE

> Serves 4

Our Rangers Valley grain-fed beef is from big animals — they're approaching 30 months old at slaughter. That's why we also split the rib down the middle on these ones, as we do with our grass-fed rib-eyes. You can always talk to your butcher about the weight of rib that suits you. The cooking time will be driven by the size of the eye of the rib and what weight it is when the one rib is cut off.

4 x 440 g (15½ oz) rib-eyes on the bone
sea salt
extra virgin olive oil, for drizzling
lemon wedges, to serve

Heat the barbecue, either using wood, charcoal or gas, or grill (broiler) until extremely hot. Season each side of the steaks with salt, drizzle with the olive oil and set aside to come to room temperature.

Cook one side of the steaks for about 6 minutes, rotating the steaks 90 degrees halfway through the cooking time so you get a crisscross pattern. Turn the steaks over and cook for another 5 minutes. Remove from the heat and set aside for a few minutes to rest.

Slice each steak into 5–6 slices, then form the meat back into its original shape and place a steak on each plate. Sprinkle with salt, drizzle with olive oil and serve with a wedge of lemon.

GRAIN-FED SIRLOIN ON THE BONE

> Serves 4

I like sirloin a lot and it's a great cut for those who, unlike me, don't enjoy the fat and connective tissue of the rib-eye. Here the eye is all meat so it's a bit easier to eat.

4 x 450 g (1 lb) sirloins on the bone
sea salt
extra virgin olive oil, for drizzling
lemon wedges, to serve

Heat the barbecue, either using wood, charcoal or gas, or grill (broiler) until extremely hot. Season each side of the steaks with salt, drizzle with the olive oil and set aside to come to room temperature.

Cook one side of the steaks for about 5 minutes, rotating the steaks 90 degrees halfway through the cooking time so you get a crisscross pattern. Turn the steaks over and cook for another 3 minutes. Remove from the heat and set aside for a few minutes to rest.

Slice each steak into 5–6 slices, then form the meat back into its original shape and place a steak on each plate. Sprinkle with salt, drizzle with olive oil and serve with a wedge of lemon.

SLOW COOKING

At Rockpool Bar & Grill we have private rooms where various functions and parties are held. The menus are generally set and we offer a very special beef dish — either a rib-eye or sirloin that is cooked in a whole piece. It's seasoned, vacuum-sealed and cooked sous vide in a water bath at 53°C (127°F) for 4 hours. It's then seared on the wood-fired grill to create a gorgeous crust and smoky flavour. To serve, we slice it into 200 g (7 oz) portions and top it with my modern béarnaise (see page 345). It's a truly wonderful, melt-in-the-mouth dish.

As most of you won't have this equipment at home, I have included a method for the home cook where all you need is an oven and thermometers, simple inexpensive devices. I think it's a fantastic way to cook beef for a party at home and once you buy a meat thermometer you'll never look back. I've had a long time to perfect this method. You'll need to do a little adjusting yourself, but the good news is that with meat and oven thermometers you'll always be in control of the situation — it's foolproof.

CONTROLLED COOKING

To follow this method successfully, two things are essential: an oven thermometer and a digital meat thermometer. The first is needed to keep a check on your oven's true temperature, and the latter is so you can check the core temperature of large joints and birds to make sure they're cooked to your liking every time.

Controlled cooking is a matter of knowing what core cooking temperature you need to reach to achieve rare, medium and well-done meat after allowing for the residual cooking that occurs during resting. Refer to the temperature chart below illustrating the different final core temperatures and corresponding states of doneness for meat and poultry. Keep in mind the chart refers to the final core temperatures after resting so you will need to remove your meat from the heat source several degrees before your desired doneness and let the residual heat finish off the cooking process. The amount of residual cooking will vary depending on the temperature at which the meat or poultry is cooked. Remember, the higher the oven temperature you cook at, the more the temperature of the meat will rise during resting. These final core temperatures are international standards and are a very good guide to doneness.

When checking the temperature of a piece of meat with your thermometer, make sure you push the thermometer into the fleshy part of the joint but don't let it touch the bone if there is one, as it will give you a false reading and you'll probably overcook the meat.

	RARE	MEDIUM	WELL-DONE
BEEF	55°C (131°F)	62°C (144°F)	70°C (158°F)
LAMB	55°C (131°F)	62°C (144°F)	70°C (158°F)
VEAL		64°C (147°F)	70°C (158°F)
PORK			74°C (165°F)
CHICKEN			70°C–75°C (158°F–167°F)

SLOW-ROASTED RIB OF BEEF

> Serves 4

1 x two- or three-bone rib of beef
sea salt & freshly ground black pepper
80 ml (2¹/₂ fl oz/¹/₃ cup) extra virgin olive oil, plus extra for drizzling
modern béarnaise (see page 345), to serve

This slow, gentle cooking allows the juices to set through the beef and not be sent rushing into the centre as the beef's outside cells are destroyed by high heat. After the beef has finished slow cooking, give it a good sear on the barbecue or in a pan to add another level of complexity. In this way, you achieve the best of both worlds — a delicious crust and a melting interior. The one thing this recipe does demand, though, is time, maybe up to 3 hours.

First, you're going to have to see how your oven performs. I have carried out functions at people's homes where the oven won't even start until around 100°C (212°F) and gas ovens tend to cut in and out at low temperatures and can be a bit flaky in terms of consistency. The most important thing to do is to check your oven temperature with an oven thermometer. It doesn't matter if the lowest your oven can go is around 90°C (194°F; this will just vary the cooking time), as you'll be able to test the meat's core temperature with your meat thermometer.

I like to serve this dish rare, although it may look very rare. The texture of the meat is set all the way through so it will be meltingly tender and very moist. To do this, we want to slowly take the meat's core cooking temperature to about 53°C (127°F) only, as it will rise to about 55°C (131°F) while resting. At this temperature, all the connective tissue will soften and the internal fat will be like jelly. If you want to take it a bit further than rare, consult the temperature chart (see opposite) for doneness and remember to calculate in the residual cooking, especially if you're having trouble keeping your oven low.

Remove the beef from the refrigerator a couple of hours before you intend to cook it. Season each side of the steak with salt and set aside to come to room temperature. (Alternatively, season the beef the night before as we do at the restaurant.)

Preheat the oven to 75°C (167°F/Gas ¹/₄) or to the lowest possible temperature. Drizzle the beef with the olive oil and rub in. Place in a large roasting tray and roast for 1¹/₂ hours, turning the tray every 30 minutes. After 1¹/₂ hours, insert a meat thermometer into the centre of the beef to check the core temperature. Remove the thermometer and continue roasting until the core temperature has reached 53°C (127°F) — keep in mind that if your oven is a little hotter, then you'll need to take the meat out a degree or two earlier. The entire slow cooking should take at least 3 hours. When the beef is done, remove from the tray and place on a chopping board. Carefully remove the bones from the beef and discard. Reduce the oven to 60°C (140°F) — you may need to leave the door slightly ajar — to create a warm environment to rest the meat.

Heat a large frying pan over high heat. Add the olive oil and heat to just below smoking. Add the beef and sear, turning 3 cm (1¹/₄ inches) at a time, until the entire rib has a lovely crust. Return to the roasting tray and rest in the oven for about 30 minutes while you get the other parts of the meal together (or at least get your guests a drink). Alternatively, you can sear the beef as it is and serve on the bone.

Cut the beef into 4 rosy red slices and place a piece on each plate. Season with pepper, drizzle with olive oil and top with a dollop of béarnaise.

WHITE ROCKS VEAL,
AUSTRALIAN-BRED CHAMPIONS

White Rocks Veal is quite simply the most amazing veal produced in Australia. I was going to write a story on it, when I came across this article in Spice *magazine by* Carole Watson *— I couldn't possibly have put it any better.*

For many people, veal is associated with dubious practices, akin to battery farming. David Partridge, of White Rocks Farm at Brunswick Junction in Western Australia, understands how this idea has taken hold, but is adamant that it doesn't have to be that way. "The veal industry has got a rotten reputation in Europe," he says "and it deserves it. They used to keep the calves in little pens. The calves could lie down and stand up, but they couldn't turn around."

In America their treatment hasn't been much better. "I've been to the States and looked at the veal industry there. I was not impressed," says David. "They chain the calves so they can't walk around and they just have to drink milk alone." And "milk" typically means a powdered milkshake mixture that makes them grow artificially faster. By contrast, Australian veal producers abide by a code of practice that states that calves must be in open pens with freedom to move. "They must have contact with animals their own size, that's important," says David, "and they can gambol around."

David says that veal farmers in Europe have been known to keep calves in complete darkness. At White Rocks the animals live in a shed that runs north and south, so they all receive their daily dose of sunshine. "The ones on the east side

get the sun on them in the morning, while the calves on the other side get it in the afternoon," says David.

"They live a very happy life, albeit short. You can't grow calves or any other animals as well as we do unless they're cared for. They turn into great big sooks. They love me so much. And then I take them to the butcher.

"A couple of guys on the farm make pets of them. I'm usually the one that picks the calves that have to go so they ask, 'Oh, you haven't sent Popeye?' I always say no, even if Popeye was on the truck. You must not do this. Farming is a business.

"These calves are a sort of by-product of the dairy industry, where males would normally go for processing as bobby calves at two weeks old, whereas our ones get the chance to grow."

White Rocks calves have as much milk as they can drink and they are also fed a very sophisticated, "semi-secret" formula of low-iron grains. They flourish on this diet for 20 or more weeks. David describes milk as "the best food in the world", perfectly balanced and designed to make animals grow quickly. The difference between the White Rocks method and others is that the light coloured flesh is achieved without feeding them milk exclusively. "Now what we have done on

White Rocks is pioneered, quite frankly for the rest of the world, the use of low-iron grains to keep the calf meat a light colour. This is milk-fed veal but by the time the calves are three weeks old there's a natural craving for some harder food, so we give them low-iron grains as well. The rest of the world is going to have to follow because they're not going to be allowed to keep doing what they're doing in Europe."

David says that when calves eat grass, hay or grains, they absorb the iron and this is what makes their flesh red. "Then people say, 'this is notta good veal!' You have to say it in an Italian accent," he grins. "Itsa black, itsa white. They like to have white. We can sell veal and get a very top price for it if it's a nice light colour." Chefs and consumers have always shown a clear preference for "white" veal but David insists that it doesn't taste any different.

"We occasionally get one that's red," says David. "Now this guy probably hasn't drunk his milk at all, he's just living on grain." David keeps these carcasses for family use and says even this red veal cooks up white. "If you've had anything to do with politics, perceptions are much harder to fight than facts. So that perception needs changing."

Back in the sixties David read about the white veal industry in a Dutch magazine so he grew some and tried to sell it to Perth butchers. All agreed it was very good veal, but they were reluctant to pay a premium for it. Vealers (what young calves raised for veal production are called) consume a great deal of milk making it a very expensive meat to produce, so at that time he didn't pursue it any further.

Then, in 1989, David sat on a plane next to master butcher, Vince Garreffa of Perth's Mondo Di Carne, who complained that he couldn't buy enough good veal in Australia. David responded that he could grow good veal but couldn't market it. This chance meeting was the beginning of White Rocks' journey from the south-west to the finest restaurants in Australia and beyond. David says that while they've been careful to guarantee the quality and supply of the meat, the promotion has all been down to Vince.

For all their innovation in rearing and marketing veal, David maintains that the Partridges are primarily dairy farmers. His grandfather established White Rocks farm in 1887 and David's son Michael now runs it. "Michael's doing a very good job and he's got a son who will be fifth generation if he's interested in carrying it on. Although, I think I'm still quite useful," he laughs.

WOOD-FIRE GRILLED WHITE ROCKS VEAL CUTLET

> Serves 4

You can of course use any veal you wish. If it's from smaller vealers then just use two chops per person. The most important thing to remember is to cook it about medium and ensure it's well rested; I find rare veal unappetising.

4 x 300 g (10½ oz) veal cutlets
sea salt
extra virgin olive oil, for drizzling
lemon wedges, to serve

Heat the barbecue, either using wood, charcoal or gas, or grill (broiler) until extremely hot. Season each side of the cutlets with salt, drizzle with oil and set aside to come to room temperature.

Cook one side of the cutlets for about 8 minutes, rotating the cutlets 90 degrees halfway through the cooking time so you get a crisscross pattern. Turn the cutlets over and cook for another 8 minutes. Remove from the heat and set aside for a few minutes to rest.

Place a cutlet on each plate. Sprinkle with salt, drizzle with the olive oil and serve with a wedge of lemon.

MAYLANDS FARM LAMB,
SETTING THE AUSTRALIAN STANDARD

Where a lamb comes from and what its diet has been is very important. I really believe that true grass-fed lamb is superior in every way to grain-fed lamb. I do acknowledge that there is a need to finish on grain when grass is at a premium price through drought. However, to me the pure taste of lamb that is not too strong only comes from grass feeding. I also love the fat on grass-fed lamb as, surprise, surprise, it tastes like lamb; as you're eating the lamb, it's almost impossible to tell where the meat stops and the fat starts as it doesn't have that greasy taste typical of grain-fed lamb. We use Brian Croser's *Maylands Farm lamb. Here is his story.*

I grew up on a sheep farm in the Clare Valley in South Australia where we raised merinos for wool. The wool was first-class, but the meat was awful. When I turned my back on sheep farming as a schoolboy in 1964 and embraced grapes and wine as a career, I never dreamt sheep would again be part of my life.

During my wine endeavour I learnt that careful matching of vine type to terroir creates the uniqueness characterised by the world's finest wines. I learnt to make great wine. I sought out special sites and grew the grapes to my own standards.

The winding path of life brought me back to sheep after the takeover of my wine company, Petaluma, in 2001. I found solace in returning to my roots and in applying the lessons of wine terroir to finding the best site to grow grass-fed lamb.

When I purchased Maylands Farm on the Fleurieu Peninsula, just south of Adelaide, in 2002, the manager, Phil, who is originally from the South Island of New Zealand, persuaded me (after I got my head around his accent and learnt his language) that Tefrom, a cross-breed from his cool, wet and foggy homeland, would be ideally suited to the cool, foggy terroir of the property and would produce the finest grass-fed lamb all year round. He was right about that. Maylands Farm proved to be a win not only for my sheep but for my wine too; I identified Foggy Hill vineyard on the property as one of the best sites on the Australian mainland on which to grow pinot noir.

Now here I am growing Tefrom sheep and achieving the highest standards. Maylands Farm's pastures, 350 metres (1150 feet) above sea level, and the pure, cool Great Southern Ocean air that washes over them imparts a unique flavour and texture to the lamb. Most satisfying of all, is achieving the very high quality levels and uniqueness of product that is demanded by Neil. It's not just about achieving the conventional quality standards for meat that can be churned out in well-run feedlots.

Tefrom lambs and pinot noir vines grow calmly alongside one another on my farm, derived from the same terroir and grown with the same dedication to natural quality. On the table, they provide a truly integrated culinary experience.

WOOD-FIRE GRILLED LAMB CUTLETS WITH MINT JELLY

> Serves 4

I love lamb. Perhaps it's being Australian, but I grew up with it as part of Mum's weekly menu plan. Whether chops and cutlets on weekdays or a Sunday roast of leg, Mum always seemed to pair it with mint jelly (only she used to buy hers). The taste of grass-fed lamb, charry from the grill, and mint jelly is a nostalgic nod to my childhood. You can, of course, buy mint jelly (and that's the simplest way to do it). However making it can be fun and it isn't taxing.

MINT JELLY

You will need to begin this recipe the day before.

3 large Granny Smith apples, quartered, cores & stems reserved
1 bunch mint leaves
250 ml (9 fl oz/1 cup) white wine vinegar
550 g (1 lb 4 oz) caster (superfine) sugar

Place the apple, reserved cores and stems and 250 ml (9 fl oz/1 cup) of water in a large saucepan over medium heat. Cover and simmer for 20 minutes or until softened.

Place the mint and vinegar in a blender and blend until finely chopped. Add to the apple and simmer for 5 minutes. Remove from the heat and set aside for 2 hours for the flavours to infuse.

Hang the mixture overnight in muslin (cheesecloth) in the refrigerator. Place over a bowl to catch the juices.

Measure out 500 ml (17 fl oz/2 cups) of the juices and place in a saucepan over high heat. Add the sugar and stir until completely dissolved. Bring to the boil, reduce the heat to a simmer and cook for 15–20 minutes, skimming the scum from the surface regularly. Pour into a 1 litre (35 fl oz/4 cup) capacity sterilised jar and refrigerate overnight before using. Store for up to 1 month.

TO SERVE

12 x lamb cutlets or loin chops
sea salt
extra virgin olive oil, for drizzling
lemon wedges, to serve
mint jelly, to serve

Heat the barbecue grill plate, either using wood, charcoal or gas, or grill (broiler) until extremely hot. Season each side of the cutlets with salt, drizzle with the olive oil and set aside to come to room temperature.

Cook one side of the cutlets for about 4 minutes, rotating the cutlets 90 degrees halfway through the cooking time so you get a crisscross pattern. Turn the cutlets over and cook for another 3 minutes. Remove from the heat and set aside for a few minutes to rest.

Place 3 cutlets on each plate. Sprinkle with salt, drizzle with the olive oil and serve with a wedge of lemon and mint jelly.

CONDIMENTS
AND
SIDES

I wanted to have a condiment service that would go well with the steaks and would give the waiters a chance to interact with the guests. If you are a total purist, I guess you wouldn't put anything on a great steak, but then people do expect something. I felt we should offer a variety. They should reflect the classics and also include a good representation of sauces we make in house. At the very least we had to make a cracking barbecue sauce, horseradish cream and béarnaise.

BARBECUE SAUCE

The barbecue sauce at Rockpool Bar & Grill is a very important part of the DNA of the restaurant. A signature condiment to complement and enhance the enjoyment of our dry-aged beef, it's a very important thing to consider. So where do you start when you want to make a sauce that is different, but still reminiscent of what a great barbecue or steak sauce is? How do you stay in character but make it your own? Well the starting point was to track down some real benchmark sauces, do a tasting and see what we liked.

My business partner David Doyle is a very thorough man, so when I said I would like to set up a tasting he did all the research, found out which sauce is considered the best —turns out barbecue and steak sauces are an art form in the States — and had them shipped over from there. We then sat down and held a tasting of seven very interestingly named sauces. First we tried them without steak. Our shortlist included: Head Red (sweet tamarind flavours with a mild heat), Grumpy's Black Label (penetrating, hard, raw heat, smoky chipotle flavour with notes of cumin, not particularly sweet), Grumpy's Bold Kansas Style (sweeter than the Black Label but not as smoky and more balanced), Russ & Franks "Mild" (sweet with mild heat and not much depth of flavour), Russ & Franks "Sassy" (much like the mild with a shortness of flavour), Bone Sucking Sauce (sweet and tomato chutney-like without much heat) and Mad Dog (well balanced with caramelised sweetness, smoky heat and a rich cumin flavour).

Then we tasted the sauces with meat and the flavour certainly did change. Grumpy's Black Label and the Mad Dog really sung out. Perhaps we had to build a sauce that seemed strong and almost out of balance when tasted by itself, so that when you added steak, they come together and the sauce still manages to shine through the richness of the aged beef?
That is what we did. We built a big bold sauce that was smoky and hot with a good background of spice. It also had a lovely balance of sweetness and tang of vinegar. I really believe we have built one of the great steak sauces in the world to complement our great beef. It took about three months to get it right. We changed the recipe only by a small amount each time to get the balance spot on. The way it is thickened, the amount of smoke and chilli, the background spices — all of these had to be tweaked bit by bit.

> Makes about 3 litres (105 fl oz)

You will need to begin this recipe the day before.

60 g (2¼ oz) chipotle chillies (see notes)

80 ml (2½ fl oz/⅓ cup) vegetable oil

80 ml (2½ fl oz/⅓ cup) extra virgin olive oil

400 g (14 oz) brown onions, finely diced

75 g (2⅔ oz) garlic, chopped

2 tablespoons sea salt

2.8 kg (6 lb 4 oz) tinned whole Roma (plum) tomatoes, roughly chopped, juices reserved

550 g (1 lb 4 oz/2½ cups) soft brown sugar

100 g (3½ oz) honey

35 g (1¼ oz) mild chilli powder

460 ml (16¼ fl oz) red wine vinegar

1.5 kg (3 lb 5 oz) oranges, freshly squeezed

250 ml (9 fl oz/1 cup) tomato ketchup

125 ml (4 fl oz/½ cup) Worcestershire sauce

¼ teaspoon white peppercorns

¼ teaspoon liquid smoke (see notes)

1 teaspoon xanthan gum (see notes)

Soak the chipotle chillies overnight in 300 ml (10½ fl oz) of hot water. The next day, remove the chipotle chillies from the water and roughly chop. Reserve the soaking water.

Heat the vegetable oil and olive oil in a large saucepan over low heat. Add the chipotle chilli, onion, garlic, season with salt and cook for 10 minutes or until the onion has softened.

Add the reserved chilli soaking water and remaining ingredients, except the xanthan gum, and bring to the boil, then reduce the heat to a simmer and cook for 20 minutes or until the tomato is soft.

Pass the mixture through a mouli (food mill), then return the mixture to a clean pan. Cook for 15 minutes to allow the flavours to infuse.

Combine the xanthan gum with 200 ml (7 fl oz) of cold water in a bowl and blend until combined. Whisk into the sauce and check the seasoning. Pour into sterilised bottles and seal with the lids. Store in a cool dark place for up to 1 month. Refrigerate after opening and use within 1 week.

NOTES

Chipotle chillies are available from Latin American grocers, gourmet food stores and delicatessens.

Liquid smoke is available from Herbie's Spices.

Xanthan gum is available from Simon Johnson.

MY HARISSA

> Makes about 2 cups

This is a sauce I made up at Rockpool back in the early nineties. I was inspired by the wonderful Moroccan condiment, harissa. I loved the spiciness and heat from the chilli, but it was way too aggressive to use more than a spoonful in anything other than a tagine. So I decided to trick it up a bit, add lots of fleshy capsicum and, as I was having a major love affair with Thai food at the time, I decided to season it with palm sugar and fish sauce. The result was a sauce that was hot and spicy as well as salty and sweet and not too punchy so you could use a fair bit of it. It was an absolute cracker with a steak.

2 tablespoons fennel seeds

2 tablespoons cumin seeds

2 tablespoons coriander seeds

6 red capsicum (peppers), cut into strips

2 teaspoons sea salt

500 ml (17 fl oz/2 cups) extra virgin olive oil, plus extra to cover

6 garlic cloves, sliced

70 g (2¹/₂ oz/¹/₂ cup) grated palm sugar (jaggery)

2 tablespoons fish sauce

1 tablespoon medium-strong chilli powder

1 tablespoon freshly squeezed lemon juice

Preheat the oven to 150°C (300°F/Gas 2). Place the fennel, cumin and coriander seeds on a baking tray and roast for 10 minutes or until lightly coloured and fragrant. Set aside to cool, then grind to a fine powder in a spice grinder.

Place the capsicum, salt and oil in a large frying pan over low heat and cook for 1¹/₂–2 hours or until very soft and caramelised.

Add the garlic and cook for 2 minutes. Add the palm sugar, fish sauce, chilli powder and ground spices and cook for 5 minutes, then process in a food processor or blender until smooth. Mix in the lemon juice. (You can at this stage strain off the excess oil to make harissa oil.)

Spoon the mixture into a sterilised jar, cover with a thin layer of olive oil, seal with the lid and refrigerate for up to 1 month.

HORSERADISH CREAM

> Makes 1 cup

I love the taste of fresh horseradish. It is at its best and most plentiful in winter. It's wonderful grated over raw or cooked fish or try it grated over steak drizzled with extra virgin olive oil and a sprinkle of salt. It makes a great compound butter or you can fold grated horseradish through whipped cream, as I've done here, or crème fraîche to create a lovely condiment for beef or lamb.

When I want a bit more of a hit, I use a good-quality prepared horseradish relish and fold it through mayonnaise and whipped crème fraîche. I always go for a relish that packs a punch.

¹/₃ cup grated horseradish root

125 g (4¹/₂ oz/¹/₂ cup) mayonnaise (see page 431)

125 ml (4 fl oz/¹/₂ cup) pouring (single) cream

freshly ground black pepper

Place the mayonnaise in a bowl. Whisk the cream to soft peaks in a separate bowl, then gently fold it through the mayonnaise. Add the horseradish and gently fold through. Season to taste with pepper.

MODERN BÉARNAISE

> Makes 1 cup

We had a bit of fun creating this one. It's a classic béarnaise, but I wanted it to be a bit lighter than the sauce usually is. Enter Ferran Adrià, culinary genius and pusher of boundaries. In the nineties he started using cream guns to aerate sauces and create foams. I had grown up with my father making his own soda water and one of my early restaurant experiences was gassing cream for Irish coffees, so it seemed that a cream gun was a very good way of getting a full-flavoured béarnaise with a wonderful lightness. It seemed to change the sauce for the better, I think. It has since become a bit of a signature. Thank you Ferran, for that one.

You'll need a 1 litre (35 fl oz/4 cup) heat-sensitive cream siphon and 2 gas cartridges for this recipe. If you don't have one, simply serve the sauce as is.

2 sprigs tarragon, plus 2 tablespoons chopped tarragon extra
2 French shallots (eschalots), sliced
5 black peppercorns
125 ml (4 fl oz/^{1}/$_2$ cup) dry white wine
125 ml (4 fl oz/^{1}/$_2$ cup) tarragon vinegar
3 egg yolks
250 g (9 oz) unsalted butter, cubed, & at room temperature

Place the tarragon, shallot, peppercorns, wine and vinegar in a saucepan over medium–high heat and cook until reduced to 80 ml (2^1/$_2$ fl oz/^{1}/$_3$ cup).

Place the egg yolks in a heatproof bowl that sits comfortably over a saucepan. Strain the tarragon reduction and discard the solids.

Pour the reduced liquid over the egg yolks, whisking to incorporate. Place the bowl over a saucepan of barely simmering water and start whisking. The mixture will thicken and double or triple in size as it approaches the point at which it is fully cooked.

Once the sauce has reached this point, start adding 3–4 cubes of butter at a time, whisking to incorporate after each addition.

When all the butter is incorporated, remove the bowl from the heat, pour the sauce into the cream siphon and screw on the lid. Screw in one cartridge, at a time, to aerate the sauce, then shake vigorously.

Place the siphon in a warm water bath until ready to serve.

To serve, pump the sauce from the siphon and stir through the chopped tarragon.

When you add flavours to butter and melt it over fish, poultry, meat or even vegetables, you get a wonderful burst of flavour and moisture. Flavoured butters are really easy to make either in a food processor or in a mortar with a pestle. The best thing is that these freeze well. Wrap them up and you'll always have a little pat ready to add to a barbecue, roast or sauté. Simply place a slice of flavoured butter over a piece of grilled fish, meat or poultry, or add it to a pan reduction and make a delicious sauce. If I'm using the butter to make a sauce, then I usually put the sauce through a sieve. Remember to always bring the butter to room temperature, but never melting, before using.

ANCHOVY BUTTER

> Makes 35–40 portions

This butter is great with anything that has a nice bit of crust on the outside. Anchovies and barbecued rib of beef go well together — it may seem a bit odd, but it really works.

250 g (9 oz) unsalted butter, cubed & at room temperature
125 g (4¹/₂ oz) anchovy fillets
juice of ¹/₂ lemon
freshly ground black pepper

Process the butter and anchovy in a food processor until smooth. Add the lemon juice, season to taste with pepper and process for another minute.

If using immediately, transfer the butter into a serving bowl, ready to spoon over your dish. Set aside at room temperature until ready to serve.

Otherwise, spoon onto a sheet of baking paper or aluminium foil and roll into a log shape about 35 cm (14 inches) long and 4 cm (1¹/₂ inches) in diameter. Wrap in plastic wrap, twisting the ends to secure and refrigerate. Cut into 1 cm (¹/₂ inch) thick slices and bring to room temperature to serve. Refrigerate for up to 2 weeks or many months in the freezer.

ROASTED GARLIC BUTTER VARIATION

Substitute the anchovy fillets with 100 g (3¹/₂ oz) roasted garlic and season to taste with sea salt.

HERB BUTTER

> Makes 35–40 portions

250 g (9 oz) unsalted butter, cubed & at room temperature
3 large handfuls mixed herbs, such as flat-leaf (Italian) parsley, chervil, tarragon & chives
4 French shallots (eschalots), sliced
2 garlic cloves, finely chopped
juice of 1 lemon

Bring a saucepan of water to the boil and blanch the herbs and shallot for 2 minutes. Remove and refresh in iced water, then place in a tea towel and gently wring out.

Place the herbs and shallot in a food processor, add the remaining ingredients and process until just combined. Check the seasoning.

If using immediately, transfer the butter into a serving bowl, ready to spoon over your dish. Set aside at room temperature until ready to serve.

Otherwise, spoon onto a sheet of baking paper or aluminium foil and roll into a log shape about 35 cm (14 inches) long and 4 cm (1¹/₂ inches) in diameter. Wrap in plastic wrap, twisting the ends to secure and refrigerate until firm. Cut into 1 cm (¹/₂ inch) thick slices and bring to room temperature to serve. Refrigerate for up to 2 weeks or many months in the freezer.

CAFÉ DE PARIS BUTTER

> Makes 35–40 portions

Along with anchovy butter, this would have to be my favourite on a steak, especially a barbecued steak that has a nice charred exterior and is perfectly cooked. No one does Café de Paris butter better than Damien Pignolet at Bistro Moncur in Sydney. Don't be scared to give it a bash on just about anything, not just beef. I used to dollop this on barbecued fish at my first restaurant, Blue Water Grill. As I'm writing this, the thought of melting it over some peas or sugar snaps just popped into my head. Perfect.

250 g (9 oz) unsalted butter, cubed & at room temperature

1¹/₂ tablespoons vegetable oil

¹/₂ white onion, finely diced

¹/₃ cup Indian curry powder

6 anchovy fillets

3 garlic cloves

1 large egg yolk (from a 60 g/2¹/₄ oz egg)

2 large handfuls flat-leaf (Italian) parsley leaves

1 very small handful basil leaves

1 small handful thyme leaves

2¹/₂ tablespoons Worcestershire sauce

1 tablespoon ground ginger

3 teaspoons lemon juice

2¹/₂ teaspoons freshly ground black pepper

1¹/₂ teaspoons sea salt

1 teaspoon salted baby capers, rinsed

Heat the vegetable oil in a large frying pan over low heat. Add the onion and curry powder and cook for 10 minutes or until the onion has softened and the mixture is fragrant. Remove from the heat and set aside to cool.

Place the onion mixture in a food processor, add the remaining ingredients and process until just combined. Check the seasoning.

If using immediately, transfer the butter into a serving bowl, ready to spoon over your dish. Set aside at room temperature until ready to serve.

Otherwise, spoon onto a sheet of baking paper or aluminium foil and roll into a log shape about 35 cm (14 inches) long and 4 cm (1¹/₂ inches) in diameter. Wrap in plastic wrap, twisting the ends to secure and refrigerate until firm. Cut into 1 cm (¹/₂ inch) thick slices and bring to room temperature to serve. Refrigerate for up to 2 weeks or many months in the freezer.

MARCHAND DE VIN BUTTER

> Makes 35–40 portions

This red wine butter is great on minute steaks or whipped into a sauce for meat, poultry or even seafood such as salmon and tuna. This is a great flavour enhancer to use when creating a sauce from pan juices — just add a little water to the pan and simmer, scraping up the cooked-on bits from the base of the pan, then add some red wine butter and season to taste.

250 g (9 oz) unsalted butter, cubed & at room temperature

500 ml (17 fl oz/2 cups) red wine

3 French shallots (eschalots), finely chopped

80 ml (2½ fl oz/⅓ cup) veal glaze (see page 438)

juice of ½ lemon

2 tablespoons flat-leaf (Italian) parsley leaves

sea salt

Place the wine and shallot in a saucepan over medium–high heat and simmer for 20–30 minutes or until reduced to 125 ml (4 fl oz/½ cup).

Add the veal glaze and cook, stirring continuously, for 15–20 minutes or until reduced to 80 ml (2½ fl oz/⅓ cup) and you have a syrupy sauce. Towards the end of the cooking time, be careful not to burn the reduction. Remove the pan from the heat and cool.

Transfer the sauce to a food processor, add the remaining ingredients and process until just combined. Season to taste with salt.

Spoon onto a sheet of baking paper or aluminium foil and roll into a log shape about 35 cm (14 inches) long and 4 cm (1½ inches) in diameter. Wrap in plastic wrap, twisting the ends to secure and refrigerate until firm. Cut into 1 cm (½ inch) thick slices and bring to room temperature to serve. Refrigerate for up to 2 weeks or many months in the freezer.

Side dishes are an important part of the Bar & Grill concept. Sure we're a steakhouse, but in reality we have to be a whole lot more than that, so by having a large selection of side dishes it gives the customer a great choice.

The best thing about sides is that they allow you to cook simply at home, prepare food that is all about the quality of the ingredients and, above all, share a meal. It's a wonderfully generous way to eat. I love to have a few sides in the middle of the table so everyone can help themselves. It really gets the interaction going and is the perfect setting to indulge in a love of food.

SAUTÉED ZUCCHINI WITH GARLIC & MINT

> Serves 4–8

Zucchini are one of my favourite vegetables in summer. I love to barbecue them for salads, they're great pickled in a burger or fabulous simply sautéed with lots of garlic and finished with a touch of fresh mint, as I've done here. I think any green vegetable works well cooked in this fashion.

1 kg (2 lb 4 oz) zucchini (courgettes), cut into 6 rounds

2 tablespoons extra virgin olive oil

2 garlic cloves, thinly sliced

sea salt & freshly ground black pepper

100 ml (3½ fl oz) white chicken stock (see page 436)

1 handful mint leaves, chopped

Heat the olive oil in a large frying pan over low heat. Add the garlic, season to taste with salt and pepper and cook for 5 minutes or until softened but not coloured. Add the stock before the garlic starts to colour, then the zucchini. Cook until the stock has reduced by half and the zucchini is tender. Stir through the mint and check the seasoning.

LONG-BRAISED, MELTING ROMAN BEANS WITH HERBS

> Serves 4–6

This dish comes from my Executive Chef Khan Danis, whose heritage is Turkish. In Turkey, they cook their vegetables for a long time to get the best flavour out of them. The bean becomes full-flavoured but mellow. People who are used to eating crisp, very green beans freak out and ask me, "How could you overcook such beautiful beans?" All I can really do is laugh to myself and thank heaven that most people let their tastebuds decide. This recipe is great using many types of beans. We often braise them with tomato, as well.

20 Roman beans, halved

80 ml (2½ fl oz/⅓ cup) extra virgin olive oil

10 garlic cloves, finely diced

sea salt & freshly ground black pepper

1 small handful dill leaves

1 tablespoon freshly squeezed lemon juice

Heat the olive oil in a heavy-based saucepan over low heat. Add the garlic, season to taste with salt and cook, stirring, until the garlic starts to colour. Add 900 ml (31⅔ fl oz) of water and the beans. Cover and simmer, stirring often, for about 35 minutes or until the beans are very tender. The beans will lose their colour.

Add the dill and lemon juice, season to taste with salt and pepper and mix well.

BRAISED CAVOLO NERO & SILVERBEET
WITH CHILLI, GARLIC & PARMESAN

> Serves 4–8

This is one of my favourite sides and very hard for me to go past if I'm dining at Bar & Grill. I just love that deep rich dark green flavour. It's a great match with steak and don't underestimate its magic under a piece of grilled fish. I love this topped with a slow-cooked egg, too (see page 209).

3 bunches cavolo nero (black kale)

3 bunches silverbeet (Swiss chard)

80 ml (2½ fl oz/⅓ cup) extra virgin olive oil

1 red onion, finely diced

10 garlic cloves, finely diced

2 anchovy fillets, finely diced

2 dried chillies, seeds removed & finely diced

200 ml (7 fl oz) white chicken stock (see page 436)

1 tablespoon freshly squeezed lemon juice

sea salt & freshly ground black pepper

freshly grated parmesan, to serve

Remove the stems from the silverbeet and cavolo nero. Slice the leaves into 2 cm (¾ inch) thick strips and set aside.

Heat the oil in a large heavy-based saucepan over low heat. Add the onion, garlic, anchovy and chilli and cook, stirring, until the onion and garlic starts to colour. Add the stock, silverbeet and cavolo nero and stir to combine. Cover and simmer, stirring regularly, for about 25 minutes or until the leaves are very tender. The leaves will lose their vibrancy and turn a deep green.

Add the lemon juice, season to taste with salt and pepper and mix well. Serve scattered with the parmesan.

CREAMED SILVERBEET

> Serves 6

This classic is traditionally held together with a béchamel sauce, but I find it lighter and more delicious to thicken it simply with cream. This is equally yummy with English spinach. You may see this dish with a grating of nutmeg but I'm not a big fan of it.

2 bunches silverbeet (Swiss chard), washed well, stems removed

2 tablespoons extra virgin olive oil

½ brown onion, finely chopped

1 garlic clove, crushed

500 ml (17 fl oz/2 cups) pouring (single) cream

50 g (1¾ oz) unsalted butter

freshly squeezed lemon juice, to taste

sea salt & freshly ground black pepper

Bring a large saucepan of salted water to the boil. Cook the silverbeet for 5–6 minutes or until softened. Drain and refresh in iced water. Drain again and squeeze out all of the liquid, then chop.

Heat the olive oil in a large frying pan over low heat. Add the onion and garlic and cook until softened and translucent. Add the cream and cook until reduced by one-third.

Place the silverbeet, one-third of the reduced cream mixture and one-third of the butter in a food processor and process until combined. Repeat the process twice more until the cream and butter are all combined and the mixture is smooth. Season to taste with the lemon juice, salt and pepper.

HAND-CUT FAT CHIPS

> Serves 4

These chips are inspired by one of the great chefs walking the planet, The Fat Duck chef Heston Blumenthal, a curious and caring cook, if ever there was one. You won't find a better chef. Heston's great charm is his fascination with why: Why should it be that way? Why can't he make it better? And why not make it better? These are the questions he put to the humble chip and now we eat better chips because of it. The great thing about this thrice-cooked chip is that it's creamy on the inside, crisp on the out and it remains crisp for a very long time as it cools.

200 g (7 oz) sebago or other waxy potatoes, peeled & washed
vegetable oil, for deep-frying
sea salt

Cut the potatoes into big finger-sized chips, about 1.5 cm x 7 cm ($^5/_8$ inch x $2^3/_4$ inches). Place in a bowl and soak in cold water for 1 hour.

Drain the potatoes, place in a large saucepan and cover with cold water. Bring to the boil and cook for 5 minutes. Drain well and set aside to cool. Pat dry with paper towel.

Heat the oil in a deep-fryer or in a large heavy-based saucepan to 120°C (235°F). Deep-fry the chips for 6 minutes or until soft. Remove with a slotted spoon and drain well on paper towel. Spread out on a tray to cool.

To serve, heat the same oil to 180°C (350°F). Deep-fry the chips until golden. Remove with a slotted spoon and drain. Sprinkle with salt and serve immediately.

KIPFLER POTATOES SAUTÉED WITH WAGYU FAT & ROSEMARY

> Serves 6–8

Fat is flavour. When you buy 1500 kilograms (one-and-a-half tonnes) of Fullblood Wagyu bodies every month, you have a little fat left over. We render the fat and cook potatoes in it, as the French would do with duck fat. This makes for a very tasty potato indeed. Add rosemary and sea salt and it's just about as good as it gets. This is the best way to use new-season kipflers or pink-eyes, when their flesh is dense and creamy.

350 g (12 oz) kipfler potatoes, unpeeled & washed

1½ cups rendered Wagyu fat (see page 436; see note)

4 garlic cloves, blanched (see right)

2 sprigs rosemary, leaves picked

sea salt & freshly ground black pepper

Place the potatoes in the top of a double boiler and steam over simmering water for about 50 minutes or until tender. Alternatively, place the potatoes in a saucepan of cold salted water, bring to a gentle boil and cook for about 25 minutes or until tender, then drain. Set aside to cool completely. Halve lengthways. Cut each half into 2.5 cm (1 inch) long pieces. Ensure potato pieces are dry and have completely cooled before placing into hot Wagyu fat.

Heat a deep-sided saucepan over high heat until quite hot. Add the rendered Wagyu fat and heat until smoking. Add the potato very carefully to avoid splashing. Fry until evenly golden on one side, then turn over to colour the other side. When the potato is light golden, add the blanched garlic cloves and fry until lightly golden.

Carefully drain the fat, leaving the potato in the pan. Return the pan to the heat, add the rosemary and fry until the rosemary is fragrant. Season to taste with salt and pepper and serve immediately.

NOTE

If you don't want to render your own Wagyu fat, use duck or goose fat instead. A vegetarian option is to use a neutral cooking oil, such as canola. Heat the duck or goose fat or oil in the same manner as the rendered Wagyu fat.

HOW TO BLANCH GARLIC

Place the garlic cloves in a saucepan of cold water and bring to a gentle boil. Drain and repeat 2 more times. The garlic should be tender but not too soft as it will break up when fried later with the potatoes. Peel off the skins before using.

POTATO PURÉE

It's hard to go past a buttery potato purée, especially with lamb cutlets (see page 337). At the restaurant we boil the potatoes with their skins on, then peel them while they're hot. This improves the flavour. You can do this at home, too, but you will still get a delicious result if you don't want the hassle. The most important part that must be followed is pushing the puréed potatoes through the mouli. This removes any lumps and makes the purée lighter. I like to use desiree potatoes at the restaurant but you could also use nicola, Toolangi Delight or bintje.

600 g (1 lb 5 oz) large waxy potatoes, peeled
70 ml (2¼ fl oz) milk
70 ml (2¼ fl oz) pouring (single) cream
50 g (1¾ oz) unsalted butter, cubed & at room temperature
sea salt & freshly ground white pepper

Place the potaoes in a large saucepan of cold salted water, bring to the boil and cook until tender.

Meanwhile, combine the milk and cream in a small saucepan and bring to the boil. Remove from the heat and keep warm.

Drain the potatoes and pass through a mouli (food mill) back into the warm pan. Using a wooden spoon, incorporate the hot milk mixture into the potato. Add the butter, a cube at a time, stirring into the potato purée until well combined. Season to taste with salt and pepper.

MAC 'N' CHEESE

> Serves 4 as a light meal or side

Pasta and cheese is the best combo. My daughter Josephine can polish one of these off for dinner any night of the week. I first started making this years ago. I loved going to America and having mac 'n' cheese, more often than not at steakhouses. I began with a recipe from a great friend and truly one of the world's great chefs, Thomas Keller of The French Laundry and Per Se. If you start with that kind of pedigree, you're going to end up with a great dish, and a great dish I did end up with. It's a perfect marriage with a good steak but is equally at home with all of the other meats and poultry we serve at the restaurant. Use good cheese, really good quality hard Italian pasta and a smoky bacon. Your efforts will be well rewarded.

400 g (14 oz) dried macaroni

2 tablespoons extra virgin olive oil

3 rashers smoky bacon, diced

500 ml (17 fl oz/2 cups) pouring (single) cream

125 g (4$\frac{1}{2}$ oz/1$\frac{1}{4}$ cup) freshly grated cheddar

250 g (9 oz/2 cups) freshly grated Gruyère

2 garlic cloves, crushed

1 teaspoon smoked sweet paprika

2 teaspoons Dijon mustard

sea salt & freshly ground black pepper

100 g (3$\frac{1}{2}$ oz/1 cup) freshly grated parmesan

80 g (2$\frac{3}{4}$ oz/1 cup) fresh breadcrumbs

Cook the macaroni in a large saucepan of boiling salted water until al dente. Drain and refresh in iced water. Drain again and place in a large bowl.

Heat the olive oil in a saucepan over medium heat. Add the bacon and cook until golden. Drain on paper towel, then add to the macaroni.

Return the pan to the heat, add the cream, bring to the boil, then reduce the heat and simmer for 5 minutes or until thickened. Remove from the heat and gradually add the cheddar and Gruyère, stirring until melted.

Combine the garlic, paprika and mustard to form a paste, then stir into the cream mixture. Season to taste with salt and pepper. Add to the macaroni mixture and stir through.

Heat a grill (broiler) to high. Divide the mixture between individual heatproof bowls or a 1.5 litre (52 fl oz) capacity baking dish. Sprinkle over the parmesan, then the breadcrumbs. Grill (broil) until the top is golden.

CHARCOAL-OVEN ROASTED PUMPKIN & SWEET POTATO WITH GARLIC YOGHURT & BURNT BUTTER

> Serves 6–8

I love to cook vegetables in the charcoal oven, especially root vegetables to show off their earthy sweetness. This is a combination that works well but other sorts of root veggies, such as potato, white sweet potato, parsnip, carrot and celeriac. The garlic-spiked yoghurt is the knockout punch. It adds flavour, texture and a wonderful cool mouthfeel. You can just roast the vegetables, then add the garlic yoghurt as I've done here, or half-roast or blanch the vegetables in boiling water, then finish them in a roasting tray in the barbecue with the hood down. You can burn some wood chips first to get a nice smoky flavour (see page 257).

ROASTED PUMPKIN & SWEET POTATO

½ pumpkin (winter squash), unpeeled, cut into 3 cm–4 cm (1¼ inch–1½ inch) thick wedges

2 x 200 g (7 oz) pieces of sweet potato, unpeeled, cut into 2 cm (¾ inch) thick slices

1 head garlic, halved widthways

¼ bunch thyme

2½ tablespoons extra virgin olive oil

sea salt

50 g (1¾ oz) butter

Preheat the oven to 240°C (475°F/Gas 8). Place the pumpkin, sweet potato, garlic and thyme in a roasting tray, drizzle with the olive oil and season to taste with salt. Roast for 15–20 minutes.

Add the butter and roast for another 5 minutes.

GARLIC YOGHURT

2 garlic cloves

sea salt & freshly ground black pepper

200 g (7 oz) natural yoghurt

juice of 1 lemon

Pound the garlic cloves in a large mortar with a pestle with a little salt and pepper until smooth. Stir in the yoghurt and lemon juice.

TO SERVE

Place the pumpkin, sweet potato and garlic on a serving plate. Spoon over the butter from the roasting tray and the garlic yoghurt.

MUSHY PEAS WITH SLOW-COOKED EGG

> Serves 6–8

*Really good quality tinned peas are fabulous.
We use D'aucy, a French brand, but I've had good
Italian and Spanish ones as well. It's essential
for peas to be picked super fresh and processed
straight away because they only remain sweet and
fresh in the first few hours from the time they're
picked — they really start going downhill from
then onwards. In Australia, it's too hot a lot of the
time for growing sweet peas, so you really can't
go past French tinned ones. Once you start using
them, you'll find it hard to stop. They're great to
have in the pantry to add to pasta, soups, braises
or casseroles (try using them in the pea, bacon
and chilli broth with gnocchetti on page 192).*

300 g (10½ oz) tinned green peas,
drained, liquid reserved

1 egg

60 ml (2 fl oz/¼ cup) extra virgin
olive oil, plus extra for drizzling

1 French shallot (eschalot)

2 anchovy fillets

1 garlic clove

½ dried long red chilli

180 ml (6 fl oz) white chicken stock
(see page 436)

lemon juice, to taste

sea salt & freshly ground black pepper

1 tablespoon chiffonade flat-leaf
(Italian) parsley, plus extra to serve

To slow-cook the egg, heat a saucepan
of water to 60°C (140°F). Place the
egg in the pan and cook for 2 hours,
making sure the temperature remains
constant. Alternatively, poach the egg
(see glossary).

Heat the oil in a frying pan over medium–
low heat. Add the shallot, anchovy, garlic
and chilli and sauté until soft and sweet.
Add the peas, 2½ tablespoons of reserved
pea liquid and the chicken stock. Flatten
the peas with the back of a spoon and
cook until they are soft, the liquid has
reduced and the mixture has thickened.
Season to taste with the lemon juice,
salt and pepper. Stir through the parsley.
Spoon onto a serving plate.

Very carefully crack the egg on top.
Season to taste, drizzle with some olive oil
and sprinkle with the extra parsley.

POTATO & CABBAGE GRATIN

> Serves 6–8

This has been on the Rockpool menu almost since the first day. It just seemed to be perfect for a steakhouse so I had no hesitation in putting it on the Bar & Grill menu. I love the taste of the braised cabbage and potatoes baked together with cream and cheese. Hell! What's not to like about that? When we first opened, a journalist said that the gratin was too heavy for steak and that chips were best. Well, chips may well be good with steak, but serve me up this gratin and some boiled greens and I'm in steak heaven.

BRAISED CABBAGE

230 g (8 oz) Savoy cabbage, thinly sliced

1½ tablespoons olive oil

30 g (1 oz) brown onion, thinly sliced

1 garlic clove, finely chopped

1 heaped tablespoon caster (superfine) sugar

1 tablespoon red wine vinegar

150 ml (5 fl oz) white chicken stock (see page 436)

Heat the olive oil in a saucepan over medium heat. Add the cabbage, onion and garlic and cook until the vegetables begin to soften. Add the sugar, vinegar and enough stock to just cover the cabbage, reduce the heat to very low and braise for 30–40 minutes or until the cabbage is very tender. Drain and discard the liquid.

TO ASSEMBLE

500 g (1 lb 2 oz) bintje potatoes, peeled & cut into 1 mm (¹⁄₃₂ inch) thick slices

250 ml (9 fl oz/1 cup) pouring (single) cream

sea salt & freshly ground white pepper

30 g (1 oz) unsalted butter, melted

30 g (1 oz) freshly grated Gruyère

Preheat the oven to 180°C (350°F/Gas 4). Combine the potato and cream in a bowl and season to taste with salt and pepper.

Brush a shallow round baking dish or copper pan (about 20 cm x 3 cm deep/ 8 inches x 1¼ inches) or 2 small round dishes (about 16 cm x 2.5 cm deep/ 6¼ inches x ⅛ inches) with the melted butter. Arrange half of the potato slices, slightly overlapping, in a circular pattern in the dish. Spread the braised cabbage over the potato, then layer over the remaining potato slices.

Pour enough cream from the potato into the dish so the potatoes are just covered. Sprinkle over the Gruyère. Bake for about 20 minutes or until the top is lightly golden and the potato is tender when pierced with a skewer.

SAUTÉED MIXED MUSHROOMS

> Serves 6–8

A great match to steak. Mushrooms come in lots of cultivated varieties and, at certain times of the year, wild, too. This dish benefits from a wide selection of mushrooms, so add whatever you like. I love fresh shiitakes and shimejis as well as oyster mushrooms. Just make sure you brush the mushrooms; don't wash them in water as it dilutes the flavour.

400 g (14 oz) field mushrooms
400 g (14 oz) Swiss brown mushrooms
60 ml (2 fl oz/¼ cup) extra virgin olive oil
40 g (1½ oz) unsalted butter
2 garlic cloves, sliced
sea salt & freshly ground black pepper
freshly squeezed lemon juice, to taste
1 handful flat-leaf (Italian) parsley leaves, chiffonade

Cut the mushrooms into 2.5 mm (¹/₁₀ inch) thick slices.

Heat the olive oil and butter in a large heavy-based frying pan over high heat. When the butter starts to foam, increase the heat to high, add the mushrooms and stir to coat. Reduce the heat to medium and cook for 10 minutes.

Add the garlic, season to taste with salt and increase the heat. The mushrooms should start to caramelise. Cook for another 5 minutes.

Remove from the heat and add the lemon juice to taste. Add the parsley, season with pepper and mix well.

ORGANIC CARROTS INSPIRED BY ST. JOHN

> Serves 4

4 medium carrots
40 g (1 ½ oz) unsalted butter
2 teaspoons extra virgin olive oil
½ teaspoon caster (superfine) sugar
sea salt & freshly ground black pepper

This dish is in honour of Fergus Henderson of London's St. John restaurant. For seven years, Rockpool on George Street, Sydney, was included in The S.Pellegrino World's 50 Best Restaurants, which is a great privilege and honour in itself, but the best thing about the awards was the lunch that would take place the next day at St. John every year. All the celebrated chefs and restaurant owners would attend and Fergus Henderson would cook an amazing lunch for everyone. One year, legendary chef Alice Waters was honoured for her contribution to the world of gastronomy. At that lunch, Fergus served corned beef with boiled whole carrots. When Alice stood up to give her speech, she mentioned that Fergus was the only chef in the world who would serve the greatest chefs from around the globe whole boiled carrots; the crowd erupted in laughter. Since that lunch, I was inspired to find the very best carrots and honour Fergus on my Bar & Grill menu.

These carrots are a great addition to a steak and are a lot of fun to make. At the restaurant, I cook these sous vide in a vacuum-sealed bag at 90°C (194°F) to concentrate the carrot flavour, but you can boil them (as Fergus does) or to mimic sous-vide cooking at home, place the carrots and seasonings in a zip-lock bag and steam until tender, as in this recipe. This is the way I cook a lot of vegetables at home. Make sure you use carrots in season to really appreciate how sweet and wonderful they can be.

Peel the carrots and remove the hard core with a knife. Place the carrots in a Cryovac (vacuum-seal) bag with the butter and olive oil and season to taste with the sugar and salt. Seal the bag and steam the carrots for 30–45 minutes, depending on their size or until tender.

Once the carrots are cooked, remove from the steamer. Place the whole carrots on a plate, pour over the contents of the bag, grind over a good amount of pepper, sprinkle with salt and serve.

ONION RINGS

Onion rings, to me, should taste of onions first and foremost, not batter. These are soaked first in milk, then dusted in flour and dipped in a light batter and fried. They're super crisp and onion is the lead flavour. I love them with tomato ketchup. Another popular method is to thickly slice the onions, then fry them in a tempura batter — but I can't say I'm a fan, as you can't taste the onion.

3 red onions
500 ml (17 fl oz/2 cups) milk
170 g (6 oz) plain (all-purpose) flour, plus extra for dusting
375 ml (13 fl oz/1½ cups) beer
vegetable oil, for deep-frying
sea salt

Cut the onion into 1 cm (½ inch) thick slices and separate into rings. Place in a large bowl, cover with the milk and leave to soak for 3 hours.

Whisk the flour and beer together in a separate bowl until well combined and the mixture is smooth with no lumps. Strain the batter through a fine sieve.

Heat the oil in a large heavy-based saucepan or deep-fryer to 180°C (350°F). Drain the onion. Dust the onion rings with flour, shaking off any excess, then dip the rings, one at a time, into the batter, letting any excess batter drip off before placing the onion into the hot oil. Let the batter start to crisp up before turning the onion rings with tongs, otherwise the batter will break. Cook until golden and crisp all over. Remove and drain on paper towel. Season with salt and serve immediately.

CAULIFLOWER & CHEESE

This is a classic from my childhood. My dad loved to make cauliflower and cheese and we would have it often with corned beef. He thickened it with a béchamel sauce. After reading and making Thomas Keller's great cauliflower cheese from The French Laundry, I replaced Dad's traditional sauce for one thickened with the cauliflower itself.

2 small cauliflowers

50 g (1³/₄ oz) unsalted butter

2 tablespoons extra virgin olive oil

3 red eschalots

250 ml (9 fl oz/1 cup) pouring (single) cream

1 tablespoon curry powder

¹/₂ tablespoon freshly grated nutmeg

1 fresh bay leaf

2 sprigs thyme, leaves picked

sea salt & freshly ground black pepper

125 ml (4 fl oz/¹/₂ cup) white vinegar

1¹/₂ tablespoons good-quality preserved horseradish

130 g (4²/₃ oz/1 cup) freshly grated Gruyère

50 g (1³/₄ oz/¹/₂ cup) dried breadcrumbs

Preheat the oven to 180°C (350°F/Gas 4).

Cut the cauliflower into florets and thickly slice the stems. Heat the butter and olive oil in a large saucepan over medium heat. Add the shallot and cook until softened. Add the cauliflower stems and cook for 5 minutes. Add 500 ml (17 fl oz/2 cups) of water, the cream, curry powder, nutmeg, bay leaf and thyme and simmer for 20 minutes or until the stems are tender.

Meanwhile, fill a large saucepan with 10 litres (350 fl oz) of water, add a good handful of salt and the vinegar and bring to the boil. Blanch the cauliflower florets for 1 minute so they're still crunchy. Remove and set aside.

Using a stick blender, purée the cauliflower stem mixture until smooth. Season to taste with the preserved horseradish, salt and pepper.

Add the florets to the hot purée, mix to combine and season to taste. Spoon into a shallow gratin dish. Cover with the cheese and sprinkle with breadcrumbs. Bake for 8 minutes or until lightly golden.

GREEN BEANS WITH CREAMY ANCHOVY, CHILLI & LEMON DRESSING & ALMONDS

> Serves 6–8

A beautiful little salad that is great as a starter or side. The dressing is really good with any blanched green vegetables — try broccolini, cabbage, Roman beans or asparagus, and it tastes quite nice to swap the almonds for hazelnuts too.

CHILLI & LEMON DRESSING

1 lemon
125 ml (4 fl oz/$^1/_2$ cup) extra virgin olive oil
55 g (2 oz) Ortiz or other good-quality anchovy fillets
4 garlic cloves, finely chopped
pinch of ground chilli
180 ml (6 fl oz) milk

Peel the lemon with a small knife taking care to remove all of the white pith. Remove any seeds and finely chop the flesh. Place in a small food processor and add the oil, anchovy fillets, garlic and chilli. Process until well combined. With the motor running, gradually add the milk, about 1 tablespoon at a time. If you add the milk too quickly, the dressing may split. When all the milk is incorporated, add about 1 tablespoon of warm water so the dressing is a pouring consistency.

TO SERVE

400 g (14 oz) green beans
2$^1/_2$ tablespoons extra virgin olive oil
sea salt & freshly ground black pepper
40 g (1$^1/_2$ oz/$^1/_4$ cup) almonds, roasted & roughly chopped

Bring a saucepan of salted water to the boil. Blanch the beans until tender to the bite. Drain and refresh in iced water. Drain again and trim the beans. Dress with the olive oil and season to taste with salt and pepper.

Place 1 teaspoon of the chilli and lemon dressing in the bases of shallow salad bowls, pile the beans on top, spoon over the remaining dressing and scatter over the almonds.

BOILED MIXED GREENS WITH
EXTRA VIRGIN OLIVE OIL & LEMON

I eat this dish at home all the time and I really think it's the perfect match to a steak or roast for the simple reason that it pays homage to the great taste of seasonal, fresh green vegetables, enhanced with nothing more than fresh lemon juice, sea salt, quality extra virgin olive oil and lashings of freshly ground pepper. When I opened Rockpool Bar & Grill Melbourne, I just had to put it on the menu and it's since become one of the signature side dishes. Use any green vegetables you like, in any quantity that suits. My favourites are broccolini, beans and peas mixed with ribbons of leek and cabbage leaves.

mixed green vegetables
extra virgin olive oil
lemon juice
sea salt & freshly ground black pepper

Fill a large saucepan with water and salt it well — enough so the water tastes like the sea. Bring to a rolling boil.

Drop each type of vegetable into the pan and cook until tender (see below for cooking times), checking each vegetable along the way to see if it's cooked to your liking.

Drain well. Toss in olive oil and lemon juice and season to taste with salt and pepper.

COOKING TIMES

Green beans: 7–8 minutes (These take longer than you think. You want them a little soft so the starch converts to sugar.)

Broccoli: 5 minutes

Broccolini: 4 minutes

Asparagus: 3–5 minutes

Leeks, halved & cut into 3 cm (1 1/4 inch) lengths: 3–5 minutes

Young green peas: 3 minutes

Savoy cabbage leaves: 1 minute

English spinach leaves: 30 seconds

Kim A

2245   Gst 6

Four Tastes
To Share
Crudo
To Share
OZ Ham
To Share
Parm Proscu
To Share
Calamari
To Share
Braised Gree
To Share
****
Crazy Water
Seat 1
36 MTH TBONE
Med
Seat 1
RGS Fillet
Med Well
Seat 4
36 MTH 350G
2 Med Rare
Seat 5
Seat 7
36MTH Fillet
Med
Seat 8
****
Chips
LG Macaroni
Roast Pump
Mix Mushroom
bl 60/1   20:05

7625 Kim A

Chk 2237   Gst 4

12 Oyster
Rocks Only
Seat
1 Bolognese
Seat 4
1 OZ Ham
Seat 6
1 Agnolotti Pa
Seat 3
****
2 WGU Fillet
2 Med Rare/
Seat 1
Seat 6
1 36MTH Fillet
Med
Seat 3
1 RGS Fillet
Med
Seat 4
1 ***********
1 Boiled Green
Green Beans
Cabbage Sal

63/1   20:00

63

7626 Tim B

Chk 2240   Gst 2

1 Cured D/Trou
Seat 2
1 Globe Artich
Seat 1
1 ***********
1 MC Bolognese
Seat 2
1 Beef Pie
Seat 1
1 ***********
1 Chips
1 Boiled Green
Tbl 32/1   19:52

32

7815 Dylan N

Chk 2231

1 Roast S
To Sha
1 Parm Pr
To Share
1 36MTH Fill
Rare
Seat 1
1 36MTH Fill
Med Rare
Seat 2
****
Broccol
Tbl 7/1   20:

RADICCHIO, COS & ENDIVE SALAD
WITH PALM SUGAR VINAIGRETTE

> Serves 4

I love a green salad with steak or seafood. There is something about the crunch of fresh lettuce and that is why I like these three leaves particularly. The slight bitterness of the radicchio and endive is the perfect foil for the palm sugar vinaigrette. Make sure you get a deep caramel on the palm sugar or it will be too sweet but don't burn it or it will be bitter. It's really important to dry the lettuce leaves well and toss them in the dressing in a large bowl rather than just drizzling it on top — it's the best way to make sure each leaf has a light coating.

½ radicchio, leaves separated & washed

1 baby cos (romaine) lettuce, leaves separated & washed

1 endive, leaves separated & washed

PALM SUGAR VINAIGRETTE

30 g (1 oz/¼ cup) grated palm sugar (jaggery)

2 teaspoons sherry vinegar

2 coriander (cilantro) roots, scraped

1 garlic clove

sea salt

1¼ tablespoons red wine vinegar

80 ml (2½ fl oz/⅓ cup) extra virgin olive oil

2 tablespoons chopped coriander (cilantro)

To make the palm sugar vinaigrette, place the palm sugar in a small saucepan over medium heat and cook, stirring to dissolve the sugar, until it is a deep caramel colour. Carefully add the sherry vinegar, as it will spit, and cook for 2 minutes. Remove from the heat and allow to cool.

Meanwhile, pound the coriander roots, garlic and a little salt in a mortar with a pestle until you have a fine paste. Add the palm sugar mixture and red wine vinegar, then gradually whisk in the olive oil.

Tear the leaves into similar sized pieces and place in a large bowl. Drizzle with the vinaigrette and toss gently to combine. Transfer to a serving plate and serve immediately.

CABBAGE & PARMESAN SALAD

> Serves 4–8

Love it, love it, love it. So simple, yet it has such great flavour and texture. There is a reason that coleslaw is a classic, and it is as simple as cabbage rocks raw. Now take away the mayo and add a vinaigrette and shaved parmesan and you have a very easy dish that tastes like heaven. This is great as a starter, side or under a piece of fish.

1 baby cabbage or ¹⁄₂ Savoy cabbage, finely shredded

1 small handful flat-leaf (Italian) parsley leaves, cut into julienne

sea salt & freshly ground black pepper

extra virgin olive oil

red wine vinegar

freshly shaved parmesan

Place the cabbage and parsley in a large bowl, season to taste with salt and pepper. Drizzle the olive oil and vinegar over in a ratio of three parts oil to one part vinegar. Don't add so much dressing that it becomes wet, add just enough to moisten. Toss the cabbage, then toss through as much parmesan as you like.

TOMATO BASIL SALAD

> Serves 4–8

Not much to say about this other than it's a cracker with a steak. If the season is right and the tomatoes are sweet, it is about as good as it gets. If the tomatoes aren't ripe and sun-kissed... forget about it!

400 g (14 oz) mixed baby tomatoes, such as cherry, mini romas, Johnny Love Bites

¹⁄₄ punnet micro basil, leaves trimmed

8 Ligurian olives, pitted

1¹⁄₂ tablespoons Forum cabernet sauvignon vinegar

2¹⁄₂ tablespoons extra virgin olive oil

Halve or quarter the tomatoes, if necessary, so they're bite-sized pieces and place in a large bowl.

Add the remaining ingredients, season to taste with salt and pepper and toss gently to combine.

BROWN

CHEESE
AND
DESSERTS

WHITE

CAPRIFEUILLE EXPORT 25
COLIS X 6
Ean Colis: 10041844000044
Ean UVC: 0041844000047
N° Lot : 100812303
Best Before (DLUO) 05/07/20

(01)10041844000044(15)

Cheese is a very important part of the Rockpool Bar & Grill experience. Not only because it goes wonderfully well with that last bit of red wine one has before heading to the sweet world but also because it's such a pure thing. Just think of it as being made the same way as it was hundreds, if not thousands, of years ago. A consequence of mankind's need to preserve extra milk, cheese is one of the shining examples of a food in its purest form. Cheese is one of those things I appreciate more and more as I search for great flavours and textures in food. To me, one of the great joys of dining is to finish with a great cheese such as parmesan, Gruyère, cheddar or Roquefort.

THE CHEESE COURSE

Cheese expert Will Studd *knows that when it comes
to recommending a selection of cheese for Rockpool Bar & Grill,
I want the best. He works closely with many small dairies
in Europe and Australia to try and find the finest cheeses.
That means a lot of tasting because the secret of any great
cheese plate begins with flavour. He shares his knowledge here.*

CHEESE SELECTION

There are an infinite number of different combinations when it comes to making a cheese selection for the table. We try and combine several different types of cheese to produce a pleasant contrast of textures, colours and flavours. To keep it simple, we select at least one ripened soft or fresh cheese, a well-rounded blue and a carefully matured hard cheese, and to add variety I choose three additional cheeses at their peak of maturity.

The best cheeses are generally traditional farmhouse or artisan cheeses because they offer a far more interesting range of flavours and textures than their bland and predictable industrial counterparts. The finest traditional cheeses are handmade and quality varies from day to day and season to season. While there are some predictable tendencies, this overall lack of consistency means it is difficult to provide the same cheese in optimum condition week after week. To ensure we always have the best, we work with a seasonal selection that is constantly changing.

The selection is carefully paired with matching condiments and, to help everyone know more about the cheese, we provide brief notes on origin and flavour.

CHEESE STORAGE

How cheese is stored in a restaurant environment is critically important. There is no point in selecting well-crafted cheeses if they're not carefully looked after or not served at the right temperature to reveal their true flavours. The natural ripening cheeses on offer at Bar & Grill are best kept in cool, damp conditions, but these are very hard to achieve in a kitchen with constantly changing temperature extremes.

To help overcome this, we developed a very simple system of storing cheese in an insulated foam box that provides a moist environment with minimal airflow. Two holes the size of a twenty-cent coin are punched in the lid of the box. The cheeses, wrapped in wax paper to allow them to breathe, are placed inside the box, then covered with a clean damp napkin before the lid is replaced. The box is an effective "cheese safe" that can be taken in and out of the fridge and left in the hot kitchen during service without the cheese suffering frequent temperature shocks.

RAW MILK CHEESE

The best cheeses include those made from raw milk but there are restrictions in Australia on the sale of soft and blue cheeses made from unpasteurised milk. Will Studd shares with us why he is a such a passionate advocate of raw milk cheeses.

A UNIQUE TASTE

The right to enjoy a choice of cheese made from natural raw milk is one of the most important issues facing the specialist cheese industry in Australia today. You only have to taste raw milk cheese to know there is a real difference between the predictable flavours and textures of cheese made from pasteurised milk — nothing compares to the individual character, aromas and distinct flavours of cheese made from good-quality raw milk. In fact, the pleasure of authentic regional cheese is all about celebrating and experiencing these differences. The world's classic benchmark cheeses are almost entirely produced from raw milk. These owe their unique qualities to their origins or terroir — the combination of soil, climate, season, pasture composition, animal breeds and the centuries-old traditions, skills and craft of the cheesemakers.

National food standards adopted by Australia in 1996, however, introduced mandatory pasteurisation and banned the sale or production of all types of cheese made from raw milk. This extraordinary policy led to a special review the following year, granting an exemption to imported hard-cooked varieties of cheeses, including Parmigiano-Reggiano, Grana Padano and Gruyère. This was followed by a court of appeal challenge over the right to sell Roquefort in 2002. Roquefort is the world's oldest and most popular blue cheese and is made from raw ewe's milk. A special review by Food Standards Australia New Zealand (FSANZ) followed and Roquefort was finally declared "safe" to sell three years later.

The crucial question for the future is whether FSANZ will recognise the opportunity to work with local specialist cheesemakers and importers to change the regulations or continue to limit choice because of the commercial interests of large dairy companies focused on mass-produced industrial cheeses made from cooperative milk for supermarkets and export.

PASTEURISATION

The main aim of pasteurisation is to destroy pathogenic micro-organisms that might threaten public health. The French scientist Louis Pasteur discovered the method while he was experimenting on grape juice and wine fermentation during the mid-1800s. Its application to milk processing was almost a matter of chance.

In those days, milk hygiene was unreliable. Little was known about the sources of milk contamination, refrigeration was not widely available and bovine diseases, such as brucellosis and tuberculosis, were not controlled. Most communities and farms had their own milk supplies. Fresh milk for drinking was usually boiled or scalded, and cheese was made in limited quantities, either on the farm or in small dairies, using fresh raw milk from a small number of animals. Cheese was preserved by fermentation, as it had been since antiquity.

Milk quality inevitably varies from farm to farm and without pasteurisation a dangerous micro-organism from just one bad batch could contaminate the whole milk pool. This is why there is a very good reason to promote pasteurisation as a vital part of hygiene control in the mass collection of cooperative milk and processing of dairy products, including cheese, but one of the problems with mandatory pasteurisation is that it provides no incentive for a farm to produce milk of exceptional quality, but instead encourages bulk production. The question is whether specialist cheesemakers should be forced to adopt standards formulated for industrial-scale dairy processing. There are very good reasons for arguing that they should not.

The starting point for making any raw milk cheese is the selection of good, clean, raw milk from healthy animals. If milk from an individual farm is regularly monitored to ensure it is clean, there should be no need to pasteurise it for making cheese.

Catherine Adams is one of the most talented pastry chefs in the country. With her great palate, Catherine also has a very good understanding of the role of texture and, more importantly, how a dessert comes together to express its ingredients, so like the rest of the Rockpool Bar & Grill menu, her desserts reflect the best of the seasons. I often find in restaurants that if you close your eyes and eat the dessert, apart from being sweet, you would struggle to say what was in it. Not with Catherine's. Her desserts are produce, flavour and texture driven, and in the end you taste what she has lovingly put into them. Here she shares some of our favourite Rockpool Bar & Grill desserts.

A MEMORABLE ENDING

Catherine Adams is the Rockpool Group Pastry Creative Director and she does an amazing job of it. She has great skill, patience and an extraordinary ability to teach and, most importantly, she has a great palate and an ability to marry what she does with every restaurant we do together. You can be assured that all the recipes work. Such is Catherine's dedication to perfection that as she finished each recipe she gave it to the girls at head office to go home and make it as their homework. There would be a tasting the next day and she would workshop anything they didn't understand. She shares her wisdom here.

This is a little collection of recipes that I hope will help to establish what an experience at a Rockpool Bar & Grill might end with. It's a continuation of the philosophies on which the restaurants are based: freshness, produce, integrity, flavour, balance, simplicity. A lot of my initial thoughts and inspiration for the desserts I make come from within the main kitchens; walking around and seeing the produce and products that are being used and how dishes are being presented keeps me in step with what customers are enjoying before they get to dessert and enables me to maintain the continuity of the meal.

Neil has put a lot of faith in me to help create an experience for our diners that is world class. It's a hard task, but I in turn have a group of people who support me and make it possible to achieve that goal.

I would just like to make a note that at the restaurant we weigh everything when making desserts. We do not measure in tablespoons, cups or millilitres as I find there is quite a variation in the cups, jugs and tablespoon measures that are available in the marketplace and it depends on where they have been made as to their measurement. I also find people are open to variation as to how they use cups and spoons so weighing ingredients ensures more consistency across the board regardless of who is making the recipe.

At the restaurant, we make desserts in large batches. Some components of the following desserts may make more than is required for it can be difficult to size a recipe to correspond with the particular portion needed. I have offered storage advice for any leftover components.

MUSCAT DE BEAUMES-DE-VENISE GRANITA WITH MANGO ICE-CREAM & FRUIT SALAD

> Serves 4

"As soon as the Kensington Prides start coming into season, I naturally think of a pairing with Muscat de Beaumes-de-Venise, which works beautifully with tropical fruit as it is lighter and fresher than botrytis-affected wine. Over the years we have paired these two in many different ways, the combination of icy granita with fruit and ice-cream is a simple fresh variation and very achievable at home." Catherine

You will need to begin this recipe the day before.

MANGO ICE-CREAM

500 g (1 lb 2 oz) mango flesh
190 g (6 ³/₄ oz) caster (superfine) sugar
375 g (13 oz) pouring (single) cream (35% fat content)
3 egg yolks

Purée the mango flesh in a blender until smooth, then pass through a fine sieve, forcing as much purée through as possible. Discard what is left in the sieve. Add 90 g (3¹/₄ oz) of the sugar to the purée and mix to combine.

In a small heavy-based saucepan over medium heat, warm the cream.

Whisk the egg yolks and remaining sugar in a bowl until pale, then, while whisking continuously, gradually add the warm cream. Return to a clean pan over medium heat and cook, stirring continuously, until the custard coats the back of the spoon. Remove from the heat, and strain into a bowl sitting over another bowl full of ice.

Once chilled, stir through the mango purée. Refrigerate in an airtight container overnight.

The next day, churn in an ice-cream machine according to the manufacturer's instructions. Transfer to an airtight container and store in the freezer until firm enough to scoop. Makes 1 litre (35 fl oz).

MUSCAT DE BEAUMES-DE-VENISE GRANITA

75 g (2²/₃ oz) caster (superfine) sugar
375 g (13 oz) Muscat de Beaumes-de-Venise (see note)
juice of 1 lime

In a heavy-based saucepan over low heat, combine the sugar and 300 g (10¹/₂ oz) of water and cook, stirring until the sugar has dissolved, then increase the heat and bring to a boil. Remove from the heat and set aside to cool to room temperature.

Place the wine, lime juice and cooled sugar syrup in a wide-based container and stir to combine. The wider the container the better, as you want the level of the granita mixture to be quite shallow so it will freeze faster. Freeze for about 1 hour or until it begins to harden. Stir the mixture with a fork to break up the ice crystals, then return to the freezer. Give it a stir with a fork every 30 minutes for about 3 hours or until frozen.

NOTE

Muscat de Beaumes-de-Venise is available from good wine stores and online.

»

MUSCAT DE BEAUMES-DE-VENISE GRANITA WITH MANGO ICE-CREAM & FRUIT SALAD
CONTINUED

PINEAPPLE CHIPS (OPTIONAL)

8 x 2 mm ($^1/_{16}$ inch) thick slices of pineapple
220 g (7$^3/_4$ oz) caster (superfine) sugar

Combine the sugar and 500 g (17 oz) of water in a saucepan over medium heat and cook, stirring, until the sugar has dissolved, then increase the heat and bring to the boil. Add the pineapple slices and boil for 8 minutes. Remove from the heat and allow the pineapple to cool in the syrup.

Preheat the oven to 120°C (235°F/Gas $^1/_2$). Remove the pineapple from the syrup and lay flat on paper towel to absorb the excess syrup. Transfer to a baking tray lined with baking paper or a silicone baking mat. Dry in the oven for about 30 minutes or until crisp but not coloured. It helps if you turn the slices over once they start to dry. To test if they're ready, remove one and sit it on a bench for 3 minutes to cool, then bend to see if it is crisp. Store in an airtight container for up to 3 days.

FRUIT SALAD

$^1/_2$ small pineapple, peeled
1 mango, peeled
2 slices poached pineapple
4 mint leaves, finely chopped
4 lime segments, cut into 4 pieces
juice of 1 lime

Cut the fresh pineapple, mango and poached pineapple into 6 mm ($^1/_4$ inch) cubes and place in a small bowl. Add the mint and lime segments and juice and refrigerate until ready to serve.

TO SERVE

Divide the fruit salad between serving glasses. Place a scoop of mango ice-cream on top of the fruit salad, then cover with the Muscat de Beaumes-de-Venise granita. Crumble the pineapple chips into large pieces over the granita. Serve immediately.

CHOCOLATE PUDDING WITH CHERRY COMPOTE

"A little chocolate can go a long way, and that is certainly true for this pudding. It's very rich and intense. They should be baked just until the centre is still a little soft and creamy. Serve them straight from the oven."
Catherine

CHERRY COMPOTE

50 g (1³/₄ oz) dried sour cherries
110 g (3³/₄ oz) caster (superfine) sugar
1 teaspoon vanilla extract
¹/₂ cinnamon quill
20 ml (²/₃ fl oz) brandy
500 g (1 lb 2 oz) cherries, washed & pitted (see note)
10 g (¹/₃ oz) cornflour (cornstarch)
2 teaspoons balsamic vinegar

Combine the sugar, 60 g (2 oz) of water, vanilla extract and cinnamon quill in a heavy-based saucepan over medium heat, stirring occasionally until the sugar has dissolved, then increase the heat to medium–high and bring to the boil. Cook for 4–5 minutes or until golden caramel. Stir in the brandy, add the cherries and reduce the heat to medium–low. As the cherries start to release their juices, add the dried cherries. Gently turn, using a wooden spoon, being carefully not to crush the fruit. Cook for 10–15 minutes or until tender. Strain through a sieve placed over a bowl. Place the cherries in a container.

Return the juices to the pan over medium–high heat and bring to the boil. Boil for 4–6 minutes or until starting to thicken.

Mix the cornflour and 3 teaspoons of water in a small bowl. Add to the pan, whisking to combine. Boil for 2–3 minutes, ensuring it does not catch on the base. Remove from the heat and stir in the vinegar. Pour over the cherries and set aside until serving. You can make the compote 1–2 days ahead and refrigerate in an airtight container. Bring to room temperature before serving.

NOTE

The most efficient way to pit the cherries is with a cherry pitter. If you don't have a pitter, cut the cherries in half and remove the pit. The cooking time will need to be reduced for the smaller-sized cherry halves and simmering of the cherry juices.

CHOCOLATE PUDDING

185 g (6¹/₂ oz) dark chocolate, such as Valrhona Manjari (64% cocoa solids), chopped
20 g (³/₄ oz) butter, melted
55 g (2 oz) caster (superfine) sugar, plus 2 tablespoons extra for dusting
4 eggs, separated
pinch of table salt

Brush the insides of 4 x 250 ml (9 fl oz/ 1 cup) capacity ramekins (see note) with the melted butter, then dust with the extra sugar, rotating to coat evenly, and tap on a bench to remove any excess. Wipe rims to remove excess butter and sugar.

Place the chocolate in a large heatproof bowl. Bring a saucepan of water to the boil, then remove from the heat and sit the bowl of chocolate on top without letting the base of the bowl touch the water. Allow the chocolate to melt, stirring occasionally. Remove from the pan and allow to cool slightly but the chocolate should still be warm.

Whisk the eggwhite and salt in a bowl until soft peaks form. While whisking, gradually sprinkle the sugar over the eggwhite and whisk until stiff peaks form.

Using a whisk, stir the egg yolks into the warm chocolate, then stir in one-third of the eggwhite mixture. Using a rubber spatula, fold in the remaining eggwhite. Divide the mixture between the prepared ramekins. At this stage they can be refrigerated until you're ready to bake.

Preheat the oven to 200°C (400°C/Gas 6; it's preferable to use non fan-forced). Place the ramekins, evenly spaced on a baking tray and bake for 12–15 minutes or until set. They should have risen but still be moist inside. Serve immediately.

NOTE

If you do not have ramekins of this capacity, a teacup or smaller ramekins are fine. It is quite flexible what you bake them in.

TO SERVE

250 g (9 oz) pouring (single) cream (35% fat content)
1 teaspoon vanilla extract
1 tablespoon caster (superfine) sugar
pure icing (confectioner's) sugar, for dusting

Whisk the cream, vanilla extract and caster sugar in a bowl to soft peaks. Place in a serving bowl. Dust the chocolate puddings with the icing sugar and serve the vanilla cream and cherry compote on the side. Let guests break their puddings open and spoon in some compote and cream.

STRAWBERRY TART WITH BALSAMIC VINEGAR ICE-CREAM

> Serves 4

This is such a great classic combination. I remember tasting balsamic and strawberries for the first time about 20 years ago in a restaurant in the States. I thought it was so innovative, but later discovered that it was an Italian time-honoured use of their wonderful vinegar.

"Queensland's camarosa strawberries are, for me, the best," says Catherine. "They're usually in season from May to June and September to October. They're so delicious that I never want to do much to them, except add something crisp, something creamy and, for this tart, the perfect pairing of some aged balsamic vinegar."

Catherine is so right. It is the crispness, the creaminess and the depth of flavour of this tart that makes it so wonderful.

You will need to begin this recipe the day before.

BALSAMIC VINEGAR ICE-CREAM

270 g (9½ oz) milk

80 g (2 oz) pouring (single) cream (35% fat content)

35 g (1¼ oz) egg yolk

85 g (3 oz) caster (superfine) sugar

30 g (1 oz) aged balsamic vinegar

Heat the milk in a small heavy-based saucepan over medium heat until warmed. Meanwhile, whisk the egg yolk and sugar in a bowl until pale, then gradually add the warm milk, whisking continuously. Return to a clean pan over medium heat and cook, stirring, for about 12 minutes or until the custard thickens and coats the back of the spoon. Strain into a bowl placed over ice. Add the cream and stir until cooled. Refrigerate in an airtight container overnight.

The next day, add the vinegar to the custard and mix to combine well. Freeze in an ice-cream machine according to the manufacturer's directions. Transfer to an airtight container and store in the freezer until firm enough to scoop. Makes 500 ml (16 fl oz).

STRAWBERRY JAM

400 g (14 oz) strawberries, hulled & quartered

100 g (3½ oz) freshly squeezed orange juice (about 1 large orange)

55 g (2 oz) caster (superfine) sugar

juice of 1 lemon

Combine all of the ingredients in a saucepan over medium–low heat, stirring to dissolve the sugar. Increase the heat to medium and bring to a boil, then reduce the heat to maintain a steady simmer. Simmer for 45 minutes or until most of the liquid has evaporated. Spoon into warm sterilised jars and seal. Store in a cool dark place for up to 12 months. Makes 1 cup.

»

STRAWBERRY TART WITH BALSAMIC VINEGAR ICE-CREAM
CONTINUED

BALSAMIC VINEGAR DRESSING

100 g (3¹/₂ oz) balsamic vinegar
50 g (1³/₄ oz) caster (superfine) sugar
1 teaspoon vanilla extract

Place the vinegar in a small saucepan over medium heat, bring to the boil and cook for 2–3 minutes or until reduced by half.

Meanwhile, heat a separate small saucepan over medium heat until hot. Sprinkle in the sugar, a tablespoon at a time, allowing each addition to dissolve completely by itself without stirring before adding more. Cook until caramelised and a rich golden colour. Add 100 g (3¹/₂ oz) of hot water and bring to the boil, stirring to dissolve the caramel. Remove from the heat and add to the reduced vinegar. Stir in the vanilla extract. Cool and refrigerate in an airtight container until needed or for up to 2 weeks. Makes 125 g.

NOTE

You will only need 20 g (²/₃ oz) of the dressing but the recipe could be halved and any extra could be used to drizzle on ice-cream or a bowl of fresh strawberries.

TO ASSEMBLE

4 sweet pastry tartlet cases, blind-baked (see page 440)
80 g (2³/₄ oz) strawberry jam
60 g (2¹/₄ oz) crème pâtissière (see page 439)
40 g (1¹/₂ oz) softly whipped cream
160 g (5²/₃ oz) strawberries, hulled & diced
20 g (²/₃ oz) balsamic vinegar dressing
10–12 strawberries, extra, hulled & sliced
dried strawberries (see note), crumbled (optional)

Place the tart cases in the centre of each serving plate. Divide the jam between the cases and spread evenly over the bases.

Combine the crème pâtissière and cream in a bowl and mix until smooth. Spoon over the jam and spread evenly.

Combine the diced strawberries and balsamic vinegar dressing together in a bowl and spoon over the cream. Arrange the strawberry slices on top in a circular pattern keeping them in line with the edge of the tart and leaving the centre empty.

Place a scoop of ice-cream in the centre of each tart and sprinkle with the dried strawberries. Serve immediately.

NOTE

Dried strawberries are available from gourmet food stores or confectionery stores.

SUMMER FRUIT TART WITH ROSE CREAM

> Serves 6

"Summer fruit at the height of the season needs to be enjoyed and this tart would have to be one of my favourite ways of doing that. Baking the tart freeform means you can do away with a tart ring, and there's plenty of crisp, buttery pastry to enjoy with the tender, jammy fruit encased within. The fruit can be any combination you like, depending on personal preference and availability or it could just be one type of fruit." Catherine

SOUR CREAM PASTRY

210 g (7½ oz) plain (all-purpose) flour, plus extra for dusting
55 g (2 oz) fine semolina
20 g (¾ oz) caster (superfine) sugar
pinch of table salt
185 g (6½ oz) chilled unsalted butter, finely diced
60 g (2¼ oz) sour cream

Combine the flour, semolina, sugar and salt in a large bowl. Add the butter and, using your fingertips, rub it through the dry ingredients until the mixture resembles coarse breadcrumbs. Make a well in the centre.

Combine the sour cream and 45 g (1⅔ oz) of water in a separate bowl and mix until combined. Add to the well and, using a fork, toss the dry ingredients and sour cream mixture together until the flour is coated.

Turn the pastry onto a lightly floured surface and knead quickly and gently to bring it together. It should be a bit wet. Form into a disc about 20 cm (8 inches) in diameter, wrap in plastic wrap and refrigerate for at least 2 hours.

TO ASSEMBLE

4 apricots, quartered
3 peaches, cut into eighths
100 g (3½ oz) cherries, halved & pitted
120 g (4¼ oz) blackberries
40 g (1½ oz) unsalted butter, diced
55 g (2 oz) caster (superfine) sugar
120 g (4¼ oz) raspberries

Place a baking tray in the oven and preheat the oven to 200°C (400°F/Gas 6).

Roll the sour cream pastry on a lightly floured surface into a round about 4 mm–5 mm (¼ inch). Transfer to a baking tray lined with baking paper.

Combine all of the fruit, except the raspberries, in a bowl. Spread the fruit filling evenly over the sour cream pastry, leaving a 5 cm (2 inch) border. Scatter the butter over the fruit and sprinkle with two-thirds of the sugar. Fold the pastry edge up over the fruit to create a border, leaving the centre exposed. Refrigerate for 15 minutes to chill a little.

Brush the pastry border with water and sprinkle with the remaining sugar.

Place the tart and tray on top of the preheated tray in the oven — this helps the base of the tart cook — and reduce the oven temperature to 185°C (365°F/Gas 4–5). Bake for 30 minutes, then remove the tart from the oven and scatter the raspberries over the fruit filling. Bake for another 15–20 minutes or until the pastry is cooked and the fruit is tender.

Allow to cool for 5 minutes on the trays, then slide the tart onto a wire rack to cool to room temperature.

ROSE CREAM

250 g (9 oz) pouring (single) cream (35% fat content)
2 tablespoons caster (superfine) sugar
¼ teaspoon vanilla extract (optional)
½ teaspoon rosewater (optional)

Combine the cream, sugar, vanilla extract and rosewater to taste in a bowl and whisk to soft peaks.

Serve the tart with the rose cream on the side.

SYLLABUB WITH RHUBARB & STRAWBERRY COMPOTE

> Serves 4

"I like cream. Sometimes I'm guilty of having a lot of creamy desserts on the menu at the one time. The thing is, though, there are different degrees of creamy: light, heavy, baked and fresh, and then there are flavour and texture to consider. This is a fresh cream flavoured with white wine and sherry." Catherine.

RHUBARB & STRAWBERRY COMPOTE

1 bunch rhubarb, trimmed & washed (about 350 g/12 oz trimmed weight)
250 g (9 oz) strawberries, washed & hulled
230 g (8 oz) caster (superfine) sugar
20 g (²/₃ oz) freshly squeezed lemon juice
5 g (¹/₈ oz) gelatine leaf

Peel any tough strings from the rhubarb stalks with a vegetable peeler. Cut the stalks into 1.5 cm (⁵/₈ inch) thick slices and place in a bowl. Halve the strawberries or quarter, if large, and add to the rhubarb with the sugar and lemon juice. Set aside for 1 hour for the sugar to dissolve and the juices to be released.

Preheat the oven to 160°C (315°F/Gas 2–3). Transfer the fruit and juices to a baking dish, cover with aluminium foil and bake for 30–40 minutes or until the fruit is tender without being mushy. Remove from the oven, uncover and allow to cool.

Soak the gelatine in a small bowl of iced water. Measure out 200 g (7 oz) of the juices from the compote (reserving the remaining compote) and gently heat until hot, then remove from the heat. Squeeze the excess water from the gelatine and add the leaf into the hot juice. Stir briskly to dissolve the gelatine. Pour over the reserved compote and stir through. Refrigerate in an airtight container for about 1 hour or until set. You can store it for up to 4 days.

BISCUITS

60 g (2¹/₄ oz) unsalted butter, softened
80 g (2³/₄ oz) caster (superfine) sugar
1 egg yolk
¹/₂ teaspoon vanilla extract
finely grated zest of 1 lemon
pinch of table salt
70 g (2¹/₂ oz) plain (all-purpose) flour

Place the butter in the bowl of an electric mixer fitted with a beater attachment and beat on medium speed for 2 minutes.

Add the sugar and continue to beat for 5–8 minutes or until light and fluffy, occasionally scraping down the side of the bowl.

Combine the egg yolk, vanilla extract, lemon zest and salt in a small bowl, add to the butter mixture and beat for 2 minutes to ensure it is thoroughly combined.

On low speed, add the flour and mix until just incorporated. Transfer to a container and refrigerate for 1 hour.

Preheat the oven to 175°C (347°F/Gas 3–4). Roll pea-sized amounts of dough into balls and place on a baking sheet lined with baking paper, leaving a little space between each one. Bake for 5–7 minutes or until golden brown around the edges and golden in the centre. Cool on the baking sheet, then store in an airtight container for up to 3 days.

SYLLABUB

150 g (5 oz) dry white wine
40 g (1¹/₄ oz) pale, dry sherry, such as Seppeltsfield Flora Fino
40 g (1¹/₂ oz) freshly squeezed lemon juice
peel of 1 lemon
75 g (2²/₃ oz) caster (superfine) sugar
400 g (14 oz) pouring (single) cream (35% fat content)

Combine the wine, sherry, lemon juice and peel in a container, cover and set aside for 1 hour to infuse.

Strain and discard the peel. Add the sugar to the wine mixture and stir to dissolve. Add the cream and whisk to soft peaks. Use immediately.

TO SERVE

pure icing (confectioner's) sugar, for dusting

Divide the rhubarb and strawberry compote between 4 glass bowls or glasses, spoon over the syllabub, dust the biscuits with icing sugar and arrange them over the top of the syllabub. Serve immediately.

LEMON MERINGUE CUPCAKES

> Makes 12

"Of all the cupcakes we've had on the menu so far, this would have to be the most popular flavour. The curd has a nice tanginess to it so it sits happily with the cake and meringue without being dulled. When I started thinking about what recipes to put in this chapter this was probably one of the first things that got put on the pile. I gave the recipe to our exceptionally talented Administrations Manager, Lauren Treweek, with a supply of ingredients as well as a kitchen blowtorch and she went home after work that day and made a batch from start to finish and brought them in to work the next day for morning tea, thus establishing herself as our official recipe tester." Catherine

LEMON CURD

5 eggs
155 g (5¼ oz) strained freshly squeezed lemon juice
finely grated zest of 1 lemon
150 g (5½ oz) unsalted butter
265 g (9⅓ oz) caster (superfine) sugar

Whisk the eggs in a large bowl to break them up, then strain through a sieve.

Combine the lemon juice and zest, butter and sugar in a heavy-based saucepan over medium heat, stirring until the butter has melted and the sugar has dissolved. Add a little of the hot lemon mixture to the beaten egg to warm it up, then, while whisking continuously, gradually add back into the remaining lemon mixture in the pan. Cook, stirring continuously and scraping the base with a wooden spoon, for 7–8 minutes or until it has thickened and coats the back of the spoon. Do not allow to boil or it will curdle. Pour into a container and cool. Cover and refrigerate for 1 hour or until chilled.

Makes 600 g (1 lb 5 oz). This recipe makes more than you will need. You can keep the extra curd in the refrigerator for up to 2 weeks.

»

LEMON MERINGUE CUPCAKES
CONTINUED

CUPCAKES

155 g (5$^{1}/_{2}$ oz) unsalted butter, at room temperature
155 g (5$^{1}/_{2}$ oz) caster (superfine) sugar
2 eggs
1 teaspoon vanilla extract
155 g (5$^{1}/_{2}$ oz) self-raising (self-rising) flour
75 g (2$^{2}/_{3}$ oz) milk

Preheat the oven to 185°C (365°F/Gas 4–5) and line a 12-hole, 125 ml (4 fl oz/$^{1}/_{2}$ cup) capacity muffin tin with paper cases.

Place the butter in the bowl of an electric mixer fitted with a paddle attachment and beat on medium speed for 2 minutes. Add the sugar and beat on medium–high speed for 5–8 minutes or until light and fluffy, stopping the mixer occasionally to scrape down the side of the bowl.

Add the eggs, one at a time, beating well after each addition and until the batter looks smooth, about 2–3 minutes, then add the vanilla extract and beat to combine.

While beating on low speed, add the flour and milk alternately, each in 3 batches, and beat until just combined.

Divide the batter evenly between the paper cases and smooth the tops. Bake for 15–20 minutes or until dark golden brown and the cupcakes spring back when their centres are lightly touched. Cool in the tin for 10 minutes, then turn out onto a wire rack to cool until you can handle them.

ITALIAN MERINGUE

120 g (4$^{1}/_{4}$ oz) caster (superfine) sugar
70 g (2$^{1}/_{2}$ oz) eggwhite
small pinch of cream of tartar

Combine the sugar and 40 g (1$^{1}/_{2}$ oz) of water in a small saucepan over medium heat and cook, stirring until the sugar has dissolved, then increase the heat to medium–high, brush down the side of the pan with a wet pastry brush to remove any residual sugar crystals and cook, without stirring, until the sugar reaches 121°C (250°F) on a candy thermometer.

Meanwhile, place the eggwhite and cream of tartar in the bowl of an electric mixer fitted with a whisk attachment and whisk until soft peaks form, then, while whisking continuously on medium speed, steadily pour the hot sugar syrup down the side of the bowl of the mixer (not on the whisk) into the eggwhite. Continue to whisk on medium speed until cooled and the meringue is thick and glossy, about 10–12 minutes. Place in a piping bag fitted with a small plain nozzle and use immediately.

TO SERVE

150 g (5$^{1}/_{2}$ oz) lemon curd
pure icing (confectioner's) sugar, for dusting

Cut a hole from the centre of each cupcake. It should be big enough to hold $^{1}/_{2}$ tablespoon of lemon curd. Fill the holes with the curd and dust with icing sugar.

Pipe the Italian meringue onto each cupcake, covering the curd completely. Alternatively, spoon the meringue on top of each cupcake. Use a kitchen blowtorch to gently brown the meringue, if desired.

RICOTTA FRITTERS WITH
RICOTTA ICE-CREAM & CITRUS

> Serves 4

"We get beautiful fresh ricotta from a local cheesemaker. Its sweet milky flavour and soft curds are transformed into fritters and with an ice-cream of such depth and creaminess, it is hard to resist. The citrus compote adds the sparkle of acid to keep the freshness." Catherine

You will need to begin this recipe the day before.

RICOTTA ICE-CREAM

275 g (9³/₄ oz) pouring (single) cream (35% fat content)

¹/₂ vanilla bean, split & seeds scraped

finely grated zest of 1 lemon

5 egg yolks

180 g (6¹/₃ oz) caster (superfine) sugar

¹/₄ teaspoon table salt

250 g (9 oz) fresh ricotta

110 g (3³/₄ oz) double (thick) cream (55% fat content)

50 g (1³/₄ oz) mixed candied peel

Heat the cream, vanilla bean and seeds and lemon zest in a heavy-based saucepan over medium heat until hot. Remove from the heat, cover and set aside for 2 hours to infuse. Uncover and heat over medium heat until hot.

Whisk the egg yolks, sugar and salt in a bowl until pale, then, while whisking continuously, gradually add the hot cream mixture. Return to a clean pan over medium heat and cook, stirring, for 6–8 minutes or until the custard thickens and coats the back of the spoon. Strain into a bowl sitting over ice and cool.

Place the ricotta and cream in a food processor and pulse to just combine. Stir into the cooled custard, place in an airtight container and refrigerate overnight.

The next day, freeze the ice-cream in an ice-cream machine according to the manufacturer's instructions — just before it's finished churning, add the candied peel. Transfer to a container and freeze for about 4 hours or until firm enough to scoop. Makes 750 ml (26 fl oz).

»

RICOTTA FRITTERS WITH
RICOTTA ICE-CREAM & CITRUS
CONTINUED

RICOTTA FRITTER BATTER

250 g (9 oz) fresh ricotta
40 g (1 1/2 oz) plain (all-purpose) flour
7 g (1/4 oz) baking powder
pinch of table salt
2 eggs
1/4 teaspoon vanilla extract
finely grated zest of 1 lemon
1/2 teaspoon brandy

If the ricotta has a lot of moisture in it, place it in a sieve sitting over a bowl and refrigerate for a few hours to drain. To speed up the draining process, cover the ricotta with a piece of plastic wrap and place something heavy on top of it. Discard the liquid.

Sift the flour, baking powder and salt together into a small bowl.

Place the ricotta, eggs, vanilla extract, lemon zest and brandy in the bowl of an electric mixer fitted with a whisk attachment and whisk for 3–5 minutes or until combined. Fold in the flour mixture until just combined. Transfer to a clean bowl, cover and refrigerate until needed or for up to 6 hours.

CITRUS SALAD

165 g (5 3/4 oz) caster (superfine) sugar
4 cumquats, unpeeled, sliced into 5 mm (1/4 inch) thick slices, seeds removed
2 teaspoons lemon juice
1/2 cinnamon quill, lightly toasted
60 g (2 oz) orange juice
1/2 teaspoon orange blossom water
2 oranges
2 mandarins
2 blood oranges
2 mint leaves, finely chopped

Combine 110 g (3 3/4 oz) of the sugar and 125 g (4 oz) of water in a heavy-based saucepan over medium heat and stir until the sugar dissolves. Bring to the boil, add the cumquat slices, reduce the heat and simmer for about 15 minutes or until the cumquat is translucent and the syrup has thickened. Remove from the heat and cool.

Combine the remaining sugar, the lemon juice, cinnamon quill and 40 g (1 1/2 oz) of water in a small saucepan over low heat and stir until the sugar has dissolved, then increase the heat and bring to the boil. Remove from the heat and cool. Add the orange juice and orange blossom water and remove the cinnamon quill.

Peel and segment the oranges, mandarins and blood oranges (see glossary). Combine the citrus segments, mint, cumquat slices and 2 tablespoons of cumquat syrup, and the orange syrup in a bowl and mix to coat. Set aside until ready to serve.

TO SERVE

vegetable oil, for deep-frying
icing (confectioner's) sugar, for dusting

Heat 5 cm (2 inches) of the oil in a heavy-based pan over medium heat to 170°C (325°F/Gas 3). To test if the oil is hot enough, drop 1 teaspoon of ricotta fritter batter into the oil; the oil should bubble vigorously around the batter and the batter should puff up. Carefully drop 1-heaped-teaspoon amounts of batter into the oil. Cook the fritters, 3–4 at a time, turning with a slotted spoon, for 20–30 seconds or until golden all over. Drain on paper towel.

Dust the fritters with the icing sugar. Divide the citrus salad between bowls, top with a scoop of ricotta ice-cream and serve the warm fritters on the side.

PASSIONFRUIT PAVLOVA

> Serves 8

I'm totally biased but I think this is the best pav in the world. It also does nothing to clear up the argument that the pav is in fact from New Zealand and not Australia. You see Catherine is a New Zealander (although we're claiming her as our own). I have often heard New Zealand customers say, "I don't care if the pav is Australian or New Zealand, but this one must have been cooked by a New Zealander because it is so fabulous!"

PASSIONFRUIT CURD

4 egg yolks
50 g (1³/₄ oz) unsalted butter, cubed
100 g (3¹/₂ oz) caster (superfine) sugar
80 g (2³/₄ oz) passionfruit pulp
(about 4–5 passionfruit)
1¹/₂ teaspoons lime juice

Place the egg yolks in a medium bowl and whisk to combine.

Combine the butter, sugar and passionfruit pulp in a small heavy-based saucepan over low heat and stir until the butter has melted and the sugar has dissolved. Whisk one-third into the whisked egg yolks, then add back to the remaining butter mixture in the pan. Cook, stirring continuously, until it has thickened and coats the back of the spoon. Do not allow to boil.

Remove from the heat and stir through the lime juice. Pass through a coarse sieve into a bowl. Press a piece of plastic wrap onto the surface of the curd and refrigerate for 1 hour or until chilled.

PAVLOVA

315 g (11¹/₁₀ oz) eggwhites
pinch of table salt
525 g (1 lb 2¹/₂ oz) caster (superfine) sugar
3 teaspoons cornflour (cornstarch)
2 teaspoons vanilla extract
3 teaspoons white vinegar

Preheat the oven to 200°C (400°F/Gas 6). Trace a 24 cm (9¹/₂ inch) diameter circle on a sheet of baking paper, turn the paper over and place on a baking tray.

Place the eggwhite and salt in the bowl of an electric mixer fitted with a whisk attachment and whisk on low speed until they start to break up, then increase the speed to medium–low and whisk until soft peaks form.

Add one-third of the sugar and whisk until the peaks become a little firmer but not stiff, then add the remaining sugar, 1 tablespoon at time, whisking continuously. Once all the sugar has been added, increase the speed to medium–high and whisk for 2–3 minutes or until stiff peaks form. Fold through the cornflour, vanilla extract and vinegar until just combined. Spoon onto the prepared baking tray to form a round, using the circle as a guide, making the edges slightly higher than the centre.

Reduce the oven temperature to 160°C (315°F/Gas 2–3) and bake the pavlova for 25 minutes. Turn the oven off and leave the pavlova in the oven for 10 minutes, then remove from the oven and allow to cool to room temperature.

TO SERVE

1 kg (2 lb 4 oz) pouring (single) cream (35% fat content)
¹/₂ teaspoon vanilla extract
2 tablespoons caster (superfine) sugar
pulp of 4 passionfruit

Combine the cream, vanilla extract and sugar in a large bowl and whisk until stiff peaks form. Fold through the passionfruit curd until just combined.

Gently peel off the baking paper from the pavlova. Place the pavlova on a serving plate, spoon the cream mixture on top, then spoon over the passionfruit pulp.

RICE PUDDING WITH APRICOTS & CANDIED ALMONDS

> Serves 8

"By gently baking the apricots in a syrup, the flesh becomes luscious and tender without turning to pulp, the acid is brightened and the sweetness balanced. The apricot flavour really comes alive." Catherine

RICE PUDDING

150 g (5½ oz) short-grain rice
1.2 kg (2 lb 10 oz) milk
150 g (5½ oz) caster (superfine) sugar
1 teaspoon vanilla extract
30 g (1 oz) rosewater (optional)
4 egg yolks

Combine the rice and 350 g (12 oz) of water in a heavy-based saucepan over medium heat and bring to the boil. Reduce the heat to low and simmer until the water has been absorbed. Add the milk, stir to combine, increase the heat and bring to the boil, then reduce the heat to low and simmer for 7–8 minutes or until the rice is soft — there should still be a lot of liquid left in the pan. Stir in the sugar until dissolved, then stir in the vanilla extract and rosewater.

Whisk the egg yolks for 2 minutes in a bowl until pale, then, using a ladle, add about 1 cup rice to the egg yolk and whisk to combine. Add to the remaining rice mixture in the pan and cook, stirring continuously, for about 3 minutes or until thickened. Do not let it boil or it will curdle. Spoon into 250 ml (9 fl oz/1 cup) capacity serving bowls and refrigerate for 1 hour to chill and set.

BAKED APRICOTS

1 chamomile tea bag
1 vanilla bean, split & seeds scraped
330 g (11⅔ oz) caster (superfine) sugar
8 apricots, halved

Preheat the oven to 160°C (315°F/Gas 2–3).

Place the tea bag, vanilla bean and seeds and 250 g (9 oz) of water in a small saucepan over medium heat and bring to the boil. Add the sugar and stir to dissolve. Reduce the heat to low and simmer for 5 minutes.

Place the apricots, cut-side down, in a single layer in 2 large baking dishes and pour over the hot chamomile syrup including the tea bag and vanilla bean. Bake for 10–15 minutes or until starting to soften, then turn the apricots over and bake for another 10–15 minutes or until tender. You want the apricots to retain their shape without being firm still. Set aside in the syrup to cool.

CANDIED ALMONDS

2 eggwhites
85 g (3 oz) caster (superfine) sugar
1 teaspoon vanilla extract
pinch of table salt
115 g (4 oz) flaked almonds

Preheat the oven to 150°C (300°F/Gas 2). Whisk the eggwhite, sugar, vanilla extract and salt in a bowl until soft peaks form. Add the almonds and gently fold through. Spread over a baking tray lined with baking paper. Bake for 20–25 minutes or until golden, stirring frequently to ensure even colouring. Watch the mixture carefully in the last 5 minutes of cooking to ensure it doesn't burn. Set aside to cool and crisp up, then store in an airtight container for up to 4 days.

TO SERVE

65 g (2⅓ oz) caster (superfine) sugar (optional)

If desired, sprinkle the sugar evenly over each bowl of rice pudding, then, use a kitchen blowtorch, or place the puddings under a hot grill (broiler), to caramelise the sugar.

Divide the baked apricots between the bowls and spoon over some of the apricot syrup. Sprinkle generously with the candied almonds and serve.

CRÈME RENVERSÉE

> Serves 6

This is a beautiful textured dessert that I asked Catherine to make when we first opened Rockpool Bar & Grill Melbourne. I have very fond memories of it from the early eighties when I first tried it as a waiter at Gay Bilson's wonderful restaurant, Berowra Waters Inn. This was a watershed restaurant for Australia and also for me, having first dined there and then worked there for a short time; I still count it among my important early learning experiences. I was struck by the amazing texture of what is essentially a large crème caramel.

"We bake this in a cake tin," says Catherine, "and serve a wedge quite austerely on the plate with only some of the caramel from the tin spooned over, so it has to be baked just right every time — not too hard, not too soft. The caramel has to be just right, too — not too dark, not too light. For something so simple, it sets the standard and is a challenge to get it just so."

This recipe is based on one from Paul Bocuse's great 1976 book La Cuisine du Marché.

You will need to begin this recipe the day before.

800 g (1 lb 12 oz) milk
4 oranges, washed & zest finely grated (flesh reserved for another use)
220 g (7³/₄ oz) egg (not in shell)
145 g (5¹/₄ oz) egg yolk
250 g (9 oz) caster (superfine) sugar
¹/₂ vanilla bean, split & seeds scraped

CARAMEL

340 g (12 oz) caster (superfine) sugar

To make the caramel, combine the sugar and 200 g (7 oz) of water in a small saucepan over medium heat and cook, stirring, until the sugar has dissolved, then brush down the side of the pan with a wet pastry brush, increase the heat to medium–high and boil, without stirring, until the sugar has caramelised and is golden brown. Remove from the heat and carefully pour into a 26 cm (10¹/₂ inch) or 28 cm (11¹/₄ inch) round tin, swirling to coat the base and side evenly. Set aside to cool for 5 minutes.

Preheat the oven to 160°C (315°F/Gas 2–3).

Place the milk, orange zest and vanilla bean and seeds in a saucepan and bring to just a simmer. Remove from the heat, cover and allow to infuse for at least 20 minutes. Strain through a fine sieve and discard the zest. Measure out 750 g (1 lb 10 oz) of milk mixture, place in a clean pan and bring just to the boil.

Whisk together the egg, egg yolk and sugar in a bowl until pale and the sugar has dissolved, then, while whisking continuously, gradually add the hot milk. Strain through a fine sieve into a jug and set aside for 5 minutes. Skim any foam from the surface, then pour into the tin lined with caramel.

Place the tin in a roasting tray that is taller than the tin. Fill the tray with enough hot water to come two-thirds of the way up the side of the tin. Cover the tray with aluminium foil and pierce with a few holes to release the steam. Carefully, without splashing water into the custard, place the tray in the oven and bake for about 40 minutes. To test if it's ready, gently jiggle the tin; the custard should have a uniform jelly-like wobble. If the custard is not set, continue to bake until set. Remove from the oven, uncover and allow to cool slightly in the water bath. When cool enough to handle, remove the tin from the water bath and refrigerate overnight.

To serve, place a large plate on top of the tin, invert the plate and tin and remove the tin. Cut the crème renversée into wedges and serve with the caramel spooned over.

WARM RHUBARB & STRAWBERRY PUDDING

"I always think of this pudding as the self-contained pudding, with every spoonful yielding up warm cake, tangy fruit, creamy crusty meringue and melting crunchy praline, all generously doused with vanilla sauce."
Catherine

RHUBARB & STRAWBERRY COMPOTE

1 bunch rhubarb, trimmed (about 350 g/12 oz trimmed weight)
250 g (9 oz) strawberries, hulled
230 g (8 oz) caster (superfine) sugar
20 g (2/3 oz) freshly squeezed lemon juice

Peel any tough strings from the rhubarb stalks with a vegetable peeler. Cut the stalks into 1.5 cm (5/8 inch) thick slices and place in a bowl. Halve the strawberries or quarter, if large, and add to the rhubarb with the sugar and lemon juice. Set aside for 1 hour for the sugar to dissolve and the juices to be released.

Preheat the oven to 160°C (315°F/Gas 2–3). Transfer the fruit and juices to a baking dish, cover with aluminium foil and bake for 30–40 minutes or until the fruit is tender without being mushy. Remove from the oven, uncover and allow to cool. Refrigerate in an airtight container until ready to use. Store it for up to 4 days.

VANILLA CAKE ·

50 g (1 3/4 oz) unsalted butter, plus extra for greasing
1 teaspoon vanilla extract
60 g (2 1/4 oz) plain (all-purpose) flour
small pinch of table salt
2 x 60 g (2 1/4 oz) eggs
60 g (2 1/4 oz) caster (superfine) sugar

Preheat the oven to 180°C (350°F/Gas 4). Grease and line a 15 cm (6 inch) square cake tin with baking paper.

Heat the butter and vanilla extract in a small saucepan over medium heat until melted and combined. Transfer to a large bowl and set aside. Sift the flour and salt together into a separate bowl and set aside.

Place the eggs in the bowl of an electric mixer fitted with a whisk attachment and whisk on a medium speed until broken up. Add the sugar and whisk on medium–high speed for 4–5 minutes or until the mixture has tripled in volume. Using a spatula fold the flour mixture, in 3 batches, into the egg mixture, ensuring the flour is well combined after each addition.

Add one-quarter of the egg mixture to the melted butter and quickly mix together. Add back to the remaining egg mixture and fold through until just combined. Pour into the prepared tin. Bake on the centre rack in the oven for about 15 minutes or until golden and the top springs back when gently pressed. Remove from the oven and allow to cool in the tin before turning out. You can store the cake in an airtight container for up to 4 days.

> Serves 4

VANILLA SAUCE

250 g (9 oz) milk
250 g (9 oz) pouring (single) cream
(35% fat content)
$^1/_2$ vanilla bean, split & seeds scraped
6 egg yolks
85 g (3 oz) caster (superfine) sugar

Heat the milk, cream, vanilla bean and seeds in a heavy-based saucepan over medium heat until warm, then reduce the heat to low. Whisk the egg yolks and sugar in a bowl for 2–3 minutes or until pale. Gradually whisk in some of the warm milk mixture to warm the egg mixture. Then gradually whisk the egg mixture back into the remaining milk mixture in the pan over medium heat and cook, stirring continuously, for 6–8 minutes or until the mixture coats the back of the spoon. Strain into a bowl placed over ice to cool, and stir occasionally. Remove the vanilla bean from the strainer and return to the custard to continue infusing. Once completely chilled, transfer to a container, cover and refrigerate until ready to use. Store for up to 3 days.

CREAMY MERINGUE TOPPING

200 g (7 oz) milk
4 eggs, separated
90 g (3$^1/_4$ oz) caster (superfine) sugar
15 g ($^1/_2$ oz) cornflour (cornstarch)
pinch of table salt

Heat the milk in a small heavy-based saucepan over medium heat until hot.

Whisk the egg yolks and 30 g (1 oz) of the sugar together in a bowl for 3–4 minutes or until pale. Add the cornflour and whisk for 2–3 minutes to combine. Then gradually whisk in some of the warm milk mixture to warm the egg mixture. Gradually whisk the egg mixture back into the remaining milk mixture in the pan and, while whisking continuously, bring to the boil over medium–high heat, then reduce the heat to a simmer and cook for 1 minute. Remove from the heat and pass through a sieve into a large bowl. Press a piece of plastic wrap onto the surface of the custard to prevent a skin forming and refrigerate until ready to use.

Meanwhile, place the eggwhite in the bowl of an electric mixer fitted with a whisk attachment and whisk on medium–low speed. As they start getting frothy, add the salt and continue whisking until soft peaks form. Sprinkle in the remaining sugar, 1 tablespoon at a time, and continue whisking until stiff peaks form. Watch it carefully as you do not want the mixture to be dry and grainy. If it does start to become dry, increase the speed at which you add the sugar.

Stir the custard with a spatula to loosen it, then fold through one-third of the meringue. This makes the two mixtures of a similar consistency, which makes it easier to fold the remaining meringue through. Very gently fold through the remaining meringue until just combined. Use immediately or cover with plastic wrap and refrigerate for up to 1$^1/_2$ hours.

TO ASSEMBLE

$^1/_2$ cup praline (see page 441)
pure icing (confectioner's) sugar,
for dusting

Preheat the oven to 180°C (350°F/Gas 4). Cut the vanilla cake into 4 pieces and place in the base of 4 x 500 ml (17 fl oz/ 2 cup) capacity ramekins. Divide the rhubarb purée between the ramekins and spread evenly over the cake. Divide the rhubarb and strawberry compote between the ramekins. Spoon over the creamy meringue topping. Sprinkle over the praline and dust generously with some icing sugar. Place on a baking tray and bake for 12–15 minutes or until a rich golden colour.

Serve immediately with a jug of vanilla sauce. Let guests break open the pudding with a spoon and pour in the sauce themselves.

PRUNE & ARMAGNAC CRÈME BRÛLÉE

> Serves 4

"This is the classic combination of prunes and Armagnac combined with another classic, crème brûlée, which makes it that little bit more indulgent." Catherine

ARMAGNAC PRUNES

12 pitted prunes
500 g (1 lb 2 oz) freshly brewed hot black tea
250 g (9 oz) caster (superfine) sugar
1 teaspoon vanilla extract
finely grated zest & juice of 1 orange
finely grated zest of 1 lemon
80 g (2^1/$_2$ oz) Armagnac

Place the prunes and tea in a bowl, cover with aluminium foil and set aside for 1 hour to infuse. Strain and discard the liquid.

Combine the sugar, vanilla extract, citrus zest, juice and 250 g (9 oz) of water in a saucepan over medium heat and stir until the sugar has dissolved. Increase the heat to high and bring to the boil. Add the prunes, reduce the heat to a simmer and cook for 10 minutes or until the prunes are tender. Remove from the heat and set aside to cool in the liquid.

Strain the prunes, discarding the liquid. Place the prunes in a container, add the Armagnac, cover and set aside for at least 2 hours before using. You can store them in the refrigerator for up to 1 week.

VANILLA CRÈME BRÛLÉE

450 g (1 lb) pouring (single) cream (35% fat content)
^{1}/$_2$ vanilla bean, split & seeds scraped
1 quantity Armagnac prunes
20 g (^{2}/$_3$ oz) Armagnac
5 egg yolks
70 g (2^1/$_2$ oz) caster (superfine) sugar

Place the cream and vanilla bean and seeds in a saucepan over medium heat and heat until hot. Remove from the heat, cover and set aside for 1 hour to infuse.

Preheat a non fan-forced oven to 160°C (315°F/Gas 2–3). Coarsely chop the prunes and divide between 4 x shallow 250 ml (9 fl oz/1 cup) capacity ramekins. Press the prunes into the bases to help stop them floating up in the custard. Divide the Armagnac between the ramekins. Line a deep roasting tray with a folded tea towel and place the ramekins on top.

Reheat the cream over medium heat until hot. Whisk the egg yolks and sugar in a bowl until pale, then gradually add the warm milk, while whisking continuously. Strain through a fine sieve into a jug. Try and get as many vanilla seeds as possible into the custard. Set aside for 5 minutes. Skim any foam from the surface, then pour the custard evenly between the ramekins.

Fill the tray with enough hot water to come two-thirds of the way up the side of the ramekins. Cover the tray with aluminium foil and pierce with a few holes to release the steam. Carefully, trying not to splash water into the ramekins, place the tray

in the oven and bake for about 35 minutes or until set. To test if they're ready, gently shake a ramekin; the custard should have a uniform jelly-like wobble. If the custards are not set, continue to bake until set. Remove from the oven, uncover and allow to cool slightly in the water bath. When cool enough to handle, remove the ramekins from the water bath and refrigerate for at least 6 hours.

TO SERVE

50 g (1^3/$_4$ oz) caster (superfine) sugar

Sprinkle each vanilla crème brûlée with one-quarter of the sugar, then wipe the edges to remove any excess sugar. Use a kitchen blowtorch or place the ramekins under a preheated hot grill (broiler), and caramelise the sugar, but do not burn. You're aiming for a nice amber brown not black, which will make it bitter. Refrigerate for 5 minutes before serving. This will help the caramel set and crisp up.

SALTED BUTTER CARAMELS

> Makes 154 pieces

"You don't want to cook the caramel too fast; the faster it cooks, the less chance the flavour has to develop through caramelisation. It can be quite difficult having a thermometer that reads accurately, so I use two thermometers when I make it." Catherine

500 g (1 lb 2 oz) caster (superfine) sugar

250 g (9 oz) liquid glucose

435 g (15¼ oz) pouring (single) cream (35% fat content)

125 g (4½ oz) butter with sea salt flakes, such as Lescure, cubed

1 teaspoon vanilla paste

1½ teaspoons sea salt flakes, such as Murray River pink sea salt

---

Lightly grease a 22 cm (8½ inch) square cake tin with cooking spray and line with aluminium foil or baking paper. Spray again.

Combine the sugar, glucose and cream in a heavy-based saucepan over medium–low heat and cook, stirring until the sugar has dissolved, then increase the heat to medium and bring to the boil slowly. Cook gently until the mixture reaches 113°C (235°F) on a candy thermometer, then whisk in the butter, a cube at a time. Continue to boil, without stirring, until the mixture reaches 119°C (246°F). Immediately remove from the heat and whisk in the vanilla paste. Pour into the prepared tin and sprinkle with the salt. Set aside in a cool dry place for at least 3 hours or until completely cooled.

Remove the block of caramel from the tin and place on a chopping board. Using a serrated knife, cut into 1.5 cm (⅝ inch) wide strips, then cut each strip into 2 cm (¾ inch) pieces. Wrap in cellophane and store in an airtight container in a cool dry place for up to 5 days.

PASSIONFRUIT MARSHMALLOWS

These passionfruit marshmallows are so delicate and full-flavoured. They have been part of the Rockpool DNA for many years, and now belong to the Rockpool Bar & Grills too. The thing I love most about these marshmallows is their texture. Having grown up picking passionfruit off the vine for my mum's desserts, I think of this flavour as being so Australian. What a great way to finish a meal.

snow sugar (see note), for dusting

135 g (4³/₄ oz) strained passionfruit juice (from about 10 passionfruit)

15 g (¹/₂ oz) powdered gelatine

375 g (13 oz) caster (superfine) sugar

55 g (2 oz) eggwhite

pinch of table salt

Lightly grease a 22 cm (8¹/₂ inch) square cake tin with cooking spray and line with baking paper. Spray again and dust with a thin layer of snow sugar.

Combine the passionfruit juice and gelatine in a bowl and set aside to absorb.

Combine the sugar and 180 g (6¹/₃ oz) of water in a heavy-based saucepan over medium heat and cook, stirring until the sugar has dissolved, then increase the heat to high and boil rapidly until it reaches 125°C (257°F) on a candy thermometer. Remove from the heat and set aside.

Place the eggwhite in the bowl of an electric mixer fitted with a whisk attachment. Add the salt and whisk on medium–high speed for 1 minute or until frothy. Once the bubbling of the syrup has subsided, pour onto the passionfruit mixture and whisk until the gelatine is dissolved, then steadily pour the mixture down the side of the bowl of the mixer (not on the whisk) into the eggwhite until all of it is added. Continue whisking for about 5 minutes or until soft peaks form. Decrease the speed to medium and whisk for 5 minutes or until lukewarm.

Pour into the prepared tin and spread out evenly with a palette knife sprayed with cooking spray. Dust liberally with snow sugar, cover with aluminium foil and set aside in a cool dry place for about 3 hours or until set.

Turn the marshmallow out of the tin onto a chopping board dusted with snow sugar. Using a pizza cutter, cut into 2 cm (³/₄ inch) cubes. Roll each cube in snow sugar and store in an airtight container in a cool dry place for up to 3 days.

NOTE

Snow sugar is icing (confectioner's) sugar that has been treated with cocoa butter and starch. This means you can use it to dust goods with a high moisture content and it doesn't dissolve. It's available from baking and gourmet food stores. If you can't find it, simply sift together 90 g (3¹/₄ oz) pure icing sugar and 60 g (2¹/₄ oz) cornflour (cornstarch).

BASICS

SEMI-DRIED CHERRY TOMATOES

6 vine-ripened cherry tomatoes, halved
2 small garlic cloves, cut into 12 slices
1 tablespoon extra virgin olive oil
sea salt & freshly ground black pepper

Preheat the oven to 100°C (200°F/Gas ½).
Place the tomatoes, cut-side up, on a
baking tray. Top each with a slice of
garlic, drizzle with the olive oil and
season to taste with salt and pepper.
Roast for about 20–30 minutes or until
semi-dried.

**SMOKY SEMI-DRIED CHERRY
TOMATOES VARIATION**

The tomatoes are smoked on trays like
the potatoes in the salad of prawn,
calamari, octopus, mussels and clams
with rocket and smoky potato (see page
157) and you can use the same wood chip
method to smoke these over a resting
rack on an open barbecue. I use these
little smoked beauties on everything:
salad, with meats and fish and roast
chicken. They are a cracker, no doubt
about it, so just make them.

GREMOLATA

> Makes ½ cup

1 garlic clove, finely chopped
1 bunch flat-leaf (Italian) parsley, leaves
picked & finely chopped
finely grated zest of 1 lemon

Combine all of the ingredients in a small
bowl. You should have an even mix of
yellow and green.

TOMATO JELLY

> Fills a 22 cm x 11 cm tray

600 g (1 lb 5 oz) ripe tomatoes
sea salt & freshly ground black pepper
5 g (¹/₈ oz) gelatine leaf

Place the tomatoes in a blender or food processor, season to taste with salt and pepper and blend lightly until pulped. Transfer to a sieve lined with muslin (cheesecloth) placed over a container to catch the tomato water. Do not force the pulp through or squeeze the muslin as it will cloud the tomato water. Leave to hang overnight in the fridge. Discard the solids and collect the tomato water. You will need 100 ml (3¹/₂ fl oz).

Gently warm 80 ml (2¹/₂ fl oz/¹/₃ cup) of the tomato water in a small saucepan to blood temperature. Soak the gelatine in cold water until softened. Squeeze out the excess water, add to the warm tomato water and whisk to dissolve.

Add the remaining 1 tablespoon of tomato water and whisk to combine. Strain into a 22 cm x 11 cm (8¹/₂ inch x 4¹/₄ inch) tray. Refrigerate for 2 hours or until set.

PICKLED ONIONS

> Fills a 400 ml (14 fl oz) capacity jar

125 ml (4 fl oz/¹/₂ cup) rice wine vinegar
110 g (3³/₄ oz/¹/₂ cup) caster (superfine) sugar
1 fresh bay leaf
3 black peppercorns
4 small brown onions

Place all of the ingredients, except the onions, in a small saucepan and bring to the boil, then remove from the heat and set aside to cool.

Pack the onions in a sterilised jar and pour in the liquid. Use a small ramekin or small weight to make sure the onions are completely submerged. Cover with the lid and leave overnight to pickle. Store for up to 6 months in a cool dark place. Refrigerate after opening.

MAYONNAISE

> Makes about 400 g (14 oz/1²/₃ cups)

3 egg yolks
2 tablespoons freshly squeezed
lemon juice
sea salt & freshly ground black pepper
185 ml (6 fl oz/³/₄ cup) olive oil
185 ml (6 fl oz/³/₄ cup) extra virgin olive oil

Place a saucepan, large enough to hold
a stainless steel bowl, on a work surface.
Place a tea towel around the inside
edge of the pan and place the bowl
on top — this will hold the bowl steady
while you whisk.

Place the egg yolks in a bowl and lightly
whisk. Whisk in the lemon juice and
season to taste with salt and pepper.
While whisking continuously, slowly
drizzle in the combined oils. As the
mixture begins to emulsify, add the oil in
a thin stream. Don't let the oil sit on the
surface as this can cause the mayonnaise
to split. Keep whisking until all of the oil
is added and a thick mayonnaise forms.
Season to taste with pepper and check the
balance of salt and lemon juice. Store in
an airtight container in the refrigerator
for up to 1 week.

AIOLI VARIATION

Add 3 cloves of crushed garlic to the
whisked egg yolk with the lemon juice.

TOMATO & CHILLI RELISH

> Makes 1.25 litres (44 fl oz)

This sauce goes the whole nine yards. You can make it as hot as you like — just subtract or add chillies to achieve your desired level. You can use it as a sauce for just about anything you like — with barbecued seafood, on meat sandwiches and burgers, or as a base to pasta sauces and braises. You'll be surprised how fast you go through this sauce.

2 brown onions, finely chopped

4 garlic cloves, chopped

1 small knob of ginger, finely chopped

2 red capsicum (peppers), seeds removed & finely chopped

125 ml (4 fl oz/^{1}/$_2$ cup) olive oil

1 tablespoon sea salt

15 vine-ripened tomatoes, peeled, seeds removed (see glossary) & chopped

220 g (7^3/$_4$ oz/1 cup) caster (superfine) sugar

175 g (6 oz) soft brown sugar

juice of 3 lemons

2 cloves

1 cinnamon quill

8 small red bird's eye chillies, finely chopped

Combine the onion, garlic, ginger, capsicum, olive oil and salt in a large saucepan over medium heat and cook for 30 minutes or until syrupy.

Add the remaining ingredients and simmer for 1^1/$_2$ hours or until reduced to a jam-like consistency. Remove from the heat and cool. Spoon into sterilised jars. Store in the refrigerator for up to 1 week.

CROÛTONS

> Makes 2 cups

^{1}/$_4$ loaf of white bread

500 ml (17 fl oz/2 cups) vegetable oil

1 garlic clove

sea salt

Trim the crusts from the bread and discard. Slice the bread into 1 cm (^{1}/$_2$ inch) thick slices, then cut into 1 cm squares.

Heat the vegetable oil in a saucepan over high heat and add the garlic clove to infuse the oil. To test if the oil is the right temperature, add a cube of bread; the oil should start bubbling but the bread should not colour too quickly. Carefully tip the croûtons into the oil and cook, stirring continuously with a metal spoon, until golden. Strain and drain on paper towel. Season to taste with salt while hot.

TOMATO JAM

> Makes about 1$^1/_2$ cups

8 vine-ripened tomatoes
60 ml (2 fl oz/$^1/_4$ cup) extra virgin olive oil
$^1/_2$ onion, finely chopped
1 garlic clove, finely chopped
2 tablespoons white sugar
60 ml (2 fl oz/$^1/_4$ cup) red wine vinegar
sea salt & freshly ground black pepper

Preheat the oven to 180°C (350°F/Gas 4). Place the tomatoes in a roasting tray and roast for 30 minutes. Pass through a mouli (food mill).

Heat the olive oil in a large saucepan over low heat, add the onion and garlic and cook for 10 minutes or until softened and translucent. Add the tomato, sugar and vinegar and cook over low heat for about 1 hour or until the mixture is a jam-like consistency. Season to taste with salt and pepper. Spoon into a sterilised jar and store in the refrigerator for up to 2 weeks.

SALTED CHILLI PASTE

> Makes 250 g (9 oz)

You will need to begin this recipe 2 weeks ahead.

250 g (9 oz) long red chillies
35 g (1$^1/_4$ oz) sea salt

Chop the chillies into 1 cm ($^1/_3$ inch) pieces and combine with the salt. Place in a sterilised jar and leave in a cool dark place for 2 weeks. Store in the refrigerator after opening and use within 6 months.

PRESERVED LEMONS

> Fills a 2 litre (70 fl oz) capacity jar

*These are indispensable to have in the pantry.
Not only do they bring life to braises but they can
be used in salads and with barbecued meats and
poultry. They're perfectly at home with seafood
and are just as good with raw fish. I have also
included the quick version opposite because I
don't want you to get caught short and think you
have to wait six weeks before they're ready. The
quick version will not have the complexity of
flavour that the preserved ones with spices have
but they're really yum and make a great salsa.
Remember only use the rind, all the rest
is discarded.*

12 ripe lemons
195 g (6³/₄ oz/1¹/₂ cups) sea salt
1 tablespoon coriander seeds
3 cinnamon quills, roughly broken
juice of 3–4 lemons

Thoroughly wash the lemons in cold
water to remove their waxy coating.
Pat dry, then cut each lemon into quarters
without cutting all the way through,
leaving each attached at the base by
1 cm (¹/₂ inch). Place 1 tablespoon of salt in
the middle of each lemon. Squeeze each
lemon to close and place in a sterilised jar
big enough to snugly fit all the lemons,
packing them in tightly. Intersperse the
lemons with the coriander seeds and
broken pieces of cinnamon. Add the
remaining salt and enough lemon juice
to just cover, making sure no lemons are
poking out at the top or they will not cure
properly and will go mouldy. Seal the jar
with the lid and leave in a cold dark place
for at least 6 weeks.

To use the lemons, wash the preserved
lemon and remove all of the rind with a
sharp knife. Dice or thinly slice the rind
to use in an array of dressings, sauces
and dishes.

PRESERVED LEMON SALSA

> Makes about 1 cup

1 garlic clove
80 ml (2¹/₂ fl oz/¹/₃ cup) extra virgin olive
oil
juice of 1 lemon
finely chopped rind of 1 preserved
lemon
sea salt & freshly ground black pepper

Crush the garlic in a mortar with a pestle.
Transfer to a bowl, add the olive oil,
lemon juice and preserved lemon rind,
season to taste with salt and pepper and
mix well.

QUICK PRESERVED LEMONS

> Makes 4

4 ripe lemons
1 large handful sea salt

Thoroughly wash the lemons in cold water to remove their waxy coating. Fill a large saucepan with enough water to cover the lemons and bring to the boil. Add the lemons and sea salt and cook for 30–40 minutes or until soft when squeezed. Drain and set aside to cool. Once cooled, they are ready to use.

LEMON OIL

> Makes 1 litre (35 fl oz/4 cups)

finely grated zest of 8 lemons
1 litre (35 fl oz/4 cups) extra virgin olive oil

Place the lemon zest and olive oil in a saucepan over low heat and cook for 1 hour. Remove from the heat and set aside to cool. Strain and store in the refrigerator for up to 6 months. This is great in salad dressings or simply splashed over raw fish.

WHITE CHICKEN STOCK

> Makes 2.5 litres (87 fl oz)

1 x 1.6 kg (3 lb 8 oz) whole chicken

Rinse the chicken. Remove the fat from the cavity and discard. Place the chicken on a chopping board and, using a large knife or cleaver, cut off the legs at the point where the thigh and drumstick meet. Make a few slashes in the leg meat. Cut the wings off where they meet the breast. Cut down the side of the chicken so the back comes off the breast. Cut the back and breast in half and make a few slashes in the breast meat.

Fill a large saucepan with 3 litres (105 fl oz) of water and add the chicken pieces. Bring to the boil, then reduce the heat to a bare simmer and cook for about 4 hours. Skim any impurities from the surface during the cooking process. Carefully strain the stock through a fine sieve lined with muslin (cheesecloth). Discard the chicken pieces. Strain the stock through the muslin-lined sieve again, then set aside to cool to room temperature. Refrigerate for up to 2 days or freeze. Remove and discard the layer of fat before using.

RENDERED WAGYU FAT

> Makes 1¹/₂ cups

400 g (14 oz) Wagyu fat (see note)

Trim any excess meat from the fat and discard. Dice the fat into 2.5 cm (1 inch) cubes. Place in a small saucepan with enough water to just cover the base. The water prevents the fat from burning initially and will evaporate as the fat melts. Place the pan over very low heat and cook the fat, stirring occasionally so it does not catch on the base, for about 30 minutes or until all of the fat has melted. Strain into a heatproof container or jar. Use immediately or cool and refrigerate.

NOTE

You can buy Wagyu fat from select butchers, but you will need to order it in advance.

VEAL STOCK

5 kg (11 lb 4 oz) veal shanks, cut into rounds

15 garlic cloves

1 large red onion, finely diced

1 carrot, finely diced

500 ml (17 fl oz/2 cups) vegetable oil

3 sprigs thyme

3 fresh bay leaves

6 vine-ripened tomatoes, peeled, seeds removed (see glossary) & diced

Preheat the oven to 220°C (425°F/Gas 7). Place the veal bones in a large roasting tray and roast until well browned, turning once during cooking. Transfer to a saucepan large enough to fit them snugly. Pour a little water into the hot tray and scrape the residue off the base with a wooden spoon. Add this to the pan with enough water to just cover the bones. Bring to the boil over high heat, then reduce the heat to a simmer and cook for 30 minutes, skimming the scum from the surface regularly.

Pound the garlic and onion in a large mortar with a pestle for 5 minutes or until a rough paste forms. Add the carrot and pound for 2 minutes or until roughly pulped.

Heat the vegetable oil in a wok or deep-sided saucepan over high heat. Add the garlic paste and fry, stirring from time to time to stop it burning, until dark brown. It is vital that the garlic paste is dark brown but not burnt or this will impart a bitter flavour to the stock. Strain the paste through a sieve and discard the oil. Add the paste to the stock.

Add the remaining ingredients to the stock and gently simmer for 5 hours, skimming occasionally. Remove from the heat and set aside to cool. Skim the fat from the surface as it cools.

When it has cooled to lukewarm, very carefully ladle the stock through a sieve lined with muslin (cheesecloth) placed over a large bowl. Try not to squeeze or push against the bones as this will make the stock cloudy. Strain the stock again through the muslin-lined sieve into a container. Make sure it is completely cool before refrigerating. Freeze or store for up to 6 days in the refrigerator. After that time, bring the stock to the boil to kill any bacteria and you can store it for a few more days.

VEAL GLAZE VARIATION

Place 1 litre (35 fl oz/4 cups) veal stock in a clean wide saucepan over high heat and cook for 1 hour or until reduced to about 5 mm ($^1/_4$ inch) deep and beginning to thicken.

Strain into a smaller, shallow saucepan and continue to cook until reduced by half to a syrup-like consistency.

Strain through a fine sieve into a container and cool. Store in the freezer for up to 1 month. Makes about 100 ml ($3^1/_2$ fl oz).

CRÈME PÂTISSIÈRE

> Makes 2 cups

500 g (1 lb 2 oz) milk
120 g (4¼ oz) caster (superfine) sugar
½ vanilla bean, split & seeds scraped
25 g (1 oz) plain (all-purpose) flour
25 g (1 oz) cornflour (cornstarch)
6 egg yolks

Place the milk, half of the sugar, the vanilla bean and seeds in a large heavy-based saucepan over medium heat and cook, stirring occasionally, until the sugar has dissolved and the mixture is hot. Remove from the heat, cover and set aside to infuse for 1 hour.

Sift the flour and cornflour together into a bowl. Whisk the egg yolks and remaining sugar in a bowl for 3–4 minutes or until pale. Add the flour mixture and whisk for 2–3 minutes or until combined

Reheat the milk over medium heat until hot. Add a little of the hot milk to the egg mixture and whisk to warm through. Whisk the egg mixture back into the milk mixture and bring to the boil over medium–high heat. Boil for 1 minute. Give it a quick stir to ensure the custard does not stick to the base of the pan. Remove from the heat and strain through a sieve placed over a container. Press plastic wrap onto the surface of the crème pâtissière to prevent a skin forming and refrigerate until chilled. You can keep for up to 3 days, stored in the fridge.

SWEET PASTRY

This is sufficient pastry to make six tartlet cases or one 26 cm x 1 cm (10½ inch x ½ inch) tart case.

200 g (7 oz) unsalted butter, cubed

75 g (2²/₃ oz) pure icing (confectioner's) sugar

1 egg yolk, at room temperature

250 g (9 oz/1¹/₃ cups) plain (all-purpose) flour, sifted, plus extra for dusting

½ teaspoon table salt

Place the butter and sugar in the bowl of an electric mixer fitted with a paddle attachment and lightly cream — it does not need to be light and fluffy as this will make it difficult to handle later. Add the egg yolk and beat until well combined. Stop the mixer and scrape down the side of the bowl. Add the flour and beat on low speed until just combined and the mixture comes together to form a dough. Do not overmix. Remove from the bowl and form into a log about 5 cm (2 inches) thick. Wrap in plastic wrap and refrigerate for at least 2 hours.

Divide the pastry into 6 pieces. (If you do not need to use all the pastry, cut off the required portions and freeze the remainder, wrapped in plastic wrap, for up to 2 months.) Working with one piece at a time, roll out to 3 mm–4 mm (¹/₈ inch–¹/₆ inch) thick on a lightly floured surface. Refrigerate for 10 minutes to firm up a little, then use to line a 10 cm (4 inch) diameter tartlet case, trimming the edges. Repeat with the remaining pastry. Refrigerate for 2 hours.

To blind bake the tartlet cases, preheat the oven to 175°C (347°F/Gas 3–4). Line the cases with baking paper or aluminium foil and fill with dried beans, uncooked rice or pie weights. Bake for 15 minutes or until the dough looks dry and is light in colour, then remove the weights and baking paper and bake for another 5–8 minutes or until golden and evenly coloured. Remove from the oven and allow to cool in the tins. Gently remove the cases from the tins and store in an airtight container in a cool dry place for up to 3 days.

PRALINE

> Makes 2 cups

120 g (4¼ oz) almonds or hazelnuts
120 g (4¼ oz) liquid glucose (see note)
150 g (5½ oz) caster (superfine) sugar

Preheat the oven to 175°C (347°F/Gas 3–4). Spread the nuts over a baking tray and roast for 10–15 minutes or until golden and aromatic. Remove from the oven and turn the oven off. If using hazelnuts, wrap in a clean tea towel and allow them to cool, then rub off their skins. Coarsely chop the nuts and return to the oven to keep warm, but keep an eye on them as you don't want them to brown.

Meanwhile, place the glucose and sugar in a small heavy-based saucepan with just enough water to moisten the sugar, about 2 tablespoons. Cook over medium–low heat, stirring continuously to dissolve the sugar. Once the sugar has dissolved, increase the heat to medium–high and bring to the boil. Brush down the side of the pan with a wet pastry brush. Continue to boil, but do not stir until the sugar starts to caramelise. As the sugar starts to colour, decrease the heat to medium–low and continue cooking until the caramel is dark amber. Remove from the heat and quickly stir in the nuts. Scrape out onto a lightly greased baking tray and spread in a thin layer. Set aside to cool, then place in a food processor and pulse for 10–15 seconds or until finely crushed. Store in an airtight container in the freezer until ready to use.

NOTE

You can find liquid glucose in the baking aisle of supermarkets or in health food stores.

GLOSSARY

CHIFFONADE Roll the herbs tightly and place on a chopping board at a right angle to your knife. Cut across the leaves to produce thin strips.

CLARIFIED BUTTER Clarified butter is great when you want to cook things at a high heat for an extended time while retaining the flavour of butter (and not oil). Heat some diced unsalted butter in a heavy-based saucepan over low heat. When melted, simmer until the foam rises to the top. Remove from the heat, skim the foam off and drain through muslin (cheesecloth). This will keep for 6 months in the fridge and you can also freeze it.

CLEANING SQUID & CALAMARI Pull the tentacles out of the tube along with the ink sac and any insides. You can reserve the ink sac, if desired. Cut off the hard beak (its mouth), the tentacles and eyes. Set the tentacles aside.

COOKING CHICKPEAS OR DRIED BEANS Soak the chickpeas or dried beans in water for at least 2 hours or preferably overnight. Remove and discard any floaters, then drain. Place in a saucepan, cover with water and bring to the boil, then reduce the heat to a simmer and cook until tender. Drain and use as directed.

EGGS All eggs are at room temperature. Those who might be at risk from the effects of salmonella poisoning (the elderly, pregnant women, young children and those suffering from immune deficiency diseases) should consult their doctor with any concerns about eating raw eggs.

JULIENNE Otherwise known as "matchstick cut" — be sure to use a sharp knife.

OIL TEMPERATURE If you don't have an oil thermometer, you can use the bread test to check oil temperature. Heat the oil, then drop in a cube of bread. For 180°C (350°F), a cube of bread will take 15 seconds to turn golden.

OVEN GUIDE You may find cooking times vary depending on the oven you are using. For fan-forced ovens, as a general rule, set the oven temperature to 20°C (68°F) lower than indicated in the recipe.

PEELING TOMATOES Cut a small cross 2 mm ($^1/_{16}$ inch) deep at the base of the tomatoes. Bring a saucepan of water to the boil and add enough salt to make it taste like seawater. Blanch the tomatoes for 10 seconds, then refresh in iced water. Once cooled, remove the tomatoes from the water and peel off the skin — it should come away easily from the cross — while the flesh is still firm.

POACHING EGGS Fresh eggs are of the essence and make sure they are at room temperature. Bring a saucepan of water to the boil, then reduce to a gentle simmer. Break each egg into small separate bowls, then lower each gently into the water. Poach the eggs for 2 minutes or until the eggwhites are just set and the yolks are still runny.

QUENELLE A quenelle, in this book, refers to a shape and not an actual item of food as it is traditionally. To shape a quenelle, simply use two spoons of the same size to create an oval shape. Using one spoon, scoop a spoonful of the food being shaped and this forms the first side. Use the second spoon to press against one side of the existing scoop and this then creates the second side.

ROASTING NUTS Preheat the oven to 160°C (315°F/Gas 2–3). Roast different nuts separately. Place nuts on a baking tray and roast for 8–10 minutes, shaking occasionally, or until lightly coloured. Remove from the oven and set aside to cool.

SEGMENTING CITRUS Trim 1 cm ($^1/_2$ inch) from both ends, then sit the citrus on one flat end. With a small sharp knife, cut the peel away, from top to bottom, removing all the skin and white pith. Working over a small bowl to catch the juices, cut between the membranes, letting the segments fall into the bowl. Squeeze the membrane to release any remaining juice.

STERILISING JARS Preheat the oven to 170°C (335°F/Gas 3). Wash the jars and lids in hot soapy water. Rinse and dry them, then place in the oven for 10 minutes to sterilise. Turn the oven off but leave the jars in there to keep warm until you're ready to fill them. You can put them through the dishwasher if you wish but you must use them while they are still warm.

TOASTING SPICES There are two ways to toast spices, either in the oven or in a frying pan. It is easier in a pan as you can keep an eye on them. Toast different spices separately. Put the spices in a pan over medium heat and keep the pan moving to ensure the spices toast evenly and do not burn. When they become fragrant, remove them from the pan immediately to prevent the residual heat in the pan from burning the spices.

THANK YOU

This book is a reflection of three wonderful restaurants, the Rockpool Bar & Grills. Therefore I would like to thank my business partners Trish Richards and David Doyle for making it all happen, and John Alexander for having faith that we could do something special in Melbourne where Rockpool Bar & Grill was born.

Very importantly, I'd like to thank all the wonderful staff of the three restaurants who bring the spirit of these tremendous establishments to life each day with their hard work and dedication. Some staff need special mention: Khan, Catherine, Angel, Paul, Dan, Vanessa, Jeremy, Tom, Linden, Sarah, David and Sophie, thank you. And my gratitude to all the staff who contributed to this book by jotting down recipes as you worked — you know who you are, and part of you will always be in this book.

I also need to say a special thanks to all of our great suppliers, who make the restaurants what they are; the cornerstone of good cooking is indeed to source the finest ingredients. Also thanks for their words on their amazing endeavours. They are the unsung heroes.

Thank you to John Susman, seafood supremo and contributor, great friend and a man who can turn more than a few elegant words into an inspiring insight into how our fishermen work for us and the lengths to which they go to safeguard the quality of their catch.

The incomparable Sarah Swan who not only put heaps into this book but is an indispensable part of my professional life — thank you a thousand times.

Sue Fairlie-Cuninghame and Earl Carter, what a pleasure to work with two people who understand my vision so well. Love you both. Your style and focus are inspiring! I write cookbooks to hang out with you guys.

The Murdoch team: Kylie, Viv, Bel and Marcus — thanks for putting together such a wonderful book.

Most importantly, I want to thank my wife, Sam, and children Josephine, Macy and Indy. Running restaurants in three states of Australia means lots of time away from home. No one knows how hard it is on you, and as a family you never complain and only ever give me support. I know that I couldn't do it without you, so along with big thanks... lots of hugs and kisses!

INDEX

Page numbers in **bold** indicate a recipe.

A

Adams, Catherine 21, 27, 35, 47, 165, 389, 391, 397
agave plant 60
Age Good Food Guide 2007, Restaurant of the Year 29
aioli **431**
Alexander, John 17–18, 53
almonds, candied **415**
anchovies
    anchovy, baby cos & poached egg salad with
        green goddess dressing **156**
    anchovy butter **349**
    Ortiz anchovies with smoky tomato
        bruschetta **172**
animal welfare 79, 287, 310, 319
Applejack 61
aqua pazza 230
Armagnac 61
Armour, Brian 38
artichokes
    artichoke & mushroom bruschetta **167**
    globe artichokes sautéed with minced prawn
        on soft white polenta with Fontina **191**
asparagus
    white asparagus with shiitake mushrooms,
        slow-cooked egg, burnt butter
        & parmesan **209**
    wood-fire grilled asparagus bruschetta with
        tomato, ricotta & basil **174**
Australian Gourmet Traveller Restaurant Guide
    Awards dinner 27, 31
    New Restaurant of the Year 29, 31, 47
Avruga 142
awards 29, 31, 41, 47, 255, 367

B

balsamic vinegar dressing **398**
balsamic vinegar ice-cream **397**
barbecue sauce **342–3**
barbecues
    charcoal 257
    gas 257, 280, 292
bars
    speakeasy drinks list 63
    stock of spirits 59–61
basil oil **138**
beans
    clams steamed with jamón serrano, white wine
        & flageolet beans **205**
    green beans with creamy anchovy, chilli & lemon
        dressing & almonds **373**
    long-braised, melting Roman beans
        with herbs **354**
    preserved tuna, white bean, chilli & silverbeet
        bruschetta **173**
    seared crisp snapper with smoky cherry tomatoes,
        borlotti beans & green olive butter **234**
    white bean purée **147**
    wood-fire grilled swordfish with broad beans
        & olive tapenade **235**
béarnaise sauce, modern **345**
beef 17, 25, 29, 38, 297–301
    dry ageing 29, 297, 298, 313, 319
    grain-fed 297–8, 307, 319
    grass-fed 297–8, 313
    primary cuts 298
    secondary cuts 298
beef dishes
    corned Wagyu silverside with slow-cooked carrots
        & mustard sauce **247**

David Blackmore's Fullblood Wagyu hamburger
        with bacon, Gruyère & Zuni pickle **165–6**
    empanadas **185**
    grain-fed rib-eye on the bone **321**
    grain-fed sirloin on the bone **321**
    grass-fed fillet **315**
    grass-fed rib-eye on the bone **315**
    grass-fed T-bone **314**
    my steak tartare with chips **143**
    slow-roasted rib of beef **325**
    steak sandwich with tomato & chilli relish **179**
    Wagyu Bolognese with hand-cut fettuccine **225**
    Wagyu bresaola with mushroom toast **171**
    Wagyu chuck braised in red wine with gremolata
        and potato purée **246**
    Wagyu rump, topside or skirt **303**
    Wagyu sirloin, rib-eye or fillet **303**
beer, and sick cattle 311
beer batter **177**
beetroot
    beetroot jelly **136**
    beetroot, mâche & feta salad with pistachio
        nut dressing **136**
    roasted beetroot **136, 147**
    salad of baby beetroot, pickled onion, grilled
        zucchini, farro, feta & white beans **147**
Berowra Waters Inn 417
Black Angus cattle 319
Blackmore, David 128, 297
    Fullblood Wagyu beef 165, 246, 307, 310–11
    Wagyu beef bresaola 128, 171
Bloody Mary 72
blue nose mackerel escabeche **115**
Blue Water Grill 17
Blumenthal, Heston 38, 47, 358
Bombay Sapphire 59
Bordeaux wines 45
Bourbon 60
brand 21, 25, 29
brandy 60–1
bruschetta
    artichoke & mushroom bruschetta **167**
    Ortiz anchovies with smoky tomato
        bruschetta **172**
    preserved tuna, white bean, chilli & silverbeet
        bruschetta **173**
    sardines with chilli on bruschetta **172**
    wood-fire grilled asparagus bruschetta with
        tomato, ricotta & basil **174**
burgers 165
Burgundy wines 45
Burrawong 283, 287
butter, clarified **445**
butter lettuce, avocado, cherry tomato & jalapeño
    chilli salad **140**
butters *see* flavoured butters

C

cabbage & parmesan salad **379**
cabbage & potato gratin **365**
cabbage, braised **365**
cachaça 60
Café de Paris butter **350**
Calvados 61, 75
Campbeltown 59–60
Canadian whiskey 60
Cannavo, Peter 27
Cape Grim beef 298, 313
Caprese salad, modern-day, with burrata **138**
capsicum
    flathead ceviche **113**
    red capsicum sauce **248**
    smoked capsicum juice **66**
caramel
    crème renversée **417**
    salted butter caramels **424**

care philosophy 57, 79
carrots, organic, inspired by St. John **367**
Carter, Earl 25, 38
cauliflower & cheese **372**
caviar 125
cavolo nero & silverbeet, braised, with chilli, garlic
    & parmesan **355**
Champagne dressing **135**
charcoal ovens 255
charcoal-oven roasted king prawns **187**
charcoal-oven roasted pumpkin & sweet potato with
    garlic yoghurt & burnt butter **362**
charcoal-oven roasted squid & pork belly **200**
cheese 383, 385, 387
    cauliflower & cheese **372**
    mac 'n' cheese **361**
chermoula **251**
cherry compote **395**
cherry tomatoes
    roasted **222**
    semi-dried **428**
    smoky semi-dried **428**
Cheyne, Grant 21, 38, 53
chicken
    white chicken stock **436**
    wood-fired rotisserie chicken with Tuscan bread
        salad **280**
chicken farming 283
chickpeas, cooking 445
chiffonade 445
chilli
    butter lettuce, avocado, cherry tomato & jalapeño
        chilli salad **140**
    chilli & lemon dressing **373**
    chilli mayonnaise **177**
    pea, bacon & chilli broth with gnocchetti **192**
    salted chilli paste **433**
    sardines with chilli on bruschetta **172**
    tomato & chilli relish **432**
    wood-fire grilled eggplant, roasted pumpkin &
        chilli salad with goat's curd **148**
Chipotle Margarita 70
chips, fat, hand-cut **358**
chocolate pudding with cherry compote **395**
citrus, segmenting 445
citrus salad **408**
City Mutual Cocktail 66
clams 203, 256
    clams, steamed with jamón serrano, white wine
        & flageolet beans **205**
clarified butter **445**
classic lobster thermidor **243**
Clean Seas Aquaculture 99
cocktails 63
Cognac 60–1
condiments 341
confit duck with roasted mango **245**
Coorong yellow-eye mullet 271, 272, 273
corned Wagyu silverside with slow-cooked carrots
    & mustard sauce **247**
Courmadias, Jeremy 47
court-bouillon **247**
Craigie, Rowen 17–18, 53
cream of oyster, leek & potato soup **206**
creamed silverbeet **355**
crème brûlée, prune & Armagnac **421**
crème pâtissière **439**
crème renversée **417**
Crichton, Vanessa 21, 28, 29, 31, 35, 38
Crinis, Peter 53
crisp leatherjacket with 'crazy water' **230**
Croser, Brian 333
croûtons **432**
Crown, Melbourne 17, 25, 26, 27, 28
crudo of kingfish, ocean trout & tuna with horseradish,
    shallot, coriander & lemon oil **109**
cumin mayonnaise **120**
cured meats 127–8

D

Dalrymple, Laura 287
Danis, Khan 21, 28, 29, 35, 47, 267, 354
Dark & Stormy **69**
David Blackmore's Fullblood Wagyu hamburger with
    bacon, Gruyère & Zuni pickle **165–6**
desserts 391
    chocolate pudding with cherry compote **395**
    crème renversée **417**
    lemon meringue cupcakes **405–6**
    Muscat de Beaumes-de-Venise granita with mango
        ice-cream & fruit salad **393–4**
    passionfruit pavlova **413**
    prune & Armagnac crème brûlée **421**
    rice pudding with apricots & candied
        almonds **415**
    ricotta fritters with ricotta ice-cream
        & citrus **407–8**
    strawberry tart with balsamic vinegar
        ice-cream **397–8**
    summer fruit tart with rose cream **399**
    syllabub with rhubarb & strawberry compote **402**
    warm rhubarb & strawberry pudding **418–19**
Doyle, David 25, 35, 50, 71, 243, 342
    wine connoisseur 38, 41, 42–7, 71
Doyle, Greg 109, 267
dressings
    aioli **431**
    balsamic vinegar dressing **398**
    basil oil **138**
    Champagne dressing **135**
    chilli & lemon dressing **373**
    chilli mayonnaise **177**
    green goddess dressing **156**
    mayonnaise **143**
    palm sugar vinaigrette **377**
    pistachio nut dressing **136**
    spicy mayonnaise **176**
    spicy prawn oil **221**
    see also sauces
drinks
    Bloody Mary **72**
    Chipotle Margarita **70**
    City Mutual Cocktail **66**
    Dark & Stormy **69**
    House Martini **69**
    Italian Sour No. 3 **72**
    Jack Rose **75**
    Mexican Sour No. 1 **66**
    New Fashioned **74**
    Our Pink Lady **74**
    Rockpool Mai Tai **71**
    Rockpool Tonic **64**
    Scorched Almond Sidecar **67**
dry ageing 29, 297, 298, 313, 319
dry filleting 257
duck confit with roasted mango **245**

E

Easson, Paul 35
Eather, Mark 93, 266–7
eau-de-vie 61
eggplant
    eggplant salad **120**
    lentil & ricotta eggplant moussaka **248, 250**
    wood-fire grilled eggplant, roasted pumpkin
        & chilli salad with goat's curd **148**
eggs
    anchovy, baby cos & poached egg salad with
        green goddess dressing **156**
    lemon curd **405**
    lobster omelette with prawn sauce **199**
    mushy peas with slow-cooked egg **363**
    poaching 445
    white asparagus with shiitake mushrooms,
        slow-cooked egg, burnt butter
        & parmesan **209**
empanadas **185**
entrées, hot 183
escabeche marinade **115**

F

farming, sustainable 79, 287, 311
Felsted, Barry 53
fennel & herb butter **238**
Fernandez, Angel 185
finger limes 109
fish 84, 253
    buying 256
    cooking 257
    cutting raw 96
    filleting 256–7
    handling 256, 266–7
    overcooking 256, 257
    serving 255
    see also raw fish; seafood
fish dishes
    blue nose mackerel escabeche **115**
    Coorong yellow-eye mullet **273**
    crisp leatherjacket with "crazy water" **230**
    crudo of kingfish, ocean trout & tuna with
        horseradish, shallot, coriander
        & lemon oil **109**
    flathead ceviche **113**
    four raw tastes of the sea **117–18**
    fried fish burger with chilli mayonnaise **177**
    grilled swordfish steak **274**
    hiramasa kingfish tartare **100**
    hiramasa kingfish with smoked oyster
        dressing **117**
    lemongrass sugar-cured ocean trout **124**
    ocean trout with preserved lemon salsa
        & harissa **117**
    pickled blue nose mackerel, apple
        & potato salad **95**
    raw flounder with fresh horseradish **119**
    raw leatherjacket with cherry tomato & chilli **112**
    salmon tartare with olives **103**
    sardines with chilli on bruschetta **172**
    seared crisp snapper with smoky cherry tomatoes,
        borlotti beans & green olive butter **234**
    seared swordfish with red braised vegetables **101**
    snapper **263**
    Sterling Caviar with toast & crème fraîche **125**
    tuna tartare, Moroccan eggplant, cumin
        mayonnaise & harissa **120**
    tuna with ginger, jalapeño chilli & coriander
        dressing **118**
    whole John Dory **265**
    whole red mullet **268**
    wood-fire grilled swordfish with broad beans
        & olive tapenade **235**
Fish Forever (Johnson) 106
fishing, sustainable 79, 258–9, 272
flathead ceviche **113**
flavoured butters 347
    anchovy butter **349**
    Café de Paris butter **350**
    fennel & herb butter **238**
    garlic butter **349**
    green olive butter **234**
    herb butter **349**
    marchand de vin butter **351**
flounder, raw, with fresh horseradish **119**
four raw tastes of the sea **117–18**
Fratelli Galloni prosciutto di Parma 128
Free Range Pig Farming (McCosker) 291
Freeman, Eben 67

G

garlic, blanching 359
garlic butter **349**
garlic yoghurt **362**
Garreffa, Vince 330
gin 59
ginger beer, house-made **69**
Glenloth pigeons 288
globe artichokes sautéed with minced prawn on soft
    white polenta with Fontina **191**
grain-fed cattle 297–8, 307, 319
grain-fed rib-eye on the bone **321**
grain-fed sirloin on the bone **321**
grappa 61
grass-fed cattle 297–8, 313
grass-fed fillet **315**
grass-fed lamb 333
grass-fed rib-eye on the bone **315**
grass-fed T-bone **314**
green beans with creamy anchovy, chilli & lemon
    dressing & almonds **373**
green goddess dressing **156**
green lip abalone steak meunière **233**
green olive butter **234**
Greenham, Peter 297, 313
gremolata **428**
grenadine **75**
Guidera, Brendie 89

H

ham 127, 128
    clams steamed with jamón serrano, white wine
        & flageolet beans **205**
    ham plates 127, 128
    steamed mussels with Joselito jamón Ibérico,
        chilli, tomato & chickpeas **198**
hamburgers 165
harissa **344**
Henderson, Fergus 367
Hera-Singh, Garry 271
herb butter **349**
herb salad **255**
herrings 95
Hilliard, Grant 287
hiramasa kingfish 99
    crudo of kingfish, ocean trout & tuna with
        horseradish, shallot, coriander
        & lemon oil **109**
    hiramasa kingfish tartare **100**
    hiramasa kingfish with smoked oyster
        dressing **117**
hirazukuri method, of cutting raw fish 96
Hodges, Stephen 109, 267
Hogan, Paul 188
homogenisation 79
horseradish cream **344**
House Martini **69**
house-chopped salad **135**
Hunter Street, Sydney 35, 38

I

ice-cream
    balsamic vinegar **397**
    mango **393**
    ricotta **407**
iki-jime 266–7
Irish whiskey 60
Islay whiskies 59

Italian meringue **406**
Italian Sour No. 3 **72**

J

Jack Daniel's 60
Jack Rose **75**
Jamón Ibérico de bellota Joselito Gran Reserva 128
Jamondul jamón serrano Millenium Gran Reserva 128
Japanese beef 307, 319
jars, sterilising 445
John Dory, whole **265**
Jolliffe, Grant & Trudi 283
julienne 445

K

Katelysia clam 203
Keller, Thomas 38, 47, 361, 372
king prawn Russian salad with Avruga **142**
kingfish farming 99
Kinkawooka Shellfish Mussel Farm 197
kipfler potatoes sautéed with Wagyu fat & rosemary **359**
Kumamoto-style oysters 89
Kurobuta capocollo 128
Kurobuta prosciutto 128

L

La Cuisine du Marché (Bocuse) 417
Lakes & Coorong Fishery 271–2
lamb 333
    wood-fire grilled lamb cutlets with mint jelly **337**
leatherjacket
    crisp, with "crazy water" **230**
    raw, with cherry tomato & chilli **112**
lemon meringue cupcakes **405–6**
lemon oil **435**
lemongrass sugar-cured ocean trout **124**
lemons, preserved **434–5**
lentil & ricotta eggplant moussaka **248, 250**
lobsters
    classic lobster thermidor **243**
    grilled lobster with fennel & herb butter **238**
    killing 106
    lobster omelette with prawn sauce **199**
    raw lobster with chilli & mint **107**
lot-fed beef 297

M

mac 'n' cheese **361**
Mackay, Don 319
mango ice-cream **393**
marchand de vin butter **351**
Margarita 70
Marine Stewardship Council 272
Martini **69**
Marubeni 319
Maylands Farm 333
mayonnaise **143, 431**
    chilli **177**
    garlic **431**
    spicy **176**
McCosker, Lee 291
meat 17, 295
    composition 298
    cured 127–8

resting 301
    slow-roasted 301
    and stress 310, 311, 319
    tempering 301
    vacuum-packed 298
    see also beef; lamb; pork; veal
Melanda Park Pork 291
Melbourne 27
Melicertus latisulcatus 188
metabisulphite 188, 189
Mexican Sour No. 1 **66**
mignonette sauce **87**
milk 79, 387
mint jelly **337**
modern béarnaise **345**
modern-day Caprese salad with burrata **138**
molasses 60
Mondo di Carne pancetta 128
Murray–Darling Basin 271–2
Muscat de Beaumes-de-Venise granita with mango
    ice-cream & fruit salad **393–4**
mushrooms
    mushroom spread **167**
    sautéed mixed mushrooms **366**
    Wagyu bresaola with mushroom toast **171**
    white asparagus with shiitake mushrooms,
        slow-cooked egg, burnt butter
        & parmesan **209**
mushy peas with slow-cooked egg **363**
mussels 197, 256
    bouchot-style 197
    steamed mussels with Joselito jamón Ibérico,
        chilli, tomato & chickpeas **198**
mustard sauce **247**
my harissa **344**
my steak tartare with chips **143**

N

Nesbit, Todd 53
New Fashioned **74**
new-style prawn cocktail **139**
Nguyen, David 74
North American whiskey 60
nuts, roasting 445

O

ocean trout
    crudo of kingfish, ocean trout & tuna with
        horseradish, shallot, coriander
        & lemon oil **109**
    lemongrass sugar-cured ocean trout **124**
    ocean trout with preserved lemon salsa
        & harissa **117**
octopus 256
    octopus braised in red wine, tomato & olives
        with saffron pappardelle **219**
    salad of prawn, calamari, octopus, mussels &
        clams with rocket & smoky potato **157**
    wood-fire grilled baby octopus with olives and
        hand-pounded pesto **145**
oil temperature, bread test 445
The Old Waldorf-Astoria Bar Book 75
olives
    green olive butter **234**
    olive tapenade **235**
    salmon tartare with olives **103**
    warm salad of wood-fire grilled quail with smoky
        tomato & black olives **159**
onions
    onion rings **370**
    pickled onions **429**
    red onion pickle **166**

organic carrots inspired by St. John **367**
orgeat syrup **71**
Ortiz anchovies with smoky tomato bruschetta **172**
Otton, Sophie 47
Our Pink Lady **74**
Oxenham, Will 63, 70
oyster farming 89
oysters 256
    cream of oyster, leek & potato soup **206**
    freshly shucked **87**
    Kumamoto-style 89
    Sydney rock oysters 91

P

Packer, James 17, 53
Packer, Kerry 17
palm sugar vinaigrette **377**
Partridge, David 329–30
passionfruit marshmallows **425**
passionfruit pavlova **413**
pasta 213
    mac 'n' cheese **361**
    octopus braised in red wine, tomato & olives
        with saffron pappardelle **219**
    seared king prawns with goat's cheese tortellini,
        burnt butter, pine nuts & raisins **215–16**
    spanner crab, roasted cherry tomato & spicy
        prawn oil with semolina noodles **221–2**
    Wagyu Bolognese with hand-cut fettuccine **225**
Pasternak, David 109
pasteurisation 387
pastry
    sour cream **399**
    sweet **440**
peas
    mushy peas with slow-cooked egg **363**
    pea, bacon & chilli broth with gnocchetti **192**
pebre sauce **185**
Percuoco, Armando 192
Perry, Neil 18, 27, 31, 45, 49, 50, 189, 259, 267
Perth 53
pesto, hand-pounded **145**
Petaluma 333
philosophy 29, 47, 57, 79, 297, 391
pickles
    pickled blue nose mackerel, apple
        & potato salad **95**
    pickled onions **429**
    pickled vegetables **129**
    red onion pickle **166**
    zucchini pickle **166**
pig farming 291
pigeon with roasted red capsicum, red grape & radicchio
    salad **288**
Pignolet, Damien 350
pisco 61
pistachio nut dressing **136**
Pollard, Ben 35
pork 291
    charcoal-oven roasted squid & pork belly **200**
    wood-fired rotisserie loin of pork **292**
potatoes
    cream of oyster, leek & potato soup **206**
    hand-cut fat chips **358**
    kipfler potatoes sautéed with Wagyu fat
        & rosemary **359**
    potato & cabbage gratin **365**
    potato purée **360**
    salad of prawn, calamari, octopus, mussels &
        clams with rocket & smoky potato **157**
praline **441**
prawn farming 188
prawns 188, 197
    charcoal-oven roasted king prawns **187**
    globe artichokes sautéed with minced prawn on
        soft white polenta with Fontina **191**

king prawn Russian salad with Avruga **142**
new-style prawn cocktail **139**
prawn, nectarine & hazelnut salad **152**
prawn roll **176**
prawn sauce **199**
raw school prawns **100**
salad of prawn, calamari, octopus, mussels &
    clams with rocket & smoky potato **157**
seared king prawns with goat's cheese tortellini,
    burnt butter, pine nuts & raisins **215–16**
spicy prawn oil **221**
preserved lemons **434**
quick **435**
salsa **434**
Pride, Linden **47, 63**
product knowledge **57**
prosciutto **128**
provenance **258**
prune & Armagnac crème brûlée **421**
Puglisi, Andrew "Pugs" **189, 197**
Puharich, Anthony **297, 298**
Puharich, Vic **298**
pumpkin
    charcoal-oven roasted pumpkin & sweet potato
        with garlic yoghurt & burnt butter **362**
    wood-fire grilled eggplant, roasted pumpkin
        & chilli salad with goat's curd **148**

Q

Qantas **25**
quail
    quail farming **283**
    warm salad of wood-fire grilled quail with smoky
        tomato & black olives **159**
queen scallops with lemon & coriander **94**
queen scallops with preserved lemon salsa & harissa **94**
quenelle (shape) **445**

R

radicchio, cos & endive salad with palm sugar
    vinaigrette **377**
Rangers Valley **297, 319**
raw fish **83, 109, 266–7**
    crudo of kingfish, ocean trout & tuna with
        horseradish, shallot, coriander
        & lemon oil **109**
    cutting **96**
    four raw tastes of the sea **117–18**
    raw flounder with fresh horseradish **119**
    raw leatherjacket with cherry tomato & chilli **112**
    raw tuna **97**
raw lobster with chilli & mint **107**
raw milk cheese **387**
raw school prawns **100**
red braised vegetables **101**
red capsicum sauce **248**
red mullet, whole **268**
red onion pickle **166**
Reeves, Peter "Reevso" **203**
Reimers, Nicole **38, 41**
rhubarb & strawberry compote **403**
rhubarb & strawberry pudding, warm **418–19**
rhum agricole **60**
rice pudding with apricots & candied almonds **415**
Richards, Trish (Neil's business partner) **17, 18, 21,
    25, 29, 35, 38, 45, 49–50**
ricotta béchamel **250**
ricotta fritters with ricotta ice-cream & citrus **407–8**
Rockpool Bar & Grill Melbourne **17–18, 29, 35, 47**
    building **21, 31**
    funding **25**
    General Manager **31**

opening night **28–9, 31**
staffing **21, 27, 31, 47**
wine list **45**
Rockpool Bar & Grill Perth **53**
Rockpool Bar & Grill Sydney **27, 35, 38, 41, 255**
    Art Deco premises **38**
    and the GFC **41, 47**
    opening week **47, 50**
    staff **47**
    wine list **41, 42, 45, 47**
Rockpool Mai Tai **71**
Rockpool (Sydney) **17, 25, 49, 255**
Rockpool Tonic **64**
Rodely, Gary & Jo **91**
Rodgers, Judy **165**
Rodriguez Bros chorizo **128**
Romesco sauce **207**
Roquefort **387**
rose cream **399**
rotisseries, wood-fired **279, 280**
rum **60**
rye whiskey **60**

S

saffron pappardelle **219**
salads **133**
    anchovy, baby cos & poached egg salad with
        green goddess dressing **156**
    beetroot, mâche & feta salad with pistachio
        nut dressing **136**
    butter lettuce, avocado, cherry tomato & jalapeño
        chilli salad **140**
    cabbage & parmesan salad **379**
    citrus salad **408**
    fried squid, radicchio & chilli salad with Romesco
        sauce **207**
    green beans with creamy anchovy, chilli & lemon
        dressing & almonds **373**
    herb salad **255**
    house-chopped salad **135**
    king prawn Russian salad with Avruga **142**
    modern-day Caprese salad with burrata **138**
    pickled blue nose mackerel, apple &
        potato salad **95**
    prawn, nectarine & hazelnut salad **152**
    radicchio, cos & endive salad with palm sugar
        vinaigrette **377**
    salad of baby beetroot, pickled onion, grilled
        zucchini, farro, feta & white beans **147**
    salad of prawn, calamari, octopus, mussels
        & clams with rocket & smoky potato **157**
    tomato basil salad **379**
    warm salad of wood-fire grilled quail with smoky
        tomato & black olives **159**
    wood-fire grilled baby octopus with olives and
        hand-pounded pesto **145**
    wood-fire grilled eggplant, roasted pumpkin
        & chilli salad with goat's curd **148**
    wood-fire grilled vegetables & goat's curd
        salad **155**
salinity **271, 272**
salmon **257**
salmon tartare with olives **103**
salted butter caramels **424**
salted chilli paste **433**
sandwiches **163**
    see also bruschetta
sardines with chilli on bruschetta **172**
sauces
    barbecue sauce **342–3**
    crazy water **230**
    horseradish cream **344**
    mignonette sauce **87**
    modern béarnaise **345**
    mustard sauce **247**
    my harissa **344**

pebre sauce **185**
prawn sauce **199**
red capsicum sauce **248**
ricotta béchamel **250**
roasted tomato sauce **237**
Romesco sauce **207**
vanilla sauce **419**
white sauce **243**
see also dressings; mayonnaise
scallops **93**
    queen scallops with lemon & coriander **94**
    queen scallops with preserved lemon salsa
        & harissa **94**
    shucking **93**
    with ceviche dressing **93**
scampi ceviche **114**
Scorched Almond Sidecar **67**
Scottish whisky **59–60**
seafood **79, 83, 256–7**
    cured **84**
    frozen **84**
    live **87, 93**
    raw **83, 84, 93, 266**
    sustainable **258–9**
    see also fish
seafood dishes
    charcoal-oven roasted king prawns **187**
    charcoal-oven roasted squid & pork belly **200**
    clams steamed with Jamón Serrano, white wine
        & flageolet beans **205**
    classic lobster thermidor **243**
    cream of oyster, leek & potato soup **206**
    freshly shucked oysters **87**
    fried squid, radicchio & chilli salad with
        Romesco sauce **207**
    globe artichokes sautéed with minced prawn on
        soft white polenta with Fontina **191**
    green lip abalone steak meunière **233**
    grilled lobster with fennel & herb butter **238**
    king prawn Russian salad with Avruga **142**
    lobster omelette with prawn sauce **199**
    new-style prawn cocktail **139**
    octopus braised in red wine, tomato & olives
        with saffron pappardelle **219**
    prawn, nectarine & hazelnut salad **152**
    prawn roll **176**
    raw lobster with chilli & mint **107**
    raw school prawns **100**
    salad of prawn, calamari, octopus, mussels &
        clams with rocket & smoky potato **157**
    scampi ceviche **114**
    seafood stew with spicy mussel
        & saffron broth **237**
    seared king prawns with goat's cheese tortellini,
        burnt butter, pine nuts & raisins **215–16**
    spanner crab, roasted cherry tomato & spicy
        prawn oil with semolina noodles **221–2**
    squid ink ceviche **114**
    steamed mussels with Joselito jamón Ibérico,
        chilli, tomato & chickpeas **198**
    Sterling Caviar with toast & crème fraîche **125**
    wood-fire grilled baby octopus with olives
        & hand-pounded pesto **145**
    see also fish dishes
semolina noodles **221**
service **57**
shellfish **256**
side dishes **353**
    boiled mixed greens with extra virgin olive oil
        & lemon **374**
    braised cavolo nero & silverbeet with chilli,
        garlic & parmesan **355**
    cabbage & parmesan salad **379**
    cauliflower & cheese **372**
    charcoal-oven roasted pumpkin & sweet potato
        with garlic yoghurt & burnt butter **362**
    creamed silverbeet **355**
    green beans with creamy anchovy, chilli & lemon
        dressing & almonds **373**
    hand-cut fat chips **358**

kipfler potatoes sautéed with Wagyu fat & rosemary **359**

long-braised, melting Roman beans with herbs **354**

mac 'n' cheese 361

mushy peas with slow-cooked egg **363**

onion rings **370**

organic carrots inspired by St. John **367**

potato & cabbage gratin **365**

potato purée **360**

radicchio, cos & endive salad with palm sugar vinaigrette **377**

sautéed mixed mushrooms **366**

sautéed zucchini with garlic & mint **354**

tomato basil salad **379**

Sidecar 63, 67

silver tequila 60

silverbeet

braised **173**

creamed **355**

single malts 59

slow cooking 324

slow-roasted rib of beef **325**

smallgoods 128

snapper 263

seared crisp, with smoky cherry tomatoes, borlotti beans & green olive butter **234**

soup

cream of oyster, leek & potato soup **206**

pea, bacon & chilli broth with gnocchetti **192**

sour cream pastry **399**

southern bluefin tuna 99, 197

Southern Fishermen's Association 271, 272

southern king prawn (*Melicertus latisulcatus*) 188

spanner crab, roasted cherry tomato & spicy prawn oil with semolina noodles **221–2**

speakeasy drinks list 63

Spencer Gulf Prawn Fishery 188–9, 197

Speyside whiskies 59

Spice Temple 31, 38, 41

spices, toasting 445

spicy mayonnaise **176**

spicy prawn oil **221**

spirits, range of 59–61

Springbank 60

squid 256

charcoal-oven roasted squid & pork belly **200**

cleaning 445

fried squid, radicchio & chilli salad with Romesco sauce **207**

squid ink ceviche **114**

Starlight Children's Foundation, Ultimate Dinner 38, 47

steak sandwich with tomato & chilli relish **179**

steakhouse concept 17, 18, 21, 25, 29, 35, 41, 83

Stehr, Hagen 99

Sterling Caviar with toast & crème fraîche **125**

Sterns, Talis 21

stock

veal **438**

white chicken **436**

strawberry tart with balsamic vinegar ice-cream **397–8**

Studd, Will 385, 387

sugar syrup **72**

spiced **74**

summer fruit tart with rose cream **399**

Susman, John 89, 188, 197, 203, 255

on sustainable seafood 259

sustainability 258–9, 272, 287, 311

swordfish 274

grilled swordfish steak **274**

seared swordfish with red braised vegetables **101**

wood-fire grilled swordfish with broad beans & olive tapenade **235**

Sydney 35

Sydney Morning Herald Good Food Guide, Best New Restaurant 47

Sydney rock oysters 91

Sykes, Tom 47

syllabub with rhubarb & strawberry compote **402**

Takeda, Shogo 310

Tasmania 313

Taste of Morocco (Carrier) 120

Tathra Oysters 91

tequila 60

Tetsuya's 25, 38

The Waiting Room 31

Thompson, Greg 255

tomatoes

Ortiz anchovies with smoky tomato bruschetta **172**

peeling 445

roasted tomato sauce **237**

seared crisp snapper with smoky cherry tomatoes, borlotti beans & green olive butter **234**

spanner crab, roasted cherry tomato & spicy prawn oil with semolina noodles **221–2**

tomato & chilli relish **432**

tomato basil salad **379**

tomato jam **433**

tomato jelly **429**

warm salad of wood-fire grilled quail with smoky tomato & black olives **159**

see also cherry tomatoes

tonic water, house-made **64**

Tonks, Mitch 255

Treweek, Lauren 405

Tsukiji Market, Tokyo 266, 267

tuna 84, 257

preserved tuna, white bean, chilli & silverbeet bruschetta **173**

raw tuna **97**

southern bluefin 99, 197

tuna tartare, Moroccan eggplant, cumin mayonnaise & harissa **120**

tuna with ginger, jalapeño chilli & coriander dressing **118**

tuna ranching 99

usuzukuri method, of cutting raw fish 96

vanilla sauce **419**

veal 329–30

veal glaze **438**

veal stock **438**

wood-fire grilled White Rocks veal cutlet **331**

vegetables

boiled mixed greens with extra virgin olive oil & lemon **374**

pickled vegetables **129**

red braised vegetables **101**

vegetable tagine **251**

wood-fire grilled vegetables & goat's curd salad **155**

vision 57

vodka 59

vongole 203, 256

Wagyu 297, 298

corned Wagyu silverside with slow-cooked carrots & mustard sauce **247**

rendered Wagyu fat **436**

Wagyu Bolognese with hand-cut fettuccine **225**

Wagyu bresaola with mushroom toast **171**

Wagyu chuck braised in red wine with gremolata and potato purée **246**

Wagyu rump, topside or skirt **303**

Wagyu sirloin, rib-eye or fillet **303**

see also Blackmore, David

wait staff 29, 31, 57

Wakuda, Tetsuya 38, 267

warm salad of wood-fire grilled quail with smoky tomato & black olives **159**

Waters, Alice 367

Watson, Carole 329

whisky, Scottish 59–60

white asparagus with shiitake mushrooms, slow-cooked egg, burnt butter & parmesan **209**

white bean purée **147**

White Rocks Veal 329–30

white sauce **243**

wine collecting 42, 45, 47

wine lists 38, 41, 47

Wine Spectator, Grand Award 41

wood-fire grilled asparagus bruschetta with tomato, ricotta & basil **174**

wood-fire grilled baby octopus with olives & hand-pounded pesto **145**

wood-fire grilled eggplant, roasted pumpkin & chilli salad with goat's curd **148**

wood-fire grilled lamb cutlets with mint jelly **337**

wood-fire grilled swordfish with broad beans & olive tapenade **235**

wood-fire grilled vegetables & goat's curd salad **155**

wood-fire grilled White Rocks Veal cutlet **331**

wood-fired grills 295, 301

wood-fired rotisserie chicken with Tuscan bread salad **280**

wood-fired rotisserie loin of pork **292**

yellow-eye mullet 272

Young, Naren 72

Zenwa 311

zucchini

grilled zucchini **147**

sautéed zucchini with garlic & mint **354**

zucchini pickle **166**

Published in 2011 by Murdoch Books Pty Limited
Reprinted in 2012

Murdoch Books Australia
Pier 8/9
23 Hickson Road
Millers Point NSW 2000
Phone: +61 (0) 2 8220 2000
Fax: +61 (0) 2 8220 2558
www.murdochbooks.com.au

Murdoch Books UK Limited
Erico House, 6th Floor
93–99 Upper Richmond Road
Putney, London SW15 2TG
Phone: +44 (0) 20 8785 5995
Fax: +44 (0) 20 8785 5985
www.murdochbooks.co.uk

Publisher: Kylie Walker
Designer: one8one7
Project Manager & Editor: Belinda So
Production: Karen Small

National Library of Australia Cataloguing-in-Publication Data

Author:	Perry, Neil.
Title:	Rockpool Bar and Grill / Neil Perry.
ISBN:	978 1 74196 829 3 (hbk.)
Notes:	Includes index.
Subjects:	Rockpool Bar and Grill (Restaurant) Cooking.
Dewey Number:	641.5

A catalogue record for this book is available from the British Library.

Printed by 1010 Printing International Limited, China